T3-BNX-345

CONTEMPORARY APPROACHES TO MORAL EDUCATION

THE GARLAND BIBLIOGRAPHIES
IN CONTEMPORARY EDUCATION
(GENERAL EDITOR: JOSEPH M. MC CARTHY)
(VOL. 2)

GARLAND REFERENCE LIBRARY
OF SOCIAL SCIENCE
(VOL. 117)

CONTEMPORARY APPROACHES TO MORAL EDUCATION:
An Annotated Bibliography and Guide to Research

James S. Leming

GARLAND PUBLISHING, INC. • NEW YORK & LONDON
1983

Library of Congress Cataloging in Publication Data

Leming, James S., 1941–
Contemporary approaches to moral education.

(The Garland bibliographies in contemporary education; v. 2) (Garland reference library of social science ; v. 117)
Includes indexes.
1. Moral education—Bibliography. 2. Moral development—Bibliography. 3. Values—Study and teaching—Bibliography. 4. Socialization—Bibliography.
I. Title. II. Series.
Garland bibliographies in contemporary education; v. 2.
Z5814.M7L45 1983 [LC268] 016.37011′4 81-48422
ISBN 0-8240-9389-5

Printed on acid-free, 250-year-life paper
Manufactured in the United States of America

To
Joan,
Jimmy,
&
Jessica

CONTENTS

ACKNOWLEDGMENTS

This work could not have been completed without assistance from many sources. The completion of the task was greatly expedited due to the excellent holdings of Morris Library on the campus of Southern Illinois University at Carbondale. I was constantly surprised by the extensiveness of the library's collection in moral education. Thanks should also go to the fourth-floor staff for their valuable assistance in overcoming my own weaknesses as a library researcher. Thanks also go to the Department of Curriculum, Instruction and Media and the College of Education for their encouragement and assistance. Janice Mayo and Beth Snider, who typed the body of the bibliography, deserve special recognition for their efficiency, good humor and incredible ability to decipher my handwriting. Thanks also go to Chris Martin and Kelly Crombar for their typing assistance. Finally, and most importantly, my appreciation goes to Joan, Jimmy and Jessica Leming whose encouragement and good-natured tolerance of my benign neglect and work-induced neuroses during critical writing periods made the effort bearable.

INTRODUCTION

In 1966 two works appeared which signaled the beginning of the recent surge of interest in moral education. In that year Raths, Harmin, and Simon published their highly influential book on values clarification, *Values and Teaching* (item 227), and Lawrence Kohlberg in the *School Review* wrote the first article in which he discusses moral education (item 402). Up to the present time the values clarification and the cognitive developmental approaches to moral education remain the most coherent, well-developed and popular approaches to moral education. The 1970's were banner years for those interested in moral education. Journals were filled with articles on moral education, graduate theses examined the field, national projects and centers were set up, and both scholars and practitioners worked together to create programs and curricula. It was during the 1970's that two journals which focused exclusively on moral education were first published: the *Journal of Moral Education* (1971) and *Moral Education Forum* (1976).

The quantity of discourse concerning moral education produced during the late 60's and the decade of the 70's has been great. On a yearly basis since 1977 the *Moral Education Forum* has published an extensive annual bibliography on works related to moral education (item 1773). This bibliography indicates that since 1977 an average of twenty-five books, six special issues of journals and over 200 articles have appeared annually on the subject of moral education. Another index of the extent of interest in moral education is the level of research in graduate schools. Between 1964 and 1971 in *Dissertation Abstracts International* approximately ten doctoral dissertations per year were completed on moral education and related topics. Since 1972, the number of dissertations has increased gradually from 20 per year in 1972 to 82 in 1979. Since 1979 the number has dropped off only slightly.

That moral education has become a major movement in the field of education can not be argued. The reasons for its rise are somewhat less clear. No doubt, in part, the movement is the result of bright, articulate, prolific, and driven individuals who, through their writing and speaking, have kept the subject in the public and academic eye. No educational movement, however, can attract the attention that moral education has without a strong base of support from school personnel and the general public. In 1975, a Gallup poll sponsored by Phi Delta Kappa (item 1335) revealed that approximately 80 percent of the adult population felt that the schools should be directly involved in moral education. The reasons for this interest in moral education are to a great extent a result of the times we live in. Neither the family nor the Church seems as firmly in control of the moral instruction of youth as in the past. The social and political turmoil of the late 60's no doubt raised serious questions in the minds of many citizens regarding the character of contemporary youth. In addition, the narcissistic ethos of the 80's coupled with the increasing incidence of divorce, single-parent families, and dual-career families has made the role of the family in the moralization of youth a chancy social phenomena.

Whatever the reasons, moral education is an educational movement of significant social interest and importance. The purpose of this bibliography is to present, in an organized and annotated manner, the important thinking and research surrounding the practical side of the moral education movement of the 60's and 70's. The time frame of this bibliography corresponds to that of the resurgence of interest in the topic: the mid 1960's to 1981. The bibliography was compiled through the following resources: the reference sections of the most salient works in the field, *Dissertation Abstracts International, Current Index to Journals in Education* (1969–1981), *Education Index* (1965–1968), the ERIC documents system, and other major bibliographies on the topic. This bibliography is not limited to post-1965 sources; however, it is most exhaustive of the literature during this period.

The Scope of the Bibliography

In the opening line of one of the early seminal works on moral education (item 167), John Wilson observes "'Moral Education' is a name for nothing clear," The attempt to compile a bibliography on the subject convinces one of the wisdom of Wilson's comment. Any bibliographer, in order to make this task manageable, the product useful, and to maintain his own sanity, must place reasonable parameters on the field under study. However, clearly some fields of inquiry are more susceptible to delimitation than others. The field of moral education is an area of inquiry in which it is exceedingly difficult to set firm parameters. A single example will illustrate the problem. Imagine a teacher, Mrs. Jones, sitting in her fourth-grade classroom near the end of the school day. A number of events have transpired this warm September day which have given her cause to reflect on what lies ahead for the year. In this single day, the milk money has been stolen out of her desk over recess, eight students were detected cheating on a multiplication test, and Jimmy and Paul were noticed cruelly taunting a tall angular fifth-grade girl who happens to be physically handicapped. Mrs. Jones, in reflecting about what has happened this day, interprets these incidents as ones which involve questions of morals or values. By examining some of the questions Mrs. Jones might ask about the incidents which occurred, one begins to get a feel for the breadth and complexity of the issues embedded in the concept of moral education.

Some of the questions Mrs. Jones, or any teacher or parent, might reasonably ask of an "expert" in moral education are:

> Why do children behave this way? Are they born cruel, immoral, evil, or does the society make them this way? Are these sorts of behaviors solely the result of childrearing practices, television, peer group norms, or do the schools play a part in the development of these sorts of immoral behaviors? Are these behaviors the result of naturally occurring developmental trends in chidren's moral development?

Am I overreacting? Can I be sure that these acts by my students are really wrong? How do I know, or can I know for sure, what a moral or good act is? Is it something I intuitively know; is it the result of societal consensus; is it divinely revealed; etc.? Certainly before I attempt to teach children what right actions consist of, I must know myself. How do I obtain such knowledge? And on what basis is it grounded?

Suppose I've decided to attack the problem head on and implement a program in moral education in the classroom. What assumptions do I base such a program on? Do I assume that moral behavior is rational behavior? If so, what psychological evidence exists on the issue of the role of thought in moral behavior? Should I attempt to operantly condition my students to perform moral acts and attempt to extinguish immoral acts? Do my students have the potential for autonomous, reflective choice or do they need someone to tell them what is right?

What educational materials are available to me on this issue? What's the best available thinking on moral education curricula? Do experts agree? What's the track record of the major approaches. What works—if anything? What are the arguments, pro and con, for moral education in the schools?

I've heard that the Church and the home are the proper locations for moral education and that the schools should only focus on academics. Is this a respectable position? Can the schools avoid being involved in moral education? When I punish students, am I not acting as a moral educator? Am I effective when I act this way? How about the Church? Is all morality ultimately based on religion, and, if so, then can there be such a thing as a secular morality? If there is no such thing as morality divorced from religion, then wouldn't it violate separation of Church and State to engage in moral education in the classroom?

Should I ever tell my students what I think, or should I always remain neutral?

The above reflections and questions by Mrs. Jones by no means exhaust all the avenues one might explore in an attempt to clarify one's response to the issue of moral education; however, this series of questions should illustrate the breadth of issues and disciplines centrally related to the practice of moral education. It is my position that none of the questions asked by Mrs. Jones are trivial or irrelevant to the enterprise of moral education. However, due to length restrictions this volume will focus on the practice of moral education. Questions regarding the philosophic, cultural, psychological and historical foundations of the field are not presented in this volume. This is not to say that these are unimportant, for certainly an analysis of how individuals acquire morality or reflections on the nature of morality are important areas for the understanding of moral education. Due to the vastness of the literature on the foundations of moral education they will comprise the subject of a second volume.

Even with the above delimitations additional restrictions were necessary to keep the length of this volume manageable and enhance its utility. This bibliography is not a guide to available moral education curriculum materials. There are a number of reasons for not including moral education curricula in this bibliography. First, as the values or moral education movement grew in significance and popularity, almost every educational publisher either put the word "values" into his available curricula or created new materials with a "values" emphasis. Second, curriculum materials are not indexed in any central source. Third, the availability and price of these materials fluctuate in such a way that any attempts at cataloging are almost immediately obsolete. It was the author's judgment that because of the eclectic nature of most of the commercially published curricular materials, these entries would add little of substance to an understanding of the movement. The reader will note, however, that in the subject index under "curricular materials" items are included which will lead one to sources of information on curriculum materials. Of course, published professional literature which discusses specific curricular approaches is included.

A second major area not included in this bibliography is unpublished materials. If the materials were not published in a journal, book, or as part of the ERIC microfiche system, they were not included. Accessibility of materials was held to be of great importance if this bibliography was to be of use to the reader. The author's own experiences in attempting to obtain unpublished materials suggests that the reader of this bibliography should be spared the same frustrations. Also, it has been my experience that very few significant ideas or research studies remain unpublished. In the field of moral education, I can think of fewer than a dozen such manuscripts, and these have been included. The major exception to this rule is the inclusion of selected papers from the forthcoming volumes by Lawrence Kohlberg, the *Psychology of Moral Development* (item 1800) and *Education and Moral Development* (item 395). In the introduction to the first volume of this three-volume series (item 1799), Kohlberg lists, with annotations, the contents of the two forthcoming volumes. Since this three-volume series represents the culmination of twenty years work by one of the of major figures in the field, I have listed these items. This was done with some apprehension, however, for within the literature on moral education, one observes a frequently cited book (Kohlberg, L., and E. Turiel, Eds. *Recent Research in Moral Development*, New York: Holt, Rinehart and Winston, 1973). Although this book was never published, it has been cited repeatedly in the literature. How this phantom volume came to be a part of the literature on moral education constitutes a fascinating problem in the sociology of knowledge. I am trusting that history will not repeat itself, and that the contents of the last two volumes of the Kohlberg series will appear as promised. The reader is, however, urged to compare the listings in this bibliography against the actual contents of these volumes when they appear.

A Guide to Using the Bibliography

There are two ways in which this bibliography is designed to be used. First, through the author and subject indices, the user will be able to identify items and authors of interest. Because this first method may sometimes be time consuming, the body of the bibliography is organized into significant topical sections.

This enables the user, rather than going repeatedly from index to item to track down items on a given topic, to peruse items in a selected topic within a set number of pages. This topical method may constitute the most efficient way to use the bibliography; however, there are two obvious limitations to exclusive use of the bibliography in this manner. First, the topic of the reader's interest may not be presented with the degree of precision desired by the topical headings. These headings are general headings and subsume under them broad but related collections of references. Second, seldom if ever is an article or book adequately defined by a single descriptor. Entries are placed under a topical heading in the body of the bibliography based on its primary focus. In this bibliography, items are only entered once in the main body. The multiple nature of items is reflected only in the subject index where items are listed by major descriptors. Therefore, the reader is urged not to assume that the items collected under the topical headings are the only items in the bibliography dealing with that topic. It may well be that there are a substantial number of additional related items; however, in these items the topic of interest is not the major focus. The use of the subject index, therefore, is called for to exhaust all included items related to the reader's interest.

The only abbreviations used in this bibliography follow the listing of the individual items. "NR" is used to indicate that the listed item was not reviewed by the author. A few items were included even though not reviewed because of the significance of the author or the topic. Occasionally, some items which were reviewed did not receive an annotation. In these cases an annotation would add little to the information already in the title. The letters "NI" follow collections of readings in which the individual articles are not entered into the bibliography. In collections of readings not followed by "NI" the individual articles germane to the study of moral education are included within the bibliography.

In order to allow the reader to easily access the abstracts of doctoral dissertations, each dissertation is followed by the volume number and page number in *Dissertation Abstracts International* (e.g., 34/06, p. 2318). Unless indicated by a "B" following the volume number, one should reference the humanities and social sciences volumes of DAI. If the letter B follows the volume number, the abstract is to be found in the sciences and engineering volumes.

Entries available through the ERIC microfiche document system are followed by the access number of that item within the ERIC system (e.g., ED 101 063).

As the scope and breadth of this bibliography will attest, one of the reasons why moral education is a name for nothing clear is because moral education is in a way a name for a central task of all peoples in all times. In this sense, there is no dimension of the study of the human experience which does not shed light on mankind's efforts to bring successive generations into the moral life of society. Although this volume is the most extensive extant bibliography on the topic, the discovery of important sources at the last minute convinces me that some few but nonetheless important sources may have been overlooked. I would appreciate hearing from anyone using this bibliography concerning any omissions which fall within the inclusive criteria used.

The Organization of the Bibliography

The first subheading of this bibliography, "general analyses" (items 1–174), consists of those sources that present a broad overview of the state of the field. Also discussed in this section are general arguments concerning the need for moral education. This section's analysis is directly linked to the current practice of moral education in schools. The "values clarification" sections (items 175–245, 246–335, and 336–361) present sources on the theory and practice, the curricular effectiveness, and critiques of the values clarification approach with rejoinders. The "cognitive development" section contains sources in the applications of the cognitive developmental approach as developed by Lawrence Kohlberg. Included here are sections on theory and practice (items 362–458), curricular effectiveness (items 459–605), just community programs (items 606–650), and critiques and rejoinders (items 651–761).

Following the two most widely discussed and practiced approaches are sections on other recent approaches to education which have a strong moral or values emphasis: psychological or developmental education (items 762–842), humanistic or affective education (items 843–924), value analysis (items 925–975), directive moral education (items 976–1063), and a series of other coherent, but not widely practiced approaches (items 1064–1116). The "directive" section contains a collection of sources which argue that children should learn and exemplify in their behavior certain values that are viewed by the community as essential to adequate socialization. This perspective is frequently slighted by academics, yet is probably what most parents and teachers have in mind when they picture moral education.

The next two sections contain sources which compare and contrast the above approaches (items 1117–1132) or empirically test the comparative effectiveness of the approaches (items 1113–1157). This section of the bibliography closes with sources on moral education in specific school subject matter areas (items 1158–1312).

The second major section of the bibliography contains sources on a variety of topics directly related to moral education but not easily subsumed under the above sections. Included here are sources on the current status of moral education movement (items 1313–1342), issues and instruments in the evaluation of moral education efforts (items 1343–1446), educating teachers to be moral educators (items 1447–1507), the role of the school counselor in moral education (items 1508–1526), moral education in higher education (items 1527–1639), moral education of the handicapped, incarcerated, retarded, etc. (items 1640–1664), moral education as practiced in religious settings (items 1665–1720), and the relationship and interconnections between civic and moral education (items 1738–1769).

The volume concludes with a listing of bibliographies on moral education (items 1770–1783), collections of readings related to moral education (items 1784–1822), and special editions and sections of journals (items 1823–1858).

Contemporary Approaches to Moral Education

THE PRACTICE OF MORAL EDUCATION

General Analyses, Issues, and Approaches

1. Allegheny Intermediate Unit. Moral Reasoning: A School Administrator's Handbook. Pittsburgh: Allegheny Intermediate Unit, 1976. ED 132 702.

   Reviews several of the more popular forms of moral education, presents a rationale and process for a moral education program, and suggests ways to deal with the administrative requirements involved in implementing a moral reasoning approach.

2. Aubry, Roger. "Moral Development in Elementary School Classrooms." Moral Education: A First Generation of Research and Development (item 428), pp. 250-262.

   Discusses a variety of issues that must be faced in designing a program to educate teachers in stimulating the moral development of children in their classrooms.

3. Barrs, Stephan, et al. Values Education: A Resource Booklet. Toronto: Ontario Secondary School Teachers Federation, 1975. ED 154 307.

   Intended to introduce teachers to values education and provide them with activities and exercises. Contains sections on all the standard approaches and includes a useful bibliography and guide to resources.

4. Beck, Clive. "Value Education Notes." Religious Education, 69 (1974): 379-381.

Contains four statements on the scope of value education and seven statements regarding the content of values education. These notes originate from the Moral Education Project of the Ontario Institute for Studies in Education.

5. Bell, Julia, Sarah Bennett and James Fallace. "From Inculcation to Action: A Continuum for Values Education." Values Concepts and Techniques (item 1784), pp. 95-102.

Presents a view of values education as a continual process that combines inculcation, clarification analysis, moral reasoning, and action learning.

6. Bell, Terrel H. "Morality and Citizenship Education: Whose Responsibility?" Occasional paper No. 1. Philadelphia: Research for Better Schools, 1976. ED 134 522.

Consists of three parts: a sketch of the present moral climate of the United States, background information on the values upon which the United States was founded and methodological developments that enable educators to be effective moral educators.

7. Benson, George, and Thomas S. Engeman. Amoral America. Stanford, CA: Hoover Institution Press, 1975.

Presents the case that America is suffering through an ethical malaise. The sources of this malaise are seen in such social institutions as the media, government, business, in widespread criminal activity, etc. Argues that the family, the church, and the school can reverse this amoral trend. The present status of ethical instruction in America and other countries is reviewed, along with religious approaches to ethical instruction. Argues that moral education should focus on individual moral choice rather than on a social ethic. Although the authors advocate no specific approach and tend toward eclecticism, they obviously favor a Deweyan formulation.

8. Benson, George, and Joseph Forcinelli. "Teaching Ethics in High School." NASSP Bulletin, 59 (May 1975): 80-89.

Discusses six methods of teaching ethics: case discussion, law as a basis of values, conduct of the school, individual virtues, historical examples, and sociological experience.

9. Berson, Robert J. "Ethics and Education in the Freshman Year: Impact and Implications of an Experimental Value Oriented Curriculum." Ed.D. dissertation, Columbia University, 1979. 40/05, p. 2495.

An experimental value-oriented curriculum is found to have no significant effect on moral judgment. The nature of the curriculum is not well described in the abstract.

10. Berstein, Jean, et al. "Examining Values in the Upper Grades." Social Education, 35 (1971): 906-910.

Discusses the efforts of a Park Forest, Ill., school district to assist children in understanding value conflicts and experience value choices.

11. Black, Algernon D. "A Secular Approach to Moral Education." Educational Leadership, 21 (1964): 505-508; 553-554.

Discusses the obstacles that confront school efforts at moral education and presents a program of discussion topics which, it is argued, will develop moral sensibilities in children.

12. Blackham, H., ed. Moral and Religious Education in County Primary Schools. Slough, Berks, England: NFER Publishing Co., 1976.

Contains a report by teachers in infant and junior schools on the purposes of religious and moral instruction in schools. Contains sections on principles and aims, the school community, methods of teaching, contributions of subject areas, and religious education.

13. Blum, Mark E. "Public Policy Considerations in Ethical Education." Paper presented at the annual meeting of the American Educational Research Association, New York, 1977. ED 146 097.

Discusses the background of public policy considerations related to the place of moral education in schools. Concludes that there are many problems (e.g., specifying content in a pluralistic society), but advantage should be taken of this public demand.

14. Brewer, James H. A Mini-Guide for Students on Setting Values. Clinton, MS: J.B. Publishers, 1976. ED 121 710.

Designed to help students understand moral concepts and values so they can better evaluate their own behavior, and to increase awareness of consequences.

15. Burgess, Evangeline. Values in Early Childhood Education. Washington, DC: National Education Association, 1965. ED 088 565.

Summarizes research evidence for the impact of early childhood education on children's social, personal, emotional, and intellectual development. Contains resumes of selected sources and a detailed bibliography.

16. Burnham, B. "Human Values Education: The New Dynamic in Program Development." Education Canada, 15 (Spring 1975): 4-10.

Discusses the rationale for and practice of "Human Values Education" in the schools of the province of Ontario.

17. Burnham, B. "Values Education at a Turning Point in History." Education Canada, 15 (Winter 1975): 23-27.

Presents a rationale for values education and two criteria for an effective values education program.

18. Burton, William. "Behavioral Morality? A Critique of William Kay's Moral Development." Religious Education, 67 (1972): 298-304.

Kay's proposals for moral development in education (item 1011) are criticized as being behavioristic and likely to lead to the inculcation of an authoritarian and deterministic morality.

19. Carbone, Peter F. "Objective Morality: Teaching Students to Think Critically." NASSP Bulletin, 59 (January 1975): 64-72.

Argues that secondary schools should be doing more with moral education. The approach suggested would initiate students into the language and structure of morality, preferably as moral issues come up during regular classes. No specific values should be foisted on students.

20. Carmon, Arye. "Teaching the Holocaust as a Means of Fostering Values." Curriculum Inquiry, 9 (1973): 209-228.

Describes a program focused on the Holocaust, designed to teach adolescents, through the students' confrontation with the meaning of the Holocaust, specific values that will prepare them for initiation into a democratic society.

21. Carter, John. "Trends in the Teaching of Values." Contemporary Education, 44 (1973): 295-297.

Describes three ways values are currently taught (traditional, scientific, and process approaches) and presents an alternative approach.

22. Clark, David B. "The Academic, the Interpersonal, and the Role of the Teacher in Social and Moral Education." Journal of Moral Education, 5 (1976): 145-157.

Argues that the major reason for adolescent dissatisfaction in schools is neglect of social and moral education. How this problem can be addressed by schools through greater interpersonal learning and increased pupil authority is discussed.

23. Clauss, William R. "New York State Education Department Fosters Inquiry about Values." Moral Education Forum, 1 (May 1976): 10-11.

Describes the efforts of the New York State Education department to encourage moral education in the state.

24. Cleaver, Betty. "A Brief Survey of Values Education." Charlotte: University of North Carolina-Charlotte, 1975. ED 109 041.

Presents a brief history of moral education, reviews values clarification, analyzes the role of the school in values education, and assesses the state of research in the field.

25. Cochrane, Donald B. "Moral Education and the Curriculum: An Introduction." Development of Moral Reasoning (item 1332), pp. 59-67.

Discusses the implications for curriculum development of taking moral education seriously. Cochrane is somewhat pessimistic regarding the chances of his suggestions being implemented, but is concerned about what will happen if they are not.

26. Cochrane, Donald B., and Michael Manley-Casimir, eds. Development of Moral Reasoning: Practical Approaches. New York: Praeger Publishers, 1980.

Contains a series of papers presented at a Summer Institute on the "Practical Dimensions of Moral Education" held at Simon Fraser University in 1978. The focus of the papers is on the practice of moral education in the school and home. The organizing question posed by the editors was, "What strategies can the classroom teacher or parent adopt to foster the development of principled thinking and moral action in students or children?"

27. Crabtree, Walden. "A Clarification of the Teacher's Role in Moral Education." Religious Education, 69 (1974): 643-653.

Argues that there are right ways and wrong ways to handle values in the schools. The wrong way is by indoctrination, the right way is to advance the ability to value wisely.

28. Dalis, George T., and Ben B. Strasser. "A Concept of Value for the Classroom." Health Education, 7 (March/April 1976): 12-13.

Presents a concept of value (a preferred or important quality characteristic, attribute, or property) and shows how it is useful in analyzing individuals' value decisions.

29. Daniels, L.B. "Moral Education in the Context of Lifelong Learning." Journal of Educational Thought, 15 (1981): 34-40.

The approach of the Association for Values Education and Research is offered as an example of a program that instills a moral "critical mass" that will ensure lifelong growth in the moral domain.

30. Daubner, Edith S. "Making Moral Education Possible." Elementary School Journal. 70 (1969): 61-73.

Advocates use of J.S. Mill's ethical theory to settle moral disputes in the classroom. Principles of ethical theory should be made a reality in the classroom.

31. DiGiacono, James J. "Ten Years as Moral Educator in a Catholic High School." Values/Moral Education: The Schools and the Teachers (item 1794), pp. 51-71.

Discusses the author's approach, through Socratic dialogue, to the moral education of young men between the ages of 13 and 18. Contains many interesting examples of topics used to stimulate conflict and discussion. Discusses the problems of moral education in a Catholic school.

32. Diller, Ann. "On a Conception of Moral Teaching." Growing Up with Philosophy (item 1075), pp. 326-338.

Argues that an appropriate setting for moral education is the parent-child setting. Using everyday events and literature as a basis for dialogue the child can be led to his/her own realization of the moral issues involved.

33. DiStefano, Ann. "Dissertations in Review: A Brief Survey of Studies Spanning the Last Ten Years." Moral Education Forum, 4 (1979): 14-16.

A short overview of 200 dissertations. The types and incidence of topics in moral education are reported. Observations on the state of the field are made. No bibliography is included.

34. Dressel, P.L. "Values: Cognitive and Affective." Journal of Higher Education, 42 (1971): 402-404.

Argues that objectives in the cognitive and affective domains are not separable. Educated behavior always involves both affective and cognitive elements. The focal problem for education is the recognition of values in all behavior and the resolution of value conflicts within and among individuals.

35. Dunfee, Maxine, and Claudia Crump. Teaching for Social Values in Social Studies. Washington, DC: Association for Childhood Education International, 1974.

Using a combination of Laswell's eight universal values (item 1018) and values clarification, practical classroom activities are presented. Contains chapters on building self-concept, friendship, overcoming bias, making democracy a reality, and renewing the environment.

36. Etzioni, Amitoi. "Can Schools Teach Kids Values?" Today's Education, (September/October 1977): 29-38.

Reviews the major approaches to values education and concludes that what is likely to have the greatest impact is that which restructures the hidden curriculum. Four reactions, one by Simon and the others by public school teachers, follow this article.

37. Ezer, Melvin. "Value Teaching in the Middle and Upper Grades: A Rationale for Teaching But Not Transmitting Values." Social Education, 31 (1967): 39-40.

Presents examples of classroom activities designed to assist children in reaching informed and rational decisions.

38. Fairburn, Doug. "An Approach to Moral Education." History and Social Science Teacher, 11 (1975): 4-14.

Describes the use of values clarification and moral development strategies in the classroom.

39. Farmer, Rodney. "Maslow and Values Education." Social Studies, 69 (1978): 69-74.

Argues that schools should teach students to discover and analyze values found in themselves and others and teach students universal values that are derived from human basic needs and metaneeds. How the teacher is to go about this is touched on but not discussed in any great detail.

40. Ferguson, Patrick, and John W. Frieser. "Values Theory and Teaching. The Problem of Autonomy versus Determinism." Theory and Research in Social Education, 2 (December 1974): 1-24.

Five theoretical models of values teaching are identified and analyzed in terms of their philosophical tenets. The implications of each model for teaching are discussed and a possible integration is offered.

41. Fielder, William R. "Two Styles of School Talk about Values." Social Education, 31 (1967): 34-3.

Orthodox talk (value inculcation) is contrasted with radical talk about values education. Radical talk holds that the discovery of self and learning to examine what one finds are at the heart of values education.

42. Forisha, Bill E., and Barbara E. Forisha. Moral Development and Education. Lincoln, NB: Professional Educators Publications, 1976.

Presents a general overview of the history of and current approaches to moral education. Of special interest are chapters on Adlerian and Rogerian approaches. Also included are sections on Kohlberg, behaviorism, and values clarification.

43. Fraenkel, Jack R. "Goals for Teaching Values and Value Analysis." Journal of Research and Development in Education, 13 (Winter 1980): 93-102.

Identifies some of the differences in viewpoint that permeate the field of values education and then offers some suggestions as to what a more comprehensive viewpoint might include. The more comprehensive view is seen as involving four sorts of objectives: knowledge, cognitive skill, affective (interpersonal) skill, and motivational skill.

44. Fraenkel, Jack R. "Values Clarification Is Not Enough." History and Social Studies Teacher, 13 (1977): 27-32.

Following a short critique of values clarification three objectives are offered as additional goals of values education: sensitivity to value claims, consideration of alternatives and points of view of others, and consideration of the effects and consequences of action.

45. Frazier, Alexander. Values, Curriculum and the Elementary School. Boston: Houghton Mifflin Company, 1980.

Outlines three approaches to values development: Piaget and Kohlberg, values clarification, and humanistic attempts to offset what is seen as a repressive social environment. An analysis of the content of the values curriculum for the elementary school is presented. This content is presented under three headings: everyday living, cultural heritage, and the moral-ethical-political realm. Some suggestions for classroom activities are presented.

46. Frick, R. "Values: Games Are Not Enough." Teacher, 91 (December 1973): 8-9.

Points out that current approaches are too superficial. Argues that an approach to values education should be built around the study of values and should emphasize that consequences follow from decisions.

47. Friedlander, Henry. "Toward a Methodology of Teaching about the Holocaust." Teachers College Record, 80 (1979): 519-542.

Discusses why the Holocaust ought to be taught and what topics are essential to its treatment in schools. Many useful sources are footnoted.

48. Gantt, Walter N. "Teacher Accountability for Moral Education." Social Education, 39 (1975): 29-32.

Argues that in order for teachers to be accountable for the moral education of children there must be public agreement about and acceptance of goals and anticipated outcomes. There must also be agreement as to how such a program is to be evaluated.

49. Glashagel, Jerry; Mick Johnson; and Bob Phipps. Introduction to Values Education. New York: Young Men's Christian Association, 1977. ED 166 092.

Describes teaching methods and learning activities to help youth develop value-decision skills. Intended for use by staff of youth and family organizations as they develop values education workshops. The emphasis is on values clarification.

50. Glenn, Allen D., and Eugene D. Gennaro. "An Interdisciplinary Approach for Exploring Values and Value Questions for Social Studies and Science Teachers." High School Journal, 58 (1975): 208-223.

Three approaches to exploring values are presented: affective clarification, and analytical and moral reasoning. Exemplars of materials developed by teachers at a workshop on valuing illustrate each of the approaches.

51. Gold, Leo. "The Value/Moral Education Movement and Alfred Adler." Values/Moral Education: The Schools and the Teachers (item 1794), pp. 193-209.

Adler's emphasis on usefulness to society, social interest, democratic approach and positive motivation is applied to the concerns of moral education.

The educational applications are illustrated in practices of Family Education Centers.

52. Goldbecker, Sheralyn S. Values Teaching. Washington, DC: National Education Association, 1976.

In a very short space (22 pages) the author presents the values clarification and cognitive development approaches to values education and reviews research related to the teaching of values.

53. Goodwin, Robert D. "Morality: How Can We Teach It If We Cannot Define It?" Religious Education, 73 (1978): 678-685.

Argues that if we are to escape the morass of moral relativism that pervades public school systems, we must define morality and elucidate those principles upon which a moral system can be built. It is concluded that Rawls has provided a workable definition, Kohlberg the psychology, and Simon many helpful techniques.

54. Grainger, A.J. The Bullring: A Classroom Experiment in Moral Education. Oxford: Pergamon Press, 1970.

Reports on a technique in which children and a teacher discuss their own behavior with a view to understanding how they function in groups. The children in the two groups (bullrings) were early adolescents. The book consists of descriptions of the rules used to structure the groups, what happened in the groups, and an analysis of the moral growth that occurred as a result of the group experiences.

55. Hall, Robert T. Moral Education: A Handbook for Teachers. Minneapolis: Winston Press, 1979.

Following the rejection of hardline and softline approaches to moral education--the former involving indoctrination and the latter relativism and unwillingness to take a stand--a middle way is proposed but not spelled out in any great detail. Five teaching strategies are presented and illustrated: the awareness, debate, rational, concept, and game strategies.

The book concludes with five teaching units from differing disciplinary areas.

56. Hall, Robert, and John Davis. Moral Education in Theory and Practice. Buffalo: Prometheus Books, 1975.

Following a discussion of the nature of indoctrination and the presentation of a principle for avoiding it, an approach to moral education is presented which emphasizes inducing students to consider the morally relevant consequences of their decisions. The approach incorporates relevant philosophical and psychological insights into the teacher's handling of moral decision making in the classroom. Following chapters on the relevant philosophic issues (the analytic school is emphasized) and psychological issues (Kohlberg is emphasized), a case study approach is recommended and illustrated.

57. Harding, Thomas R. "Moral Education in Adulthood." Ph.D. dissertation, University of Toronto, 1975. 38/09, p. 5190.

Presents an analysis of the adult moral agent and offers some approaches to adult moral education. Argues that major blocks to adult moral development are low self-concept, limited self-discipline, and absence of the support of others.

58. Harmin, Merrill. What I've Learned about Values Education, Fastback 91. Bloomington, IN: Phi Delta Kappa Educational Foundation, 1977.

Suggests that the teacher ought to offer a model of one willing to examine his/her own values. Suggestions are offered for helping others to understand and clarify their own values.

59. Harris County Department of Education. "Pattern of Healthful Living: A Values Curriculum." Houston, TX: Harris County Department of Education, 1974. ED 118 500 - ED 118 508.

Contains curriculum guides for K-8 which are intended to assist students in the development of a positive self-concept, rational thinking processes and a personal and societal value system. The activities emphasize role playing, solving dilemmas, and classroom discussion. Many practical activities are included.

60. Hartoonian, H. Michael. "Working with Value and Moral Teaching Strategies." Paper presented at the Annual Meeting of the National Council for the Social Studies, 1975. ED 115 562.

Presents four models for interpreting values education strategies and examines six examples from curriculum projects in light of these models. A disclosure model which synthesizes the other three models (value position, psychological precepts, and valuative-objective) is proposed.

61. Havinghurst, Robert J. "What Research Says about Developing Moral Character." National Education Association Journal, 51 (January 1962): 28-29.

Presents a typology of character development and suggests two things schools can do to help develop moral character: provide models for character development and the opportunity for reflective thinking.

62. Hawley, Robert C. Human Values in the Classroom. Amherst, MA: Education Research Associates, 1973.

Presents a sequence of value-related teaching concerns for teacher consideration in educational planning: orientation, community-building, achievement motivation, fostering open communication, information seeking, gathering, and sharing, value exploration and clarification, and planning for change.

63. Healey, Robert M. "Instruction in Values: Some Unfinished Business." Religious Education, 64 (1969): 163-171.

Two programs for the teaching of values in public schools are analyzed and evaluated: the Educational Policies Commission report (item 997) and the Kentucky Movement. The discussion of the two approaches is thorough and insightful.

64. Hendryx, Steven W. "In Defense of the Homosexual Teacher." Viewpoints in Teaching and Learning, 56 (Fall 1980): 74-84.

Argues that teachers can strengthen their students' commitment to the value of human dignity by openly affirming the homosexual teacher's right to teach.

65. Hersh, Richard H.; John P. Miller; and Glen D. Fielding. Models of Moral Education: An Appraisal. New York: Longman, 1980.

Presents six models of moral education in separate chapters: the rationale building model, the consideration model, the valuing process and clarification model, the value analysis model, the cognitive moral development model, and the social action model. Also included is a discussion of the historical context of moral education as well as a discussion of how each of the models relates to three themes (caring, judging and acting) that the authors see as essential to morality.

66. Hill, Russell A., and Joan D. Wallace. Recommendations for Research, Development and Dissemination for Ethical-Citizenship Education Planning for Moral/Citizenship Education. Philadelphia: Research for Better Schools, 1976. ED 134 524.

Recommendations are presented for organizing research, development, and dissemination activities around the concept of a school-community effort at an Ethical Citizenship Education program. The recommendations involve general objectives (short and long range), a list of tasks, a strategy, and a schedule.

67. Hoffman, Alan J., and Thomas F. Ryan. "Developing Values Awareness in Young Children." Values Concepts and Techniques (item 1704), pp. 171-176.

Presents an approach to values education based on a psychosocial model of development of three to eight year olds. The model is drawn largely from Piaget and Bruner.

68. Hoffman, Martin L. "Fostering Moral Development." Toward Adolescence: The Middle School Years. Yearbook of the National Society for the Study of Education, Vol. 79, Part I. Edited by M. Johnson. Chicago: University of Chicago Press, 1980, pp. 161-181.

After reviewing the major theories of and research on moral development, a framework for adolescent moral development is presented. This framework incorporates the adolescent's awareness of others, fears of ubiquitous authority, capacity for empathy, ability to cognitively process information, and ability to actively construct new moral concepts.

69. Holmes, Mark. "Moral Education--What Can Schools Do?" Interchange, 7 (1977): 1-10.

Argues that moral education must be taken seriously, but that all of the current approaches are limited in their practical application. A moral education program is presented which uses elements from the different approaches but avoids their inherent weaknesses is presented.

70. Holroyd, Peter R. "Different But Fun--An Experience with Values." Independent School Bulletin, 35 (October 1975): 25-26.

Describes a program in values education offered to sophomores at Taft School in Watertown, CT. The approach was to discuss the issues with the adults who provided the children with the benefit of their experiences.

71. Hunt, David E. "Matching Models and Moral Training," Moral Education: Interdisciplinary Approaches (item 3166), pp. 231-251.

Presents theoretical background for the need for person-environment matching in education. Illustrates with examples of matching: moral maturity matching model; conceptual level matching model; and community treatment project matching model.

72. Jantz, Richard K., and Trudi A. Fulda. "The Role of Moral Education in the Public Elementary School." Social Education, 39 (1975): 24-28.

Argues that developmental psychology is a good place to begin any reexamination of the role of moral education in public schools. Summarizes the work of Piaget and Kohlberg and sets forth some possible implications of these theories for social studies instruction in elementary schools.

73. Jenkins, Robert E. The Moral and Spiritual Development of a Free People. Fullerton: California State University, Fullerton, 1977. ED 155 097.

Argues that the schools should be teaching for values, that directive methods won't work, and that values clarification holds out great promise.

74. Jensen, Larry C., and Karen M. Hughston. Responsibility and Morality: Helping Children Become Responsible and Morally Mature. Provo, UT: Brigham Young University Press, 1979.

Following a description of the conditions in the home and school that contribute to a climate conducive to moral development, ten virtues or area of moral concern are presented along with practical suggestions for developing these moral characteristics in children. The suggested techniques are eclectic involving modeling, induction, discussion, role playing, reinforcement of desired behavior, low power techniques, etc. Typical virtues are kindness, respect for property, sharing, truth telling, etc. The activities are suitable for elementary schools.

75. Johannesen, Richard L. "Teaching Ethical Standards for Discourse." Journal of Education, 162 (Spring 1980): 5-20.

Argues that complex and difficult ethical problems lurk in human discourse. Methods of securing student interest in such issues are presented, along with perspectives for assessing ethicality in discourse.

76. Johnson, Henry C. The Public School and Moral Education. New York: Pilgrim Press, 1980.

Argues that schools should be involved in moral education and that the focus should be on developing thoughtful conduct. The content of moral education has four principal sources: the moral presuppositions of our democratic social/political tradition; the moral presuppositions that underlie education as a process; the content of the "moral conversation" that has gone on from the beginning of human history; and the students' own experience of a particular moral tradition.

77. Jones, V.A. Character and Citizenship Training in the Public Schools. Chicago: University of Chicago Press, 1936.

200 seventh- and eighth-grade students were instructed for a year on rules, values, manners, and virtues. Three teaching methods were used: experience in concrete situations, discussion only, and a combination of the two. Only the third method demonstrated any impact on honesty, cooperation and moral knowledge, but the gains observed were short term.

78. Jones, Vernon. "Character Education." Encyclopedia of Educational Research, edited by Chester Harris. New York: Macmillan, 1960, pp. 184-191.

Presents a discussion of basic factors in character development and general principles of learning and teaching in character education, and reviews specific methods and programs.

79. Kavanagh, Harry B. "Moral Education at the Elementary School Level." Value/Moral Education: The Schools and the Teachers (item 1794), pp. 95-118.

Discusses the preconditions of morality which are deeply influenced in early childhood (personal identity, self-acceptance, moral models, conscience, and competence) and how these affect moral factors. Presents ideas of how parents and teachers can effectively influence children's early moral development.

80. Kentucky Department of Education. "Character Education: Some Questions and Answers." Frankfort: Kentucky Department of Education, 1977. ED 159 107.

Presents thorough guidelines for the planning, implementing, and evaluating of character education. This document is meant to assist staff development. It contains detailed statements of goals and teaching approaches. A specific "common core" of values is spelled out. These values are based on Laswell (item 1018).

81. Kirkendall, Lester A. "Reflections on Sexual Morality." The Humanist, 32 (November/December 1972): 11-13.

Presents four principles basic to the successful inculcation of moral concepts.

82. Kniker, Charles R. You and Values Education. Columbus, OH: Charles E. Merrill, 1977.

Presents an introduction to values education covering such topics as preparation of value objectives, construction of value activities, evaluation of value positions, and approaches to values education. The book also suggests a framework for constructing and analyzing values lessons and curricula. Includes references to and addresses for many commercially available materials.

83. Koberg, Dan, and Jim Bagnall. Values Tech: A Portable School for Discovering and Developing Decision Making Skills and Self-Enhancing Potentials. Los Altos, CA: William Kaufmann, 1976. ED 127 241.

Contains a multitude of activities designed to lead to greater awareness of one's values and to help one develop one's full potential. Intended to be an individualized, systematic experience.

84. Kyle, Judy A. "Educative Discipline." Progress and Problems in Moral Education (item 1820), pp. 159-177.

Describes how an outside-class Critical Review Board made up of students and teachers can be used to deal with discipline problems and can be a valuable educational arena. Children need a responsible role in the organization of social life.

85. Lachman, Seymour P., ed. Proceedings: Fourth Annual Conference on Public and Non-Public Schools: Value Education. New York: Center for Advanced Study in Education, City University of New York, 1977. ED 162 928.

Contains the keynote address, "Four Approches to Values Education" by Edwin Fenton and a variety of reactions from participants to the question of values education in the schools.

86. Lamborn, Robert L. "Values and the Private Schools." Religious Education, 70 (1975): 158-162.

The Executive Director of the Council for American Private Education discusses the nature and extent of values education in private schools. Four current models of values education are discussed.

87. Lavaroni, Charles, and Richard Togni. "Values Education: A Framework and Exercises." Social Studies, 70 (1979): 133-137.

Based on their experiences as practitioners, the authors propose a four-phase values education program, consisting of values awareness at the primary level, values clarification in the intermediate grades, values analysis at the junior high level, and values reasoning at the high school level.

88. Leary, William. "The Introduction and Administration of a Law Program as a Form of Moral Education in a Boston High School." Ed.D. dissertation, Boston University, 1972. 33/04, p. 1367.

No gain in moral reasoning was detected as a result of the Law Program. A teacher's strike interfered with the successful completion of the study.

89. Lengel, James. "Explanations of Developmental Change Applied to Education: Atmospheres for Moral Development." Montpellier: Vermont State Department of Education, 1974. ED 104 738.

Presents a proposal for "developmental atmospheres" --viewing the elementary classroom as a total social environment where a student's moral development occurs. A four-phase model is presented.

90. Lewis, Justin, and Albert Korbal. "On Sensitizing Youth to Moral Imperatives: The Holocaust as Case Study." Religious Education, 72 (1977): 657-663.

Argues that the study of the Holocaust can create a sense of the need for a humane milieu. A select bibliography of materials for teachers is presented.

91. Lickona, Thomas. "Fostering Moral Development in the Family." Development of Moral Reasoning (item 26), pp. 169-191.

Discusses strategies parents may employ to become more systematic and deliberate about the moral development of their children. Moral development is defined as involving thought, feeling, and action. The strategies presented focus on the moral example of parents, a fairness approach to rules and discipline, democratic family meetings, the development of positive affective relationships with children, and the use of moral perspectives.

92. Los Angeles City Schools. The Teaching of Values: An Instructional Guide. Los Angeles: Los Angeles City Schools, 1978. ED 171 611.

Identifies value concepts that should be integrated into the education of all children and suggests learning activities for use in the classroom. The values identified are integrity, courage, responsibility, justice, reverence, love, and respect for law and order. The approach appears to rely on the teacher's guiding the children to understand the reasonableness of these values.

93. Lovin, Paul. Anecdotes to Develop Social and Self Awareness with Elementary School Children. Midland, MI: Pendell Publishing, 1973.

Presents 24 stories designed to help elementary school children gain insights into the reasons for their actions and to help them understand how their behavior affects other persons. Also included is a copy of the Lovin scale of social adjustment, which attempts to assess the degree to which children are socially adjusted, i.e., behaving appropriately.

94. Lunn, Alma J. "The Effects of Group Techniques on the Attitudes Held by Children Toward Moral and Spiritual Values." Ed.D. dissertation, Colorado State College, 1967. 28/05, p. 1734.

Using role playing, discussion, and lecture an attempt was made to change children's moral and spiritual values. The lecture and discussion groups produced changes, but not the role-playing group.

95. Lush, Robert. "Contract and Discipline in Society." Progress and Problems in Moral Education (item 1820), pp. 178-183.

Discusses the role of a contract between free individuals as the basis for discipline in society and schools. Exercising choice, making decisions, and abiding by them are the basis of the current state of society and determine the acceptable limits of human behavior.

96. MacLean, John D. "Values Theory and Values Education Curricula Materials: An Examination." Ed.D. dissertation, Boston University, 1977. 38/04, p. 2074.

Points out that little rationale/procedures consistency exists in recent values education curricula. Discusses two equally sound approaches to values education: emphasize practices and imply rationale and justification, or emphasize premises and imply practices.

97. McPhail, Peter. "To Play Roles or Do Your Own Thing?" History and Social Science Teacher, 11 (1975): 27-31.

Describes the ways in which role playing and simulation can assist students to clarify values and develop more adequate values.

98. May, Phillip R. Moral Education in School. London: Methuen Educational Ltd., 1971.

Discusses a wide range of issues related to the place of moral education in schools. Reports the results of a survey in England in which teachers gave their opinions on the place of moral education. Finally, May presents his own views. He holds that teachers must assist society by teaching a clear moral code to supplement instruction received at home. Suggestions for content and method are presented.

99. Meaney, Marie H. "A Guide for Implementing Values Education in the Primary Grades." Ed.D. dissertation, Seattle University, 1979. 40/03, p. 1159.

Develops a program in values education for use in the primary grades, focusing on values for self, others, country, and environment.

100. Meeker, David L. "Measuring Attitude and Value Changes in Selected Humanities and Human Relations Programs." Ph.D. dissertation, Kent State University, 1969. 30/12, p. 5292.

Attitudes and values did not change as a result of student participation in selected high school humanities and human relations classes. Gordon's Survey of Interpersonal Values instrument was used.

101. Meyer, John. "Projects and Prospects: Applied Research in Values Education." Values Education: Theory/Practice/Problems/Prospects (item 1805), pp. 95-102.

Presents a survey of the more identifiable projects in Great Britain, Canada, and the United States.

102. Meyer, John R. "Where Are We and Where Might We Go in Values Education?" Reflections on Values Education (item 1804), pp. 213-221.

Discusses the current state of the art in Canada, Great Britain, and the United States and identifies a number of problematic areas that need more attention: definitions, learning theory, moral agents, evaluation, and collaboration.

103. Middleton, Drew. "West Point Seeks to Eliminate Moral 'Corruption' in Army Enlistees." New York Times, August 6, 1978, p. 38.

Discusses how the honor code is no longer adequate in controlling immoral behavior at West Point and describes courses in morals and ethics now implemented.

104. Milgram, Roberta M. "A Study of the Inquiry-Discovery Method in Teaching Moral Concepts." Ed.D. dissertation, The American University, 1969. 30/05, p. 1887.

Examines the effects of an inquiry-discovery versus a teacher-centered approach on the learning of moral concepts. Both methods were equally effective.

105. Morain, L.L. "California's Moral Guidelines for Children." Humanist, 39, 5 (1979): 36-38.

Critically reviews Guidelines for Moral Education in California Schools. Argues that the humanism the document deplores is a figment of the authors' imagination.

106. Mosher, Ralph. "Moral Education: Seven Years Before the Mast." Educational Leadership, 38 (1980): 12-15.

Mosher describes the current status of moral education, based on his experiences of the preceding seven years. He discusses the major problems currently facing the movement and suggests new directions for the future of moral education.

107. Newell, Peter. "Discipline." Progress and Problems in Education (item 1820), pp. 169-177.

Argues that discipline is essentially compulsion and that the imposition of any value system is propaganda and requires authoritarian structures. Argues for a system of discipline based on knowledge of the child's family and outside social life.

108. Newman, Arthur J. "Aesthetic Sensitizing and Moral Education." Journal of Aesthetic Education, 14, 2 (1980): 93-101.

Argues that there is some evidence to suggest a marked affinity between aesthetically inclined personality configurations and those that would characterize the morally mature. Argues that a curriculum that focuses on aesthetic development could nicely complement a curriculum focusing on moral development. In this way the overly rational-analytic world view of Kohlberg could be broadened into a more adequate view of the moral personality.

109. Nicholes, Daniel R. and Cheryl L. Kubelick. "Creating Classroom Community." Pittsburgh: Allegheny Intermediate Unit, 1979. ED 198 029.

A manual for elementary school teachers. Discusses William Damon's stages of social reasoning and suggests methods for establishing a classroom and school-wide community to aid students in social reasoning and self-governance.

110. Northview Public Schools. The Project on Student Values. A Report to Interested Citizens. Grand Rapids, MI: Northview Public Schools, 1970. ED 041 334.

Contains an extensive final report of a curriculum effort in values education. Strategies, materials, rationales, and a bibliography of 2,000 entries are included. The activities have a values clarification emphasis.

111. Nyquist, Ewald B. "The American 'No-Fault' Morality." Phi Delta Kappan, 58 (1976): 272-277.

Presents a general polemic on the need for values education and briefly describes the efforts of project SEARCH in New York state.

112. Ojemann, R., and A. Campbell. "The Development of Moral Judgment-I." Journal of Experimental Education, 42 (Spring 1974): 65-73.

A rationale and a planned instructional sequence were developed for teaching the process of making moral judgments. The instruction focused on developing sensitivity to long-range consequences of behavior and on finding alternative means for achieving one's goals. Students exposed to the program become more consequences-oriented and less arbitrary, judgmental, and prone to unproved conclusions. Subjects were fifth graders.

113. Oliver, R.G. "Knowing the Feelings of Others: A Requirement for Moral Education." Educational Theory, 25 (1975): 116-124.

Demonstrates that knowing the feelings of others is essential if children are to be rational about morals. Also discusses the cognitive processes and dispositions related to this understanding and the implications for education.

114. Olmo, Barbara G. "Value Clarification or Values Analysis?" Clearing House, 50 (1976): 122-124.

Discusses the use of values clarification and values analysis strategies in the classroom.

115. Oregon Department of Education. "Ethics and Morality: Suggested Activities for Instruction as Required by ORS 336.067." Salem: Oregon Department of Education, 1978. ED 165 252.

A booklet intended to aid school administrators and teachers in their curriculum development efforts in response to an Oregon law requiring instruction in specific aspects of ethics and morality. There is no apparent theoretical uniformity underlying the suggested activities.

116. Pannwitt, Barbara. "Admittance to the Moral Domain ... Where Schools Have Feared to Tread." Curriculum Report, Vol. 6, No. 2, December 1976. ED 131 565.

This curriculum report from the National Association of Secondary School Principals presents an overview of values education, a section on steps to allay community apprehensions, and reports on school districts with successful programs.

117. Parker, Kathryn E. "With Liberty and Justice for All--From Recitation to Reality." Educational Horizons, 56 (Winter 1977-78): 90-94.

Explores the issue of appropriate curriculum strategies for teaching justice. Self-development of teachers (becoming an agent of justice) and the educational setting are seen as the most important variables.

118. Paterson, R.W.K. Values, Education, and the Adult. Boston: Routledge and Kegan Paul, 1979.

Chapter 5 (pp. 123-152) presents a philosophic analysis of the appropriate goals of moral education with adults. Moral autonomy, moral awareness and the capacity to make reasoned and perceptive moral judgments are at the heart of the discussion.

119. Peckenpaugh, Donald H. "Moral Education: The Role of the School." The School's Role as Moral Authority. Washington, DC: Association for Supervision and Curriculum Development, 1977, pp. 31-50.

Reviews a wide variety of approaches to moral/values education and draws together strands that run through each. Concludes with the characteristics of a quality program of moral education.

120. Platek, Theresa F. "The Responses of Six Adolescents to Value Situations in Selected Short Stories: A Case Study of the Valuing Process." Ed.D. dissertation, State University of New York at Buffalo, 1975. 36/06, p. 3245.

Describes the valuing process that adolescents go through while reading short stories. The process was found to have five dimensions: identification, definition, compatibility, judgment, and modification.

121. Porwoll, Paul J. Values Education. Arlington, VA: Education Research Service, 1976. ED 132 678.

Presents a brief overview of the values education field and offers a section on beginning a values education program. Contains 15 accounts of values education programs currently in place in public schools.

122. Presno, Vincent. "Strategies for Value Teaching." Ed.D. dissertation, Columbia University, 1975. 36/08, p. 5000.

Demonstrates that Robert Hartman's theory of value is a sound basis for organizing teaching strategies for value teaching. Develops teaching strategies around three different types of values.

123. Proefriedt, William A. "Teaching Value Issues: The Challenge to Rationality." Ed.D. dissertation, Columbia University, 1970. 31/10, p. 5043.

Discusses three alternatives to the rational approach to the teaching of moral values: indoctrination, conditioning, and an affective model.

124. Purpel, David, and Kevin Ryan. "Moral Education: What Is It and Where Are We." Moral Education ... It Comes With the Territory (item 1811), pp. 3-10.

Discusses historical and social reasons for the need for moral education and the considerations necessary before implementation of any moral education program.

125. Purpel, David, and Kevin Ryan. "Moral Education: Where Sages Fear to Tread." Phi Delta Kappan, 56 (1975): 659-662.

Sketches out the vast terrain involved in moral education, schools' current responses, and difficulties inherent in implementing moral education in a democratic, pluralistic society.

126. Purpel, David, and Kevin Ryan. "What Can Be Done?" Moral Education ... It Comes with the Territory (item 1811), pp. 387-391.

Attempts to outline what the schools can do to get started in the tricky terrain of moral education. Indicates how to take a moral inventory of the school and establish long-range goals.

127. Quinn, Richard T. "An Approach to Teaching/Learning Moral Values and Valuation in Kindergarten Through a Computer-Based Resource Unit." Ed.D. dissertation, State University of New York at Buffalo, 1979. 40/03, p. 1251.

A survey of kindergarten teachers found that they felt that moral education without indoctrination was possible, and that many favored values clarification. Although a computer-based resource unit was not developed, Quinn concluded that it would be possible to develop one.

128. Reilly, Kathryn C. "Strategies of Values Education in Schools: A Review, Analysis and Proposal." Ph.D. dissertation, Saint Louis University, 1978. 39/03, p. 1505.

Four approaches to values education were found to be quantitatively and qualitatively similar. It was concluded that the notion of heterogeneity among these approaches in terms of content or underlying values may be a myth.

129. Ross, John A. "Values Education and the Role of the Community." Religious Education, (March/April 1978).

Discusses an example of ineffective school/community cooperation in values education and sets forth some guidelines for an effective and appropriate role for the community.

130. Ryan, Kevin. Questions and Answers on Moral Education, Fastback 153. Bloomington, IN: Phi Delta Kappa Educational Foundation, 1981.

Reviews four approaches to moral education and offers a synthesis.

131. Sessons, Isaiah. "The Development, Design and Testing of an Instrument Designed to Bring About Value Awareness." Ph.D. dissertation, Cornell University, 1975. 36/06, p. 3372.

A slide-music production on value conflict was found to produce 50% positive change and 50% negative change in values awareness.

132. Shannon, Gary J., and Alphonse D. Selinger. "Values Transmission: Some Issues and an Answer." Interchange, 11, 2 (1980-81): 39-55.

In an effort to make sense of the welter of materials and approaches to values education, the authors analyzed issues in the field are analyzed in four categories: philosophical, psychological, pedagogical, and socio-political. They argue that there exists some common agreement among practitioners, and they proposes a "values transmission" model that reflects these commonalities. The approach consists of personalizing the environment, building community, learning cooperatively, developing awareness of and respect for others, and respect for the processes of society.

133. Shaver, James P. "Values and Schooling Perspectives for School People and Parents." Logan: Utah State University, 1972. ED 067 320.

Attempts to provide a perspective from which parents and school personnel can formulate reasoned opinions on what the school's role should be in regard to values education. Central to thinking about this question is a democratic society's commitment to human dignity and the need for a rational basis for values. However, the parents' desires in this matter must also be considered.

134. Shaver, James, and William Strong. Facing Value Decisions: Rationale Building for Teachers. Belmont, CA: Wadsworth, 1976.

Presents readings and exercises designed to facilitate teacher reflection on the role of a values educator. The theoretical framework presented consists of three parts: a definition of values, a discussion of the nature of democracy, and an analysis of moral education in a democratic society.

135. Shibles, Warren. Ethics: A Critical Analysis for Children. Whitewater, WI: The Language Press, 1978. ED 171 640.

Part of the "Teaching Young People to Be Critical" series, this volume is intended to introduce children to the field of ethics and modes of philosophical inquiry about ethical questions.

136. Shockley, Foster B. "Implications of Pestalozzi's Epistemology for Contemporary Early Childhood Moral Development." Ph.D. dissertation, George Peabody College for Teachers of Vanderbilt University, 1980. 41/09, p. 3940.

Pestalozzi's ideals for moral instruction, with emphasis on teacher conduct and behavior, are presented.

137. Short, Edmund C. "No Rights Without Right Actions." Educational Leadership, 35 (1978): 434-438.

Presents some guidelines on an effective moral education program and suggests that only through reflective moral action by all will our rights be protected.

138. Shrank, Jeffrey. Media in Value Education: A Critical Guide. Chicago: Argus Communications, 1970.

Provides a comprehensive guide to approximately 100 films that could be used in values education along with suggested questions for discussion.

139. Silver, Michael. Values Education. Washington, DC: National Education Association, 1976.

Presents an overview of the field. Contains sections on the nature of values, how values are learned, and the teacher's role in values education. Six approaches to the teaching of values are presented, along with a bibliography on each approach and references to curriculum materials based on the approaches. Also included is a list of addresses for project newsletters and clearinghouses.

140. Sizer, Theodore R. "Values Education in the Schools: A Practitioner's Perspective." Religious Education, 70 (1975): 138-149.

Argues that the basis of values education is rational--the unending analysis of values. However, there are two touchstones of a sound school--justice and charity--that educators are obliged to exhibit fully. A response by Philip Phenix follows, in which he argues that more attention should be paid to the affective in values education.

141. Smith, Barbara L. "The Teaching of Morality: Does It Have a Legal Basis or Is It Legally Sanctioned?" Educational Horizons, 56 (1977-78): 66-70.

Holds that morality is law, therefore the educator must recognize trends in the law for then and only then can one be sure one's teaching of morality is legally sanctioned. Preserving neutrality within this legal framework is discussed.

142. Smith, B.O. "We Need a New Discipline of Judgment." Educational Leadership, 35 (1978): 419-422.

Argues that given the extent of moral perplexity in contemporary society, there is a need for a new discipline of judgment. Youth and adults should engage in joint deliberation about pressing personal and social problems.

143. Smith, Philip G. "What Is Moral Education?" Viewpoints, 51 (November 1975): 17-29.

Argues that "the moral aspects of education" are not only the more basic but also the more powerful meaning of "moral education." Two key ideas underlie moral education understood as moral aspects of education: sensitivity to other persons and a feeling of obligation to act on principle rather than entirely on self-interest. Possible aids to achieving the goals of moral education are discussed.

144. Smith, Philip. "What Is Value?" Chapter 7 in Philosophy of Education by Philip Smith. New York: Harper and Row, 1965.

Presents a detailed analysis of the value concept and attempts to set forth the conditions for a science of valuation. Offers suggestions for education for improved valuing.

145. Snook, I.A. "John Locke's Theory of Moral Education." Educational Theory, 20 (1970): 364-367.

Esteem and disgrace, praise and blame, are to be the chief means of securing right conduct. The child should find that virtuous acts lead to esteem and that esteem leads to pleasure. Early training is based on habit, but later the child must come to see the reasonableness of moral law.

146. Steiner, Elizabeth, and Ruth Hitchcock. "Teaching Moral Criticism in the Sciences." Viewpoints in Teaching, 56 (Fall 1980): 63-73.

Finds the value analysis, values clarification, and cognitive-developmental approaches all inadequate. The moral criticism approach is introduced. In this approach elements of criticism and moral reasoning are combined and applied in a form of scientific reasoning.

147. Stuhr, David, and Louise Rundle. "Moral Education in the Elementary School: Unconventional Methods for Conventional Goals." Moral Education: A First Generation of Research and Development (item 428), pp. 237-249.

Discusses the rationale and curriculum developed to stimulate elementary school children's moral reasoning. The results of the curriculum and issues raised by the approach are discussed.

148. Sullivan, Paul. "A School Rules Unit Designed to Foster Moral Development in the Elementary School." Moral Education Forum, 4 (1979): 21-28.

Describes the Ethical Quest Project in the Tacoma, Wash. School District. The focus of the project is on rules: what they are, why they exist, how to decide if they are fair or not, how to change them, etc. A School Rules Unit used on the elementary level is described. Examples of classroom discussions are presented.

149. Sullivan, Paul J., and Mary F. Dockstader. "Values Education and American Schools: Worlds in Collision?" Value Development ... As the Aim of Education (item 1816), pp. 135-155.

Presents a progress report (as of June 1977) on the Ethical Quest in a Democratic Society curriculum project in the Tacoma School District (funded by the national Endowment for the Humanities). Documents the efforts of a large school district to implement a largely developmental approach to moral education K-12. Discusses building community and school support, curriculum development, and in-service training for teachers.

150. Sullivan, Paul J., and Mary D. Sullivan. "Establishing Moral Education Programs: A Priority for Guidance." Personnel and Guidance Journal, 58 (1980): 622-626.

The Ethical Quest in a Democratic Society Project of Tacoma, Wash. is offered as a possible model for curriculum development in moral education. The cognitive-developmental basis of the approach is explained, followed by descriptions of how to build community support, curriculum development, classroom materials, and staff development.

151. Superka, Douglas P., et al. Values Education Sourcebook. Boulder: Social Science Education Consortium, 1976.

Presents a typology of six approaches to values education: Inculcation, Moral Development, Analysis, Clarification, Action Learning, and Evocation and Union. Each of the six approaches is described and examples of student and teacher materials are presented. An annotated bibliography of values education materials classified by approach and a selected bibliography of related works on values education are presented.

152. Taylor, B.L., and R.C. McKean. "Values Curriculum Being Developed." Educational Leadership, 32 (1974): 238.

Describes a three-year values education project in Aurora, Ill. The curriculum utilizes the ideals of values clarification, Kohlberg, and Rokeach.

153. Thomas, Donald, and Margaret Richards. "Ethics Education Is Possible." Phi Delta Kappan, 60 (1979): 579-582.

Describes the efforts of the Salt Lake City, Utah, school district to develop and implement ethics education in their school district. A program of individual ethics, based on the philosophical writings of Kant, and 12 democratic values was developed. A description of the various components of the curriculum is included.

154. Toffler, Alvin; June G. Shane; and Harold G. Shane. "Interview: Alvin Toffler on the Role of the Future and Values in Education." Values Concepts and Techniques (item 1784), pp. 268-276.

155. Torkelson, Gerald M. "Using Learning Resources in Teaching Values." Social Education, 31 (1967): 41-42; 48.

How learning resources can contribute to children engaged in the processes of differentiation and integration as objective ways of examining values and attitudes.

156. Vance, Barbara. "Toward a Theory of Moral Values Instruction for Children." Journal of Research and Development in Education, 13, 1 (1979): 43-49.

Argues that effective social and moral values education requires attention to the interrelationships of the moral values already known, ability, and motivation. All three must be considered for each student individually for instruction for values to be effective.

157. Vare, Jonatha W. "Moral Education for the Gifted: A Confluent Model." The Gifted Child Quarterly, 23 (1979): 487-499.

A confluent model for moral development is described in which cognitive and affective goals and appropriate instructional strategies are defined. The strategies focus on discussion and problem solving through the use of reasoning in an atmosphere of openness, tolerance, and concern for others.

158. Wagschol, Harry. "Education and the Study of Values." Educational Studies, 5 (1975): 205-209.

Briefly reviews 25 books on values. Concludes that the rigorous study of values in society and the classroom is much needed.

159. Wagschol, Harry. "Values Education. Towards a Theory and Practice of Cultural Transformation." Quebec: Dawson College, 1976. ED 133 274.

Examines some of the major theoretical considerations and pedagogical applications of values education. Attempts to explore some of the major sociological dimensions of this type of education. It is seen as a manifestation of anti-technocratic currents in modern culture, suggesting actual criticism of the scientific paradigm. A case study of an interdisciplinary Humanities course at the undergraduate level is described.

160. Weikart, David. "Influencing Children's Values, Feelings and Morals: Program Development and Problems." <u>Values, Feelings and Morals</u> (item 1791): pp. 86-102.

Presents a matrix for viewing program development in moral education based on varying degrees of teacher and student response. Four types of curricula are discussed: programmed, open framework, custodial, and child-centered.

161. Weinstein, J., and M.S. Schwartz. "Values Education Without Indoctrination." <u>Educational Forum</u>, 43 (1979): 203-211.

Presents a theoretical and philosophical model for values education drawn from the ideals of Martin Buber. The model emphasizes a relationship of reciprocal trust.

162. Westerhoff, J.H., ed. "Moral Development." <u>Religious Education</u>, 75 (March-April 1980).

Presents a series of papers originally delivered at the 1979 annual meeting of the Association of Professors and Researchers in Education.

163. Williams, David M. "A.V.E.R. in Surrey: An Approach to Research and Development in Moral Education." _The Teaching of Values in Canadian Education_ (item 1797), pp. 62-74.

Reports the results of a moral education project in Surrey, B.C., schools initiated by A.V.E.R. The thrust of the intervention is to promote rational morality as defined by the A.V.E.R. "Components of Moral Competency." Three experimental conditions were involved: Kohlbergian dilemma discussions, the Meux self-paced programmed text on value reasoning, and the A.V.E.R. treatment. The results were on the whole discouraging; this was attributed to weaknesses in the implementation of the approaches due to poor teacher training.

164. Wilson, John. "How to Study 'Value Education.'" _Values Education: Theory/Practice/Problems/Prospects_ (item 1805), pp. 165-167.

Presents a brief guide to becoming clear about the nature of values education.

165. Wilson, John. "Moral Education: Retrospect and Prospect." _Journal of Moral Education_, 9 (1979): 3-9.

Argues that for moral education to progress, a nonpartisan approach and methodology must be developed, research must be interdisciplinary and linear, and teacher education and school time must be addressed. Fragmentation between the theoretical and practical is one of the most serious threats to the future of moral education.

166. Wilson, John. "Research and Development: Some Problems in Co-operation." _Journal of Moral Education_, 3 (1974): 137-141.

There is a need for a movement against sectarianism in the field of moral education. There is also a need for more precise definition of terms and aims.

167. Wilson, John; Norman Williams; and Barry Sugarman. _Introduction to Moral Education_. Baltimore, MD: Penguin Books, 1967.

This book consists of three sections. The first, "What is Moral Education?" by Wilson, is comprehensive, focusing on other people's interests, being reasonable, the problems of justifying methods, indoctrination, religion, and assessing the morally educated person. Williams' "What the Psychologist Has to Say" section focuses on factors in moral development and moral behavior. "What the Sociologist Has to Say," by Sugarman, discusses mass society, youth culture, home, and school as they impact on the development of moral character. Wilson closes the book with a discussion of practical possibilities for moral education.

168. Windishar, Frank L. "The Education of Judgment: A Rationale." Educational Leadership, 35 (1978): 430-433.

Schools cannot present solutions to contemporary and future problems, but can help to provide the skills needed to arrive at necessary moral and spiritual standards.

169. Wisconsin State Department of Public Instruction. Knowledge Processes and Values in the New Social Studies. Madison: Wisconsin State Department of Public Instruction, 1970. ED 048 023.

A guide for K-12 teachers with an emphasis on the teaching of values. A variety of theoretical frameworks for the teaching of values is presented, along with practical suggestions for classroom activities.

170. Wolf-Wasserman, Miriam, and Linda Hutchinson. Teaching Human Dignity: Social Change Lessons for Every Teacher. Minneapolis, MN: Education Exploration Center, 1978.

A practical book for teachers who are interested in social change, including lessons on virtually every topic concerning what is wrong with life in the United States: racism, sexism, economic oppression, chemical additives in food, militarism, etc. The authors hope, by stimulating teachers' and students' awareness of the bankruptcy of contemporary life, to stimulate radical social change and achieve greater dignity for all people.

171. Wolfson, Bernice. "Values and the Primary School Teacher." Social Education, 31 (1967): 37-38.

Presents a values clarification approach to the teaching of values. Argues that teachers need to be aware of their own values because these influence the values that students learn.

172. Wright, Derek. "Discipline a Psychological Perspective." Progress and Problems in Moral Education (item 1820), pp. 143-158.

Discusses contrasting views on the necessity of discipline and the major generalizations to be drawn about the topic from psychological research. Discusses ways that discipline can be improved.

173. Zatz, Julie. "The Right to Privacy: An Issue in Moral Development." Moral Development and Politics (item 1821), pp. 190-191.

Discusses how privacy based on the prior principle of respect for persons can foster moral development. Argues that legal moralism overly restricts individuals and therefore hinders moral development.

174. Zigler, Ronald L. "Toward a Holistic Model of Morality and Moral Education." Ed.D. dissertation, University of Cincinnati, 1977. 38/05, p. 2641.

A holistic and organic model of moral education is proposed, incorporating such diverse ideals as Dewey's aesthetic/imaginative experience, transcendental meditation, and biological stress.

Values Clarification: Theory and Practice

175. Abramowitz, Mildred W., and Claudia Macari. "Values Clarification in Junior High School." _Educational Leadership_, 29 (1972): 621-626.

Describes the authors' efforts at implementing a values clarification program in Niles Junior High School, the Bronx, N.Y. Although no data is presented, the authors claim the program has helped both students and faculty. Examples of actual curricula are presented. Also in _Readings in Values Clarification_ (item 212), pp. 297-306.

176. Berson, M.B. "Valuing, Helping, Thinking, Resolving." _Childhood Education_, 49 (1973): 242-245.

Pays tribute to Louis E. Raths. Reviews his life and major work including his several books on values, emotional needs, and thinking.

177. Boyer, Evelyn P. "Value-Clarification as an Approach to Moral Development." _Educational Horizons_, 56 (1977-78): 101-106.

Discusses the benefits of using values clarification in the classroom.

178. Casteel, J. Doyle, and Clemens Holiman. "Cross Cultural Inquiry: Value Clarification Exercises." Gainesville: Center for Latin American Studies, University of Florida, 1974. ED 107 536.

Ten examples illustrating an integrated multi-disciplinary and practical values clarification approach to teaching about Latin America are presented.

179. Cogan, John J., and Wayne Paulson. "Values Clarification and the Primary Child." _Social Studies_, 69 (1978): 20-24.

Applies values clarification to the primary level. Stresses that the issues considered must be within the students' frame of reference and at their level of interest. Practical examples of appropriate activities are provided.

180. Curwin, Richard L. "Values Clarification Approach to Teaching Secondary English Methods." Ed.D. dissertation, University of Massachusetts, 1972. 33/09, p. 4999.

A case study of an attempt, using the Tyler rationale, to design a course in secondary English methods based on the values clarification model. It was found that students enjoyed the course.

181. Curwin, R.L., and A. Curwin. Developing Individual Values in the Classroom. Palo Alto, CA: Learning Handbooks, 1974.

A handbook for implementing values clarification in the elementary school classroom. Contains sections on building trust, integrating values and curriculum areas, creating activities for the classroom, record keeping, etc.

182. Engle, David E. "Some Issues in Teaching Values." Religious Education, 65 (1970): 9-13.

Argues that there is no single correct answer in the consideration of values. Any approach to the study of values must focus on the clarification of values.

183. Evans, Clyde. "Facing Up to Values." Teacher, 92 (December 1974): 16-18; 72-73.

Basically urges that teachers adopt a position of helping students to clarify the values they want to hold. Teachers are urged not to create the impression that there are right answers to value questions. The emphasis is on values clarification. Do's and Don't's are listed.

184. Gellatt, H.B., B. Varenhorst; and R. Carey. Deciding: A Leader's Guide. New York: College Entrance Examination Board, 1972.

Presents a decision-making unit for high school students, much of which is based on values clarification techniques. The student booklet is very attractively packaged.

185. Goodman, Joel. "Sid Simon on Values: No Moralizers or Manipulators Allowed." Nation's Schools, 92 (December 1973): 39-42.

In an interview with Goodman, Simon discusses his theory and how teachers and administrators can begin to implement values clarification strategies.

186. Goodman, Joel, ed. Turning Points: New Developments, New Directions in Values Clarification, Vols. I and II. Saratoga Springs, NY: Creative Resources Press, 1978. NI

Contains 45 articles and 30 strategies that represent, according to the editor, "state-of-the-art" thinking about values clarification. The articles vary widely, from responses to the critics of values clarification, to applying values clarification to a wide range of schooling concerns, to testimonials on "Why I Love Values Clarification." Includes an extensive bibliography and guide to sources. Most of the articles are by non-academics and have a practical bent.

187. Goodman, Joel. "Values Clarification: Some Thoughts on How to Get Started." Values Concepts and Techniques (item 1784), pp. 144-147.

188. Goodman, Joel and Laurie Hawkins. "Value Clarification: Meeting a Challenge in Education." Readings in Values Clarification (item 212), pp. 307-316.

Describes an eight-week course, taught in a dormitory setting, on how values clarification can be used to help college undergraduates deal with value related concerns.

189. Gray, Farnum. "Doing Something about Values." Readings in Values Clarification (item 212), pp. 317-326.

A report on the philosophy and work of Sid Simon. Describes Simon's workshops for teachers, which provides a sense of his personal style of values clarification.

190. Greene, Diane; Pat Stewart; and Howard Kirschenbaum. "Training a Large Public School System in Values Clarification." Readings in Values Clarification (item 212), pp. 348-357.

Describes how values clarification came to the Akron, Ohio, public schools in 1969, and traces the first four years of involvement. The workshops presented and the role of specialists in keeping the program going are discussed.

191. Hall, Brian P. Value Clarification and Learning Process: A Guidebook of Learning Strategies. New York: Paulist Press, 1973.

Presents an introduction to values clarification, 49 different strategies, suggestions on organizing workshops for training value clarifiers, and a section on potential problems in using values clarification exercises.

192. Harmin, Merrill, and Sidney B. Simon. "How to Help Students Learn to Think ... About Themselves." High School Journal, 55 (1972): 256-264.

Suggests values clarification activities to help students to learn to think, to think about life, and to think about themselves.

193. Harmin, M., and S.B. Simon. "The Subject Matter Controversy Revisited." Peabody Journal of Education, 42 (1965): 194-205.

Describes three levels of subject matter (facts, generalizations, and values) and suggests that schools move from a focus on facts to a greater emphasis on the other levels as a means of making learning more exciting and meaningful.

194. Harmin, Merrill, and Sidney B. Simon. "Values." Readings in Values Clarification (item 212), pp. 4-15.

Reviews a variety of approaches that assume that absolute goods exist and are known and then reviews approaches based on clarifying values without promoting specific values.

195. Harmin, Merrill, and Sidney B. Simon. "Values and Teaching: A Humane Process." Educational Leadership, 24 (1967): 517-525.

Standard values clarification fare.

196. Harmin, Merrill; Howard Kirschenbaum; and Sidney B. Simon. Clarifying Values Through Subject Matter. Minneapolis, MN: Winston Press, 1973.

Discusses the need for teachers to teach at three levels: facts, concepts, and values. Guidelines for values level teaching are presented, followed by examples from 20 different subject areas ranging from art to physics. The final section of the book presents a variety of values clarification techniques.

197. Hawley, Robert C. Value Exploration Through Role Playing: Practical Strategies for Use in the Classroom. New York: Hart, 1975.

A practical guide to role playing designed to clarify student values.

198. Hawley, Robert C.; Sidney B. Simon; and D.D. Britton. Composition for Personal Growth: Values Clarification Through Writing. New York: Hart Publishing Co., 1973.

A guide for teaching writing with a focus on values clarification. Personal growth is seen as the major focus of writing activities.

199. Howe, Leland W. "Group Dynamics and Value Clarification" Readings in Values Clarification (item 212), pp. 358-361.

Discusses the importance of the arrangement of the group (a circle is best) in facilitating student discussion and involvement.

200. Howe, Leland W., and Mary M. Howe. Personalizing Education: Values Clarification and Beyond. New York: Hart Publishing Co., 1975.

Attempts to extend values clarification so that it becomes an integral part of every dimension of the classroom. Contains sections on personalizing human relationships, personalizing goals in the classroom, personalizing the curriculum, and personalizing classroom organization and management. Contains many practical activities for helping the teacher make his/her classroom total values clarification.

201. Huggins, Kenneth B. "Alternatives in Values Clarification." National Elementary Principal, 54 (November/December 1974): 76-79.

Argues that teachers can achieve a balance between overdirecting students and freely offering alternatives, which, the author feels, makes students feel lost.

202. Johnson, Bruce D., and Bryce Nelson. "Values Clarification: A Critical Perspective." Morality Examined (item 1818) pp. 121-140.

Presents the history, rationale, procedures, and assumptions of the values clarification approach. A mild critique is offered, focusing primarily on whether or not it is possible or desirable for value-free education to occur.

203. Kingman, Barry. "The Development of Value Clarification Skills: Initial Efforts in an Eighth Grade Social Studies Class." Stony Brook: State University of New York, 1975. ED 108 979.

A candid account of the problems, successes, and failures involved in attempting to implement values clarification in the classroom.

204. Kirschenbaum, Howard. Advanced Values Clarification. La Jolla, CA: University Associates, 1977.

Designed for those who train others to use the values clarification approach. The first chapter attempts to clarify theoretical issues and to respond to common criticisms of the approach. Chapters on current research, designing values clarification experiences for use in workshops, and suggestions for building values clarification into the curriculum follow. One chapter answers 18 commonly asked questions about values clarification. Contains a fairly complete chronological annotated bibliography.

205. Kirschenbaum, Howard. "Beyond Values Clarification." Readings in Values Clarification (item 212), pp. 92-110.

In an attempt to incorporate the wider goals of humanistic education within the values clarification movement, Kirschenbaum discusses the limitations of the original 3-level process and discusses a 5-level, 19-step process. Communicating and feeling are given important roles in the new processes by which individuals achieve humanistic goals--achieving identity, developing values, and deciding what they stand for and what they wish to live for.

206. Kirschenbaum, Howard. "Clarifying Values at the Family Table." Readings in Values Clarification (item 212), pp. 265-270.

Discusses the technique of the family circle where at dinner the family discusses values topics. A list of 52 suggested topics is included.

207. Kirschenbaum, Howard. "The Listening Game." Readings in Values Clarification (item 212), pp. 288-294.

Discusses two structured-listening exercises (Rogerian listening and the Free-Choice game) designed to help people learn more fully to understand and experience one another.

208. Kirschenbaum, Howard. "Values Clarification and Civil Liberties." Moral Education Forum, 5 (Fall 1981): 29-33.

Discusses the political ramifications of values clarification in the classroom. Argues that teachers and students have the right to discuss controversial issues in the classroom and they should exercise this right.

209. Kirschenbaum, Howard. "Values Clarification in an Organizational Setting." Readings in Values Clarification (item 212), pp. 327-335.

In a letter to the United Presbyterian Women's Planning Committee Kirschenbaum describes how values clarification techniques can be used to achieve specific organizational goals of the group.

210. Kirschenbaum, Howard. "Values Education: 1976 and Beyond." The School's Role as Moral Authority. Washington, DC: Association for Supervision and Curriculum Development, 1977, pp. 51-69.

Argues that all approaches to values education share two common goals: (1) to help people become more satisfied with their lives and (2) to help people become more socially constructive. States that there are five valuing skills or valuing processes which are common to all approaches: thinking, feeling, choosing, communicating, and acting. When these processes are followed the goals of values education will be achieved.

211. Kirschenbaum, Howard, and Barbara Glaser-Kirschenbaum. "An Annotated Bibliography on Values Clarification." Readings in Values Clarification (item 212), pp. 366-383.

Traces the major publications in values clarification from 1965 to 1973.

212. Kirschenbaum, Howard, and Sidney B. Simon, eds. Readings in Values Clarification. Minneapolis, MN: Winston Press, 1973.

Contains 37 articles on values clarification and related topics. Includes sections on values clarification and school subjects, values in religious education, values in the family, and other approaches to valuing.

213. Kirschenbaum, Howard, and Sidney B. Simon. "Values and the Futures Movement in Education" Readings in Values Clarification (item 212), pp. 17-30.

Reviews the theory and method of values clarification and discusses how it can help students to control their futures.

214. Lawhead, Victor B. "Values Through Identification." Educational Leadership, 21 (1964): 515-519.

Argues that there are two avenues by which individuals arrive at their values: identification with a respected other, and valuing process. Since the first is not susceptible to major influence, it is argued that teachers should be involved in the process of values clarification.

215. Lieberman, Phyllis, and Sidney Simon. "Values and Student Writing." Educational Leadership, 22 (1965): 415-421; 438.

Discusses the use of values cards (a values clarification technique) in the teaching of writing. This technique requires one to write down each week something that has been on his/her mind during the past week. The guidance emphasis of values clarification is very apparent in this article.

216. Liles, Jesse. "A Dilemma of Teaching Values to Young Children." Contemporary Education, 45 (1974): 296-298.

Poses the dilemma of either indoctrinating or doing nothing with values. Values clarification is seen as a way out of the dilemma.

217. Mears, Michael. "Who's Sid Simon and What's All This about Values Clarification?" Media and Methods, 9 (1973): 30-37.

Following an explanation of why teachers should clarify values, many values clarification strategies are presented.

218. Michalak, D.A. "The Clarification of Values." Improving College and University Teaching, 18 (1970): 100-101.

Argues that what is needed in society is clarified values. Only then can we begin to solve society's problems.

219. Nevin, Hugh G. "Values Clarification: Perspectives in John Dewey and Paulo Freire." Ed.D. dissertation, Columbia University, 1977. 38/02, p. 691.

Analyzes the Raths version of values clarification and concludes that it is representative of John

Dewey's thought. Paulo Freire's thought is then introduced as an aid in considering the relation of values clarification to Dewey's social philosophy.

220. Olmo, Barbara G. "Threat of New Ideas: A Values Clarification Lesson." Adolescence, 10 (1975): 456-462.

Presents a two-day values clarification lesson for secondary school students centered around the topic of enthusiasm.

221. Pozdol, Marvin D., and Marvin Pasch. "Values Clarification in Teacher Education: An Explanation and an Evaluation." Contemporary Education, 47 (1976): 202-205.

Reports on a course taught on the graduate level at Cleveland State University: "Introduction to Values Clarification in the Schools." Reports the results of a survey indicating that the course is well-received and has an impact on classroom teaching.

222. Raths, James. "A Strategy for Developing Values." Educational Leadership, 21 (1964): 509-514; 554.

Discusses the four methods most commonly used in schools to teach values: lecture, example, peer pressure, and rewards and punishment. Finds them all ineffective. Presents values clarification as a potential approach with some promise.

223. Raths, Louis E. "Freedom, Intelligence, and Valuing." Values Concepts and Techniques (item 1784), pp. 9-17.

Discusses the theoretical background for values clarification, citing Dewey and Whitehead.

224. Raths, Louis E.; Merrill Harmin; and Sidney B. Simon. "Helping Children to Clarify Values." National Education Association Journal, 56 (October 1967): 12-15.

Presents a short review of values clarification theory and practice.

225. Raths, Louis; Merrill Harmin; and Sidney B. Simon. "Selection from Values Clarification." Moral Education ... It Comes with the Territory (item 1811), pp. 75-115.

Contains key sections from Values and Teaching (item 227) which describe, justify, and give examples of values clarification.

226. Raths, Louis; Merrill Harmin; and Sidney Simon. "Teaching for Value Clarity." Moral Education (item 171), pp. 170-182.

A selection from Values and Teaching (item 227) which discusses traditional approaches to values education, their weaknesses, and a new approach--values clarification.

227. Raths, Louis E.; Merrill Harmin; and Sidney B. Simon. Values and Teaching: Working with Values in the Classroom, 2nd ed. Columbus, OH: Charles E. Merrill, 1978.

In this updated and slightly revised edition of the authors' 1966 book, values clarification theory and suggestions for practice are presented in a readable and persuasive manner. In the revised edition the seven-step definition of the valuing process remains unchanged, but the authors do attempt to respond to criticisms leveled against the approach. The strength of the book lies in the many practical and engaging strategies presented and the practical advice for beginning values clarification in the classroom.

228. Simms, Richard. "Pop Music and Values Clarification." Values Concepts and Techniques (item 1784), pp. 243-247.

Three popular songs are used to demonstrate how values clarification can be used in the classroom.

229. Simon, Sidney B. Caring, Feeling, Touching. Niles, IL: Argus Communications, 1976.

Discusses the lack of affection in society. "Skin hunger" is held to be a major source of psychological malaise. Describes a variety of techniques for providing physical affection lacking in the family.

230. Simon, Sidney B. "Dinner Table Learning." Readings in Values Clarification (item 212), pp. 271-279.

Discusses the use at the dinner table of selected values clarification activities: value sheets, coat of arms, rank orders, and 20 things you like to do.

231. Simon, Sidney. "Election Year and Dinner Table Learning." Readings in Values Clarification (item 212), pp. 280-287.

Discusses a variety of values clarification techniques geared to an election year and suitable for the family dinner table.

232. Simon, Sidney B. Meeting Yourself Halfway. Niles, IL: Argus Communications, 1976.

Presents 31 values clarification strategies for junior and senior high school students.

233. Simon, Sidney. "Values and Teaching." Religious Education, 68 (1973): 183-194.

Appears to be a transcript of an informal presentation to teachers. Gives a good feel for "Sid Simon in Action" as a leader of workshops.

234. Simon, Sidney B. "Values Clarification vs. Indoctrination." Moral Education ... It Comes With the Territory (item 1811), pp. 126-135.

In an article written for social studies teachers Simon rejects indoctrination and presents five examples of values clarification techniques. Also in Social Education, 35 (1971): 902-905.

235. Simon, Sidney, and M.B. Bohn. "What Schools Should Be Doing about Values Clarification." NASSP Bulletin, 58 (February 1974): 54-60.

Describes a self-evaluation process that helps students answer the questions of who they are and where they are going.

236. Simon, Sidney B., and Jay Clark. *More Values Clarification: A Guidebook for the Use of Values Clarification in the Classroom*. San Diego: Pennant Press, 1975.

237. Simon, Sidney B., and Polly de Sherbinin. "Values Clarification: It Can Start Gently and Grow Deep." *Values Concepts and Techniques* (item 1784), pp. 36-47.

A definition, a rationale, and an exposition of the way in which values clarification works in the school. Also in *Phi Delta Kappan*, 56 (1975): 679-683.

238. Simon, Sidney, and Sara Massey. "Value Clarification." *Educational Leadership*, 30 (1973): 738-739.

Students explore who they are by making their own value questionnaires and trading them with each other.

239. Simon, Sidney B., and Sally W. Olds. *Helping Your Child Learn Right from Wrong*. New York: McGraw-Hill, 1976.

Presents values clarification for parents. The title is misleading, for under the theory children's choices are not limited to what parents judge as "right."

240. Simon, Sidney B., and Robert O'Rourke. "Getting to Know You." *Educational Leadership*, 32 (1975): 524-526.

Argues that the basis for effective learning is students' making themselves known to teachers and teachers' making themselves known to students. Illustrates four values clarification activities for exposing oneself (psychologically) to others.

241. Simon, Sidney; Leland Howe; and Howard Kirschenbaum. *Values Clarification: A Handbook of Practical Strategies for Teachers and Students*. New York: Hart Publishing Co., 1972.

79 practical and fun strategies for use in the classroom. Contains the controversial Alligator River and other activities that have been the focus of much of the criticism of the approach.

242. Simon, Sidney; Myra Sadker; and David Sadker. "Where Do They Stand?" Instructor, 84 (August 1974): 110.

Presents examples of strategies that can be used to help students explore their beliefs about sexuality.

243. Taffee, Stephen J. "Values Clarification Ten Years Later: Changes and Futures as Perceived by Selected Experts." Ph.D. dissertation, Michigan State University, 1976. 37/09, p. 5582.

Interviews with nine experts in values clarification and values education provide the basis for analyzing the current status and potential future of values clarification.

244. Woodhouse, M., and D.B. Fleming. "Moral Education and the Teaching of History." History Teacher, 9 (1976): 202-209.

Discusses ways that values clarification can be integrated into the study of history.

245. Yonker, Mary M. "Humanizing Through Value Clarification." Values Concepts and Techniques (item 1784), pp. 130-134.

Discusses how values clarification can make schooling more humanistic.

246. Balcruz, Emmanuel. "Group Process in Retreat Ministry Focusing on Values Clarification." D.Min., The Catholic University of America, 1980. 41/02, p. 613.

Values clarification was found to be an effective tool in achieving the goals of a retreat experience using group process.

247. Barman, Charles R. "The Influence of Values Clarification Techniques on Achievement, Attitudes and Affective Behavior in High School Biology." Ph.D. dissertation, University of Northern Colorado, 1974. 35/11, p. 7139.

No significant differences were detected on attitudes toward science, attitudes toward biology, and affective behavior as a result of exposure to values clarification activities.

248. Bernreuter, John D. "A Study of Self Concept and Achievement of Inner City Black Seventh Grade Students as Influenced by Values Clarification Lessons in Science." Ed.D. dissertation, University of Northern Colorado, 1980. 41/08, p. 3973.

It was found that values clarification lessons do not increase the self-concept of Black inner city students.

249. Berry, Paul M. "The Relationship Between Some Value Clarification Programs and Pupil Achievement." Ph.D. dissertation, United States International University, 1974. 34/10, p. 6347.

Concludes that a strong and positive relationship may be inferred between effects of innovative teaching strategies involving values clarification programs and academic achievement.

250. Blake, Bonnie J. "An Investigation into the Effects of Selected Values-Clarifying Strategies on the Valuing Behaviors of Students in a Teacher Education Program." Ed.D. dissertation, George Washington University, 1977. 38/06, p. 3246.

Found that participation in a semester of value-clarifying strategies had no significant impact on the student's application of the valuing process to teaching-problem situations.

251. Blokker, William; Barbara Glaser-Kirschenbaum; and Howard Kirschenbaum. "Values Clarification and Drug Abuse." Health Education, 7 (March/April 1976): 6-8.

In a study using 607 fourth-, fifth- and sixth-grade students it was found that exposure to a values clarification approach had no significant impact on self-esteem or on a school behavior rating scale. The connection of this study with student drug abuse is tenuous.

252. Bloom, Ronald L. "Development of Competency in the Use of the Value-Clarification Technique by Master of Arts in Teaching Interns for the Clarification of Value-Related Problem Behavior of Selected Secondary School Students." Ed.D. dissertation, New York University, 1969. 30/07, p. 2875.

Interns practiced values clarification individually with selected students. No changes in value-related problem behaviors were detected.

253. Boyle, Jackie L. "A Study of the Effects of Simon's Valuing Process on Seventh and Eighth Grade Students." Ed.D. dissertation, Oklahoma State University, 1978. 39/08, p. 2724.

No statistically significant difference was found between participation in values clarification strategies and ease in making value-related choices or incidence of value-related behavior problems.

254. Chamberlain, Virginia M. "A Description of the Use of a Value Clarification Approach in the Teaching of Earth Science Classes." Ph.D. dissertation, Michigan State University, 1971. 32/06, p. 3148.

Contains a purely descriptive study of the utilization of values clarification techniques in the teaching of Earth Science.

255. Chapman, Alice L. "The Effects of a Values Clarification Program on the Academic Achievement and Self-Concept of Students in Grade Six." Ed.D. dissertation, Boston University, 1979. 40/05, p. 2441.

It was found that only girls, and only in language and math, achieved higher grades as a result of values clarification experiences. No changes in self-concept were detected as a result of values clarification.

256. Clark, J., et al. Operation Future: Third Annual Report. San Diego, CA: Pennant, 1974.

Often referred to as "the largest and most important study on values clarification to date" by values clarification proponents. The sample consisted of 851 fifth through tenth graders, two groups of pregnant minors, two church groups, and 65 young people on probation. The study measured the effect of values clarification experiences on character traits and on the students' use of drugs. In the decrease of drug use the gains were highly significant.

257. Cobb, Gerald W. "The Effects of Values Clarification on the Self Concept and Values of Teachers." Ed.D. dissertation, Northeastern Louisiana University, 1977. 38/11, p. 6656.

Found that self-concept of graduate students in education improved significantly as a result of values clarification training. Other significant shifts in values were also found.

258. Collis, Anthony G. "Perspectives of Values-Clarification Within a Small Training Group and Within the Professional Community." Ed.D. dissertation, Temple University, 1978. 39/05, p. 2751.

It was found that graduate students, as a result of a five-week intensive program in values clarification, experienced significant moral development as measured on the Defining Issues Test. A national survey of professional educators yielded varying responses on the proper goals of moral education and their involvement.

259. Colucci, Jeffrey J. "The Measurement of Values Clarification in Middle Class Adolescents." Ph.D. dissertation, Boston College, 1979. 40/03, p. 1354.

Attempts to devise measures that would assess the constructs of value clarity and "non-value-based-behavior." Student- and teacher-based instruments were designed. Results indicated that value clarity and "non-value-based-behavior" did not appear to be homogeneous constructs.

260. Compton, Myrna J. "The Effects of Values Clarification Upon Reading Achievement, Biology Content Achievement, Cognitive Levels of Development and Expressive Language and Other Factors." Ed.D. dissertation, University of Northern Colorado, 1979. 40/10, p. 5413.

Participation in values clarification had no effect on the prediction of reading achievement. Combinations of the other variables also had no effect on the prediction of reading achievement.

261. Cooney, Timothy M. "The Effects of Values Clarification Techniques in College Physical Science on Critical Thinking Ability, Open-Mindedness and Achievement." Ed.D. dissertation, University of Northern Colorado, 1976. 36/07, p. 4252.

Values clarification lessons produced significantly greater gains in critical thinking than did traditional methods. With respect to achievement and open-mindedness, values clarification offered no advantage over traditional methods.

262. Covault, Thomas J. "The Application of Values Clarification Teaching Strategies with 5th Grade Students to Investigate Their Influence on Students' Self-Concept and Related Classroom Coping and Interacting Behaviors." Ph.D. dissertation, The Ohio State University, 1973. 34/05, p. 2199.

Found that after 11 sessions of values clarification students improved in self-concept, self-direction, positive attitude toward learning, and eight value-related behaviors.

263. Coy, Michael N. "The Effects of Teacher In-Service Training in Values Clarification on Attitudes of Elementary School Students Toward Themselves, School and the Teacher." Ed.D. dissertation, University of the Pacific, 1974. 35/10, p. 6507.

Found that after teachers' in-service training in values clarification, students' self-concept did not increase, but positive attitude toward the teacher did.

264. Crellin, David W. "Learning and Attitude Change During an In-Service Workshop in Value Clarification." Ed.D. dissertation, University of Rochester, 1968. 29/06, p. 1803.

It was found that students' attitudes toward and knowledge about values clarification increased as a result of the in-service workshop with teachers.

265. DePetro, Henry M. "Effects of Utilizing Values Clarification Strategies on the Self Esteem of Secondary School Students." Ed.D. dissertation, University of Northern Colorado, 1975. 36/02, p. 775.

The experimental group had a small but significant increase in self concept as a result of involvement in values clarification activities.

266. Dixon, Beverly R. "An Investigation into the Use of Rath's Values Clarification Strategies with Grade Eight Pupils." Ph.D. dissertation, Michigan State University, 1978. 39/10, p. 5987.

Using an ethnographic approach it was found that values clarification strategies have a significant impact on those behaviors associated with value clarity.

267. Dunbar, Louise H. "The Utilization of Values Clarification in Multicultural Education as a Strategy to Reduce Prejudicial Attitudes of Eighth Grade Students." Ed.D. dissertation, Northern Arizona University, 1980. 40/03, p. 920.

The values clarification technique did not significantly reduce the racial prejudice of eighth-grade students.

268. Dye, Joan C. "Values Clarification as a Discipline Alternative for the Middle School." Ph.D. dissertation, University of Florida, 1979. 40/04, p. 1773.

Students who were disciplinary problems received one of three treatments: self-study, group values clarification experience, or no treatment. Exposure to treatment did not affect the disciplinary referral rate of any of the subjects.

269. Edwards, Henry B. "The Effects of Selected Values Clarification Experiences on the Self Acceptance of 8th Grade Students." Ed.D. dissertation, Virginia Polytechnic Institute and State University, 1976. 37/07, p. 4313.

Found that exposure to values clarification resulted in significantly lower self-acceptance than was the case with a control group.

270. Ellison, Robert J. "A Study of the Effects of Values Clarification on Political Attitudes." Ed.D. dissertation, University of Rochester, 1974. 35/03, p. 1550.

Found that exposure to values clarification resulted in increased agreement with democratic norms.

271. Fitch, Andrew E. "Values Clarification in the Classroom and Its Effect on Student Self-Concept, Dogmatism, Classroom Attitude, Absenteeism and Grade-Point Average." Ph.D. dissertation, Indiana State University, 1979. 41/06, p. 2568.

Results indicated no significant differences between the treatment group and the control group on any of the five dependent variables.

272. Fitzpatrick, Karen. "An Experimental Study to Investigate the Effects of Selected Values Clarification Strategies on the Self-Concept and Reading Achievement of 7th Grade Students in Non-public Schools of a Large Roman Catholic Diocese." Ph.D. dissertation, The Catholic University of America, 1975. 36/04, p. 1994.

Values clarification activities yielded significantly higher scores on self-concept and test of reading comprehension and efficiency.

273. Foltz, Louis G. "An Examination of the Influence of Classifying Ability upon Success with One of Two Selected Values Clarification Activities." Ph.D. dissertation, 1978. 39/08, p. 4690.

Students with high entry ability in classification who were exposed to values clarification activities developed more complex ability in classifying their own values. Students of modal ability did not experience significant growth.

274. Foster, Georgie A. "The Effect of Values Clarification Training on Counselor Behavior." Ed.D. dissertation, Wayne State University, 1975. 36/11, p. 7204.

Exposure to values clarification yielded no significant differences in self-acceptance, acceptance of others, or dogmatism.

275. Gillihan, Carolyn L. "The Effectiveness of Value Clarifying Methodology Presented to Sixth Grade Students." Ed.D. dissertation, University of Arkansas, 1975. 36/6, p. 3233.

No significant differences in subjects' values or self-concept were found to be associated with experiences in values clarification.

276. Godfrey, Robert J. "The Effects of Values Clarification Techniques upon 9th Grade Students." Ed.D. dissertation, Lehigh University, 1976. 36/11, p. 7064.

Little impact was noted on the variables of satisfaction of values and risk taking as the result of values clarification experiences.

277. Gordon, John E. "The Effects on White Student Teachers of Value Clarification Interviews with Negro Pupils." Ed.D. dissertation, New York University, 1965. 27/02, p. 486.

Found that values clarification was no more effective than other forms of one-on-one relationships in reducing perceived social distance.

278. Graham, Marion D. "The Process of Teaching Decision Making Through Values Clarification and Its Effect on Students' Future Choices as Measured by Changes in Self-Concept." Ph.D. dissertation, St. Louis University, 1976. 37/04, p. 1885.

High school seniors exposed to values clarification yielded significant differences on all five dimensions of Shostrom's Personal Orientation Inventory.

279. Gray, Russell D. "The Influence of Values Clarification Strategies on Student Self-Concept and Sociometric Structures in Selected Elementary School Classrooms." Ph.D. dissertation, University of Southern California, 1975. 36/06, p. 3404.

It was found that the use of an outside specialist to teach values clarification for one hour per week was not an effective approach with sixth-grade students. No changes were noted in self-concept or on other variables.

280. Greco, Salvatore. "Values Clarification Methodology: Instrumentation, Predictability and Effectiveness." Ed.D. dissertation, State University of New York at Albany, 1977. 38/07, p. 4012.

Values clarification activities failed to yield significant differences as measured on scales of personal and interpersonal values and on the Values Related Behaviors Scale.

281. Gullo, Joseph F. "Effects of Videotaped Value Clarification Encounters upon Tests of Alternativism and Divergent Thinking." Ed.D. dissertation, University of Rochester, 1971. 32/07, p. 3860.

No significant differences were found in high school students' formulation of alternatives and consequences or performance on tests of divergent production of semantic content as a result of participation in videotaped values clarification encounters.

282. Guziak, Sigmund J. "The Use of Values Clarification Strategies with 5th Grade Students to Investigate Influence on Self-Concept and Values." Ph.D. dissertation, The Ohio State University, 1975. 36/03, p. 1389.

In a replication of the Covault dissertation (item 262) it was found that values clarification has no impact on self-concept, but does influence the eight values-related behaviors.

283. Handfinger, Robert. "The Effectiveness of Values Clarification Exercises Initiated by Lyrics with Music." Ed.D. dissertation, Temple University, 1979. 41/01, p. 84.

Neither values clarification initiated with popular music, values clarification without popular music, nor no values clarification yielded significant differences on the other-directed and inner-directed scales of Shostrom's Personal Orientation Inventory.

284. Hash, Virginia R. "An Evaluation of a Values Clarification Seminar in Preservice Education of Teachers." Ph.D. dissertation, Iowa State University, 1975. 36/10, p. 6472.

Found that a one-semester course on values clarification had no significant impact on interpersonal relations orientation or dogmatism.

285. Hobstettler, Lynne E. "The Effectiveness of Values Clarification Experiences for Seventh Grade Students." Ph.D. dissertation, The Ohio State University, 1980. 41/07, p. 3011.

Values clarification was found to result in no change in students' ranking of values on the Rokeach Values Survey.

286. Hopp, Norma J. "The Applicability of Value Clarifying Strategies in Health Education at the 6th Grade Level." Ph.D. dissertation, University of Southern California, 1974. 35/05, p. 2838.

It was found that teachers reacted enthusiastically to values clarification and that those students who were most confused about their values showed the greatest increase in value clarity.

287. Johnson, Rodney E. "The Effects of Utilizing Values Clarification Strategies on the Achievement of Junior High School Students." Ed.D. dissertation, University of Northern Colorado, 1977. 37/11, p. 6925.

No significant differences were detected in school achievement or the Test of Academic Skills as a result of values clarification.

288. Jonas, Arthur H. "A Study of the Relationship of Certain Behaviors of Children to Emotional Needs, Values and Thinking." Ed.D. dissertation, New York University, 1960. 21/10, p. 3018.

An early values clarification study which found that when values become more clear, behaviors associated with lack of values clarification become less acute and less frequent.

289. Kelly, Felorese W. "Selected Value Clarification Strategies and Elementary School Pupils' Self Concept, School Sentiment and Reading Achievement." Ed.D. dissertation, Fordham University, 1976. 37/05, p. 2543.

A "pronounced effect" was detected in self-concept and attitude toward school, but not in reading achievement, as a result of six months of values clarification activities.

290. Kirschenbaum, Howard. Current Research in Values Clarification. Saratoga Springs, NY: National Humanistic Education Center, 1975. ED 113 237.

Presents research reports on the effectiveness of values clarification. Most reports are positive, but few have yet made it into the published literature.

291. Kirschenbaum, Howard. "Recent Research in Values Clarification." Values Education: _Theory/Practice/Problems/Prospects_ (item 1805), pp. 71-78.

Presents a review of research on values clarification with a focus on outcomes for students, outcomes of teacher training, and methodological developments. A small number of studies are cited, most of which have not been published.

292. Klevan, Albert. "An Investigation of a Methodology for Value Clarification: Its Relationship to Consistency in Thinking, Purposefulness, and Human Relations." Ed.D. dissertation, New York University, 1957. 18/05, p. 1732.

Finds that exercises directed at clarifying values result in greater consistency in thinking and greater purposefulness. Social acceptance, however, was found to decline in the experimental group.

293. Kozlowska, Mary V. "A Study of the Effects on Racial Attitudes of Exercises in Values Clarification and Identification in Conjunction with the Poetry of a White Poet and a Black Poet." Ed.D. dissertation, Temple University, 1973. 34/07, p. 3695.

After values clarification activities and reading and discussing poetry it was found that although some individual lessening of racial tensions and increase in racial understanding occurred among the Black girls, the White girls remained unchanged in their attitudes.

294. Lang, Melvin. "An Investigation of the Relationship of Value Clarification to Underachievement and Certain Other Behavioral Characteristics of Selected College Students." Ed.D. dissertation, New York University, 1962. 23/04, p. 1288.

College students were exposed to either directive counseling or indirect values-clarification-oriented counseling. It was found that underachievers marginally increased their academic achievement under values clarification, but apathetic and dissenting students experienced no positive change.

295. Lingis, Mary. "The Effects of a Group Values Clarification Procedure on Low-Income Adolescent Girls." Ed.D. dissertation, Clark University, 1981. 42/03, p. 1041.

Finds that as a result of values clarification activities there is no significant change in self-concept and acceptance of others scores.

296. McCormick, Shirley D. "The Effects of the Use of Selected Valuing Strategies on the Personal Adjustment of Sixth Graders." Ed.D. dissertation, Memphis State University, 1975. 36/08, p. 5021.

Positive change in self-concept was found as a result of 16 sessions of values activities designed to get students to analyze, clarify, and derive values.

297. McKenzie, Gary. "A Theory-based Approach to Inductive Value Clarification." Journal of Moral Education, 4 (1974): 47-52.

Children were asked to apply steps of Taba's open-ended concept elaboration model to form operational definitions of a value concept. The approach was judged successful in teaching value concepts. Concludes that value concepts can be taught the same way as cognitive concepts.

298. Martin, Roberta P. "The Effects of Values Clarification on Change in Value Priorities as Measured by Rokeach's Value Survey." Ed.D. dissertation, Mississippi State University, 1976. 37/07, p. 4137.

On a delayed post-test no significant difference was found on the Rokeach Value Survey as a result of a weekend seminar featuring values clarification.

299. Moore, Mary L. "Effects of Values Clarification on Dogmatism, Critical Thinking and Self Actualization." Ed.D. dissertation, Arizona State University, 1976. 37/02, p. 907.

Finds that dogmatism decreased as a result of values clarification in three of four classes. In only one of four classes was critical thinking influenced.

300. Musgrave, Gary L. "The Relative Effects of Academic Skills Therapy and Values Clarification on Selected Personality Variables." Ed.D. dissertation, Mississippi State University, 1977. 38/04, p. 1897.

Two methods--values clarification and academic skills therapy--were compared regarding their effectiveness with underachieving students. It was found that the values clarification group became more adaptable and flexible, while the skills group became more moderate and conventional. We are not told if achievement was affected.

301. Neely, Veronica D. "A Comparison of Rath's Method for Values Clarification with the Traditional Method of Teaching Literature in the Eighth Grade." Ph.D. dissertation, New York University, 1978. 38/12, p. 7328.

No shift on the Rokeach Value Survey was detected as a result of an eighth-grade values clarification literature course which used values clarification strategies. Some ancillary hypotheses were confirmed, however.

302. Niblett, James O. "Measuring the Effects of a Training Sequence in Transactional Analysis, Self Awareness and Values Clarification on Educators." Ph.D. dissertation, Georgia State University, 1979. 40/06, p. 3029.

No significant differences were found in the 16 hypotheses that predicted a more positive orientation to human relations.

303. Ohlde, C.D. and M.H. Vinitsky. "Effect of Values-Clarification Workshop on Value Awareness." Journal of Counseling Psychology, 23 (1976): 489-491.

Gains in values awareness and self-esteem were detected following a seven-hour values clarification workshop with college undergraduates.

304. Olson, Gerald. "A Study of Theoretical Implications and Outcomes of a Values Clarification Process with a Group of Ninth Graders." Ph.D. dissertation, University of California, Berkeley, 1974. 35/10, p. 6464.

Finds that the longer the valuing process, the less likely the subjects were to agree or to follow the valuing methodology prescribed by values clarification.

305. Osman, Jack D. "The Use of Selected Value-Clarifying Strategies in Health Education." Readings in Values Clarification (item 212), pp. 207-216.

Presents the results of a study in which values clarification techniques were integrated into a health education unit. With a pre-post (no control) design it was found that students increased significantly in self-actualization as a result of the curriculum. It was also found that students were satisfied with the values curriculum.

306. Perlmutter, Rosanne. "The Effects of the Values Clarification Process on the Moral and Ego Development of High School Students." Ed.D. dissertation, Boston University, 1980. 40/12, p. 6208.

Values clarification activities were found to have no significant impact on students' moral reasoning or ego development.

307. Pracejus, Eleanor L. "The Effect of Values Clarification on Reading Comprehension." Ph.D. dissertation, University of Pittsburgh, 1974. 35/04, p. 2058.

It was found that reading comprehension increased when values clarification stories supplemented regular reading assignments. Subjects were eighth-grade middle- and lower-class public school pupils.

308. Quinn, Raphael E. "Evaluation of a Technique for Clarifying Environmental Values with High School Sophomores." Ph.D. dissertation, Texas A & M University, 1973. 34/10, p. 6371.

Value sheets on environmental issues used in the classroom did not result in any significant change in students' attitudes toward the environment.

309. Raths, James. "Underachievement and a Search for Values." Journal of Educational Sociology, 34 (1960): 422-424.

Although the level of significance achieved was only .109 it was concluded that a values clarification experience has a significant impact on the achievement of underachievers.

310. Redmon, George L. "An Exploratory Study of the Effects of Inservice Values Clarification Training on Openness of Teacher Assessing Behavior." Ph.D. dissertation, University of Minnesota, 1975. 36/09, p. 5876.

Training in values clarification was found to be positively related to an increase of expression of concern for the needs and interests of students as individuals.

311. Reynolds, Larry J. "Developing a Sense of Faculty Community Through Values Clarification Strategies." Ed.D. dissertation, University of Northern Colorado, 1976. 37/01, p. 118.

It was found that on selected dimensions of a sense of community scale, values clarification exercises produced significant growth among public school teachers.

312. Richardson, Michael D. "Effects of Values Clarification Strategies upon the Values and Behaviors of Alcohol Abusers in Treatment." Ed.D. dissertation, University of Maine, 1978. 39/06, p. 3381.

No significant differences on any of 11 psychological variables was found as a result of six values clarification sessions.

313. Ruebel, Marvin V. "The Effects of Valuing Process Training on the Self-Concept of Pregnant Teenage Girls Attending a Special School for Pregnant Minors." Ph.D. dissertation, United States International University, 1975. 36/03, p. 1314.

Values clarification was found to have no significant impact on self-concept.

314. Schiraldi, Frank R. "The Effects of Values Clarification Strategies on the Self-Esteem of Secondary School Students." Ph.D. dissertation, Temple University, 1978. 39/02, p. 690.

Values clarification was found to have no significant impact on self-esteem.

315. Schmedinghoff, Gerald. "A Study of the Effect of Values Clarification Strategies and Values Self Confrontation on Selected Self Concept Factors." Ph.D. dissertation, Washington State University, 1977. 38/3, p. 1234.

Neither values clarification activities nor being told that one's values are different from the group's (values confrontation) was found to have any impact on students' values or self-actualization.

316. Sheppard, Ronnie L. "Affecting Children's Value Claims by Using High-Level Questioning Focused in Selected Poetry." Ed.D. dissertation, North Texas State University, 1976. 36/07, p. 3400.

It was found using values clarification experiences using high level questioning on selected poems resulted in significant changes in eighth-grade boys' values as measured by a values inventory.

317. Simmons, John B. "An Evaluation of Values Clarification Techniques with Respect to Ecological Achievement and Attitudes." Ed.D. dissertation, University of Northern Colorado, 1974. 35/09, p. 5953.

No significant differences were found either in academic achievement or in positive attitudes toward science and ecology as a result of an experimental values clarification section of high school biology.

318. Simon, Sidney B. "Value Clarification: Methodology and Tests of an Hypothesis in an In-service Program Relating to Behavioral Changes in Secondary School Students." Ed.D. dissertation, New York University, 1958. 20/01, p. 228.

Simon's doctoral dissertation was completed under the direction of Louis Raths. Hypothesized that if students' values are clarified, their behavior will undergo positive self-directed change. The results, according to Simon are "cast in confusion" and the hypothesis was not supported.

319. Sklare, Gerald B. "The Effects of Values Clarification Process upon the Values, Clarity of Values, and Dogmatism of High School Juniors and Seniors." Ed.D. dissertation, Wayne State University, 1974. 35/12, p. 7664.

No differences in dogmatism were noted, but over ten weeks students did become clearer about their values as the result of a values clarification experience.

320. Sklare, Gerald B., et al. "Values Clarification: It's Just a Matter of Timing." Personnel and Guidance Journal, 55 (1977): 245-248.

Reports the results of a study of the effectiveness of a values clarification process with high school youth. After ten weeks students exposed to values clarification found it easier to choose between values than did controls. A two-week intervention had no significant impact.

321. Smith, Bryan C. "Values Clarification in Drug Education: A Comparative Study." Journal of Drug Education, 3 (1973): 369-376.

Compares two approaches to drug education: traditional teacher-centered and values clarification. Values clarification was found to be superior in increasing independent reading, increasing scores on cognitive and affective tests, and developing community.

322. Smith, Janice L. "The Effectiveness of Values Clarification Training on Selected Personality Dimensions and Clarification of Work Values in Women." Ph.D. dissertation, University of Missouri-Kansas City, 1979. 40/02, p. 682.

Individual and group values clarification was not found to be effective in promoting change in level of self-acceptance, locus of control, sex-role identity, or work values.

323. Solomon, Richard D. "The Effect of Values Clarification Instruction on the Values of Selected Junior High School Students." Ph.D. dissertation, University of Maryland, 1977. 38/09, p. 5228.

Values clarification did not result in any significant change in student values as measured by the Survey of Ethical Attitudes.

324. Superka, Douglas P., and Norris Harms. "A Comparative Evaluation of Values-Oriented and Non-Values-Oriented Environmental Education Materials." Boulder: Social Science Education Consortium, 1977. ED 175 777.

Compares the effectiveness of an inquiry approach and a values-oriented approach at the secondary level. The values approach was based on the methodology of values clarification. It was concluded that as a result of participation in the two approaches, there was no difference in students' gains in knowledge and only a slight difference in attitudes toward environmental issues.

325. Swanson, Jon C. "Junior High Student Evaluations of Drug Education by Values and Tradition Oriented Teachers." Journal of Drug Education, 4 (1974): 43-50.

Reports the results of student impressions of teachers trained in two different ways: traditional and values clarification. The results are mixed, and it is concluded that a mix of the two approaches is best.

326. Temple, Annette K. "The Effects of a Values Clarification Process on Students' Views of Their Own and Peer Values." Ed.D. dissertation, Wayne State University, 1979. 40/11, p. 5816.

Students did not view their own values more positively after values clarification activities, but they did view their classmates' values more positively. Following values clarification students did not want to change their present values.

327. Thompson, David G. "Effectiveness of Values Clarification and Broad-Spectrum Behavioral Group Counseling with Ninth-Grade Boys in a Residential School." Ph.D. dissertation, Pennsylvania State University, 1978. 39/08, p. 4742.

No differences were found between the effectiveness of broad-spectrum group counseling and values clarification. Both were effective in reducing the incidence of observed negative behaviors.

328. Tolliver, James H. "A Description of the Effect of Values Clarification on the Self-Actualization of a Group of Urban High School Teachers as Measured by Shostrom's Personal Orientation Inventory." Ed.D. dissertation, Temple University, 1980. 41/01, p. 213.

Teachers who engaged in values clarification workshops did not change significantly in self-actualization from teachers who did not attend such workshops.

329. Vance, Harvey E. "An Exploratory Study in Values Clarification and Its Relationship to a More Unified Valuing Process." Ph.D. dissertation, The Ohio State University, 1974. 35/05, p. 2663.

Results suggest that values clarification leads to greater consistency between thought, feeling, and action.

330. Vander Wert, Frank E. "The Effects of Values Clarification Training on the Self Concept of Selected Secondary Students." Ed.D. dissertation, Ball State University, 1979. 41/09, p. 3978.

No significant differences in self-concept were found between students subjected to values clarification lessons and students in regular classes.

331. Watkins, David D. "The Effects of Values Clarification Training on Dogmatism and Changes in Value Systems." Ph.D. dissertation, University of Missouri at Kansas City, 1977. 38/11, p. 6550.

Values clarification has no impact on dogmatism, but may result in changed values if the method is presented in a positive manner.

332. Wilgoren, Richard A. "The Relationship Between the Self Concept of Preservice Teachers and Two Methods of Teaching Values Clarification." Ed.D. dissertation, University of Massachusetts, 1973. 34/07, p. 4072.

Both values clarification and the jurisprudential approach of Oliver produced gains in positive self-concept among pre-service teachers.

333. Wilson, Edward B. "A Proposed Curriculum Model for the Development of a Process of Valuing at the Secondary School Level." Ph.D. dissertation, Florida State University, 1971. 32/09, p. 5119.

A values clarification-like course was found to have no significant impact on high school students' critical thinking, locus of control, or professed values.

334. Woess, Eileen K. "A Workshop in Values Clarification for Teachers of Adults: A Prototypical Study." Ed.D. dissertation, Indiana University, 1975. 36/09, p. 5747.

A five-day workshop in values clarification is described in detail, and feedback from an expert jury is discussed.

335. Young, Robert A. "Results of Values Clarification Training on the Self Concept of Black Female Upper Class Residence Hall Students at Mississippi State University." Ed.D. dissertation, Mississippi State University, 1977. 38/07, p. 3967.

No significant difference was found in self-concept of Black female undergraduates as a result of three weeks of values clarification.

Values Clarification: Critiques and Rejoinders

336. Baer, Richard J. "Values Clarification as Indoctrination." Educational Forum, 41 (1977): 155-165.

In a wide-ranging critique Baer argues that values clarification makes significant assumptions about man and the world which are not subject to examination. It therefore commits a form of indoctrination.

337. Caldwell, Robert L. "Values Clarification: A Case of Doublespeak." Paper presented at the annual meeting of the National Council of Teachers of English, Kansas City, 1978. ED 173 779.

Argues that the problem with values clarification is that while it is based on the thesis of moral subjectivity, in practice the moral intuitions of the proponents propel them in a different, conflicting direction. According to Caldwell the approach is hopelessly conceptually confused.

338. Chng, C.L. "A Critique of Values Clarification in Drug Education." Journal of Drug Education, 10 (1980): 119-125.

The use of values clarification in drug education programs is criticized on the grounds of ethical relativism, lack of content, danger of indoctrination, and pressure to conform.

339. Freiberg, Jo Ann. "Is Values Clarification Really Deweyan?" Philosophical Studies in Education, Proceedings-1979, Annual Meeting of the Ohio Valley Philosophy of Education Society. Terre Haute: Indiana State University, 1980, pp. 117-123.

Argues that contrary to what the proponents of values clarification would have us believe, a comparison of Dewey's valuational process and that of values clarification reveals marked differences.

340. Griffin, Robert. "Worries about Values Clarification." Peabody Journal of Education, 53 (1976): 194-200.

In a soft-hearted critique of values clarification, expresses concern that overuse of values clarification could lead to a content-free approach to teaching and learning.

341. Harrison, George J. "Values Clarification and the Construction of the Good." Educational Theory, 30 (1980): 185-191.

Argues that the second edition of Values and Teaching (item 227) is no improvement over the first and, more importantly, that the theory of valuation in values clarification is not Deweyan at all. Claims that values clarification can only lead to values confusion.

342. Harrison, John L. "Values Clarification: An Appraisal." Journal of Moral Education, 6 (1976): 22-31.

A critique of values clarification is offered. Argues that the theory is not well developed and its methods rest on untried empirical assumptions.

343. Heller, Sherri A. "Do Values Clarification Programs Help or Hinder Social and Emotional Growth?" Teacher, 96 (February 1979): 18-26.

Argues from a Piagetian perspective that although young children can describe their feelings, they are incapable of describing their value systems because of the limitations of the concrete operational stage of mental development.

344. Kazepides, A.C. "The Logic of Values Clarification." Journal of Educational Thought, 11 (1977): 99-111.

Traces the origin of the values clarification movement and exposes its unwarranted ethical stance. An exemplary episode of values clarification is examined and the theoretical confusions of the proponents are revealed.

345. Kirschenbaum, Howard. "Clarifying Values Clarification: Some Theoretical Issues." Moral Education ... It Comes With the Territory (item 1811), pp. 116-125.

Addresses some of the major misunderstandings regarding values clarification: is it value free, is it relativistic, does it have a theoretical base? Kirschenbaum also presents his expanded version of the seven-step clarifying process.

346. Kirschenbaum, Howard, et al. "In Defense of Values Clarification." Phi Delta Kappan, 59 (1977): 743-746.

Argues that the critics of values clarification have construed the technique too narrowly and misunderstood their perspective on moral relativism.

347. Kirschenbaum, Howard. "In Support of Values Clarification." Social Education, 41 (1977): 398; 401-402.

Defends values clarification against its critics. Claims that values clarification has changed since its earliest presentation, and as a result, many of the earlier criticisms do not hold up.

348. Lockwood, Alan L. "A Critical View of Values Clarification." Moral Education ... It Comes With the Territory (item 1811), pp. 152-175.

Lockwood criticizes values clarification on the grounds that it has an inadequate conception of value, a therapeutic emphasis, and a questionable moral point of view. Shows the similarity of Rogerian theory to values clarification and makes a particularly telling analysis of its relativism (can be used to justify any moral action) and its inability to adjudicate interpersonal conflicts of value. Also in Teacher's College Record, 77 (1975): 35-50; and in Developmental Counseling and Teaching (item 784).

349. Lockwood, Alan L. "Values Education and the Right to Privacy." Journal of Moral Education, 7 (1977): 9-26.

General reasons for protecting the right to privacy are developed and two approaches to values education--values clarification and moral development--are examined for their potential threat to students' right to privacy. It is discovered that values clari-

clarification methods and materials comprise a threat to students' privacy.

350. Lockwood, Alan. "What's Wrong with Values Clarification." Social Education, 41 (1977): 399-401.

Criticizes values clarification on the grounds that it fails to distinguish the moral from the non-moral, it espouses ethical relativism, it resembles therapy in practice, it jeopardizes privacy rights, and it lacks research to support its claims.

351. Loggins, Dennis. "Clarifying What and How Well?" Health Education, 7 (March/April 1976): 2-5.

In a critical analysis of the claims of values clarification, concludes that the approach is superficial in its treatment of values, it does not lead to the internalization of the required valuing process, and there is only weak evidence for changes in students' values-related behaviors.

352. Lukinsky, Joseph. "Two Cheers for Value Confusion." Religious Education, 75 (1980): 682-685.

Argues that the self must be created and that this creation arises out of facing complex problems and having to choose without having all one needs to have to choose and knowing it. This kind of confusion needs to be nurtured. There is more to valuing than being clear, and this indicates a weakness of values clarification.

353. McGough, Kris. "Values Clarification: Your Job or Mine?" Social Education, 41 (1977): 404-406.

Argues from a parent's perspective that values clarification threatens the parents' right to instill selected values in their children and the child's right to privacy.

354. McKnight, Richard. All Values Are Equal, But Some Are More Equal Than Others. Monograph Series Number 102. Code C-9. Philadelphia: Temple University Center for the Study of Psychoeducational Processes, 1977. ED 155 517.

Critiques the values clarification definition of values, theory of valuation, theory of morality, and theory of practice.

355. Nevin, Hugh. "Values Clarification: Perspectives in John Dewey with Implications for Religious Education." <u>Religious Education</u>, 73 (1978): 661-677.

Argues that in the emphasis on prizing, values clarification turns its back on Dewey's conception of value. Suggestions for making values clarification more Deweyan are presented.

356. Peters, R.S. "'Mental Health' as an Educational Aim." <u>Aims in Education</u>, Edited by T.H.B. Hollins, Manchester, England: Manchester University Press, 1964, pp. 71-90.

Critiques the view that mental health or adjustment should be a central concern of educators. Argues that this view confuses the function of the educator with that of the doctor. The main function of the teacher is to train and instruct; it is not to help and care.

357. Shaver, James P. "Moral Development and Ethical Decision Making: Theory and Faddism." Paper presented at Inter-Institutional Seminar in Childhood Education, Snowbird, VT, 1977. ED 144 868.

Presents a critique of values clarification and cognitive-developmental theory.

358. Smitch, Gordon C. "A Historical and Logical Analysis of the Values Clarification Movement." Ph.D. dissertation, Michigan State University, 1977. 38/03, p. 1281.

Claims that values clarification, regardless of what Simon, et al., say, is not value free: it does make value judgments and it does prescribe proper modes of conduct. Values clarification is in fact moral education and should come out and confront this reality.

359. Smith, John K. "Values Clarification and Moral Nonexistence." <u>Journal of Thought</u>, 12 (1977): 4-9.

Argues that by alleging that all values are equal, values clarification not only condones but even advocates the nonexistence of man. Presents an example from a class where genocide was condoned. Concludes that values clarification legitimates the individual and social flight from the struggle with age-old categories of good and evil.

360. Stewart, John S. "Problems and Contradictions of Values Clarification." Moral Education ... It Comes With the Territory (item 1811), pp. 136-151.

Argues that values clarification is deceptively and dangerously superficial. The sources of this superficiality lie in its reification of value, focus on content rather than structure in thought, failure to separate content from process, and ethical relativism. Values clarification is also criticized for its tendency in practice to result in a coercion to the mean for students, hidden value content, and failure to develop a sound theoretical base. Also in Phi Delta Kappan, 56 (1975): 684-688.

361. Wynne, Edward. "Put Your Mind Where Your Mouth Is: A Moral Story." Character, 1 (December, 1979): 7-8.

Presents a critical account of a Simon presentation to high school teachers in which high school students, on stage, had their values clarified by Simon.

Cognitive Development: Theory and Practice

362. Arbuthnot, Jack B., and David Faust. Teaching Moral Reasoning: Theory and Practice. New York: Harper & Row, 1981.

A detailed and thorough explication of the cognitive developmental approach to moral education intended for classroom teachers. A practical guide for implementing Kohlbergian moral education in schools follows a discussion of Piagetian and Kohlbergian theory. Also covered are assessing the moral stage of students, designing moral education programs, assessing moral education, and special problems and issues.

363. Bergman, Marvin. "Moral Decision Making in the Light of Kohlberg and Bonhoeffer: A Comparison." Religious Education, 69 (1974): 227-243.

Compares and contrasts the views of Kohlberg and Bonhoeffer on moral decision making and concludes that they share a desire to enable human beings to live as responsible people in a world marked by justice and reconciliation.

364. Beyer, Barry K. "Conducting Moral Discussions in the Classroom." Readings in Moral Education (item 449), pp. 62-75.

Offers practical suggestions on how to structure moral discussions for the classroom. Also in Values Concepts and Techniques (item 1784) and Social Education, 40 (1976): 194-202.

365. Birchall, Gregory B. "A Cultural Critique of 'Values Education' and the Social Studies." Melbourne, Australia: State College of Victoria at Coburg, 1978. ED 162 941.

Argues that social studies education should foster critical consciousness that will contribute to social change. Kohlberg's approach to moral education is seen as one way to foster this critical consciousness. Kohlberg and Marx are discussed in the same breath, and seen as compatible.

366. Boyd, D. "The Moralberry Pie: Some Basic Concepts." Theory into Practice, 16 (1977): 67-72.

Presents an analysis of the basic value concepts around which theories of moral education are built. It is held that there are three basic ingredients comprising the moralberry pie: the concept of good/bad, the concept of right/wrong, and the concept of praise/blame. The moralberry pie is then applied to Kohlberg, and it is concluded that he is concerned only with questions of right/wrong.

367. Boyd, Dwight R. "The Problem of Sophomoritis: An Educational Proposal." Journal of Moral Education, 6 (1976): 36-42.

Describes the period of adolescence, in which all kinds of moral questions are raised and all answers are doubted. The standard solution--introduction to ethics courses--is criticized. Instead it is urged that education adopt the developmental approach of Kohlberg.

368. Bull, Barry L. "Kohlberg's Place in a Theory of the Legitimate Role of Value in Public Education." Philosophy of Education 1978 (item 1792), pp. 70-4.

Reinterprets the broad features of Kohlberg's theory in light of an understanding of morality in general and of public morality in particular. Argues that in spite of Kohlberg's failure to incorporate an account of the development of benevolence into his cognitive view, it is the only acceptable basis for moral education in America's schools.

369. Craig, Robert P. "Can Virtue Be Taught? Some Contemporary Educational Implications." The Clearing House, 50 (1976): 147-151.

Presents a developmentalist view of the goals of moral education and suggests ten ways that teachers can help to facilitate moral growth.

370. Craig, Robert P. "Education for Justice: Some Comments on Piaget." Contemporary Education, 47 (1976): 69-73.

Presents the Piagetan perspective that moral development is best facilitated through interaction of peers and discusses ten specific implications for the educator.

371. Doris, Dennis A. "Teaching Moral Education: Principles of Instruction." Peabody Journal of Education, 56 (1978): 33-44.

Presents a summary of Kohlbergian theory on the goals and methods of moral education.

372. Duska, Ronald and Mariellen Whelan. Moral Development: A Guide to Piaget and Kohlberg. New York: Paulist Press, 1975.

Sandwiched between an introduction to the cognitive-developmental perspective on moralization and the practical educational applications of the theory is a chapter on moral development from a Christian perspective, which emphasizes the compatibility of Christianity and Kohlbergian theory.

373. Galbraith, Ronald E. "Teaching for Moral Development in Schools: Reason for Caution But Reason to Proceed." Social Education, 43 (1979): 233.

Discusses five cautions for schools using moral reasoning discussions in the classroom, but concludes that it is still the best technique available.

374. Galbraith, Ronald E., and Thomas M. Jones. Moral Reasoning: A Teaching Handbook for Adopting Kohlberg to the Classroom. Minneapolis, MN: Greenhaven Press, 1976.

A very practical "nuts and bolts" approach to developmental moral education. A brief introduction to Kohlberg's theory is presented, followed by a step-by-step process. Representative curricular materials and examples of classroom activities are included.

375. Galbraith, Ronald E., and Thomas M. Jones. "Teaching Strategies for Moral Dilemmas." Social Education, 39 (1975): 16-22.

Presents Kohlberg's theory and then an application of the theory to the social studies classroom. A sample lesson plan and a description of the teaching process are included.

376. George, Paul S. "Discipline, Moral Development and Levels of Schooling." Educational Forum, 45 (November 1980): 57-67.

Presents hypothetical relationships that may exist between moral development, classroom discipline, and school level. Argues that the classroom discipline strategy should be compatible with the level of schooling. Corporal punishment and obedience will dominate lower grades, with self-discipline the dominant mode in graduate school.

377. Hagen, Lyman B. "Billy Budd and Kohlberg's Stages of Moral Development." Journal of Thought, 12 (1977): 318-325.

Places the characters in Melville's Billy Budd in stage categories and uses this analysis to illuminate the moral themes of the work.

378. Hennessy, Thomas C., ed. Values and Moral Development. New York: Paulist Press, 1976.

The papers in this book are revisions of lectures given at the Institute in Moral and Ethical Issues in Education held at Fordham University in the Spring of 1975. The book contains three sections. Part I introduces the philosophical groundwork for the analysis of moral and ethical growth. Part II is devoted primarily to papers that emphasize programs directed to fostering growth among students in moral-related areas. Part III is devoted to papers that describe and report research in moral education and related areas.

379. Hersh, Richard H., ed. "Moral Development." Theory into Practice, 16 (April 1977).

A collection of papers on the developmental approach to moral education that hope to reflect the complexity of theory in such a way as to avoid the disastrous effects of a bandwagon phenomenon.

380. Hersh, Richard H., and Diana Pritchard Paolitto. "Moral Development: Implications for Pedagogy." Readings in Moral Education (item 449), pp. 140-146.

Discuss the importance of the teacher's educational philosophy in successful programs in moral development. Also in Contemporary Education, 58 (Fall 1976).

381. Hersh, Richard and Diana P. Paolitto. Moral Development in the Classroom. OSSC Bulletin. Eugene: Oregon School Study Council, 1977. ED 132 734.

Presents an introduction to how to approach cognitive developmental moral education in the classroom.

382. Hersh, Richard H., and Diana Pritchard Paolitto. "The Teacher as Moral Educator." Values/Moral Education: The Schools and the Teachers (item 1794), pp. 9-49.

Attempts to articulate a conception of the teacher's role as implied by moral development research. States what the teacher should be able to do to facilitate the moral development of students: stimulate conflict and students' ability to take the perspective of others. Discusses intervention research and gives examples of a concept of teaching.

383. Hersh, Richard H.; Diana P. Paolitto; and Joseph Reimer. Promoting Moral Growth: From Piaget to Kohlberg. New York: Longman, 1977.

This book attempts both to communicate a thorough understanding of the theory of moral development and to present the educational implications. Kohlberg has called this book the "best introduction to the cognitive-developmental approach to moral education."

384. Isaksson, Andri. "Kohlberg's Theory of Moral Development and Its Relevance to Education." Scandinavian Journal of Educational Research, 23 (1979): 47-63.

Reviews research on the cognitive development theory and finds it correct in its view of the development of moral reasoning--a laudatory review.

385. Kohlberg, Lawrence. "Changing Perceptions on Theory and Practice." Moral Education Forum, 4 (1979): 2-6.

Discusses the reasons for a shift in emphasis from stage-change intervention to moral atmosphere of the school. Also the introduction to Promoting Moral Growth: From Piaget to Kohlberg (item 383).

386. Kohlberg, Lawrence. "A Cognitive-Developmental Approach to Moral Education." The Humanist (November-December 1972): 13-16.

A basic introduction to the theory and a few words regarding planned moral education in the schools. Also in Collected Papers (item 1798).

387. Kohlberg, Lawrence. "The Cognitive-Developmental Approach to Moral Education." Moral Education ... It Comes With the Territory (item 1811), pp. 176-195.

Presents a general overview of the theory, research, and educational implications of Kohlberg's work in moral education. Also in Education and Moral Development (item 395), Readings in Moral Education (item 449), Developmental Counseling and Teaching (item 784), Values Concepts and Techniques (item 1784), and Phi Delta Kappan, 56 (1975): 670-677.

388. Kohlberg, Lawrence. "Cognitive-Developmental Theory and the Practice of Collective Moral Education." Group Care: The Education Path of Youth Aliyah. Edited by M. Wolins and M. Gottesman. New York: Gordon and Breach, 1971, pp. 342-371.

Discusses a variety of approaches to kibbutz education in Israel and how the relativistic trap can be avoided. Differences between kibbutz-born and kibbutz-placed youth are noted, along with the educational implications of cognitive-developmental theory. Also in Collected Papers (item 1798), Education and Moral Development (item 395), and Readings in Moral Education (item 449).

389. Kohlberg, Lawrence. "Cognitive Stages and Preschool Education." Human Development, 9 (1966): 5-17.

Using sequence in development of dream concept in American and Atayal children, argues that preschoolers' orientation to reality is a developmental stage that should be integrated into later stages of development. Preschool activities should encourage the gradual transformation of preschool thought structures into more adult forms.

390. Kohlberg, Lawrence. "The Concepts of Developmental Psychology as a Central Guide to Education: Examples from Cognitive, Moral and Psychological Education." Moral and Psychological Education: Theory and Research (item 448), pp. 5-59.

Builds the case for development as the end goal of all education. Discusses development from his own moral perspective as well as from the perspective of Piaget and Loevinger. Also discusses the relation of cognitive and moral stages and the relation of cognitive stages to the raising of IQ as an educational end.

391. Kohlberg, Lawrence. "Counseling and Counselor Education: A Developmental Approach." Counselor Education and Supervision, 14 (1975): 250-256.

Reviews the need for a developmental conception as the aim of educational intervention. This view is compared with a mental health treatment approach, and a case is made for the importance for education and counseling of a primary prevention approach with the focus on ego and moral development.

392. Kohlberg, Lawrence. "Early Education: A Cognitive-Developmental Approach." Child Development, 39 (1968): 1013-1062.

Reviews the implications for preschool education of the cognitive-developmental theories of Baldwin, Dewey, Piaget, and Vygotsky. Empirical studies supporting the validity of the interactional view of intellectual development are reviewed.

393. Kohlberg, Lawrence. "Educating for a Just Society: An Updated and Revised Statement." Moral Development, Moral Education and Kohlberg (item 432), pp. 455-470.

Traces how his original call for stage 6 as the goal for moral education has been successively retrenched to stage 5 and now to stage 4. Kohlberg states clearly why he currently espouses indoctrinative methods and goals as part of the moral education process. The Meism and Privatism of contemporary life make it imperative that moral educators help children to positive stage 4 conceptions and attitudes toward citizenship. Concludes by stressing that social participation in school democracy can lead to the necessary stage 4 citizenship role orientation.

394. Kohlberg, Lawrence. "Education for Justice: A Modern Statement of the Platonic View." Moral Education: Five Lectures (item 1814), pp. 58-83.

In this often-cited paper Kohlberg discusses his Platonic (justice) view of morality and why he rejects an Aristotelian view (virtues). He concisely presents his developmental theory of moral reasoning and its educational implications. Also in Collected Papers (item 1798) and The Philosophy of Moral Development (item 1799).

395. Kohlberg, Lawrence. Essays in Moral Development. Volume 3: Education and Moral Development. New York: Harper and Row, forthcoming.

A collection of papers that focus on the implications of stage theory for the understanding and practice of moral education.

396. Kohlberg, Lawrence. "Foreword to Readings in Moral Education." Readings in Moral Education (item 449), pp. 2-15.

Presents his personal historical perspective on the evolution of the cognitive-developmental approach to moral education. Discusses the role of Blatt and of the Stone Foundation project in crystallizing his ideas on moral education. After discussing the prison studies and just community efforts he places his theory within the Platonic justice ideal and Deweyan developmental notions.

397. Kohlberg, Lawrence. "Implications of Developmental Psychology for Education: Examples from Moral Education." Educational Psychologist, 19 (1973): 2-14.

Argues that the developmental-philosophic strategy is the only clear nonrelativistic strategy for educational aims. Since behavior changes are of reversible character they cannot define genuine educational objectives. A progessive longitudinal perspective is offered in which the worth of an educational effect is determined by its effects on later behavior and development.

398. Kohlberg, Lawrence. "The Implications of Moral Stages for Adult Education." Religious Education, 72 (1977): 183-201.

Argues that little is being done to stimulate the moral development of adults and makes suggestions for future efforts.

399. Kohlberg, Lawrence. "The Implications of Moral Stages for Problems in Sex Education." Collected Papers (item 1798).

Attacks a relativistic view of moral values in decision making and presents the cognitive-developmental approach to decision making in sexual matters.

400. Kohlberg, Lawrence. "Moral Development and Education of Adolescents." Adolescents and the American High School. Edited by Richard Purnell. New York: Holt, Rinehart and Winston, 1970, pp. 144-162.

Standard treatment of all the central tenets of cognitive-developmental theory.

401. Kohlberg, Lawrence. "Moral Education for a Society in Transition." Educational Leadership, 33 (1975): 46-54.

Presents the cognitive-developmental theory of moral reasoning and demonstrates its use as an educational technique through moral discussions and just community environments.

402. Kohlberg, Lawrence. "Moral Education in the Schools: A Developmental View." School Review, 74 (1966): 1-30.

Presents the cognitive-developmental perspective on moral character and develops a view of moral education as involving the stimulation of children's moral judgment and character.

403. Kohlberg, Lawrence. "Moral Education Reappraised." The Humanist, 38 (November/December 1978): 13-15.

Argues that there is a necessary philosophic and psychological unity in the objectives of moral education. Adds that he no longer takes a negative view of indoctrinative moral education; in fact, the goals of moral education must be partly indoctrinative.

404. Kohlberg, Lawrence. "A Moral Experiment Is Not Ethical Unless Educative." Phi Delta Kappan, 55 (1974): 607; 644.

Argues that the Milgram experiment, which demanded conformity to commands that apparently severely punished others, was unethical.

405. Kohlberg, Lawrence. "Moral Stages and Moralization: The Cognitive-Developmental Approach." Moral Development and Behavior (item 1801), pp. 31-53.

Presents in some detail his stage theory and explains how one scores interviews to assess an individuals stage of moral reasoning. Includes brief sections on the environmental stimulation of moral development and moral development within an ego development framework.

406. Kohlberg, Lawrence. "The Quest for Justice in 200 Years of American History and in Contemporary American Education." Contemporary Education, 48 (1976): 5-16.

Presents an overview of cognitive-developmental theory and argues that moral education, by fostering a sense of justice, can contribute to the actualizing of the American Creed.

407. Kohlberg, Lawrence. "The Relation Between Theory and Teachers Is a Two-Way Street." Education and Moral Development (item 295), Chapter 1.

Traces growing awareness of the "psychologist's fallacy." Describes the resulting effort to build a theory meaningful to teachers through collaboration in an evolving alternative school.

408. Kohlberg, Lawrence. "The Relationship of Moral Education to the Broader Field of Values Education." Values Education: Theory/Practice/Problems/Prospects (item 1805), pp. 79-86.

Stresses the limits of values clarification: it often focuses on nonmoral issues and has no universal conception of moral principles. Moral reasoning is suggested as the distinctively moral component in moral education. It contains a universal moral principle, justice.

409. Kohlberg, Lawrence. "Relativity and Indoctrination in Value Education." Zygon, 6 (1971): 285-310.

Discusses "cop out" solutions to the relativity problem in teaching values and offers cognitive developmental theory as a solution. Also in Collected Papers (item 1798) and The Philosophy of Moral Development (item 1799).

410. Kohlberg, Lawrence. "Revisions in the Theory and Practice of Moral Development." New Directions for Child Development, No. 2: Moral Development (item 1789), pp. 83-87.

Kohlberg states and gives reasons for two major revisions in his theory: moral education must be partly indoctrinative and there exist only five stages of moral development.

411. Kohlberg, Lawrence. "Stages of Moral Development as a Basis for Moral Education." Moral Education: Interdisciplinary Approaches (item 1785), pp. 23-92.

An extensive and wide-ranging introduction to cognitive-developmental theory. Also in Moral Development, Moral Education and Kohlberg (item 432).

412. Kohlberg, Lawrence. "This Special Section in Perspective." Social Education, 40 (1976): 213-215.

Presents a general discussion of his theory with commentary on articles in this special issue (item 1852).

413. Kohlberg, Lawrence, and Richard S. Hersh. "Moral Development: A Review of the Theory." Theory into Practice, 16 (1977): 53-59.

Presents Kohlberg's developmental theory and discusses the implications for educational practice.

414. Kohlberg, Lawrence, and Thomas Lickona. "Early Social and Moral Education." Education and Moral Development (item 395), Chapter 4.

Makes the claim that Socratic discussions and classroom community are viable and exciting strategies for moral development and education in the early years.

415. Kohlberg, Lawrence, and Rochelle Mayer. "Development and Its Implications for Moral Education." The Domain of Moral Education (item 1788), pp. 220-230.

A much edited version of "Development as the Aim of Education" (item 416).

416. Kohlberg, Lawrence, and Rochelle Mayer. "Development as the Aim of Education." Harvard Educational Review, 42 (1972): 449-496.

After reviewing two prominent educational ideologies (the romantic and the cultural transmission) the authors conclude that only progressivism, with its cognitive-developmental psychology, its interactionist epistemology, and its philosophically examined ethics, provides an adequate basis for an understanding of the process of education. Probably the best statement of the relationship of cognitive-developmental theory to the mainstream of educational thought and practice. Also in Adolescents' Development and Education (item 1806) and The Philosophy of Moral Development (item 1799).

417. Kohlberg, Lawrence, and Robert Selman. Preparing School Personnel Relative to Values: A Look at Moral Education in the Schools. Washington, DC: ERIC Clearinghouse on Teacher Education, 1972. ED 058 153.

Argues that internalized principles of moral judgment cannot be taught, but their development, through open discussion, can be encouraged. Discusses how the teacher can be an effective moral educator. Argues that the teacher should be concerned about children's moral judgments rather than about conformity with the beliefs and judgments of the teacher.

418. Kohlberg, Lawrence, and Elliot Turiel. "Moral Development and Moral Education." Psychology and Educational Practice. Edited by G. Lesser. New York: Scott, Foresman, 1971, pp. 410-465.

Presents an overview of approaches to moral education and demonstrates that the cognitive-developmental approach is the only method that deals adequately with the problem of value relativity. Discusses how to teach moral reasoning and judgment. Also in Collected Papers (item 1790) and Education and Moral Development (item 395).

419. Kuhmerker, Lisa. "Social Interaction and the Development of a Sense of Right and Wrong in Young Children." Journal of Moral Education, 5 (1976): 257-264.

The implications of Hoffman's stage theory of empathy, Selman's theory of social perspective taking, and Damon's account of "positive justice" for early childhood moral education are discussed.

420. Lewis, Frank W. "What the Value/Moral Educator Can Learn from Piaget." Values/Moral Education: The Schools and the Teachers (item 1794), pp. 167-191.

Covers Piaget's conclusions about learning and the learner, specific teachings about cognitive development that pertain to moral education, moral developmental research data, and implications of the data for moral educators.

421. Lickona, Thomas. "Moral Development and Moral Education: Piaget, Kohlberg, and Beyond." Knowledge and Development: Piaget and Education, Vol. 2. Edited by Jeanette M. Gallagher and J.A. Easley. New York: Plenum Press, 1978, pp. 21-74.

Presents the case for moral education in schools, compares the theories of Piaget and Kohlberg on moral development, and discusses how to put developmental theory to work in the classroom.

422. Mackey, James. "A Better Values Education Through Social Research." High School Journal, 57 (1974): 215-225.

Argues that the results of social research can help schools improve their values education efforts. The implications of Kohlberg's cognitive-developmental theory are presented as among the more useful findings of social research.

423. Mackey, James. "Discussing Moral Dilemmas in the Classroom." English Journal, 64 (December 1975): 28-30.

Presents three principles of Kohlbergian moral education programs and four dilemmas for use in the classroom.

424. Mackey, James A. "Moral Insight in the Classroom." The Elementary School Journal, 73 (1973): 233-238.

Presents Kohlberg's theory and discusses its implications for teaching in the elementary school.

425. Mattox, Beverly A. Getting It Together. San Diego: Pennant Press, 1975.

A very brief, sketchy introduction to Kohlbergian moral education is followed by a description of a number of techniques and dilemmas for use at the elementary level.

426. Miller, J. "Schooling and Self-Alienation: A Conceptual View." The Journal of Educational Thought, 7 (1972): 105-120.

Develops suggestions for decreasing the self-alienation impact schools have on youth. The recommendations are drawn from the models of human development of Piaget, Erickson, and Kohlberg.

427. Mosher, Ralph L. "Funny Things Happen on the Way to Curriculum Development." Adolescents' Development and Education (item 1806), pp. 306-326.

Discusses problems and benefits to be derived from implementing developmental curricula in schools.

428. Mosher, Ralph L., ed. Moral Education: A First Generation of Research and Development. New York: Praeger Publishers, 1980.

Contains a series of papers describing the framework for and practices of the Danforth project in moral education. This project has as its foci Kohlbergian moral development and the guidance work of Mosher and Sprinthall (item 810). This volume is not an impartial appraisal of the field as a whole. All of the authors were involved in the project, and therefore there is little detached critical analysis of it.

429. Mosher, Ralph. "Moral Education: The Next Generation." Moral Education: A First Generation of Research and Development (item 428), pp. 369-385.

A lively, candid, spirited discussion of what has happened, what should not have happened, and what ought to happen in the future of moral education.

430. Mosher, Ralph. "Theory and Practice: A New E.R.A.?" Theory into Practice, 16 (1977): 81-88.

Argues that through applying developmental principles to practice in schools, knowledge can be generated. Summarizes what has been learned from the practice of developmental education.

431. Mosher, Ralph. "An Uncommon Cause." Moral Education: A First Generation of Research and Development (item 428), pp. 3-19.

Discusses the rationale for and the steps in the formation of the Danforth Moral Education Project. Includes a brief guide to the book (item 1744).

432. Munsey, Brenda, ed. Moral Development, Moral Education and Kohlberg. Birmingham, AL: Religious Education Press, 1980.

A collection of 16 papers dealing with basic issues in philosophy, psychology, religion, and education as they relate to the Kohlbergian perspective on moral development and moral education.

433. Munsey, Brenda. "Multidisciplinary Interest in Moral Development and Moral Education." Moral Development, Moral Education and Kohlberg (item 432), pp. 1-11.

Introduction to item 432 which is intended as a forum for the interdisciplinary analysis of Kohlberg's developmental theory and proposals for moral education.

434. Munson, Howard. "Moral Thinking: Can It Be Taught?" Psychology Today, 12 (February 1979): 48-68; 92.

Presents Kohlberg's theory of moral development and discusses its educational implications. Special attention is given to the just community concept as applied to schools and prisons. Criticisms of Kohlbergian theory are also discussed.

435. Muuss, Rolf E. "Kohlberg's Cognitive-Developmental Approach to Adolescent Morality." Adolescence, 11 (1976): 39-59.

An uncritical summary of Kohlberg's views on moral development and moral education.

436. Nucci, Larry P. "The Distinction Between Morality and Social Convention: Implications for Values Instruction." Phi Delta Kappan, 62 (1981): 489-493.

Presents evidence for the claim that morality and social convention are discrete conceptual and developmental systems. This implies that the content presented to the student, as well as the nature of teacher instructions and classroom discussion, will be appropriate to the topics or issues under consideration. Discusses how "domain-appropriate" values education can be implemented.

437. Oja, Sharon N., and Norman A. Sprinthall. "Psychological and Moral Development for Teachers: Can You Teach Old Dogs?" Value Development ... As the Aim of Education (item 1816), pp. 117-134.

Using elementary and secondary school personnel enrolled in an in-service Developmental Education workshop the authors attempted to stimulate teacher growth in the realms of Ego Development (Loevinger), Moral Development (Rest's Defining Issues Test) and Conceptual Development (Hunt). On all three measures a post test revealed a significant difference in favor of the experimental group over the control group.

438. Otto, Robert. "The Development of Moral Reasoning in Students." Psychology, 17 (Summer 1980): 43-46.

A short introduction to Kohlbergian moral development and its applications to education.

439. Pagliuso, S. Understanding Stages of Moral Development: A Programmed Learning Workbook. New York: Paulist Press, 1976.

440. Paolitto, Diana P. "The Role of the Teacher in Moral Education." Theory into Practice, 16 (1977): 73-80.

Explores the implications of developmental theory for the role of the teacher as moral educator and for educational practice.

441. Paolitto, Diana P., and Richard H. Hersh. "Pedagogical Implications for Stimulating Moral Development in the Classroom." Reflections on Values Education (item 1804), pp. 113-129.

A brief overview of Kohlbergian theory accompanied by a section on using moral discussion to stimulate moral development. Also in Developmental Counseling and Teaching (item 784).

442. Porter, Nancy, and Nancy Taylor. How to Assess the Moral Reasoning of Students. Toronto: Ontario Institute for Studies in Education, 1972.

Following a brief discussion of how to score the moral judgment questionnaire, five dilemmas and examples of stage-scorable responses to each dilemma are presented.

443. Power, Donald. "Moral Education for Post Conventional Thinking." Journal of Moral Education, 4 (1975): 111-116.

The ideas of Kohlberg, Beck, and Wilson are compared concerning the development of post-conventional moral thinking.

444. Proudfoot, Merrill. "Socrates, Kohlberg, and Plato: Method of Moral Education." Philosophy of Education 1977 (item 1817), pp. 146-155.

Examines Plato's vision of moral education and finds that it is less intellectual and makes a less radical distinction between moral opinion and moral knowledge than does Kohlberg's distinction between conventional and principled levels. Kohlberg is only selectively a Platonist.

445. Rest, James. "Developmental Psychology and Value Education." Moral Development, Moral Education and Kohlberg (item 432), pp. 101-129.

Discusses the major assumptions of developmental psychology (structural organization, developmental sequence, and interactionism) and the research evidence for each of these. Also presents sections on

Rest's Defining Issues Test, the relationships between moral judgment values and behavior, and findings related to educational interventions based on developmental theory.

446. Rosenzweig, Linda W. "A Selected Bibliography of Materials about Moral Education Based on the Research of Lawrence Kohlberg." Social Education, 40 (1976): 208-212.

Annotates 40 items related to Kohlbergian moral education.

447. Scharf, Peter. "Creating Moral Dilemmas for the Classroom." Readings in Moral Education (item 449), pp. 76-81.

Offers practical suggestions on how to develop appropriate and valuable dilemmas for classroom use.

448. Scharf, Peter, ed. Moral and Psychological Education: Theory and Research. No location: R F Publishing, 1978.

A collection of readings, all originally published elsewhere, on the cognitive-developmental approach to moral education.

449. Scharf, Peter, ed. Readings in Moral Education. Minneapolis, MN: Winston Press, 1978.

A collection of readings dealing primarily with the developmental approach to moral education. Contains a section on criticism of Kohlbergian programs.

450. Selman, Robert L., and Marcus Lieberman. "Primary Level Curriculum: Cognitive-Developmental Theory of Moral Reasoning." Values, Feelings and Morals (item 1791), pp. 70-85.

Presents the applications of cognitive-developmental theory to moral education in the primary grades.

451. Simon, Frank. "Moral Development: Some Suggested Implications for Teaching." Journal of Moral Education, 5 (1976): 173-178.

Describes the overall process of moral development as consisting of the movement from heteronomy to autonomy. Describes implications of Kohlberg's theory for schooling. Emphasizes the need to focus on ego-strength.

452. Sperber, Robert, and David Miron. "Organizing a School System for Ethics Education." Moral Education: A First Generation of Research and Development (item 428), pp. 58-82.

Describes the history of the Brookline Moral Education Project (1974-1977) which was a part of the larger Danforth Project. Includes descriptions of curriculum to increase moral reasoning, establishment of a just community (School-Within-A-School), and teaching parents to be better moral educators.

453. Sullivan, E.V., and C.M. Beck. "Moral Education." Must Schools Fail? Edited by P. Byrne and J. Quarter. Toronto: McClelland and Stewart, 1972.

Presents Kohlberg's moral development theory and discusses how it might be applied in the classroom.

454. Sullivan, Paul J. "Implementing Programs in Moral Education." Theory into Practice, 16 (1977): 118-12.

Discusses some of the administrative issues involved in the implementation of developmental moral education programs. The Ethical Quest in a Democratic Society program is used as a case study to illustrate the problems involved. The integration within the curriculum and the necessity of building support in the school and community are discussed.

455. Thompson, Mary L. Moral Education: A Developmental Approach. Cincinnati, OH: Pamphlet Publications, 1978.

The first half of this short pamphlet consists of an account of Kohlbergian theory and its application to education. In the second part of the pamphlet a three-stage theory of emotional development is presented.

456. Waldron, Martin C. "A Model for Integrating Values Education Approaches According to Cognitive-Developmental Theory." Ph.D. dissertation, University of California, Berkeley, 1977. 39/02, p. 791.

Describes a model that attempted to interrelate a variety of values education approaches within a developmental perspective. A combination Kohlberg-Simon teaching process was field tested, but the results were not significant.

457. Wallin, Gloria J. "Fostering Moral Development Through Creative Dramatics." Personnel and Guidance Journal, 58 (1970): 630.

Describes the use of creative dramatics in inner-city schools to foster moral development. Children created their own dramatic situations for role playing.

458. Weinreich, Helen. "Kohlberg and Piaget: Aspects of Their Relationship in the Field of Moral Development." Journal of Moral Education, 4 (1975): 201-213.

Traces the historical relationship of Kohlberg to Piaget. Examines the ways in which Kohlberg extends or departs from Piaget's system of moral growth.

459. Alexander, Robert C. "A Moral Education Curriculum on Prejudice." Ed.D. dissertation, Boston University, 1977. 37/12, p. 7497.

A 16-week developmentally-based course on prejudice was found to induce a significant change in ego and moral development and to reduce prejudice.

460. Alozie, Chukwuma. "An Analysis of the Interrelationship of Two Measures Used in the Measurement of Moral Judgment Development: The Kohlberg Moral Judgment, Interview and the Rest Defining Issues Test." Ph.D. dissertation, University of Minnesota, 1976. 37/06, p. 3505.

A strong relationship was found between the two tests. Subtle differences between the two tests revealed by the findings are discussed.

461. Arbuthnot, Jack. "Modification of Moral Judgment Through Role Playing." Developmental Psychology, 11 (1975): 319-324.

Both immediate and delayed increases in moral judgment maturity were observed when subjects engaged in role playing in a moral dilemma situation where the opponent in the dilemma used +1 reasoning.

462. Azrak, Robert C. "Parental Discipline and Early Adolescent Moral Development." Ed.D. dissertation, Boston University, 1978. 39/05, p. 2747.

Found that parents trained to use discipline situations to lead moral discussions with children could stimulate the moral development of the children.

463. Azrak, Robert. "Parents as Moral Educators." Moral Education: A First Generation of Research and Development (item 428), pp. 356-365.

Reports the results of a study in which parents of early adolescents were trained to isolate the moral aspects of family discipline situations and to use these experiences to promote the moral development of children.

464. Bauer, Luanne J. "Moral Reasoning and the Decrease of Dogmatism in the Communication Classroom: Small Group Discussions and Creative Drama as Methods of Instruction." Ph.D. dissertation, Northwestern University, 1979. 40/06, p. 2980.

Examined whether small group discussions of moral dilemmas and creative drama experiences contribute to growth in moral reasoning and decreases in dogmatism. It was found that only small group discussions contributed to moral growth.

465. Beck, Clive; Edmund Sullivan; and Nancy Taylor. "Stimulating Transition to Postconventional Morality: The Pickering High School Study." Interchange, 3 (1972): 28-37.

Reports the results of a four-month intervention with high school students. No immediate change in level of moral development was detected; however, on a one-year-delayed post-test a significant increase in principled moral reasoning was observed.

466. Bennett, Allen C. "A Cognitive Developmental Orientation Toward Moral Education: An Experimental Study in Developing Moral Judgment Through the Comparable Effects of Two Teaching Strategies." Ph.D. dissertation, The Pennsylvania State University, 1975. 36/11, p. 7146.

Using pre-service teachers it was found that a social interactive approach was superior to an individually programmed approach in stimulating moral development.

467. Bennett, Susan G. "The Relationship Between Adolescents' Levels of Moral Development and Their Responses to Short Stories." Ph.D. dissertation, University of California, Berkeley, 1978. 40/01, p. 34.

Principled thinkers were found to choose interpretive responses more frequently than subjects below the principled level.

468. Berkowitz, Marvin. "The Role of Transactive Discussion in Moral Development: The History of a Six-Year Program of Research--Part I." Moral Education Forum; 5 (Summer 1980): 13-26.

Studied moral reasoning and moral development through the use of pairs of subjects discussing moral dilemmas without the intervention of experimenters. Discusses the many procedures that were developed. Found that the optimal dyadic disparity for moral development was + one third stage.

469. Berkowitz, M.W.; J.C. Gibbs; and J.M. Broughton. "The Relation of Moral Judgment Stage Disparity to Developmental Effects of Peer Dialogues." Merrill-Palmer Quarterly, 26 (1980): 341-357.

Finds that dyadic college-age peer discussion can lead to moral judgment development. Optimally the disparity in stages of the partners should be one minor stage or one-third of a stage. A larger disparity produced less marked change. No stage disparity produced no change.

470. Berman, Ethel V. "Approaches to Altruism: An Experimental Investigation of Factors Influencing Sharing Behavior and Moral Judgment." Ph.D. dissertation, Georgia State University, 1974. 35/08, p. 4853.

Four treatments--moral dilemma filmstrips with discussion, moral dilemma filmstrips with moral reinforcement, moral dilemma filmstrips alone, and morally neutral filmstrips--had no effect on moral judgment or on donations to the March of Dimes. Subjects were females between the ages of 7 and 12.

471. Biskin, D.S., and K. Hoskisson. "An Experimental Test of the Effects of Structured Discussions of Moral Dilemmas Found in Children's Literature on Moral Reasoning." Elementary School Journal, 77 (1977): 407-416.

Using fourth- and fifth-grade students who discussed moral dilemmas found in children's literature once a week for seven weeks, it was found that level of moral reasoning increased for the treatment group, but only at the .14 level of significance.

472. Blatt, Moshe. "The Effects of Classroom Discussion upon Children's Level of Moral Judgment." Ph.D. dissertation, University of Chicago, 1970.

One of the first studies to find that classroom discussion of moral dilemmas can facilitate growth in moral reasoning

472. Blatt, Moshe M., and Lawrence Kohlberg. "The Effects of Classroom Moral Discussion upon Children's Level of Moral Judgment." Journal of Moral Education, 4 (1975): 129-161.

A study which tests the hypothesis that discussion of moral dilemmas will stimulate movement toward higher stages of moral reasoning. This paper reports results from a Jewish Sunday school and public junior and senior high schools. It was found that moral discussions did have a significant impact on the moral reasoning of children. Also in Collected Papers (item 1798), Education and Moral Development (item 395), and Moral and Psychological Education (item 448).

474. Boutet, Prosper J. "A Critical Analysis of Adolescent Values and Emergent Utopian Thought." Ed.D. dissertation, University of California, Berkeley, 1976. 37/09, p. 6088.

Utopianism, the notion of the "good life" that emerges in a group, was found to be the result of two forces: the social group and the level of cognitive moral development. The educational implications are discussed.

475. Bower, Michael F. "A Sexuality Curriculum to Promote the Moral Reasoning and Ego Development of Adolescents." Ed.D. dissertation, Boston University, 1980. 40/12, p. 6149.

It was found that a systematic course using moral dilemmas, role playing, discussion, and learning of sexual information had no significant impact on students' level of moral reasoning or ego development.

476. Boyd, Dwight R. "The Condition of Sophomoritis and Its Educational Care." Journal of Moral Education, 10 (1980): 24-39.

Describes an experimental course designed around the problem of sophomoritis. Sophomoritis is defined as a problematic phase in the transition from conventional to principled moral judgment. An average development of one-third of a stage was observed to be a result of the course.

477. Boyd, Dwight R. "Education Toward Principled Moral Judgment: An Analysis of an Experimental Course in Undergraduate Moral Education Applying Lawrence Kohlberg's Theory of Moral Development." Ed.D. dissertation, Harvard University, 1976. 37/07, p. 4304.

Finds that a one-semester undergraduate course featuring discussion of moral dilemmas can stimulate moral development.

478. Bridston, Elizabeth O. "The Development of Principled Moral Reasoning in Baccalaureate Nursing Students." Ed.D. dissertation, University of San Francisco, 1979. 40/04, p. 1237.

No significant growth in principled moral reasoning was detected as a result of nurses' participation in intensive discussion of moral dilemmas that arise in the practice of nursing.

479. Brock, Annette K. "The Effects of Utilization of Discussions of Moral Dilemmas on Cognitive Gain and Attitude Change in a History Classroom." Ph.D. dissertation, University of South Carolina, 1978. 39/10, p. 6049.

High school students exposed to moral discussion activities scored significantly higher in mastery of curriculum content and attitude toward the curriculum than did students whose history classes did not include moral dilemma discussions.

480. Byrne, Patrick M. "Stage and Sex Differences in Moral and Ego Development Prior and Consequent to Independence Training." Ph.D. dissertation, University of Toronto, 1973. 35/09, p. 5918.

It was found that training a subject to be aware of aversive significant others controlling his/her life and developing alternative strategies for coping with these others can stimulate moral and ego development.

481. Colby, Anne; Lawrence Kohlberg; Edwin Fenton; Betsy Speicher-Dubin; and Marcus Lieberman. "Secondary School Moral Discussion Programmes Led by Social Studies Teachers." Journal of Moral Education, 6 (1977): 90-111.

Classrooms in Boston & Pittsburgh, 39 in all, comprised the sample. Two variables were manipulated within the Kohlbergian model of moral education: type of teacher preparation and number of moral discussions. Subjects in Boston achieved significant stage change, but students in Pittsburgh (all "slow learners") did not. The teacher preparation variable seemed not to be significant. The number of discussions seemed to have an impact. Also in Education and Moral Development (item 395).

482. Connaster, Larry A. "A Study of the Effect of an Academic Program on the Moral Development of Incarcerated Young Adults in the Bland Correctional Center, Bland County, Virginia." Ed.d. dissertation, Virginia Polytechnic Institute and State University, 1977. 38/03, p. 1175.

A regular academic program is found, not surprisingly, to have no impact on incarcerated youths' moral development when compared with the moral development of youths not attending an academic program.

483. Copeland, Terry F. "An Attempt to Enhance the Moral Development of Offenders." Ph.D. dissertation, Kansas State University, 1979. 40/06, p. 3194.

Moral dilemma discussion sessions failed to enhance the level of moral reasoning of young male incarcerated soldiers.

484. Copeland, Terry F., and Thomas S. Parish. "An Attempt to Enhance Moral Judgment of Offenders." Psychological Reports, 45 (1979): 831-834.

Attempts to apply, without success, Kohlbergian principles to enhance the moral reasoning of 134 young men incarcerated in a military training program.

485. Corella, Stephen D. "Discipline Judgments of Disruptive Behaviors by Individuals and Dyads Differing in Moral Reasoning." Ph.D. dissertation, University of Oklahoma, 1977. 38/04, p. 1550.

Mixed moral dyads and matched moral dyads watched two vignettes depicting classroom disturbances. Higher-principled subjects viewed the disturbances as less severe than did lower-principled subjects. There was no evidence that change in moral reasoning occurred as a result of the mixed pairs.

486. Cornett, Claudia E. "A Descriptive Study of the Moral Development of Selected Teachers and Their Students." Ph.D. dissertation, Miami University, 1976. 37/12, p. 7629.

Sixth-grade teachers' and students' stage of moral reasoning was identified. The majority of teachers were at stage 3; all students were at or below their teachers' stage.

487. Dettoni, John M. "Increasing the Classifiability of Moral Judgment Verbalizations in Discussions Based on Moral Development Curricular Experiences." Ph.D. dissertation, Michigan State University, 1976. 37/12, p. 7504.

Sought to increase the classifiable moral verbalizations in classes so that teachers might more easily "stage" their students. Found that none of the proposed approaches worked very well.

488. DiStefano, Ann M. "Adolescent Moral Reasoning After a Curriculum in Sexual and Interpersonal Dilemmas." Ed.D. dissertation, Boston University, 1977. 38/09, p. 5348.

Students in an experimental group discovered ethical issues encountered in their interpersonal relationships when compared with a control group. The hypothesis that this activity would stimulate moral judgment was upheld only at the .10 level.

489. Dockstader, Mary F. "Comparative Study of Developmental Sex Differences in Moral Reasoning." Ed.D. dissertation, Seattle University, 1979. 40/03, p. 1239.

No significant difference between males and females at the seventh- and eleventh-grade levels was detected. A 12-week intervention designed to stimulate development of the subjects' moral reasoning was not successful.

490. Dodd, Betty N. "A Study of the Effects of Values Development Program on Elementary School Emotionally Disturbed Students." Ed.D. dissertation, East Texas State University, 1981. 44/02, p. 547.

Emotionally disturbed subjects who experienced a six-week Kohlbergian program were found to demonstrate a higher level of moral judgment, more internality of control, and increased self-concept than their counterparts not involved in a program of values development.

491. Dunagan, Arthur E. "The Relationship among Instructional Preferences of Adolescent Students, Their Moral Reasoning Ability and Their Perceived Level of Psycho-Social Development." Ph.D. dissertation, Georgia State University, 1975. 37/08, p. 5024.

Attempted to determine if there was a relationship between preferred instructional preferences and two theories of human development (Kohlberg's and Hoffman and Ryan's Theory of Psycho-Social Instructional Stages). No significant correlation was obtained.

492. Edwards, Ned W. "A Study of the Relationship Between Curriculum Divisions in Christian Education and Moral Judgment of Teachers." Ph.D. dissertation, Case Western Reserve University, 1978. 39/07, p. 4016.

Explores whether stage of moral reasoning is related to person-centered or subject-centered curriculum decisions and whether it is a factor in preference for grade level to teach at. It was found that stage of moral reasoning was significantly related to person-centered curriculum decisions and to choice of preferred grade level.

493. Endo, Todd I. "The Relevance of Kohlberg's Stages of Moral Development to Research in Political Socialization." Ed.D. dissertation, Harvard University, 1973. 34/11, p. 7041.

Using eighth- and eleventh-grade students, and assessing their reasoning on public policy dilemmas as well as moral dilemmas, it was found that on selected topics, as Easton & Hess claim, political socialization is largely complete by eighth grade.

494. Erickson, V. Lois. "Psychological Growth for Women: A Cognitive-Developmental Curriculum Intervention." Ph.D. dissertation, University of Minnesota, 1973. 34/07, p. 3829.

The study was designed to produce movement on the developmental stages of growth in high school women. In studying women's development in history, literature, and individual interviews, it was found that stage growth on Kohlberg and Loevinger ego development scales was produced.

495. Erney, Thomas A. "The Effects of a Peer Facilitator-Led Group on the Moral Development, School Attitudes, and Self-Esteem of Middle School Subjects." Ph.D. dissertation, University of Florida, 1979. 40/08, p. 4408.

Peer-led groups were designed to encourage clarification of students' values as well as to enhance feelings of self-worth. It was found that the peer-led group produced a significant change in moral reasoning and self-esteem.

496. Evans, Charles S. "Relationship of Stages of Moral Development to Knowledge of Kohlberg's Theory of Moral Development in High School Students." Ph.D. dissertation, University of Missouri-Columbia, 1980. 44/02, p. 648.

It was found that exposing students to the tenets of Kohlberg's theory over three class periods has no effect on stage of moral development.

497. Farrelly, Thomas M. "Peer-Group Discussion as a Strategy in Moral Education." Ph.D. dissertation, University of South Florida, 1980. 41/06, p. 2422.

Peer-group discussion was found to be no more effective than an individual study strategy in effecting changes in level of moral reasoning.

498. Faust, D., and J. Arbuthnot. "Relationship Between Moral and Piagetian Reasoning and the Effectiveness of Moral Reasoning." Developmental Psychology, 14 (1978): 435-436.

Piagetian cognitiveand moral stage were assessed prior to a moral education program. It was found that the Piagetian stage does set a limit on the individual's potential for moral growth at a given point in time.

499. Fedoroko, Rose A. "Effects of Parent Training on the Moral Development of Five-, Six-, and Seven-Year-Olds." Educational Horizons, 56 (1977-78): 77-83.

Describes the results of a program in which parents were trained to facilitate the moral development of their children.

500. Fenton, Edwin. "Moral Education: The Research Findings." Readings in Moral Education (item 449), pp. 52-59.

An uncritical presentation of 11 generalizations regarding developmental moral education which, according to Fenton, are supported by the research on cognitive development. Also in Social Education, 40 (1976): 188-193.

501. Fleetwood, Robert S. "A Study of the Relationship Between Moral Development Test Scores of Juvenile Delinquents and Their Group Membership in Structured Situations." Ph.D. dissertation, Oklahoma State University, 1975. 36/10, p. 6548.

Juvenile delinquents who engaged in three hours of discussion of moral dilemmas experienced significant growth in moral reasoning.

502. Fleetwood, R.S., and T.S. Parish. "Relationship Between Moral Development Test Scores of Juvenile Delinquents and Their Inclusion in a Moral Dilemma Discussion Group." Psychological Reports, 39 (1976): 1075-1080.

Following six 90-minute discussion sessions on moral dilemmas the experimental group experienced significant growth in moral reasoning compared with the control group. Rest's Defining Issues Test was used.

503. Gagliardo, Ettore S. "A Determination of the Relationship Between Kohlberg's Moral Development Training and Hall Advisors' Effectiveness." Ph.D. dissertation, University of Pittsburgh, 1978. 39/08, p. 4691.

It was found that participation in moral development training resulted in higher levels of moral reasoning but this did not, in turn, result in higher ratings of residence hall advisors' effectiveness.

504. Gallagher, William J. "Implementation of a Kohlbergian Value Development Curriculum in High School Literature." Ph.D. dissertation, Fordham University, 1978. 38/12, p. 7111.

It was found that eleventh- and twelfth-grade students made significant advances in their moral reasoning as a result of guided peer discussion of literary conflicts.

505. Geis, George T. "An Experimental Study in the Effects of Varying Types of Peer Group Interaction upon Growth in Principled Moral Judgment of College Students." Ph.D. dissertation, University of Southern California, 1977. 38/03, p. 1299.

Groups of college students, some instructed to reach consensus, others to develop individual rationales for the dilemma, were pre- and post-tested on Rest's Defining Issues Test. No significant differences were found as a result of the varying treatments.

506. Gibson, Jerry C. "A Study of the Relationships among Stages of Moral Reasoning, Sociometric Placement, Self-Concept, Academic Achievement, and Age of Students in a Public Elementary School." Ph.D. dissertation, St. Louis University, 1977. 38/08, p. 5216.

Reveals that sociometric status is positively correlated with level of moral reasoning. Argues that "social stars" if placed carefully can be important agents in the moral growth of groups.

507. Grant, Gerald C. "Some Effects of Moral Discussion on Clinical Pastoral Education Students." Ed.D. dissertation, Boston University, 1975. 36/03, p. 1597.

No significant difference was found between subjects exposed to 10 ninety-minute moral discussions and control groups.

508. Gredler, Yvonne S. "The Effects of Film and Discussion on Facilitating Shift in Kohlberg's Stages of Moral Development among Adolescents." Ph.D. dissertation, University of South Carolina, 1976. 37/10, p. 6363.

There were no significant differences between the experimental and control groups, although subjects exposed to film and discussion experienced significantly more gain than those exposed to discussion alone. Results were probably due to four-day time span of study.

509. Green, Judith A. "A Study to Investigate the Effects of Empathy Instruction on Moral Development." Ph.D. dissertation, George Peabody College of Vanderbilt University, 1980. 44/02, p. 568.

Explores the effects of a cognitive developmental approach to empathy instruction on the moral and empathy development of nurse trainees. It was found that the treatment did not have a significant effect.

510. Green, Thomas G. "Moral Thinking in Dental Students." Ph.D. dissertation, Michigan State University, 1979. 40/10, p. 5387.

A general decline in moral reasoning was detected as students moved through the program. A Dental Dilemmas Test was created, but it did not correlate well with the Rest instrument.

511. Grimes, Patricia. "Teaching Moral Reasoning to Eleven Year Olds and Their Mothers. A Means of Promoting Moral Development." Ed.D. dissertation, Boston University, 1974. 35/03, p. 1498.

It was found that mothers trained in Kohlbergian developmental methods can be effective moral educators with their children.

512. Haber, Roslyn A. "Moral Education and Alternative Schools." Ed.D. dissertation, Columbia University, 1978. 39/01, p. 48.

Experimental classes within an alternative school were exposed to a literary-based curriculum focusing on moral dilemmas. The experimental classes experienced significant moral development when compared with control groups.

513. Harmon, Carolyn P. "The Development of Moral and Political Reasoning among 10, 13, and 16-Year-Olds: A Test of the Cognitive-Developmental Approach to Political Socialization." Ph.D. dissertation, Yale University, 1973. 34/05, p. 2718.

It was found that development in both moral and political reasoning go hand in hand and both are age-related.

514. Harris, David. "A Curriculum Sequence for Moral Development." _Theory and Research in Social Education_, 5 (1977): 1-21.

Hypothesizes that a sequence of deliberate psychological education followed by moral discussion will have a synergistic effect on students' moral development. Using eleventh-grade students it was found that both the moral discussion group (18 weeks) and the psychological education (9 weeks) followed by moral discussion (9 week) effected the same amount of change, but the latter intervention effected all of the change during the last 9 weeks. See also item 1141.

515. Harris, Kenneth L. "The Effects of Training and Age on the Moral Judgments of Institutionalized Mentally Retarded Persons." Ph.D. dissertation, Brigham Young University, 1975. 36/07, p. 4351.

Mentally retarded subjects significantly improved in their ability to make moral judgments as a result of a sample reinforcement procedure.

516. Harvey, Francis S. "The Use of the Quaker Consensus Decision-Making Process in Facilitating Moral Development." Ph.D. dissertation, Union for Experimenting Colleges and Universities, 1979. 40/07, p. 3656.

Analyzed methodology of the consensus decision-making process in a Quaker secondary school student council. Concluded that the process contains all the conditions necessary for moral development to occur among its participants.

517. Hayden, Brian, and Daniel Pickar. "The Impact of Moral Discussions on Children's Level of Moral Reasoning." Journal of Moral Education, 10 (1981): 131-134.

Attempted to replicate the Kohlbergian intervention for moral development. Found that the experimental group experienced significant moral development.

518. Hickey, Joseph E. "The Effects of Guided Moral Discussion upon Youthful Offenders' Level of Moral Judgment." Ed.D. dissertation, Boston University, 1972. 33/04, p. 1551.

Guided moral discussions with incarcerated youth using real life issues are found to be effective in stimulating moral development.

519. Hoffman, Darlene H. "The Effects of Structured Role-taking Experiences on the Level of Cognitive and Moral Development of Young Adults." Ph.D. dissertation, Southern Illinois University, 1978. 39/10, p. 6015.

Using college students it was found that limited role-taking experiences did not result in significant moral development.

520. Holman, Raquel B. "The Effects of a Discussion Course on Pre-Student Teachers' Moral Reasoning." Ph.D. dissertation, University of New Mexico, 1979. 40/08, p. 4382.

It was found that moral dilemma discussions resulted in a significant gain of stage 4 reasoning.

521. Iozzi, Louis A. "Moral Judgment, Verbal Ability, Logical Reasoning Ability, and Environmental Issues." Ed.D. dissertation, Rutgers University, 1976. 37/12, p. 7662.

Principled moral reasoning was found to be significantly related to verbal ability and logical reasoning ability. Conventional moral reasoning was found to be negatively related to verbal ability and logical reasoning ability. Subjects were also found to reason differently according to different specific moral situations.

522. Jacobson, Lowell T. "A Study of Relationships among Mother, Student and Teacher Levels of Moral Reasoning in a Department of Defense Middle School." Ph.D. dissertation, Michigan State University, 1977. 38/10, p. 5824.

On the Defining Issues Test it was found that teachers scored higher than both mothers and students.

523. Jensen, Larry, and Steve Chatterley. "Facilitating Development of Moral Reasoning in Children." _Journal of Moral Education_, 9 (1979): 53-54.

Finds that brief training programs with kindergarten and first-grade children using an indirect approach can facilitate moral development.

524. Jensen, Larry C., and Barbara Vance. "Effects of Training on the Ethical Reasoning of Children." Provo, UT: Brigham Young University, 1972. ED 071 762.

Reports the results of a number of studies analyzing the factors which affect the moral reasoning of pre-school children. For example, it was found that when children are trained to focus on intentions, shifts in moral reasoning will occur. The findings are discussed in terms of cognitive-developmental theory and in terms of the authors' own comprehension preference model.

525. Johnson, Dale A. "An Experimental Study in Developing Moral Judgment Using Different Instructional Patterns with Locus of Control and Religious Attitudes as Learner Characteristics." Ph.D. dissertation, University of California, Riverside, 1978. 39/05, p. 2724.

A significant relationship was detected between patterns of instruction (role playing and moral discussion) and moral judgment, but no significant relationship was detected between locus of control and moral judgment or between religious attitudes and moral judgment.

526. Justice, Gary E. "Facilitating Principled Moral Reasoning in College Students: A Cognitive-Developmental Approach." Ph.D. dissertation, St. Louis University, 1977. 39/03, p. 1406.

Discussion of moral dilemmas is found to stimulate moral development among college students.

527. Kavanagh, Harry B. "Moral Development in Adolescent Peer Interaction." Ph.D. dissertation, Fordham University, 1975. 36/03, p. 1394.

After viewing four moral conflict films subjects were divided into groups for three activities: peer-led discussion, counselor-led discussion, and writing out one's resolution of the conflict. The peers and the writers both showed significant gain in moral development.

528. Kavanagh, Harry B. "Moral Development in a High School Program." Values and Moral Development (item 378), pp. 124-141.

Reports the results of a study (see item 527) in which peer discussions and writing experiences were more effective than counselor-led discussions or the control group in stimulating moral development.

529. Kavanagh, Harry B. "Moral Education: Relevance, Goals and Strategies." Journal of Moral Education, 6 (1977): 121-130.

The effects of a moral education program based on Kohlberg's work are reported.

530. Keasey, Charles B. "Experimentally Induced Changes in Moral Opinions and Reasoning." Journal of Personality and Social Psychology, 26 (1975): 30-38.

The moral reasoning of fourth- and fifth-grade students was modified by exposure to conflict and +1 stage reasoning. Change observed was both short and long term.

531. Keefe, Donald R. "A Comparison of the Effect of Teacher and Student Led Discussions of Short Stories and Case Accounts on the Moral Reasoning of Adolescents Using the Kohlberg Model." Ph.D. dissertation, University of Illinois, 1975. 36/05, p. 2734.

Differences in moral development as a result of discussion of short stories or case accounts was not statistically significant. Biased versus neutral teachers likewise made no significant difference in moral development. However, when compared with control groups there was a major treatment effect.

532. Kennon, Cassandra K. "Effects of Kohlberg's Cognitive Developmental Approach to Moral Education on Development of Literal and Inferential Comprehension." Ed.D. dissertation, Auburn University, 1978. 39/10, p. 6031.

Literal and inferential sub-test scores for sixth-grade students did not differ significantly for the moral dilemma discussion group and the comparison groups.

533. Kennon, Cassandra K. "Utilizing Moral Dilemmas to Enhance Comprehension." Paper presented at the annual meeting of the International Reading Association, St. Louis, 1980. ED 189 548.

Finds that using Kohlbergian moral dilemmas in the classroom with sixth-grade children enhances inferential comprehension scores in reading.

534. Kenwin, Willard A. "A Study of the Effect of Systematic Value Instruction on Level of Moral Judgment." Ed.D. dissertation, Rutgers University, 1981. 42/04, p. 1582.

Finds no significant difference in level of moral judgment between high school students exposed to a Kohlbergian program, students exposed to programmed religious instruction, and students in the regular school program.

535. Lamberg, Roland A. "Effects of Moral Education Strategies on Increased Subject Matter Content of Secondary School Social Studies Students." Ph.D. dissertation, The Catholic University of America, 1980. 41/01, p. 218.

Finds that a cognitive-developmental intervention not only stimulates natural developmental trends in moral judgment, but also increases academic achievement, student attitude toward learning, and self-concept.

536. Lawrence, Jeanette A. "Moral Judgment Intervention Studies Using the Defining Issues Test." Journal of Moral Education, 9 (1980): 178-191.

14 moral judgment intervention studies are reviewed and evaluated. Factors contributing to upward moral growth are identified and discussed. The vast majority of references cited are unpublished.

537. Lieberman, Marcus. "Evaluation of a Social Studies Curriculum Based on an Inquiry Method and a Cognitive-Developmental Approach to Moral Education." Paper presented at the annual meeting of the American Educational Research Association, 1975. ED 106 175.

Finds that with eighth-, ninth-, and tenth-grade students, exposure to inquiry and moral development components in a social studies classroom leads to increases in inquiry skills, subject knowledge, and growth in moral reasoning.

538. Lockley, Ora E. "Moral Reasoning and Choice of Values among Students at Rutgers University." Ed.D. dissertation, Rutgers University, 1976. 36/12, p. 7663.

Using the Defining Issues Test and Rokeach's Value Survey it was found that significant differences appeared between level of moral judgment and choice of terminal and instrumental values.

539. McKenzie, Timothy. "A Curriculum for Stimulating Moral Reasoning in High School Students Using Values Clarification and Moral Development Interventions." Ed.D. dissertation, Boston University, 1980. 41/05, p. 2020.

Finds that with high school juniors a combination of values clarification and moral development intervention has a significant impact on moral reasoning. No difference was found with regard to increases in moral reasoning between the two treatments and a control group.

540. Mackie, Peter A. "Teaching Counseling Skills to Low Achieving High School Students." Ed.D. dissertation, Boston University, 1974. 35/06, p. 3427.

Attempts to determine the impact of a counseling course on the moral reasoning of low-achieving students. Half of the students were found to have increased one-third of a stage.

541. Maitland, Karen A., and Jacquelin R. Goldman. "Moral Judgment as a Function of Peer Group Interaction." Journal of Personality and Social Psychology, 30 (1974): 699-704.

A moral judgment scale was developed and used to study the effects of three different levels of peer group interaction on the moral judgments of high school students. The instrument has students choose their response to moral dilemmas from stage-scored options. The conditions were: come to consensus in a group, discuss only in a group, and individually consider a moral dilemma. The consensus group experienced the greatest change in moral development.

542. Mandelbaum, David I. "A Comparative Study of Role-Taking Training for the Enhancement of Moral Development." Ph.D. dissertation, The Pennsylvania State University, 1975. 37/02, p. 859.

Is stage mixture leading to cognitive conflict (Kohlberg) or is stage mixture alone (Piaget) the crucial variable in moral development? It was found that neither training was more effective than the other or than no training at all. Results probably due to 30 minutes of treatment.

543. Mayshack, Gail. "Cognitive Moral Development as Related to Field Independence with Delinquent, Status Offending and Normal Adolescent Males." Ph.D. dissertation, Georgia State University, 1977. 38/11, p. 6623.

Moral discussion groups were found to produce significant gains in moral reasoning for both delinquent and non-delinquent subjects.

544. Menitoff, Michael N. "A Comparative Study of Moral Development in Jewish Religious School Settings." Ph.D. dissertation, University of California, Los Angeles, 1977. 38/06, p. 3396.

Found that the more a school engaged students in examination of problematic moral situations the more the students of that school experience moral growth.

545. Murphy, Herbert J. "The Contribution of Role-Playing to the Social Perspective Taking Levels and Moral Reasoning Levels of Elementary School Pupils." Ed.D. dissertation, University of Virginia, 1976. 37/04, p. 1994.

Support was not found for the thesis that moral reasoning levels and social perspective-taking levels are influenced by role playing.

546. Nedich, Sanford I. "A Study of the Relationship of Transcendental Meditation to Kohlberg's Stages of Moral Reasoning." Ed.D. dissertation, University of Cincinnati, 1975. 36/07, p. 4361.

Meditators' scores on moral reasoning were found to be significantly higher than those of nonmeditators.

547. Novogrodsky, Jacob. "Teachers' Moral Development and Their Expressed Attitudes Toward Students." Ph.D. dissertation, Yeshiva University, 1977. 38/04, p. 2006.

It was hypothesized that the higher the teacher's stage of moral reasoning the more harmonious the interpersonal relations would be with students. The hypothesis was confirmed.

548. Oberlander, Keith J. "An Experimental Determination of the Effects of a Film about Moral Behavior and of Peer Group Discussion Regarding Moral Dilemmas upon the Moral Development of College Students." Ph.D. dissertation, University of Southern California, 1980. 41/04, p. 1496.

Viewing films dealing with moral conflict and a variety of approaches to making decisions (independent to group consensus) are found to have no significant impact on subjects' moral development as measured by the Defining Issues Test.

549. Ostarch, Valerie. "Cross-Age Teaching: Stimulus to Moral Development." Moral Education Forum, 6 (Fall 1981): 24-29.

Describes the case of a high school senior trained to conduct moral dilemma discussions with fifth-grade students. No formal evaluation of the effort was conducted but the author views the results optimistically.

550. Panowitsch, Henry R. "Change and Stability in the Defining Issues Test: An Objective Measure of Moral Development." Ph.D. dissertation, University of Minnesota, 1975. 37/01, p. 201.

A college ethics course produces significant growth on the Defining Issues Test (D.I.T.). Subjects in a logic course did not experience significant growth.

551. Paolitto, Diana P. "The Moral Education of Early Adolescents." Moral Education: A First Generation of Research and Development (item 428), pp. 205-215.

Through the use of a role-taking curriculum significant growth in level of moral reasoning was achieved with junior high students.

552. Paolitto, Diana. "Role Taking Opportunities for Early Adolescents: A Program in Moral Education." Ed.D. dissertation, Boston University, 1976. 36/11, p. 7214.

An experimental course featuring role-taking activities was found to stimulate moral development but did not increase subjects' role-taking abilities.

553. Pembroke, Eileen. "Parent Education as a Means of Fostering Moral Development in Beginning Primary Age Children." Ph.D. dissertation, Loyola University of Chicago, 1980. 41/03, p. 994.

Found that participation in the parent education program did not significantly alter children's self-concepts or their levels of social reasoning in the areas of justice and authority.

554. Perine, Maxine H. "The Response of Sixth-Grade Readers to Selected Children's Literature with Special Reference to Moral Judgment." Ed.D. dissertation, Columbia University, 1977. 39/05, p. 2729.

A relationship was found between literary responses (using the Purves schema) and moral interpretations. Data suggests that Kohlberg stages are present in some degree at all times in the minds of students, but some stages are more prominent at one time than another.

555. Piburn, Michael D. "Teaching about Science and Society: Moral Judgment and the Prisoner's Dilemma." Theory and Research in Social Education, 5 (August 1977): 20-30.

Using the Prisoner's Dilemma game--a two-person, non-zero sum game that requires repeated socio-moral choices on the part of participants--it was found that cooperators show a greater preference for principled moral reasoning and defectors a greater preference for preconventional moral reasoning.

556. Pierce, Sterling L. "The Effect of Group Discussion on Statements of Moral Judgment of Seventh Graders." Ed.D. dissertation, State University of New York at Albany, 1972. 34/03, p. 1085.

Using Johnson's Test of Moral Judgment it was found that among seventh-grade subjects, discussion in groups with a variety of stages of reasoning did produce changes in moral reasoning.

557. Pillar, Arlene M. "Dimensions of the Development of Moral Judgment as Reflected in Children's Responses to Fables." Ph.D. dissertation, New York University, 1980. 41/06, p. 2441.

Studied whether second-, fourth- and sixth-grade students' responses to questions about the moral dilemmas in fables reflect developmental trends in moral judgment. The data showed a clear developmental pattern across age levels.

558. Plymale, Sallie C. "The Effects of a Developmental Teacher Training Program on the Moral Reasoning Ability of 3rd and 6th Grade Students." Ed.D. dissertation, West Virginia University, 1977. 38/04, p. 2062.

Only with sixth-grade classes were teacher-led moral discussions found to stimulate moral development. No growth was detected with third-grade classes.

559. Preston, D. Diane. "A Moral Education Program Conducted in the Physical Education and Health Education Curriculum." Ed.D. dissertation, University of Georgia, 1979. 40/11, p. 5740.

No significant moral development was detected as a result of 12 weeks of Kohlbergian programs in ninth-grade health and physical education classes.

560. Reck, Carleen J. "A Study of the Relationship Between Participation in School Service Programs and Moral Development." Ph.D. dissertation, Saint Louis University, 1978. 39/03, p. 1504.

Greater growth in moral development was found to be associated with greater amount of service (15-, 42-, or 105-hour program).

561. Rest, James R. "Moral Judgment Research and the Cognitive-Developmental Approach to Moral Education." _Personnel and Guidance Journal_, 58 (1980): 602-605.

Argues that Kohlberg's moral judgment interview and his own Defining Issues Test provide usable, reliable means of assessing moral judgment. The evidence for moral reasoning as a useful construct for understanding human behavior is presented. Also briefly reviewed is the research on developmental education interventions.

562. Rest, James R. "New Approaches in the Assessment of Moral Judgment." Moral Development and Behavior (item 1801), pp. 198-218.

Reviews current methods of assessing moral judgment and points out their inadequacies. Describes the development and validation of his own objective measure of moral judgment, the Defining Issues Test.

563. Rest, James R. "The Research Base of the Cognitive Developmental Approach to Moral Education." Values and Moral Development (item 378), pp. 102-123.

Rest briefly reviews four theoretical approaches to the study of morality and his own efforts at developing the Defining Issues Test. He concludes by reporting four major clusters of research findings and discusses their implications for education.

564. Riley, David A. "Moral Judgment in Adults: The Effects of Age, Group Discussion and Pretest Sensitization." Ph.D. dissertation, Fordham University, 1981. 42/03, p. 1066.

Subjects in the following age ranges (20-34, 35-49, 50-64, and 65-80) participated in an eight-week series of group discussions organized around hypothetical moral dilemmas. It was found that the two younger age groups experienced significantly more growth than the two older groups.

565. Rockman, Bennett. "Improving Moral Judgment Made by Educable Mentally Retarded Adolescents." Ed.D. dissertation, Columbia University, 1974. 34/12, p. 7612.

Using discussion of simplified moral dilemmas it was found that the moral development of mentally retarded youth could be stimulated over the short run.

However, a delayed post-test indicated all gains had disappeared.

566. Rosenberg, Ralph I. "The Relationship Between Moral Judgment and Classroom Behavior among Emotionally Disturbed Elementary School Children." Ph.D. dissertation, Fordham University, 1976. 37/05, p. 2753.

It was found that significant correlations existed between moral judgment and six of the classroom variables (persistence, honesty, courtesy, generosity, cooperation, and disrespect-defiance).

567. Rosenkoetter, L.I.; S. Landman; and S.G. Mazak. "Use of Moral Discussion as an Intervention with Delinquents." Psychological Reports, 46 (1980): 91-94.

Use of discussion of moral dilemmas with adolescent delinquents led to significant moral development, with most subjects achieving stage 3.

568. Rosenzweig, Linda W. "Moral Dilemmas in Jewish History." D.A. dissertation, Carnegie-Mellon University, 1976. 37/03, p. 1711.

Describes the development and field-test of text and teacher's guide for a 15-week course on Moral Dilemmas in Jewish History. There were few changes in moral stage scores as a result of the course.

569. Rundle, Louise. "Moral Development in the Fifth Grade Classroom." Ed.D. dissertation, Boston University, 1977. 38/04, p. 2008.

Inquired whether hypothetical moral dilemmas or dilemmas drawn from the child's socio-emotional experience provide the best basis for moral education. Found that significant growth in moral development occurred only when using dilemmas from the child's socio-emotional experiences.

570. Rusnak, Timothy G. "A Study of the Effects of a Listening Treatment on the Cognitive Moral Development of Eight, Nine and Ten Year Olds." Ed.D. dissertation, University of Pittsburgh, 1980. 41/06, p. 2361.

Attempted to promote listening development and then transfer those skills to the cognitive moral development domain. It was found that increasing listening skills alone does not contribute to moral development.

571. Sachs, David A. "Implementing Moral Education: An Administrative Concern." Ed.D. dissertation, Columbia University, 1978. 39/10, p. 5856.

An experimental course on moral issues in literature was taught to classes in alternative high school and regular high school settings. The students in the alternative high school setting experienced significant development in moral reasoning. Results in the regular high school classroom were less dramatic.

572. St. Denis, Helen A. "Effects of Moral Education Strategies on Nursing Students' Moral Reasoning and Level of Self-Actualizing." Ph.D. dissertation, The Catholic University of America, 1980. 40/12, p. 6078.

The impact of cognitively oriented (Kohlberg) and affectively oriented (Rogers) strategies on nurses' level of moral reasoning and self-actualization were assessed. Both strategies produced significantly greater growth in moral reasoning than the control. The Kohlbergian strategy produced significantly greater growth than the affective strategy. Neither the cognitive nor affective approaches had any impact on self-actualization.

573. Sapp, Gary L.; and Ellen Dossett. "The Utility of a Cognitive-Developmental Model in Stimulating Moral Reasoning." Paper presented at annual meeting of the American Educational Research Association, New York, 1977. ED 143 579.

Reports the results of two studies, one with college juniors, the other with high school subjects, in which moral development was significantly affected by moral dilemma discussion experiences.

574. Schaffer, Philip A. "Moral Judgment: A Cognitive-Developmental Project in Psychological Education." Ph.D. dissertation, University of Minnesota, 1974. 35/02, p. 808.

Theoretical discussion of moral dilemmas with eleventh- and twelfth-grade students was found to have a slight impact on moral judgment.

575. Schepps, Celia H. "An Examination of the High School as a Just Institution: A Program in Moral Education for Adolescents." Ed.D. dissertation, Boston University, 1977. 37/12, p. 7549.

A course on justice featuring moral discussions was found to have no significant impact on moral judgment.

576. Schlimpert, Charles E. "The Effect of Kohlberg's Theory of Moral Development in the Parochial Secondary Classroom or Levels of Moral Judgment and Dogmatism." Ph.D. dissertation, University of Southern California, 1980. 41/05, p. 2026.

A moral dilemma discussion training program was found to have no significant effect on level of moral reasoning or on dogmatism.

577. Schneiberg, Alan B. "The Efficacy of a Psycho-Educational Intervention on Moral Development." Ph.D. dissertation, Kent State University, 1979. 40/10, p. 5380.

It was found that the use of moral dilemma discussions with early adolescents is a viable educational tool for raising levels of moral reasoning.

578. Schoenrock, Nancy B. "An Analysis of Moral Reasoning Levels and the Implications for the Nursing Curriculum." Ph.D. dissertation, University of Texas, Austin, 1978. 39/07, p. 4035.

Finds that a significant number of nurses are not at the post-conventional level nor do nurse participants have much knowledge of moral development teaching strategies.

579. Selman, Robert L.; and Marcus Lieberman. "An Evaluation of a Cognitive-Developmental Values Curriculum for Primary Grade Children." Journal of Educational Psychology, 67 (1975): 712-716.

Using second-grade students, small but significant gains in moral reasoning were detected following exposure to moral conflict dilemmas in the form of film-strips. Type of teacher training did not account for significant differences between classes.

580. Serino, Robert M. "Level of Moral Reasoning as Affected by Cognitive Frustration." Ph.D. dissertation, Mississippi State University, 1977. 34/08, p. 2010.

Attempted to ascertain if earlier modes of moral thought are used when subjects are under stress. Upon administering the Defining Issues Test after a frustrating vocabulary test, it was found that there was no significant change in moral reasoning.

581. Shafer, Jeffrey E. "The Effects of Kohlberg Dilemmas on Moral Reasoning, Attitudes, Thinking, Locus of Control, Self-Concept and Perceptions of Elementary Science Methods Students." Ed.D. dissertation, University of Northern Colorado, 1978. 39/08, p. 4850.

Participation in moral discussions resulted in significantly higher principled-reasoning scores. Principled moral reasoning was found to be unrelated to either self-concept or locus of control.

582. Shor, James Michael. "Achievement versus Development: A Study of Adolescent Value Orientations in Moral Dilemmas." Ed.D. dissertation, University of Rochester, 1974. 35/01, p. 271.

Hypothesized that the pursuit of personal achievement and the development of moral maturity are at odds. Found that when adolescents are confronted with dilemmas that offer a choice between achievement and moral motivations, the achievement ethic is significant.

583. Simon, A.; and L.O. Ward. "Variables Influencing Pupils' Responses on the Kohlberg Schema of Moral Development." Journal of Moral Education, 2 (1973): 283-286.

In youth aged 11 to 16, age and intelligence were found to be significantly related to moral judgment; sex differences and concern for others were not.

584. Stanley, Sheila F. "A Curriculum to Affect the Moral Atmosphere of the Family and the Moral Development of Adolescents." Ed.D. dissertation, Boston University, 1976. 36/11, p. 7221.

Parents and adolescents engaged in discussion of differences in values and of moral dilemmas involving family members. Significant gain was found in level of moral judgment.

585. Stanley, Sheila. "The Family and Moral Education." Moral Education: A First Generation of Research and Development (item 428), pp. 341-355.

Discusses the plan and results of a study in parent education. The goal of the project was to improve the role of the family environment as a moral educator. Also in Adolescents' Development and Education (item 1806).

586. Stanley, S. "Family Education: A Means of Enhancing the Moral Atmosphere of the Family and the Moral Development of Adolescents." Journal of Counseling Psychology, 25 (1978): 110-118.

Examines the effects of a course for families in democratic conflict resolution on the families' collective decision-making abilities and on the moral reasoning of adolescents. Parents increased in their equalitarian attitudes and adolescents increased in their level of moral reasoning.

587. Stuhr, David E. "Moral Education with Children: An Examination of Related Studies." Value Development ... As the Aim of Education (item 1816), pp. 41-52.

Discusses the results of four dissertations sponsored by the author which attempted to test Kohlberg's curricular suggestions for stimulating moral development.

588. Sullivan, Edmund V.; and Clive Beck. "A Developmental Approach to Assessment of Moral Education Programs: A Short Commentary." Journal of Moral Education, 4 (1974): 61-66.

Discussions about ethics were shown to result in significant stage growth in eleventh-grade students when compared with a control group.

589. Sullivan, Edmund V.; and Clive Beck. "Moral Education in a Canadian Setting." Moral Education ... It Comes With the Territory (item 811), pp. 221-234.

Describes an experiment to apply Kohlberg's ideas in a secondary school ethics class. There was no detectable difference between experimental class and control class on the immediate post-test but on a follow-up test the experimental group had increased significantly in mean percentage of stage 5 reasoning. Also in Phi Delta Kappan, 56 (1975): 697-701.

590. Sullivan, John P. "A Curriculum for Stimulating Moral Reasoning and Ego Development in Adolescents." Ed.D. dissertation, Boston University, 1975. 36/03, p. 1320.

A full-year course featuring discussion of moral dilemmas as well as a variety of counseling and psychological education techniques was found to result in significant moral and ego development.

591. Taylor, Beverly W. "The Relationship Between Level of Moral Development and Factual Learning in Situations with Moral Overtones." Ph.D. dissertation, University of Iowa, 1975. 36/04, p. 2112.

Finds that there is a positive relationship between level of moral development and factual learning in situations where facts are embedded in events with potentially strong moral overtones.

592. Tracy, James J. "Role-Taking as an Antecedent of Shift in Moral Judgment." Ph.D. dissertation, University of Connecticut, 1971. 36/05B, p. 3019.

Finds that the moral judgment scores of subjects (seventh-grade boys) with initially high role-taking ability are affected more by role-playing experiences than are the scores of subjects with low role-taking ability.

593. Tracy, J.J.; and H.J. Cross. "Antecedents of Shift in Moral Judgment." Journal of Personality and Social Psychology, 26 (1973): 238-244.

Finds significant treatment effect for Kohlbergian intervention. Stage growth was greatest for subjects (seventh-grade males) at preconventional level.

594. Traviss, Mary P. "The Growth of Moral Judgment Through Role Playing." Ph.D. dissertation, Stanford University, 1974. 35/06, p. 3581.

It was found that role-playing activities can be as effective in facilitating moral development among fifth-grade students as discussion of moral dilemmas.

595. Turiel, Elliot. "An Experimental Test of the Sequentiality of Developmental Stages in the Child's Moral Judgment." Journal of Personality and Social Psychology, 3 (1966): 611-618.

In a seventh-grade class, a week after role playing and discussing moral dilemmas, small but significant gains were detected in those subjects exposed to +1 stage examples of moral reasoning. No changes were detected in groups exposed to +2 or -1 reasoning.

596. Tyson, David J. "Children's Understanding, Moral Evaluation, and Memory of Television Content." Ph.D. dissertation, Pennsylvania State University, 1976. 37/11, p. 7353.

Older children (fifth graders) scored highest on moral maturity and on recall of content and moral messages of family situation comedies. Younger children (first graders) did fairly well but showed some confusion on these aspects.

597. Urbschat, Gerald E. "Role-Playing: A Treatment Program for Increasing Principled Moral Judgment among Behavior Problem Adolescents." Ph.D. dissertation, Wayne State University, 1980. 41/04, p. 1504.

An intervention strategy of role playing with videotaped feedback was used as a means for raising moral judgment of seventh- and eighth-grade students with behavior problems. No significant differences were found between experimental and control groups on moral judgment, self-concept, or behavior problems.

598. Van Winkle, David B. "A Study to Assess the Relative Effects of Participation in a Moral Education Program on Selected Aspects of Students' School Behavior." Ph.D. dissertation, St. Louis University, 1977. 39/03, p. 1450.

None of the hypotheses (rejecting lower stages, change in values, or change in school behavior) was supported as a result of sixth-graders' participation in a Kohlbergian moral education program.

599. Walker, Lawrence J.; and Boyd S. Richards. "Stimulating Transitions in Moral Reasoning as a Function of Stage of Cognitive Development." _Developmental Psychology_, 15 (1979): 95-103.

Found that cognitive development (attainment of formal operations) was necessary for moral reasoning development-movement from stage 3 to stage 4.

600. White, Darrell K. "Moral Development in High School Students and Its Relationship to Success in School." Ed.D. dissertation, Utah State University, 1975. 36/09, p. 5797.

Significant relationships were found between students' level of academic achievement, educational ability, and moral development.

601. Whitely, John. "The Sierra Project: A Character Development Program for College Freshmen." _Moral Education Forum_, 3 (September 1978): 1-13.

Describes a developmental intervention for college freshmen designed to produce growth in moral reasoning, ego development, and sexual choice. Early results of the curriculum were discouraging.

602. Wilhelm, Frederich C. "The Effects of Extent of Training on Teacher Discussion Behaviors and Children's Moral Reasoning Development." Ed.D. dissertation, State University of New York at Albany, 1977. 38/03, p. 1207.

Not surprisingly, the more training teachers received, the more they demonstrated the desired moral discussion behaviors. Student moral development was also stimulated.

603. Williams, Michael R. "The Effects of the Discussion of Moral Dilemmas on the Moral Judgment of Children Aged 7 to 9 Years." Ph.D. dissertation, University of Wisconsin at Milwaukee, 1974. 36/02, p. 803.

The discussion of moral dilemmas with young children was found to result in significant moral development.

604. Winkie, Phillip A. "The Effects of an Outward Bound School Experience on Levels of Moral Judgment and Self-Concept." Ph.D. dissertation, Rutgers University, 1976. 37/12, p. 7657.

Participation in an Outward Bound experience was found to result in growth in self-concept and moral development.

605. Young, Sandye P. "The Introduction of Moral and Ethical Judgments into the Teaching of Issues in Child Development and Education to a Group of Selected College Women." Ph.D. dissertation, Georgia State University, 1974. 35/10, p. 6523.

After discussing the pros and cons of selected controversial issues in child development it was found that subjects decreased significantly in dogmatism and increased significantly in stage of moral reasoning.

606. Chesbrough, Lindsey, and Thomas Conrad. "Creating a 'Just Community': Planning, Process and Participation." Moral Education Forum, 6 (Winter 1981): 8-13.

Describes the major structural components of the Scarsdale Alternative School: orientation, core group, community meeting and fairness committee.

607. Codding, Judith, and Anthony Arenella. "Creating a 'Just Community': The Transformation of an Alternative School." Moral Education Forum, 6 (Winter 1981): 2-7.

Discusses how the introduction of Kohlbergian developmental concepts has transformed the Scarsdale Alternative School into a more valuable educational experience for all concerned.

608. Codding, Judith, and Anthony Arenella. "Supporting Moral Development with a Curriculum of Ethical Decision Making." Moral Education Forum, 6 (Winter 1981): 14-23.

Describes the efforts in the Scarsdale Alternative School Just Community to insure that the curriculum is compatible and congruent with the just community approach. To specifically promote moral development two courses were developed.

609. Cole, Peggy, and Theodore Farris. "Building A Just Community at the Elementary School Level." Moral Education Forum, 4 (1979): 12-19.

Briefly describes the Bank Street/Cottage Lane project.

610. Crockenberg, Susan B. and Jennie Nicolayev. "Stage Transition in Moral Reasoning as Related to Conflict Experienced in Naturalistic Settings." Merrill-Palmer Quarterly, 25 (1979): 185-192.

Subjects were asked to indicate the extent to which actual opportunities for decision-making and discussion of moral issues existed in two school programs (traditional and alternative). It was found that the alternative program students experienced more moral conflict and moral growth over a school year.

611. Fielding, Michael. "Democracy in Secondary Schools: School Councils and Shared Responsibility." Journal of Moral Education, 2 (1973): 221-232.

Claims that pupil school councils seldom achieve the ideal of experiencing the democratic process. "Shared Responsibility" is offered as the concept closest to the idea of direct democracy, and a better environment for healthy moral growth.

612. Hayes, Richard L. "The Democratic Classroom: A Program in Moral Education for Adolescents." Ed.D. dissertation, Boston University, 1980. 40/12, p. 6200.

Finds that an increase in level of moral reasoning can be effected by a democratic teaching style, however no significant impact on moral development was found due to the interaction of democratic teaching and moral development curriculum.

613. Kolber, William. "Living in a 'Just Community': A Student Perspective." Moral Education Forum, 6 (Winter 1981): 43-46.

A "just community" student describes his impressions of the benefits of a schooling experience which focuses on fairness and building community.

614. Kohlberg, Lawrence. "High School Democracy and Educating for a Just Society." Moral Education: A First Generation of Research and Development (item 428), pp. 20-57.

Kohlberg describes his theory of moral development and traces the major shifts which have occured in his thinking about educational questions. Major attention is given to his efforts to foster democratic school environments and develop sense of community. His shifts in emphasis from stage 6 to stage 5 and now from stage 5 to a stage 4 sense of community are discussed. The new emphases reflect revisions of theory to accommodate social and educational needs. Also in <u>Education and Moral Development</u> (item 395).

615. Kohlberg, Lawrence, Ann Higgins and Clark Power. "A Just Community Alternative in a Large Public High School: A Report on Four Years of the Cluster School." <u>Education and Moral Development</u> (item 395), Chapter 15.

Reports the structure of the Cluster alternative school and documents with interviews and community meeting records the evaluation over four years of its moral atmosphere.

616. Kohlberg, Lawrence, Clark Power, and Ann Higgins. "The Just Community Approach to Alternative High Schools: A Theory." <u>Education and Moral Development</u> (item 395), Chapter 12.

617. Kohlberg, Lawrence, Kelsey Kauffman, Peter Scharf and Joseph Hickey. "The Just Community Approach to Corrections: A Theory." <u>Journal of Moral Education</u>, 4 (1975): 243-260.

Describes an attempt to apply to the prison situation the principles of moral development intervention. An account is given of preliminary efforts to create democratic situations in prisons where moral issues can be freely discussed. Also in <u>Education and Moral Development</u> (item 395), Chapter 10.

618. Kohlberg, Lawrence, et al. "Evaluating Scarsdale's 'Just Community School' and Its Curriculum; Implications for the Future." <u>Moral Education Forum</u>, 6 (Winter 1981): 31-42.

Data was collected to assess the effectiveness of the Ethical Issues in Decision-Making course, of the just community approach, and of the combined effect. Research was collected on change in moral reasoning, and on stage of collective norms (moral atmosphere). It was found that in comparison to students not in the programs Scarsdale Alternative School students experienced significant moral growth and significant growth in stage of collective norms.

619. Krogh, Suzanne L. "Moral Beginnings: The Just Community in Montessori Pre-Schools." Journal of Moral Education, 11 (1981): 41-46.

The Kohlberg and Montessori models are compared and found to be compatible. Developmentally, it is argued, the two work well as a sequence for childrens moral growth.

620. Kubelick, Cheryl. "A Study of the Effects of a Social Skills Intervention In the Cognitive Moral Development of 8, 9 and 10 Year Olds." Ph.D. dissertation, University of Pittsburg, 1977. 38/ 04, p. 1875.

Youth, aged 8-10 participating in a just community environment made significant stage change as a result of a seven month intervention in which social skills were taught.

621. Kuhmerker, Lisa, ed. "Scarsdale Alternative School's Just Community." Moral Education Forum, 6 (Winter 1981).

Contains six articles describing the rationale, curriculum, evaluation and student perceptions of a just community intervention in Scarsdale, NY.

622. Lickona, Thomas. "Creating the Just Community with Children," Readings in Moral Education (item 449), pp. 174-185.

Recounts the efforts of primary school teachers to introduce democracy into her classroom as a part of her moral education efforts. Also contains an evaluation instrument for such programs. Also in Theory Into Practice, 16 (1977): 97-104.

623. Lickona, Thomas. "Democracy, Cooperation and Moral Education." Toward Moral and Religious Maturity (item 1793), pp. 488-515.

Attempts to set out, through seven interrelated points, the case for cooperative democracy in the classroom. A logical chain of ideas are presented which link democracy, cooperation and moral education.

624. Lickona, Thomas, and Muffy Paradise. "Democracy in the Elementary School." Moral Education: A First Generation of Research and Development (item 428), pp. 321-338.

Discusses the case for democracy in the elementary classroom. Problems and benefits involved are also discussed.

625. McCann, J. and P. Bell. "Educational Environment and the Development of Moral Concepts." Journal of Moral Education, 5 (1975): 63-70.

The impact of Freinet schools, which encourage democratic group self-discipline, and provide many and varied role-taking opportunities, on moral development was contrasted with that of a traditional Catholic school. It was found that the children attending the Freinet school exhibited more advanced moral judgments.

626. Manley-Casimir, Michael. "The School as a Constitutional Bureaucracy." Development of Moral Reasoning (item 26), pp. 69-81.

Argues that a constitutional bureaucracy is more compatible with the goal of creating autonomous purposive and self regulating adults than the more traditional authoritarian bureaucracy.

627. Mosher, Ralph. "A Democratic High School: Coming of Age." Moral Education: A First Generation of Research and Development (item 428), pp. 279-302.

Describes the genesis and development of Brookline's School-Within-A-School. Concludes with a series of observations regarding what has been learned about adolescents' capacity for self-government in a school setting.

628. Mosher, Ralph L. "A Democratic High School: Damn It, Your Feet are Always in the Water." Value Development ... As the Aim of Education (item 1816), pp. 69-116.

Presents a frank and insightful view of the authors' experiences as principal consultant to the staff of the "School Within a School" of a Brookline,

Massachusetts high school. The author presents a variety of arguments in favor of the democratic organization of students lives within schools as well as what he has learned about attempting to implement such a program.

629. Mosher, Ralph L. "Funny Things Happen on the Way to School Democracy." Development of Moral Reasoning (item 26), pp. 82-107.

Mosher discusses his impressions of experiments in school democracy gathered from his experiences as a consultant to the School-Within-A-School in Brookline, Massachusetts.

630. Power, Clark. "Evaluating Just Communities: Toward a Method for Assessing the Moral Atmosphere of the School." Evaluating Moral Development (item 1391), pp. 177-191.

Discusses the conceptual framework and research methodology behind the development of an instrument for evaluating the moral atmosphere of just community school environments.

631. Power, Clark. "The Moral Atmosphere of the School--Part I." Moral Education Forum, 4 (1979): 9-14.

Describes the evaluation of his understanding of the moral atmosphere of institutions. The philosophy and practices of the Cluster School 'just community' are described.

632. Power, Clark. "The Moral Atmosphere of the School--Part II." Moral Education Forum, 4 (1979): 21-27.

Presents the author's "Phases of Collective Normative Value and Service of Community" typology. These phases were developed from observing the evolution of the moral atmosphere of the school from nonexistent collective and community values to complete compliance and realized community.

633. Power, Clark. "Moral Education Through the Development of the Moral Atmosphere of the School." Journal of Educational Thought, 15 (1981): 4-19.

Discusses the theory, development of and evaluation of a just community approach to moral education. The stages of the collective norms and community value that develop in such a program are spelled out.

634. Power, Clark, and Joseph Reimer. "Moral Atmosphere: An Educational Bridge between Moral Judgment and Action." New Directions for Child Development, No. 2: Moral Education (item 1789), pp. 105-116.

Discusses the evolution of conceptual frameworks for analyzing the moral atmosphere of schools. Notes that as the moral atmosphere evolved in the Cluster School its influence on the actions of individual members increased.

635. Power, Francis C. "The Moral Atmosphere of a Just Community High School: A Four Year Longitudinal Study." Ed.D. dissertation, Harvard University, 1979. 41/07, p. 3017.

In a four year longitudinal study of the Cluster School moral atmosphere was defined in terms of the group's collective norms and values and a framework was developed for assessing those norms on stage of morality and behavioral dimensions. Shifts in collective norms and their relationship to individual stage of moral reasoning and behavioral conformity are noted.

636. Reimer, Joseph. "Moral Education: The Just Community Approach." Phi Delta Kappan, 62 (1981): 485-487.

This article explores the rationale behind the development of a just community and the preliminary results from research on one such just community.

637. Reimer, Joseph B. "A Study in the Moral Development of Kibbutz Adolescents." Ed.D. dissertation, Harvard University, 1977. 38/08, p. 4695.

The moral development of youth living on kibbutzin is documented. The group making greatest gains were those actively involved in the self-governing of their high school. The relationship between social participation, role taking, and moral development was borne out by this study.

638. Reimer, Joseph, and Clark Power. "Educating for Democratic Community: Some Unresolved Dilemmas." Moral Education: A First Generation of Research and Development (item 428), pp. 303-320.

Presents the authors' "phases of the collective norm" which attempts to chart the development of collective expectations which developed over four years in the Cluster School. The unresolved dilemma of democratic communal education--how one can teach others what one has yet to discover for oneself--is discussed.

639. Sachs, David, and Vicky Prusnofsky. "Supporting a 'Just Community' Concept: Sharing Moral Development Theory and Practice with Teachers." Moral Education Forum, 6 (Winter 1981): 24-30.

Describes the participation of the Scarsdale Alternative School staff members in the planning and teaching of the Harvard University Center for Moral Education Summer Institute. The institute is described and testimonials as to its effectiveness are reported.

640. Scharf, Peter. "The Democratic School on Social Curriculum." Moral and Psychological Education (item 448), pp. 303-314.

Discusses two efforts at implementing a democratic high school environment: the Cluster School of Cambridge, Massachussets and the Self School of Irvine, California. The philosophic differences between the two schools are noted.

641. Scharf, Peter. "The Developmentalists' Approach to Alternative Schooling," Values Concepts and Techniques (item 1784), pp. 121-134.

Discusses the democratic approach to school governance as exemplified in three different locations. The analysis is the just community perspective of the cognitive developmentalists.

642. Scharf, Peter. "Moral Atmosphere and Intervention in the Prison: The Creation of a Participatory Community in Prison." Ed.D. dissertation, Harvard University, 1973. 34/12, p. 7900.

Describes the creation of a "just community" within a correctional facility and the effect on moral growth and recidivism.

643. Scharf, Peter. "Moral Development and Democratic Schooling." Theory Into Practice, 16 (1977): 89-96.

Presents the Deweyan democratic ideal for schools and related its current interpretation derived from cognitive-developmental theory. The assumptions underlying developmental democratic schooling are presented. It is noted that there are dilemmas involved in democratic schooling. Among these are the conflicts with competitive achievement values and the threat posed to bureaucratic control of schools.

644. Scharf, Peter. "School Democracy: Promise and Paradox," Readings in Moral Education (item 449), pp. 186-195.

Offers a critical overview of efforts to create a participatory democratic framework for schools. Argues that a democratic framework is bound to conflict with the bureaucratic structure of most schools, and that stage 2 and stage 3 students will find the idea of constitutional democracy difficult to understand.

645. Scharf, Peter. "School Democracy: Thoughts and Dilemmas." Contemporary Education, 48 (Fall 1976): 29-34.

Describes the author's efforts at developing a just community in an Irvine, CA.

646. Stewart, John S. "The School as a Just Community: Transactional-Developmental Moral Education." Values Education: Theory/Practice/Problems/Prospects (item 1805), pp. 149-164.

Presents an analysis of the just community concept and answers potential objections. New roles for students, teachers, schools, and communities committed to just schooling are outlined.

647. Stewart, John S. "Toward a Theory for Values Development Education." Ph.D. dissertation, Michigan State University, 1974. 35/06, p. 3410.

Attempts to lay the groundwork for a theory for values development education. The theory is based largely on work of Piaget, Dewey and Kohlberg. The theory derived is compatible with democratic values and urges the schools to operate as a just moral community.

648. Wasserman, Elsa. "An Alternative High School Based on Kohlberg's Just Community Approach to Education." Moral Education: A First Generation of Research and Development (item 428), pp. 265-278.

Provides a description of the Cluster School in practice, related research about the just community and moral development, the structure of the school, and some reflections of the first graduates.

649. Wasserman, Elsa. "Implementing Kohlberg's 'Just Community Concept' in an Alternative High School." Readings in Moral Education (item 449), pp. 164-172.

Describes the authors efforts to implement a democratic school at the Cluster School in Cambridge, Massachusetts. Also in Social Education 40(1976) and Developmental Counseling and Teaching (item 784).

650. Zalaznick, Edward. "The Just Community School: A Student Perspective." Moral Education Forum, 5 (Summer 1980): 27-35.

A student discusses the hostility he felt as a result of others trying to "make us normal." Also troubling was the idea that there were "better" answers (higher stage) to moral questions. Also in Moral Development, Moral Education and Kohlberg (item 432).

651. Alston, William P. "Comments on Kohlberg's 'From Is to Ought.'" Cognitive Development and Epistemology. Edited by T. Mischel. New York: Academic Press, 1971, pp. 269-284.

Argues that Kohlberg has failed to show that stage 6 is a superior way to resolve conflict. This is so because his criterion of "moral" as the end result of moral reasoning is arbitrary. He also criticizes Kohlberg for his oversimplification of the concept of virtues and his slighting of habit and affect in moral life.

652. Arbuthnot, J. "Errors in Self-Assessment of Moral Judgment Stage." Journal of Social Psychology, 107 (1979): 289-290.

Found that teachers, even after extensive training in Kohlbergian theory, dramatically overestimate the level of moral reasoning of their students.

653. Arnove, Robert F., and Gregory Rhodes. "A Sociopolitical Critique of Moral Education." Viewpoints, 51 (November 1975): 51-70.

Argues that schools have always served a conservative function in society by instilling values that will ensure social control. Argues that Kohlberg's theories are consistent with this view in that only the children of dominant societal groups will be provided with experiences that allow them to achieve the higher stages. Contends that if the highest stages of moral reasoning are to be reached by all children there must be more just schools and a more just society.

654. Aron, Israela Ettenberg. "Moral Education: The Formalist Tradition and the Deweyan Alternative." Moral Development, Moral Education and Kohlberg (item 432), pp. 401-426.

Discusses the contributions of the formalist tradition in moral philosophy (Hare, Frankena, Peters, Rawls) and the difficulties that arise when the formalist approach is used as the entire basis for a theory of moral education. Concludes by discussing Dewey's philosophical assumptions and showing how his ideas on practical deliberation provide a more adequate framework for values education.

655. Aron, Israela E. "Moral Philosophy and Moral Education: A Critique of Kohlberg's Theory." School Review, 85 (1977): 197-217.

Questions whether Kohlberg has adequately justified his theory on philosophical grounds and whether he has adequate evidence for his claims that his moral education programs are anything other than indoctrination.

656. Atherton, Thomas. "A Critique of Lawrence Kohlberg's Theories of Moral Development and Moral Education." Ph.D. dissertation, Boston University, 1979. 40/05, p. 2727.

Criticizes Kohlberg's theory of moral development on the grounds that it is ethnocentric and commits the naturalistic fallacy. Argues that his educational proposals have the potential for indoctrination.

657. Baier, Kurt. "Moral Development." The Monist, 58 (1974): 601-615.

Argues that Kohlberg is really offering two very different models of moral development: one dealing with a premoral phase (stages 1-3) and the other as the development of practical reasoning capable of explaining and justifying the overriding portion of the peculiar mode of reasoning called moral reasoning.

658. Bailey, Charles. "The Notion of Development and Moral Education." The Domain of Moral Education (item 1788), pp. 205-219.

Contains a general discussion of the notion of development and the problems inherent when development is looked at in moral terms.

659. Beck, Clive. "Rationalism in Kohlberg's Morality and Moral Education." Philosophy of Education 1978 (item 1792), pp. 105-111.

Argues that Kohlberg's rationalist, principled, universalist approach is untenable. A more adequate approach would have a greater awareness of the complexity of moral life.

660. Bennett, William J., and Edwin J. Delattre. "Moral Education in the Schools." The Public Interest, 50 (Winter 1978): 81-98.

Argues that Kohlberg and Simon, although they prefer to be value neutral, in fact, through the "hidden curriculum" of their methodology, indoctrinate the specific values they see as important: the celebration of wants and desires, the exhortation to self-gratification, and a particular ideology of rights and "special justice."

661. Bereiter, Carl. "Educational Implications of Kohlberg's Cognitive Developmental View." Interchange, 1 (1970): 25-32.

In a critical view of Kohlbergian theory Bereiter argues that Kohlberg's conclusion that specific instruction cannot contribute significantly to cognitive development is a "category error"--an attempt to set into opposition two concepts that are not of the same type.

662. Bergling, Kurt. Moral Development: The Validity of Kohlberg's Theory. Stockholm Studies in Educational Psychology 23. Stockholm, Sweden: Almquist & Wiksell International, 1981.

Examines the validity of Kohlberg's theory of moral development through a hypothetic-deductive research strategy. The theory is synthesized into two postulates from which four hypotheses are deducted; empirical evidence is cited to examine each hypothesis.

663. Berkowitz, Marvin L. "A Critical Appraisal of the Educational and Psychological Perspectives on Moral Discussion." Journal of Educational Thought, 15 (1981): 20-33.

Presents a critical review of the research on the +1 convention in developmental theory. Suggests that student skills and student interaction are the key ingredients in stimulating moral development.

664. Berkowitz, Marvin W. "A Critical Appraisal of the 'Plus One' Convention in Moral Education." Phi Delta Kappan, 62 (1981): 488-489.

Rejects the notion that successful moral education requires a discussion leader one stage above the majority of the class. Discusses the results of research where leaderless peer discussion groups experienced nearly as much moral development as teacher-led groups.

665. Berkowitz, Marvin W. "Moral Peers to the Rescue! A Critical Appraisal of the 'Plus 1' Convention in Moral Education." Milwaukee, WI: Marquette University, 1980. ED 193 138.

Argues that students reacting to other students' reasoning is more effective in stimulating moral development.

666. Bolt, Daniel J., and Edmund V. Sullivan. "Kohlberg's Cognitive-Developmental Theory in Educational Settings: Some Possible Abuses." Journal of Moral Education, 6 (1977): 198-205.

The danger of using moral stages to "type" certain personality characteristics is discussed.

667. Braun, Claude M., and Jacinthe Baribeau. "Subjective Idealism in Kohlberg's Theory of Moral Development: A Critical Analysis." Human Development, 21 (1978): 289-301.

Analyzes the epistemological and logical foundations of Kohlberg's theory of moral development. Kohlberg's understanding of dialectics is criticized and an attempt is made to introduce a dialectical materialist outlook. Kohlberg's theory is shown to be based on a subjective idealist orientation.

668. Broughton, John. "The Cognitive Developmental Approach to Morality: A Reply to Kurtines and Greif." Journal of Moral Education, 7 (1978): 81-96.

Broughton, a doctoral student of Kohlberg, responds point by point to Kurtines and Greif's analysis (item 700) of the weaknesses of the cognitive-developmental approach of Kohlberg. In the process of responding Broughton cites 112 sources in what is a careful defense.

669. Bunzl, Martin. "The Moral Development of Moral Philosophers." _Journal of Moral Education_, 7 (1977): 3-8.

Attacks Kohlberg's theory on the basis that if psychology and philosophy are one in his theory then the capstone of his theory (Rawls's theory of justice) must be wrong because it is a purely philosophical notion.

670. Carter, Robert E. "What Is Lawrence Kohlberg Doing?" _Journal of Moral Education_, 9 (1980): 88-102.

Claims that Kohlberg, instead of attempting to establish a "best" morality, should be limiting himself to his sequential typology of development from egoism to universalism--an achievement in itself.

671. Codd, John A. "Some Conceptual Problems in the Cognitive-Developmental Approach to Morality." _Journal of Moral Education_, 6 (1977): 147-157.

Argues that Kohlberg's theory provides no satisfactory criteria for defining the moral domain; that its basic moral position is inconsistent; that the ultimate justification for the principle of justice is not established; and that the claim to logical necessity for the stage-sequence is not substantiated.

672. Collins, Clinton. "The Multiple Dimensions of Moral Education." _Philosophy of Education 1976_ (item 1819), pp. 199-208.

Argues that Kohlberg's data is concerned with the way a person's moral judgments typically evolve within the objective political dimensions of his experience. Schooling, the aims of which are within the intellectual realm, rightfully should focus on only initiating individuals into communities governed by objective inquiry. Moral education in the form of the achievement of moral autonomy is beyond the legitimate scope of schooling.

673. Conroy, Anne R., and John K. Burton. "The Trouble with Kohlberg: A Critique." Educational Forum, 45 (November 1980): 43-55.

Presents a wide-ranging critique of Kohlberg focusing on methodological problems in testing moral development, philosophical concerns, and problems certain to be encountered in attempting to implement Kohlbergian programs in local communities.

674. Craig, Robert P. "Form, Content and Justice in Moral Reasoning." Educational Theory, 26 (1976): 154-157.

Critiques the formalism of Kohlberg and Hare by showing that formal characteristics in moral reasoning cannot be separated from substantive characteristics.

675. Craig, Robert. "Lawrence Kohlberg and Moral Development: Some Reflections." Educational Theory, 24 (1974): 121-129.

Presents an overview of the key aspects of Kohlberg's theory. The major criticisms leveled against Kohlberg are reviewed and their accuracy assessed.

676. Crittenden, Brian. "The Limitations of Morality as Justice in Kohlberg's Theory." The Domain of Moral Education (item 1788), pp. 251-266.

Suggests that Kohlberg's focus is too narrow. Morality cannot be equated with justice, nor can justice necessarily be given primacy in morality.

677. DeJardins, Joseph R. "A Philosophical Analysis of Lawrence Kohlberg's Theory of Moral Development." Ph.D. dissertation, University of Notre Dame, 1980. 41/06, p. 2638.

Examines Kohlberg's theory from the perspective of practical reason, i.e., the claim that all men have reason to be moral. Concludes that in at least one sense Kohlberg's theory does support such a claim.

678. Diller, Ann. "Law, Morality and Educational Uses of Kohlberg's Scheme." Philosophy of Education 1980 (item 1802), pp. 186-189.

In responding to Freiberg (item 687) argues that Kohlberg's latest revision of stage descriptions has redefined the conventional level in nonlegal terminology.

679. Diorio, Joseph A. "Cognitive Universalism and Cultural Relativity in Moral Education." Educational Philosophy and Theory, 8 (April 1976): 33-53.

Presents a critique of Kohlberg's work which focuses on the argument that Kohlberg's formalist principles closely correspond to the moral outlook of one particular cultural orientation. An interesting comparison of Kohlberg's and the Buddhist's moral views is presented.

680. Dykstra, Craig. "Moral Virtue or Social Reasoning." Religious Education, 75 (1980): 115-128.

Presents a mild critique of Kohlberg that focuses on three claims made by Kohlberg: virtue is one (justice); a person's morality can be judged by looking at his/her judgments about situations; and there is one structure of morality (cognitive).

681. Feldman, Ray E. "The Promotion of Moral Development in Prisons and Schools." Moral Development and Politics (item 1821), pp. 286-328.

Reports the results of an evaluation of Kohlberg's just community prison programs and just community school programs. The results are highly critical of the programs. Argues that in these programs there is little talk of justice. These programs are simply another way of keeping order and exist only because people prefer the informal setting. The critique is well conceived, well documented, and essential reading for those interested in evaluating just community programs.

682. Fenton, Edwin. "The Cognitive-Developmental Approach to Moral Education: A Response to Jack R. Fraenkel." Social Education, 41 (1977): 56-61.

Fenton responds to Fraenkel's critique of cognitive-developmental theory (item 686).

683. Fishkin, James. "Relativism, Liberalism, and Moral Development." Moral Development and Politics (item 1821), pp. 85-106.

Regards Kohlberg's typology of stages as flawed because it fails to satisfactorily integrate a relativistic morality. Fishkin argues that relativistic behavior can be seen as consistent and coherent; however, once the viability of the more modest, liberal alternative to developmental theory is admitted, the relativistic arguments can be rejected.

684. Flowers, John V. "A Behavioral Psychologist's View of Developmental Moral Education." Readings in Moral Education (item 449), pp. 264-270.

Presents a critique of Kohlbergian moral education. Accuses Kohlberg of committing the naturalistic fallacy and having a teleological view of human development. Also finds weaknesses with regard to methodological, theoretical, and intervention issues.

685. Fraenkel, Jack R. "The Cognitive-Developmental Approach to Moral Education: A Response to Edwin Fenton." Social Education, 41 (1977): 57-61.

Fraenkel responds to Fenton (item 682) who is critiquing Fraenkel's critique (item 686).

686. Fraenkel, Jack. "The Kohlberg Bandwagon: Some Reservations." Moral Education ... It Comes With the Territory (item 1811), pp. 291-307.

Questions Kohlberg's theory of the universality of stages, higher stage--better stage claim, educational feasibility, research claims, and a variety of claims made by "two believers" attempting to take moral development to the classroom. Also in Social Education, 40 (1976): 216-222, and Readings in Moral Education (item 449).

687. Freiberg, Jo Ann. "Morality and the Law: Where Does Kohlberg Stand?" Philosophy of Education 1980 (item 1802), pp. 178-185.

Attempts to show that Kohlberg has tacitly assumed a particular philosophy of law and has therefore built into his stage 4 a content base. By doing so he has ruled out alternative interpretations of stage 4 reasoning.

688. Giarelli, J. "Lawrence Kohlberg and G.E. Moore on the Naturalistic Fallacy." Educational Theory, 26 (1976): 348-354.

Compares Kohlberg and G.E. Moore and finds that Kohlberg neither committed the naturalistic fallacy nor got away with it.

689. Gibbs, John C. "Kohlberg's Moral Stage Theory: A Piagetian Revision." Human Development, 22 (1979): 89-112.

Presents a reconceptualization of Kohlbergian theory in light of criticisms that the highest stages are elitist, ethnocentric and excessively abstract. The proposed revision describes moral development in adulthood as existential rather than Piagetian, and restricts moral judgment in the standard stage sense to childhood and adolescence.

690. Gibbs, John C. "Kohlberg's Stages of Moral Judgment: A Constructive Critique." Harvard Educational Review, 47 (1977): 43-61.

Distinguishes between naturalistic and existential themes in modern psychology and argues that the higher stages (5 and 6) appear to be existential or reflective extensions of the lower stages. Higher stages are not theories in action, but rather are detached reflections on one's theories in action.

691. Grover, S. "An Examination of Kohlberg's Cognitive-Developmental Model of Morality." Journal of Genetic Psychology, 136 (1980): 137-144.

Argues that people come to choose the good and act on it by not only abiding by the universal principle of justice. Courage is often required in moral decisions and knowledge of ethical principles is insufficient to account for it.

692. Hamm, Cornel M. "The Content of Moral Education, or In Defense of the Bag of Virtues." School Review, 85 (1977): 218-228.

Argues, against Kohlberg, that there is in fact a content to morality, that this content is properly conceived of as virtues, and that virtues can be taught. A list of virtues that are beyond reasonable dispute is presented.

693. Jones, Herbert T. "Kohlberg and the Deweyan Tradition." Ed.D. dissertation, Rutgers University, 1981. 42/01, p. 129.

Examines the extent to which Kohlberg's work is supported by Deweyan views on morality and moral education. Argues that Kohlberg may not have fully grasped the full force of Dewey's contextualism.

694. Kincaid, M. Evelyn. "A Philosophical Analysis of Lawrence Kohlberg's Developmental Stages of Moral Reasoning." Ph.D. dissertation, University of Florida, 1977. 38/07, p. 4016.

Criticizes Kohlberg's theory by pointing out the difficulties of simultaneously holding a Deweyan position on epistemology and a Rawlsian theory of justice. Argues that Kohlberg and Dewey are not nearly as close as Kohlberg would have us believe.

695. Kohlberg, Lawrence. "Moral Education: A Response to Thomas Sobol." Educational Leadership, 38 (1980): 19-23.

Kohlberg responds point by point to the questions raised by Sobol (item 752).

696. Kohlberg, Lawrence. "Reply to Bereiter's Statement on Kohlberg's Cognitive-Developmental View." Interchange, 1 (1970): 40-48.

Kohlberg responds to Bereiter (item 661) and argues that he has misunderstood his concept of instructional reorganization as natural and inevitable. Kohlberg's response is followed by a reply by Bereiter.

697. Kohlberg, Lawrence. "A Response to Critics of the Theory." The Psychology of Moral Development (item 1800), Chapter 7.

Summarizes and responds to criticisms of the theory.

698. Krahn, John H. "A Comparison of Kohlberg's and Piaget's Type 1 Morality." Religious Education, 66 (1971): 373-375.

Casts doubt on Kohlberg's description of Type 1 morality and argues that Piaget's description of early morality based on respect for adult authority and conformity to rules is more accurate.

699. Kuhn, Deanna. "Inducing Development Experimentally: Comments on a Research Paradigm." Developmental Psychology, 10 (1974): 590-600.

Critiques studies designed to produce developmental changes in Piagetian tasks, i.e., induce conservation in nonconserving subjects. Four major difficulties with the studies are noted, and suggestions for improving the research are presented.

700. Kurtines, William, and Esther B. Greif. "The Development of Moral Thought: Review of Evaluation of Kohlberg's Approach." Psychological Bulletin, 81 (1974): 453-470.

Examines and evaluates the research base supporting Kohlberg's theory concerning the development of moral thought. Serious questions are posed concerning the reliability and validity of assessment procedures of Kohlberg. Also noted is the absence of direct evidence for the basic assumptions of the theory. Concludes that the empirical utility of the model has yet to be demonstrated.

701. Lange, Deborah. "Kohlberg's Social Value Theory: An Ethical Analysis." Philosophy of Education 1977 (item 1817), pp. 89-99.

Argues that there is no clear notion of what values are operative at each stage and how these values can be identified within the context of a student's response. Students and teachers are asked to adjudicate moral conflict from principles containing key concepts that are vague and ambiguous.

702. Levine, C.G. "Stage Acquisition and Stage Use: An Appraisal of Stage Displacement Explanations of Variation in Moral Reasoning." Human Development, 22 (1979): 145-164.

Argues that the stage mixture perspective does not constitute a sufficient explanation for variation in stage usage. An alternative conceptualization of transformation--the nondisplacement perspective--is offered as an adequate explanation for varying stage use.

703. Locke, Don. "Cognitive Stages or Developmental Phases? A Critique of Kohlberg's Stage Structural Theory of Moral Reasoning." Journal of Moral Education, 8 (1979): 168-181.

Kohlberg's theory is criticized under the following headings: structural wholes, invariance, cultural universality, logical necessity, increasing cognitive adequacy, and increasing moral adequacy.

704. Locke, Don. "The Illusion of Stage Six." Journal of Moral Education, 9 (1980): 103-109.

705. Luizzi, Vincent. "How People Become Moral--Is Kohlberg Correct and Has He Told Us Enough?" Journal of Thought, 13 (1978): 322-330.

Challenges Kohlberg's wholesale rejection of the Aristotelian view that morality is acquired through habituation.

706. MacDonald, James B. "A Look at the Kohlberg Curriculum Framework for Moral Education." Moral Development, Moral Education and Kohlberg (item 432), pp. 381-400.

Argues that although Kohlberg's approach may be the best of many approaches to the moral education curriculum, it does have some weaknesses. Most notably, it does not fit its individualistic emphasis into a broader social and political network; thus, the developmental approach can be used to maintain the present oppressive social system.

707. McGough, Kris. "Who's Playing the Organ?" Social Education, 43 (1979): 232.

Objects to Kohlbergian moral education because it manipulates children and intrudes on parents' moral beliefs in that it teaches a morality other than that of the parents. Who's playing the organ?--Kohlberg.

Who's dancing?--teachers. Who should be directing moral education?--parents.

708. Mapel, Brenda M. "An Act-Theory Alternative to Rationalistic Moral Education." Philosophy of Education 1978 (item 1792), pp. 85-104.

Presents an ethical act-theory critique of Kohlberg's rule-theory account of moral development and argues for an alternative act-theory interpretation of cognitive moral development.

709. Margolis, Joseph. "Does Kohlberg Have a Valid Theory of Moral Education?" Growing Up with Philosophy (item 1075), pp. 240-255.

Shows that the internal structure of Kohlberg's thought is inconsistent and thus the practical consequences are not merely trivial, could well be pernicious. The history of philosophical inquiry shows that it is consistently dialectical and pluralistic. Kohlberg attempts to reduce all morality to the principle of justice and dispose of all ethical positions other than his own. Such an approach in ethics, if applied to education, could amount to indoctrination.

710. Maschette, Diane. "Moral Reasoning in the 'Real World.'" Theory into Practice, 16 (1977): 124-128.

Presents a theoretical exploration of how the reasoning one uses in hypothetical dilemmas is related to the reasoning one uses in real moral dilemmas, and of the factors to be considered in addition to reasoning in accounting for moral reasoning.

711. Matthews, Gareth. "On Talking Philosophy with Children." Growing Up With Philosophy (item 1075), pp. 225-240.

Although children are socially inexperienced and lacking in information about the world in general, it does not follow that their philosophical judgments lack insight or sensitivity or depth, as developmentalists would have us believe.

712. Meacham, John A. "A Dialectical Approach to Moral Judgment and Self-Esteem." Human Development, 18 (1975): 159-170.

Argues that moral development (from a dialectical perspective) must be conceptualized within a cultural and historical context. The reciprocal significance of individual moral development for changes in the family and society should be recognized.

713. Morelli, Elizabeth A. "The Sixth Stage of Moral Development." Journal of Moral Education, 7 (1978): 97-108.

Subjects Kohlberg's sixth stage to a dialectical critique and finds unresolved conflicts within this stage. Points to the need for a further moral stage of development.

714. Morgan, Kathryn P. "Philosophical Problems in Cognitive-Developmental Theory: A Critique of the Work of Lawrence Kohlberg." Philosophy of Education 1973: Proceedings of the Philosophy of Education Society. Edwardsville: Southern Illinois University Press, 1973, pp. 104-117.

Argues that Kohlberg equates moral principle and value. Claims that Kohlberg and other developmentalists need to learn the language of philosophy and pay attention to its distinctions.

715. Mosher, Ralph. "Who Is the Fairest of Them All?" Adolescents Development and Education (item 1806), pp. 61-65.

Reviews Kohlbergian theory and offers five problems associated with the theory.

716. Munsey, Brenda. "Cognitive-Developmental Theory of Moral Development: Metaethical Issues." Moral Development, Moral Education and Kohlberg (item 432), pp. 161-181.

Criticizes Kohlberg's formalistic interpretation of moral development and defends an alternative pragmatic interpretation which holds that as an individual encounters exceptions to the rules his/her present structure of norms would be subtly modified in ways that will make the norms a more adequate summary of his/her particular moral experience. Argues that psychology's attempt to explain the development of moral judgment would be better served if guided by a normative act theory (rather than rule theory) conception of sound moral judgment.

717. Murphy, J., and C. Gilligan. "Moral Development in Late Adolescence and Adulthood: A Critique and Reconstruction of Kohlberg's Theory." Human Development, 23 (1980): 77-104.

The persistence in late adolescence of a relativistic regression in moral development requires a revision in Kohlbergian theory. Based on a new revision of the scoring manual, the regressors are seen as progressors when evaluated against a standard of commitment in relativism instead of against absolute principles of justice.

718. Napier, John D. "The Ability of Elementary School Teachers to Stage Score Moral Thought Statements." Theory and Research in Social Education, 4 (December 1976): 39-56.

Using the Porter and Taylor manual (item 442) for assessing the stage of moral reasoning of others, it was found that 60 elementary school teachers were unable to stage score responses accurately.

719. Napier, John D. "Alternatives to the Teacher Task in 'Kohlbergian' Program of Stage Scoring Moral Judgments." Journal of Moral Education, 8 (1978): 50-51.

Argues that since teachers and pre-service teachers have been shown to be incapable of accurately stage scoring student statements, +1 modelling should be avoided.

720. Napier, John D. "The Validity of Preservice Teacher Use of Kohlberg's Issue Stage Scoring System." Theory and Research in Social Education, 6 (March 1978): 16-30.

No overall differences between intuitive and rater-guide stage scoring of moral responses was detected. It was also found that pre-service teachers also invalidly scored on the basis of content rather than structure. Concludes that teachers should refrain from stage scoring.

721. Nicolayev, Jennie, and D.C. Phillips. "On Assessing Kohlberg's Stage of Moral Development." The Domain of Moral Education (item 1788), pp. 231-250.

Examines whether or not the Kohlbergian research program is a progressive one, i.e., have its activities been content increasing? Finds that its claims for logical necessity, assertion of invariance, and even the stage assumption all lack solid evidence. Also published under a different title in Educational Theory, 28 (1978): 286-301.

722. O'Connor, Robert W. and Victor L. Worsfold. "Kohlberg's Developmental Stages as Ethical Theory: Some Doubts." Philosophy of Education 1973: Proceedings of the Philosophy of Education Society. Edwardsville: Southern Illinois University Press, 1973, pp. 118-125.

Argues that Kohlberg asks us to accept substantive moral principles (of saving a life) without advancing the sort of metaethical argument which must be used to warrant such principles.

723. Olmsted, Richard. "Was Dewey at Stage 6? Reflections in the Ethical Theory of Lawrence Kohlberg." Philosophy of Education 1977 (item 1817), pp. 156-162.

Argues that Kohlberg's claim that stages 5 and 6 exhaust morality is unwarranted.

724. Paton, James W. "An Analysis of Cognitive Moral Development Theory in Relationship to Moral Education Strategy Making Procedures." Ph.D. dissertation, Kent State University, 1980. 41/06, p. 2074.

Presents an analysis of Kohlberg's theory focusing on the form-content distinction intervention techniques, the relationship to social learning theory and possible negative effects of disequilibrium.

725. Pekarsky, Daniel. "Moral Dilemmas and Moral Education." Theory and Research in Social Education, 8 (Spring 1980): 1-8.

Argues that "escape hatching" when confronting moral dilemmas is not, as Kohlberg suggests a cop-out, but rather reflects creative method of dealing with moral quandaries.

726. Peters, R.S. "Moral Development: A Plea for Pluralism." Psychology and Ethical Development (item 1809), pp. 303-335.

After reviewing Kohlberg's theory Peters argues that virtues and habits do have a place in moral development. Many virtues are not tied down to specific situations and habit is not incompatible with intellegence and reasoning. Kohlberg is criticized for taking an overly narrow view of moral development. Originally appeared in T. Mischel, Ed. Cognitive Development and Epistemology. NY: Academic Press, 1971.

727. Peters, Richard. "The Place of Kohlberg's Theory in Moral Education." Journal of Moral Education, 7 (1978): 147-157.

Kohlberg is criticized for his general neglect of the affective side of moral development. How his work might be supplemental by a concern for others is presented. The importance of the content of morality is reaffirmed.

728. Peters, Richard. "Virtues and Habits in Moral Education." The Domain of Moral Education (item 1788), pp. 267-287.

An abridged version of "Moral Development: A Plan for Pluralism (item 726). Contains a spirited defense of the role of virtues, traits and habits in morality.

729. Peters, Richard S. "Why Doesn't Lawrence Kohlberg Do His Homework?" Moral Education ... It Comes with the Territory (item 1811), pp. 288-290.

Lists the main omissions of Kohlberg's work: holding that Kantian morality is the only acceptable morality, not taking "good-boy" morality seriously enough, paying scant attention to affective development, and not considering how ego-development occurs.

730. Philbert, P.J. "Lawrence Kohlberg's Use of Virtue in His Theory of Moral Development." International Philosophical Quarterly, 15 (1975): 455-497.

Argues that the acquisition of virtue by repeated acts has been conceived in too superficial a manner by both Kohlberg and his critics.

731. Puka, Bill. "Kohlbergian Forms and Deweyon Acts: A Response." Moral Development, Moral Education and Kohlberg (item 432), pp. 429-454.

Defends Kohlbergian views on moral education. Shows how the critics have misinterpreted Kohlberg and urges the continued use of Deweyan ideas to inform Kohlbergian theory and practice.

732. Puka, Bill. "A Kohlbergian Reply." The Domain of Moral Education (item 1788), pp. 288-301.

Replies to critics of Kohlberg's works.

733. Puka, Bill. "Moral Education and Its Cure." Reflections on Values Education (item 1804), pp. 47-87.

Presents an analysis and critique of Kohlberg's view of moral education. A major problem found with Kohlberg's views is that it does not pay adequate attention to unconscious influences on peoples choices and behavior. The focus for Puka is on a total personality development, which he feels if allowed to develop naturally will be good and moral.

734. Reid, Herbert G. and Ernest J. Yanarella. "The Tyranny of the Categorical: On Kohlberg and the Politics of Moral Development." Moral Development and Politics (item 1821), pp. 107-132.

Confronts Kohlberg's theories as a species of liberal ideology. Arguing from a modern critical theory perspective, it is concluded that Kohlberg's theory cannot be regarded as universal because it is an ideological reflection of the Anglo-American liberal tradition.

735. Rest, James. "Developmental Psychology as a Guide to Value Education: A Review of 'Kohlbergian' Programs." Moral Education ... It Comes with the Territory (item 1811), pp. 252-274.

Analyzes the fundamental ideas of Kohlberg and how these ideas have been extended into practice. Rest concludes that developmental psychology guides the educational programs in global programmatic ways, but not in day-by-day planning or analysis. Also in Review of Educational Research. 44(1974).

736. Roberts, David B. "Foundations and Implications for Adult Moral Education in Lawrence Kohlberg's Theory of Moral Development and Walter G. Muelder's Conception of Moral Laws." Ph.D. dissertation, Boston University, 1977. 38/04, 2020.

A rather critical view of Kohlberg's work coupled with a perspective on adult moral education based on Muelder's conception of moral laws.

737. Rosen, Bernard. "Moral Dilemmas and Their Treatment." Moral Development, Moral Education and Kohlberg. (item 432), pp. 232-265.

Examines the nature of moral dilemmas as a certain logical form derived from philosophical analyses of logic. In Rosen's analysis the problem of a dilemma involves knowing which of two competing antecedents or negations of consequents is true. He compares act and rule theory treatments of dilemmas and shows how the methodology of act theories, moral negotiation, fits in a most natural way the structure of moral dilemmas.

738. Rosenzweig, Linda. "Kohlberg in the Classroom: Moral Education Models." Moral Development, Moral Education and Kohlberg (item 432), pp. 359-380.

Discusses the variety of Kohlbergian developmental moral education models currently being implemented in schools and offers a critical appraisal.

739. Rubin, K.H., and Trotter, K.T. "Kohlberg's Moral Judgment Scale: Some Methodological Considerations." Developmental Psychology, 13 (1977): 535-536.

Children in grades three and five were administered the moral judgment scale and then two weeks later half were given an objective scale of moral judgment and the other half readministered the moral judgment interview scale. The results raised serious questions concerning the psychometric properties of the Kohlberg moral judgment scale.

740. Scharf, Peter. "Evaluating the Development of Moral Education: A Response to the Critiques of Flowers, Sullivan and Fraenkel." Readings in Moral Education (item 449), pp. 288-297.

741. Schleifer, M. "Moral Education and Indoctrination." Ethics, 86 (1976): 154-163.

Kohlberg is lauded for his emphasis on developing general cognitive abilities but criticized for eschewing the nonrational in moral education. Kohlberg's more recent writings (item 410) negate much of the criticism in this article.

742. Schmitt, Rudolf. "The Stages of Moral Development--A Basis for an Educational Concept?" International Review of Education, 26 (1980): 207-216.

Argues that the longitudinal evidence does not support Kohlberg's claims, that the stages are not differentiated structurally, but rather according to content on the basis of implicit moral concepts, and that the dominance of a certain ethical philosophy influences the development of moral judgment. A new arrangement of stage sequence is presented organized around ethical principles and educational climate.

743. Schur, Michael. "Achievement Need versus Moral Judgment." Journal of Moral Education, 5 (1976): 275-293.

In an experimental study it was found that the presence of competing motivations in dilemmas may increase the degree to which egocentric choices prevail when self-interest and principled morality are in conflict.

744. Schwartz, Edward. "Traditional Values, Moral Education, and Social Change." Moral Development and Politics (item 3193), pp. 221-236.

Is concerned whether moral development theories can give adequate instruction concerning the behavioral attributes of high stages. Argues that alternative visions of the good life and justice compete in a society--an abstract conception of justice does not offer a clear way to choose. Concludes that the content of an argument must be examined, not merely the structures of authority it represents.

745. Shawver, David J. "Character and Ethics: An Epistemological Inquiry with Particular Reference to Lawrence Kohlberg's Cognitive Theory of Moral Development." Ph.D. dissertation, McGill University, 1979. 40/09, p. 5087.

Kohlberg's claim that he is operating in the traditions of Piaget and Rawls is challenged it is claimed that they are incompatible traditions.

746. Sichel, Betty A. "Can Kohlberg Respond to Critics?" Educational Theory, 26 (1976): 337-347.

Indicates how in two areas (habits and reason, and passion and norm) Kohlberg's theory may be expanded to include the conceptualization necessary for any viable theory of moral development. It is stressed, however, that Kohlberg has made no such movement in that direction.

747. Sichel, Betty A. "A Critical Study of Kohlberg's Theory of the Development of Moral Judgments." Philosophy of Education 1976 (item 1792), pp. 209-220.

Focuses on four dimensions of Kohlberg's theory which are of special interest to philosophers and which have not been adequately examined: The relationship between moral judgment and moral behavior, differences between logical judgments and moral judgments, the inception of moral reasoning and moral justification and moral judgments.

748. Sichel, Betty A. "The Relation Between Moral Judgment and Moral Behavior in Kohlberg's Theory of the Development of Moral Judgments." Educational Philosophy and Theory, 8 (April 1976): 55-67.

Argues that there are empirical and logical reasons to reject Kohlbergs conceptualization of the relationship between moral judgment and moral behavior.

749. Siegal, Michael. "Kohlberg Versus Piaget: To What Extent Has One Theory Eclipsed the Other?" Merrill-Palmer Quarterly, 26 (1980): 285-297.

Based on an examination of research it is concluded that Kohlberg's theory is but a modest improvement over Piaget's. Kohlberg's evidence appears to be weakest when it strays from Piaget's formulation-stages 1, 5 and 6.

750. Siegal, M. "Spontaneous Development of Moral Concepts." Human Development, 18 (1975): 370-383.

Four types of non-spontaneous solutions to moral problems are suggested and it is argued that spontaneous, rational development of moral concepts can only occur when one perceives the pseudo-rigorousness of these non-spontaneous solutions. Moral conceptual development requires more than one moral virtue: that of courage as well as justice.

751. Simpson, Elizabeth Leonie. "Moral Development Research: A Case Study of Scientific Cultural Bias." Human Development, 17 (1974): 81-106.

Analyzes Kohlberg's claims for the cross-cultural universality of the stages and finds that the definitions of stages and the assumptions underlying them are ethnocentric and culturally-biased. Also in Moral and Psychological Education (item 448).

752. Sobol, Thomas. "An Administrator Looks at Moral Education: And if I Ask These Things, Will Ye Still Call Me Friend?" Educational Leadership, 38 (1980): 16-17.

Sobol, Superintendent of Schools in Scarsdale, NY, asks hard questions of the moral education community. The questions relate to such concerns as financing, certification of teachers, moral standards to be taught, community relations and behavior of students.

753. Stanton, Michael. "Pupils' Assessments of Social Action: A Cross-Cultural Study." *Educational Review*, 27 (1975): 126-137.

Argues that because of substantial differences in ratings of forms of positive and negative behavior among a cross-cultural sample there does not appear to be a basis for postualating universal stages of moral judgment.

754. Straughan, Roger R. "Hypothetical Moral Situations." *Journal of Moral Education*, 4 (1975): 183-189.

Drawing on the logical distinctions between different types of moral conflict, it is argued that any approach to moral education based on hypothetical moral dilemmas must have serious limitations.

755. Sullivan, Edmund V. *Kohlberg's Structuralism: A Critical Appraisal*, Monograph Series 115. Toronto: Ontario Institute for Studies in Education, 1977.

Criticizes Kohlberg from a post-critical perspective arguing that what is said to constitute disinterested and abstract fairness is in fact defined by the dominant group in the society. Moral education needs to be viewed from a much broader perspective.

756. Sullivan, Edmund V. "Structuralism per se When Applied to Moral Ideology." *Readings in Moral Education* (item 449), pp. 272-286.

Criticizes Kohlberg for not giving convincing attention to the notion of moral commitment--the fusion of thaught and action. Discusses moral blindness--where moral reasons become rationalizations. An excerpt from item 755.

757. Sullivan, Edmund V. "A Study of Kohlberg's Structural Theory of Moral Development: A Critique of Liberal Social Science Ideology." *Human Development*, 20 (1977): 352-76.

Kohlberg's stage theory is characterized as a species of liberal ideology.

758. Trainer, F.E. "A Critical Analysis of Kohlberg's Contribution to the Study of Moral Thought." Journal for the Theory of Social Behavior, 7 (1977): 41-63.

Presents a wide ranging critique of Kohlbergian theory touching on questions of whether the stages are discoveries of speculative constructions, whether high stages are somehow better, difficulties within the account of stage 6 thought, and the phenomena of adolescent regression.

759. Wilson, John. "Philosophical Difficulties and Moral Development." Moral Development, Moral Education and Kohlberg (item 432), pp. 214-231.

Offers a sympathetic but critical view of what he sees as Kohlberg's interesting data built too quickly into theory. He argues that Kohlberg's theory is not content free, contains ambiguity in interview language, especially with regard to differences between causes and reasons, and is unclear with respect to what exactly is a "stage."

760. Wilson, Richard W. "Some Comments on Stage Theories of Moral Development." Journal of Moral Education, 5 (1976): 241-248.

Based on studies of variations in moral responses of Chinese and American children it is concluded that developmental theory has ignored the type and extent of manipulation of affect. There is a crucial need for the development of internalized commitments to various types of behavior.

761. Wonderly, D.M. and J.H. Kupfersmid. "Promoting Postconventional Morality: The Adequacy of Kohlberg's Aim." Adolescence, 15 (1980): 609-631. NR

Psychological/Developmental Education: Theory, Practice and Research

762. Alschuler, Alfred S. and Allen E. Ivey. "Getting into Psychological Education." Personnel and Guidance Journal, 51 (1973): 682-691.

A wide range of materials are discussed to assist individuals interested in learning more about psychological education.

763. Alschuler, Alfred S. and Allen E. Ivey. "Internalization: The Outcome of Psychological Education." Personnel and Guidance Journal, 51 (1973): 607-610.

Argues that the valid indices of effectiveness in psychological education is not short-term knowledge and satisfaction but rather durable long-term self-chosen internalization ideas, values, skills, etc. Suggestions for measuring internalization are presented.

764. Alschuler, Alfred S., Diane Tabor, and James McIntyre. Teaching Achievement Motivation: Theory and Practice in Psychological Education. Middletown, CT: Education Ventures, 1971.

Following a brief introduction psychological education and achievement motivation a ten session achievement motivation workshop for teachers is described. The book is practical throughout, and contains bibliographies on the theory and practice of achievement motivation.

765. Arredondo-Dowd, Patricia M. "A Psychological Education Curriculum for Immigrant Adolescents." Personnel and Guidance Journal, 58 (1980): 618-621.

Describes a psychological education curriculum for immigrant adolescents. The curriculum involved introductions, social issues, the psychology of adolescence, moral reasoning and social action. The experimental group was found to have experienced significant moral growth as a result of the treatment.

766. Bernier, Joseph E. and Kenneth Rustad. "Psychology of Counseling Curriculum: A Follow-Up Study." Developmental Counseling and Teaching (item 784), pp. 101-109.

Provides an overview of a curriculum for teaching counseling skills to high school students. The curriculum is related to cognitive-developmental theory, the phases of the curriculum described, and the results of an evaluation reported. Ego development and moral reasoning were significantly stimulated by the program. Also Counseling Psychologist, 6,4 (1977).

767. Blocher, Donald H. "A Systematic Approach to Organizational Change and Its Application to Developmental Education." Developmental Counseling and Teaching (item 784), pp. 381-385.

Presents a systematic eclectic model for organizational change and describes how it can be used to incorporate developmental education into schools. Also Counseling Psychologist, 6,4 (1977).

768. Caroll, M.R. ed. "Special Feature: Psychological Education." School Counselor, 20 (May 1973).

Contains five articles which focus on the new role for the school counselor based on the principles of psychological education.

769. Cognetta, Philip. "Deliberate Psychological Education: A High School Cross-Age Teaching Model." Developmental Counseling and Teaching (item 784), pp. 110-117.

Describes a psychological education program for high school students involving a cross-age teaching and featuring responsible role-taking and active reflection within a seminar/practicum format. It was found that such a curriculum will positively affect the personal growth of adolescents. Also Counseling Psychologist, 6,4 (1977).

770. Cognetta, Philip V. and Norman A. Sprinthall. "Students as Teachers: Role Taking as a Means of Promoting Psychological and Ethical Development During Adolescence." Value Development ... As the Aim of Education (item 1816), pp. 63-68.

Reports the results of a high school cross-age teaching program on moral and ego development. It was found that the cross-age teachers experienced significant gains on the Loevinger Ego Development scale and Rests Defining Issues Test.

771. Collins, W. Andrew. "Counseling Interventions and Developmental Psychology: Reactions to Programs for Social-Cognitive Growth," Developmental Counseling and Teaching (item 784), pp. 94-98.

Makes the point that the context and evaluations of interventions should involve consideration of the child's natural social experience. Also Counseling Psychologist, 6,4 (1977).

772. Contreras, Patricia. "Staff and Organizational Development in Psychological Education: An Example." Developmental Counseling and Teaching (item 784), pp. 356-365.

Addresses the question of staff development as a part of organizational change toward psychological education, and provides a working example. Also Counseling Psychologist, 6,4 (1977).

773. Cooney, Ellen W. "Social-Cognitive Intervention: Some Thoughts on the Effects and Evaluation of an Elementary Grade Curriculum." Developmental Counseling and Teaching (item 784), pp. 69-79.

Using a series of 16 sound filmstrips a social-cognitive curriculum was implemented and evaluated with primary-grade children. Also Counseling Psychologist, 6,4 (1977).

774. Damon, William. "Some Thoughts on the Nature of Children's Social Development." Reflections on Values Education (item 1814), pp. 131-148.

Focuses on child's acquisition of social knowledge. That is, how he/she comes to understand and interpret his/her social world. Presents the four assumptions about human social development which undergird his theory. These assumptions are presented in the form of distinctions between: 1) primitive and advanced modes of knowing the world; 2) practical and moral overtations to the social world; 3) theoretical and real life social knowledge and 4) whole and partial social structures.

775. Danskin, David G. and E. Dale Walters. "Biofeedback and Voluntary Self-Regulation: Counseling and Education." Personnel and Guidance Journal, 51 (1973): 633-638.

Briefly reviews the theory and research on biofeedback and argues that it can be used to put the power of altering behavior in the hands of the individual. References on the relationship between bio-feedback and self-control are provided.

776. Dowell, Roland C. "Adolescents as Peer Counselors: A Program for Psychological Growth." Ph.D. dissertation, Harvard University, 1971.

Developing psychological sensitivity and counseling skills in adolescents is shown to be effective in stimulating moral development.

777. Enright, Robert D. "A Classroom Discipline Model for Promoting Social Cognitive Development in Early Childhood." Journal of Moral Education, 11 (1981): 47-60.

Two first grade teachers used a social cognitive model in the naturalistic context of the classroom as conflicts arose. The findings of the research support the models effectiveness in promoting children's social cognitive development.

778. Enright, Robert D. "Promoting Interpersonal and Moral Growth in Elementary Schools." Value Development ... As the Aim of Education (item 1816), pp. 27-40.

Reports the results of a program designed to teach elementary age pupils how to teach and understand their younger peers. Using Selman's social problem solving measure it was found that the students who engaged in small group social problem discussions showed significant gains in stages of interpersonal conception.

779. Enright, Robert D., Susan Colby, and Idonis McMullin. "A Social-Cognitive Developmental Intervention with Sixth and First Graders." Developmental Counseling and Teaching (item 784), pp. 80-86.

Presents a cross-age teaching program in which sixth-graders learn social-perspective-taking (Selman) by teaching first-graders. The experimental group showed dramatic changes in level of interpersonal conceptions. Also Counseling Psychologist, 6,4 (1977).

780. Erickson, V. Lois. "Deliberate Psychological Education for Women: A Curriculum Follow-Up Study." Developmental Counseling and Teaching (item 784), pp. 118-127.

Presents a method of teaching adolescent women interview, integrating and self-processing skills. Through the examination of their own basic ego components in planned social-role taking experiences and structured reflections psychological growth was promoted. Also Counseling Psychologist, 6,4 (1977).

781. Erickson, V. Lois. "Deliberate Psychological Education for Women: From Iphigenia to Antigone." Counselor Education and Supervision, 14 (1975): 297-309.

Women's psychological growth is described from a developmental perspective. Also in Moral and Psychological Education (item 448) and Adolescent's Developmental Education (item 1806).

782. Erickson, V. Lois. "The Development of Women: An Issue of Justice." Readings in Moral Education (item 449), pp. 110-122.

Examines the psychological motivation process of women from a cognitive developmental process. Discusses issues of equity in education in terms of developmental maturity, argues the need for curricula to facilitate the development of women, and reports the results of an experimental curriculum to do same.

783. Erickson, V. Lois, ed. "Developmental Counseling Psychology." The Counseling Psychologist, 6,4 (1977).

Contains twenty articles dealing with recent theoretical research and intervention issues involved with attempting to deliberately promote psychological growth through counseling and teaching programs. All articles are reprinted in Developmental Counseling and Teaching (item 784).

784. Erickson, V. Lois and John M. Whiteley, eds. Developmental Counseling and Teaching. Monterey, CA: Brooks/Cole, 1980.

Contains thirty-two papers dealing with recent theoretical research and intervention issues involved with attempting to deliberately promote psychological growth through counseling and teaching programs. Only five of the papers have not been published elsewhere. Twenty of the articles represent the complete issue of Conseling Psychologist, 6,4 (1977).

785. Felton, L. "Teaching Counseling to Adolescents and Adults." Ph.D. dissertation, Boston University, 1974. 35/12, p. 7647.

Found that moral reasoning was stimulated by teaching counseling skills to adolescents but when adolescents and adults were mixed in the training group no such growth occured.

786. Gilliland, Steve F. "Some Effects of a Human Relations Laboratory on Moral Orientation." Ed.D. dissertation, Boston University, 1971. 32/04, p. 1828.

The subjects exposed to two weeks of a human relations laboratory had little effect on moral reasoning or on specific values.

787. Gluckstern, Norma B. "Training Parents as Drug Counselors in the Community." Personnel and Guidance Journal, 51 (1973): 676-680.

Describes a program designed to educate parents with regard to drugs, to train them in counseling and human relations, and to support them with follow-up services as they enter the community.

788. Goshko, Robert. "Self-determined Behavior Change." Personnel and Guidance Journal, 51 (1973): 629-632.

Describes a project designed to determine if elementary school children can learn skills of self-observation and then select and modify behavior of their own choice. Immediate video feedback was used. It was found that children could change self-related behavior in the direction they wished. In effect children used behavior modification on themselves.

789. Greenspan, B.M. "Facilitating Psychological Growth in Adolescents through Child Development Curricula." Ph.D. dissertation, Harvard University, 1974. 36/06, p. 3353.

Finds that working with preschool children, studying their development and reflecting on ones role as helper facilitates ego, interpersonal and cognitive development.

790. Guidubaldi, John, ed. "Humanizing Education." School Psychology Digest, 1 (Summer, 1972).

Contains a collection of articles urging that school psychologists devise services that are grounded in developmental and social psychology principles.

791. Gum, May F., Armas W. Tamminen and Marlowe H. Smoby. "Developmental Guidance Experiences." Personnel and Guidance Journal, 51 (1973): 647-652.

Within a developmental framework for education three structured develomental guidance experiences are described designed to provide practical techniques for the classroom.

792. Hauser, Stuart T. "Loevinger's Model and Measure of Ego Development: A Critical Review." Developmental Counseling and Teaching (item 784), pp. 27-34.

Loevinger's seven stage theory of ego development is reviewed with examples provided illustrating responses at each of the levels. This paper is adapted from the original article in Psychological Bulletin, 83 (1976): 928-955. This version contains no critique of the theory.

793. Hurt, Bryan L. "Psychological Education for College Students: A Cognitive Developmental Curriculum." Ph.D. dissertation, University of Minnesota, 1974. 35/08, p. 5119.

A psychological education curriculum which emphasized empathy training, outside practical experience and structured reflection in that experience resulted in significant change in moral reasoning but little change in ego development or on a test of conceptual systems.

794. Ivey, Allen E. and Alfred S. Alschuler. "An Introduction to the Field." _Personnel and Guidance Journal_, 51 (1973): 591-597.

Provides a concise overview of theory, goals and strategies of psychological education. Specific suggestions for school counselors to incorporate psychological education within their school are offered.

795. Ivey, Allen E. and Alfred S. Alschuler, eds. "Psychological Education: A Prime Function of the Counselor." _Personnel and Guidance Journal_, 51 (May 1973).

Contains eleven substantive articles relating the principles of psychological/humanistic education to schooling. Contains sections on techniques, programmatic approaches and social applications. The volume is opened and closed by brief articles by the editors.

796. Katz, T. "The Arts as Vehicle for the Exploration of Personal Concerns." Ph.D. dissertation, Harvard University, 1972. 33/02, p. 619.

Anecdotal evidence suggests that psychological growth is effected by the study of the arts in an experimental high school class.

797. Kohlberg, Lawrence. "A Developmental Approach to School Psychology." _School Psychology Digest_, 1 (Summer, 1972): 3-7.

Urges that school psychologists incorporate a cognitive-developmental framework into their activities in schools.

798. Kuriloff, Peter and Mark Rindner. "How Psychological Education Can Promote Mental Health with Competence." Counseling Education and Supervision, 14 (1975): 257-267.

After establishing that competence is a necessary condition of mental health four conditions are presented which psychological education curriculums can provide for facilitating students' acquisition of cognitive competence.

799. Lawson, D.E. "Suggestions Concerning the Term 'Adjustment.'" Educational Forum, 25 (1961): 175-179.

Argues that disagreement over adjustment as an educational aim is due to the variety of meanings the word has: (1) fitting into a group, (2) personality integration, and (3) adaptable to circumstances.

800. Loevinger, Jane. Ego Development: Conceptions and Theories. San Francisco: Jossey-Bass, 1976.

Presents a theory of ego development where the ego is the keystone of personality. Its purpose is to synthesize experience and give meaning to purpose and to our lives. The ego is pictured as active and structural--an evolving intellectual framework of rules, criteria and schemata about life.

801. Loevinger, Jane. "Stages of Ego Development." Adolescent's Development and Education (item 1806), pp. 110-123.

In a section from her book, Ego Development: Conceptions and Theories (item 800) the theory of ego development is presented.

802. Lorish, R. "Teaching Counseling to Disadvantaged Young Adults." Ph.D. dissertation, Boston University, 1974. 35/09, p. 5819.

Inmates were taught counseling and problem solving skills. It was found that the inmates could master these skills and that their moral reasoning began a movement to a higher stage.

803. McDonald, William R. "The Effects of A Helping Skills Training Program on High School Students' Communication-Formulation-Discrimination-Recognition Skills, Self-Concepts and Moral Development." Ed.D. dissertation, Wayne State University, 1976. 37/05, p. 2640.

No significant gain was detected in either self concept or moral judgments as a result of training. Findings in other areas were more favorable.

804. McMullen, Ronald S. "The Achievement Motivation Workshop." Personnel and Guidance Journal, 51 (1973): 633-638.

Describes a workshop for students on achievement motivation.

805. Magara, Holly, John M. Whiteley and Karen H. Nelson. "Sequencing of Experiences in Psychological Interventions: Relationships Among Locus of Control, Moral Reasoning, and Ego Development." Developmental Counseling and Teaching (item 784), pp. 298-328.

The initial research findings on the effect of the Sierra Project (item 601) are reported. It was found that two aspects of personality (locus of control and ego development) are related to growth in moral reasoning and in turn may place limits on the individuals capacity for moral growth.

806. Maul, June P. "A High School with Intensive Education: Moral Atmosphere and Moral Reasoning." Journal of Moral Education, 10 (1980): 9-17.

Examines the impact of the moral atmostphere of a school on moral development. The high school allowed for intensive social interaction as opposed to traditional one dimensional authority relations. Dependent upon the number of years experience to intensive education, significant moral development occurred.

807. Meyer, Pierre. "Intellectual Development: Analysis of Religious Content." Developmental Counseling and Teaching (item 784), pp. 223-230.

Presents data that suggests that intellectual development can be measured cross-sectionally through analysis of religious content. Development shifts in this development were detected over the four year college experience. Also Counseling Psychologist, 6,4 (1977).

808. Miller-Tiedeman, Anna. "Explorations of Decision Making in the Expansion of Adolescent Personal Development." Developmental Counseling and Teaching (item 784), pp. 158-187.

Demonstrates that psychological growth can occur in conjunction with a course in English. Integrates ego-development and values development into a hierarchy of decision-making strategies. It was found that curriculum based on this model significantly affected ego-development and initial thinking.

809. Mosher, Ralph. "Education for Human Development." Humanistic Education (item 923), pp. 161-181.

The implications of developmental psychology for educational practice are outlined.

810. Mosher, Ralph and Norman Sprinthall. "Psychological Education in Secondary Schools." American Psychologist, 25(1970): 911-924.

Presents an overview of the rationale, assumptions, personnel, curriculum and future plans of deliberate psychological education. The thrust of the program is to promote personal and social competence during a time of change. The program has a decidedly humanistic and developmental focus. The focus of the curriculum is psychology, group process, counseling, communication and social service.

811. Mosher, Ralph and Paul Sullivan. "A Curriculum in Moral Education for Adolescents," Readings in Moral Education (item 449), pp. 82-97.

Presents a description of a moral education program for adolescents. The model is being implemented in Brookline, MA and Tocoma, WA. In addition to moral discussions this program also involves teaching counseling skills, teaching moral philosophy and psychology and having students serve as moral educators. It was found that the experimental group experienced significant growth on the Kohlberg Test of Moral Maturity and the Loevinger Test of Ego Development. Also Journal of Moral Education (item 1976), Adolescent's Development and Education (item 1806), and Moral Education ... It Comes with the Territory (item 1811).

812. Mosher, Ralph, et al. "Psychological Education: A Means to Promote Personal Development During Adolescence." Curriculum and the Cultural Revolution. Edited by David Purpel and M. Belanger. Berkeley, CA: McCutchan, 1975, pp. 284-410.

Describes a multi-faceted program of education for human development used in a high school. Such factors as openness to experience, trust, interpersonal awareness and self-awareness are seen as necessary prerequisites to growth. Described one program in peer counseling cross-age teaching, improvisational drama and a course on child development. The results of research reported confirm positive growth of students in such areas as moral development, ego development, counseling effectiveness. Also in Counseling Psychologist, 2,4 (1971).

813. Oja, Sharon N. "A Cognitive-Structural Approach to Adult Ego, Moral and Conceptual Development Through Inservice Teacher Education." Ph.D. dissertation, University of Minnesota, 1978. 39/09, p. 5356.

Evaluates a Deliberate Psychological Education curriculum for inservice teachers. It was found that as a result of the treatment significant movement occured in moral development and cognitive complexity. No movement was detected on level of ego development.

814. Palomares, Uvaldo H. and Terri Rubin. "Human Development in the Classroom." Personnel and Guidance Journal, 51 (1973): 653-657.

The Human Development Program (item 901) with its focus on awareness (knowing feelings thought and actions), mastery (self-confidence) and social interaction (knowing other people) through the use of the "Magic Circle" is described. The rationale and application of the program is discussed.

815. Perry, William G. "Comments, Appreciative and Cautionary." Developmental Counseling and Teaching (item 784), pp. 231-235.

Cautions against "tinkering" with students development. Suggests that with too great a focus on the essence of development, what happens to the value of existence? Also Counseling Psychologist, 6,4 (1977).

816. Perry, William. Forms of Intellectual and Ethical Development in the College Years. New York: Holt, Rinehart and Winston, 1970.

Using a data base of Harvard undergraduates from 1954 to 1968 a nine stage developmental trend in student's ways of perceiving knowledge and values was identified. The nine positions can be grouped into three general categories: dualism, relativism and commitment in relativism. Perry's work hints at but does not provide clear guidance for educational applications.

817. Rest, James. "Comments on the Deliberate Psychological Education Programs and the Toronto Moral Education Programs in Secondary Education." Developmental Counseling and Teaching (item 784), pp. 134-139.

Asks four questions regarding developmental programs: How much guidance can developmental psychology give anyone right now?; How closely tied to developmental psychology are these programs?; What is the distinguishing character of these programs?; and What have we learned from the evaluation research of these programs? Rest's answers to these questions reflect the judgment that there is still much work to be done. Also Counseling Psychologist, 6,5 (1977).

818. Rustad, Kenneth. "Teaching Counseling Skills to Adolescents: A Cognitive-Developmental Approach to Psychological Education." Ph.D. dissertation, University of Minnesota, 1974. 35/06, p. 3407.

Teaching counseling skills (role taking and empathy) to adolescents and having them counsel other peers was found to have a slight impact on moral judgment.

819. Rustad, Ken and Charlotte Rogers. "Promoting Psychological Growth in a High School Class." Counseling Education and Supervision, 14 (1975): 277-285.

Describes a curriculum and presents the research results of an effort to promote the personal growth of high school students. The treatment involved learning basic counseling skills, active listening, empathetic responding, and the development of role taking abilities.

820. Ryals, Kelvin R. "An Experimental Study of Achievement Motivation Training as a Function of the Moral Maturity of Trainees." Ph.D. dissertation, Washington University, 1969. 30/12, p. 5302.

Achievement motivation training with eighth grade subjects did overall produce higher academic achievement, but those highest in moral maturity achieved no higher than other subjects.

821. Selman, Robert L. "A Developmental Approach to Interpersonal and Moral Awareness in Young Children: Some Educational Implications of Levels of Social Perspective-Taking." Values and Moral Development (item 378), pp. 142-172.

Selman reports on his work in the area of social perspective-taking. He presents his stages of social perspective taking and describes how they fit into the structural-developmental approach. He discusses the educational implications and methodology which accompany his approach and describes a pilot research project. Also in Values Education (item 1805).

822. Selman, Robert L. "A Structural-Developmental Model of Social Cognition: Implications for Intervention Research." Developmental Counseling and Teaching (item 784), pp. 60-68.

Describes Selman's work in examining the role of perspective-taking in the context of reasoning about various types of interpersonal relationships. It is claimed that each level of perspective taking (social cognition) is necessary but not sufficient for each structurally parallel stage of interpersonal or moral reasoning. Also Counseling Psychologist, 6,4 (1977) and Adolescent's Development and Education (item 1806).

823. Shallcross, Doris J. "Creativity: Everybody's Business." Personnel and Guidance Journal. 51 (1973): 623-626.

Provides an introduction to the literature and methodology of creativity. Suggestions are presented for breaking down barriers to creative behavior.

824. Sprinthall, Norman A. "The Adolescent as a Psychologist: An Application of Kohlberg to a High School Curriculum." School Psychology Digest, 1 (Summer, 1972): 8-14.

Describes a high school program in psychological education emphasizing teaching counseling skills and cross-age teaching. It was found that ego and moral development were stimulated by such an approach.

825. Sprinthall, Norman A. "A Curriculum for Secondary Schools: Counselors as Teachers for Psychological Growth." School Counselor, 20 (1973): 361-369.

Contains an honest description of the successes and failures that he has encountered in the attempt to personalize cognitive learnings.

826. Sprinthall, Norman A. "Learning Psychology By Doing Psychology: A High School Curriculum in the Psychology of Counseling." Adolescent's Development and Education (item 1806), pp. 365-385.

Describes the development and implementation of a Psychology of Counseling and other classes in a high school setting designed to promote psychological (ego) development. A significant movement in students to Level 4 was noted on Loevinger's Scale of Ego Development.

827. Sprinthall, Norman A. "Moral and Psychological Development: A Curriculum for Secondary Schools." Values and Moral Development (item 378), pp. 37-73.

Sprinthall urges that the schools consider a broad range of developmental dimensions of students in addition to the moral: cognitive, ego, and personal development. He discusses the implications of the works of Piaget, Kohlberg, Loevinger, Erickson and Elkind for developmental education. Presents a summary of objectives, curriculum examples and research on psychological developmental education.

828. Sprinthall, N.A., ed. "Personal Development Through Schooling." Counselor Education and Supervision, 14 (June 1975).

Contains a series of papers which focus on the role of the counselor in promoting psychological growth. Most of the papers take a developmental perspective.

829. Sprinthall, Norman A. "A Primer on Development." Value Development ... as the Aim of Education (item 1816), pp. 1-15.

Briefly outlines the key developmental assumptions of Dewey, Piaget, Kohlberg, Loevinger and Selman as a basis for developmental education.

830. Sprinthall, Norman. "A Program for Psychological Education: Some Preliminary Issues." Journal of School Psychology, 9 (1971): 373-382.

Argues that a major focus for the recent interest in psychological education should be on the development of a careful theoretical framework. The developmental framework of Piaget and Kohlberg is offered as promising and avoiding many of the problems inherent in other theoretical frameworks.

831. Sprinthall, Norman A. "Psychology and Teacher Education: New Directions for School and Counseling Psychology." Developmental Counseling and Teaching (item 784), pp. 330-338.

Makes an argument for "giving psychology away through teacher education." It is claimed that this will improve education by leading to the connection of psychology with practice. Also Counseling Psychologist, 6,4 (1977).

832. Sprinthall, Norman. "A Reply to Jim Rest: Doonesbury's Football Team and Deliberate Psychological Education." Developmental Counseling and Teaching (item 784), pp. 140-143.

Responds to Rest (item 817) by asserting that deliberate psychological education is unlike a football team in that it is concerned with theory based action and educative and developmentally beneficial experiences.

833. Sprinthall, Norman A. and Ralph L. Mosher. "A Developmental Curriculum for Secondary Schools: Need, Purpose, and Programs." Paper presented at Moral/Citizenship Conference, Philadelphia, 1976. ED 178 457.

Presents the rationale for developmental moral education and a survey of current public school developmental programs. Also in Adolescents' Development and Education (item 1806).

834. Sprinthall, Norman A. and Ralph L. Mosher. "John Dewey Revisited: A Framework for Developmental Education." Value Development ... As the Aim of Education (item 1816), pp. 16-26.

Presents a brief and sketchy view of Dewey's historical place in the evaluation of developmental education. The authors conclude arguing that developmental education is a crucial need for the future in what may otherwise be a dismal future for mankind.

835. Stephenson, Bud W. and Christine Hunt. "Intellectual and Ethical Development: A Dualistic Curriculum Intervention for College Students." Developmental Counseling and Teaching (item 783), pp. 200-208.

Using the Perry model (item 816) as a theoretical base a curriculum program for promoting the intellectual and ethical development of college students is presented. The results of an evaluation indicate that upward movement on the Perry scheme and other developmental measures was achieved. Also Counseling Psychologist, 6,4 (1977).

836. Sullivan, Paul. "Moral Education for Adolescents." Moral Education: A First Generation of Research and Development (item 428), pp. 165-187.

Describes a one year course in psychology taught to high school juniors and seniors. The focus of the course was on moral discussions, counseling and empathy training, moral psychology and philosophy, and adolescents as moral educators. The results of an evaluation are reported as successful.

837. Thompson, Garth D. "A Theory of Counseling for Development of Moral Character." Ph.D. dissertation, University of Florida, 1976. 37/10, p. 6285.

A theory of counseling is proposed which addresses itself to counselor behaviors which may lead to increments in the development of moral character: distinguishing right from wrong, commitment to the right and implementation of the right.

838. Weinstein, Gerald. "Self-Science Education: The Trumpet." Personnel and Guidance Journal, 51 (1973): 600-606.

A technique--the trumpet--which provides the self-scientist with a cognitive map or sequence for working through a set of personal observations is presented. The goal is to lead to greater self-awareness and humaneness.

839. Whiteley, John M. "A Developmental Intervention in Higher Education." Developmental Counseling and Teaching (item 784), pp. 236-261.

Provides an overview of the Sierra Project, a developmental intervention designed to facilitate and study dimensions associated with character development in college students. The intervention centers around a course on moral development and just communities and a laboratory course on deliberate psychological education involving cross-age teaching and cross-age counseling. A research design is sketched out and relevant instruments identified, but no data is reported.

840. Whiteley, John M. and Janet C. Loxley. "A Curriculum for the Development of Character and Community in College Students." Developmental Counseling and Teaching (item 784), pp. 262-297.

Describes the Sierra Project curriculum in some detail. The curriculum modules consisted of survival skills, social perspective taking, community building, conflict resolution in society, life and career planning, socialization, asserting training and community service. Activities involved in each of the modules are described.

841. Widick, Carole. "The Perry Scheme: A Foundation for Developmental Practice." Developmental Counseling and Teaching (item 784), pp. 35-42.

Perry's developmental scheme (item 816) is succinctly reviewed and its utility for counseling/educational interventions is assessed. Six questions are posed which need investigation before the scheme's potential is realized. Also in Counseling Psychologist, 6,4 (1977).

842. Zide, Michele M. "Group Dynamics Techniques." Personnel and Guidance Journal, 51 (1973): 620-622.

Twelve group dynamics techniques that can be used in classes are briefly discussed.

Humanistic/Affective Education: Theory, Practice and Research

843. Anders-Richards, Donald. "Humanistic Psychology and Morality." Journal of Moral Education, 4 (1975): 105-110.

The potential role of the encounter group and humanistic psychology in moral education is explored. Moral objections to the technique, and to its implied moral dangers, are outlined and answered.

844. Aronson, E. The Jigsaw Classroom. Beverly Hills, CA: Sage Publications, 1978.

Describes a program designed to result in cooperative behavior. Children are placed in situations where they must treat each other as resources; no one can do well without the help of others and each person has an essential contribution to make.

845. Aronson, E., D.L. Bridgeman and R. Geffner. "Interdependent Interactions and Prosocial Behavior." Journal of Research and Development in Education, 12,1 (1979): 16-27.

Describes the jigsaw method" which attempts to incorporate the beneficial features of cooperation and peer teaching into the highly structured atmosphere of the more traditional classroom. Research on the positive effects of this method on prosocial development is reported.

846. Aspy, David N. "An Interpersonal Approach to Humanizing Education." Humanistic Education (item 923), pp. 123-140.

Argues that all must develop and use our interpersonal skills at the highest level and cites research to indicate that if teachers are trained in interpersonal skills their classrooms become more humane.

847. Aspy, David N. Toward a Technology for Humanizing Education. Champaign, IL: Research Press, 1972.

Summarizes the authors extensive work about enabling schools to humanize the educational process. The research tools and teacher training procedures used are described.

848. Berman, Louise M. and Jessie A. Roderick, eds. Feeling, Valuing, and the Art of Growing: Insights into the Affective. Washington, D.C.: Association for Supervision and Curriculum Development, 1977. ED 133 880.

A collection of papers on the role of the affective in the educational process. Definitions of the affective are presented and what schools can and are doing to foster this dimension is discussed in the papers.

849. Brown, George I. Human Teaching for Human Learning. New York: Viking Press, 1971.

Focuses on confluent education--the integration of the affective and cognitive domains of education. Many affective techniques are described and given classroom applications. A comprehensive bibliography is included.

850. Brown, G.I., M. Phillips, and S.B. Shapiro. Getting It All Together: Confluent Education, Fastback 85. Bloomington, IN: Phi Delta Kappa Education Foundation, 1976.

Defines confluent education and presents examples of curriculum approaches. Also discussed is the evaluation of confluent education.

851. Bugental, James, ed. Challenges of Humanistic Psychology. New York: McGraw-Hill, 1967.

Contains 34 articles on such topics as the nature of humanistic psychology, research areas and products, the growth encounter and the reunion of psychology and the humanities.

852. Callahan, Mary Frances. "Feeling, Reasoning, and Acting: An Integrated Approach to Moral Education." Readings in Moral Education (item 449), pp. 198-209.

853. Canfield, John and Mark Phillips. A Guide to Humanistic Education, 1970. ED 067 356.

Contains 46 annotated pages of books, articles, curricula, media, etc. on humanistic education.

854. Canfield, John T. and Mark Phillips. "Humanisticography." Media and Methods, 8 (1971): 41-56.

An annotated bibliography of books, films, tapes, curricula, etc. related to humanistic education.

855. Canfield, Jack and Harold C. Wells. 100 Ways to Enhance Self-Concept in the Classroom. Englewood Cliffs: Prentice-Hall, 1976.

As the title suggests 100 activities are presented. The activities are sure to be fun, exciting and meaningful for students and teachers alike. The book is visually attractive and a delightful and stimulating experience to read.

856. Conn, Walter E. "Affectivity in Kohlberg and Fowler." Religious Education, 76 (1981): 33-48.

Argues that Kohlberg's theory is more deeply rooted in affectivity than is commonly recognized. Fowler's theory, on the other hand, actually eliminates affectivity from analysis of faith.

857. Crisri, Pat E. "Quest: Helping Students Learn Caring and Responsibility." Phi Delta Kappan, 63 (1981): 131-133.

Describes a character education curriculum which focuses on ten areas identified by adolescents as of greatest personal concern. The curriculum focuses on developing self-esteem by enhancing the students ability to cope with these problem areas.

858. Darling, D. W. "Why a Taxonomy of Affective Learning?" Educational Leadership, 22 (1965): 473-522.

Presents a rationale for a taxonomy of affective learning. The taxonomy is seen as focusing on the interests, attitudes and values involved when a child accepts, prefers and makes a commitment to a value.

859. Dickens, Mary E. "Values Schools and Human Development." The Clearing House, 48 (1974): 473-477.

Argues that through reflection about the values we hold we can integrate our knowledge of the disciplines and relate ourselves to our experiences.

860. Dreikurs, R. Character Education and Spiritual Values in an Anxious Age. Boston: Beacon Press, 1952.

Argues for a holistic approach to moral growth, deriving from a base of social interest (Gemeinschaftegefuhl). Any approach to moral education must include an emotional appeal.

861. Dreikurs, R. Psychology in the Classroom. New York: Harper & Row, 1968.

Children become motivated toward proper behavior through a personal and direct experience. Teachers educate morally by allowing children to experience the natural consequences of their social actions.

862. Dupont, Henry. "Affective Development Stage and Sequence." Adolescents' Development and Education (item 1806), pp. 163-183.

Presents a conceptual six stage model affective development: egocentric-impersonal, heteronomous interpersonal, psychological-personal, autonomous, and integrities. This work is tied closely to other cognitive developmentists and represents a useful conceptual framework for those interested in affective education.

863. Ekstein, Rudolf. "Origins of Values." Educational Leadership, 21 (1964): 523-526.

Presents a sketchy psychoanalytic perspective on the formation of individuals and briefly discusses how the schools should deal with student values. Urges self-awareness rather than inculcation.

864. Fedell, John C. and Henry F. Bushy. "Value Changes in a Human Potential Seminar." Fargo, MD: Prince George's Community College, 1975. ED 116 082.

Finds that participants in a human development seminar showed positive value change regarding awareness of one's own value system.

865. Flynn, Elizabeth N. and John F. LaFaso. Designs in Affective Education: A Teacher Resource Program for Junior and Senior High. New York: Paulist Press, 1974.

Presents strategies for use in a variety of educational settings such as values clarification, violence, prejudice, ecology, multicultural education, drug education and city planning.

866. Ginott, Haim. Teacher and Child. New York: Macmillan, 1972.

Tools and skills are offered to help teachers deal with emotional problems in the classroom. Anecdotes and classroom scenes are presented to help teachers focus on congruent communications that fit feelings. Helps teachers find positive ways to respond to children so that self-worth and self-respect are enhanced.

867. Gordon, Ira J. "Affect and Cognition: A Reciprocal Relationship." Educational Leadership, 27 (1970): 661-664.

Argues that the affective and cognitive cannot be responsible and that they depend on each other for enhancement. Effective schooling requires both.

868. Gordon, Thomas. Teacher Effectiveness Training. New York: McKay, 1974.

Describes a humanistic model of effective teacher-student relationships. Involves teachers acquiring skills in verbal communication, active listening, and handling classroom conflict and values collisions in a non-threatening manner.

869. Hargrove, W. R. "Learning in the Affective Domain." Peabody Journal of Education, 47 (1969): 144-146.

Five affective goals for schools are presented. Among these is the development of values and behaviors necessary for sustaining democracy. Ways of implementing these goals are outlined.

870. Hart, Stuart N., ed. "Affective Education." School Psychology Digest, 7 (Spring 1978).

Contains nine articles which directly address the issue of incorporating affective concerns into school curriculum and practice. The papers describe the need for affective education as well as question the limits in schools.

871. Hartoonian, H. Michael. "A Disclosure Approach to Value Analysis in Social Studies Education: Rationale and Components." Theory and Research in Social Education, 1 (October 1973): 1-25.

Presents an approach to values education which recognizes the personalist and subjective nature of value concepts. A value-continua technique is recommended through which one comes to some self-understanding of value (disclosure) concepts.

872. Hawley, Robert C. and Isabel L. Hawley. Human Values in the Classroom: A Handbook for Teachers. New York: Hart Publishing Co., 1975.

A practical guide to humanistic teaching featuring topics such as values clarification achievement motivation, building community and fostering open communication.

873. Heath, Douglas H. "Affective Education: Aesthetics and Discipline." School Review, 80 (1972): 353-372.

Traces the reasons for the rise of the affective education movement and sketches out its dimensions. It is argued that there are dangers within the movement for we must not only let our students become more accessable to their inner world but we must also help them escape from the latent narcissim by putting their inner world in some more social communicable form.

874. Heath, Douglas H. Humanizing Schools: New Directions, New Decisions. Rochelle Park, NJ: Hayden Book Co., 1971.

Consists of an argument for the need for humanizing schools. Points to the deepening alienation of youth and societal moral and spiritual vices.

875. Henderson, T. "Review of the Literature on Affective Education." Contemporary Education, 44 (1972): 92-99.

After reviewing the affective education literature, a case is made for training teachers to recognize and express their feelings.

876. Hurst, Barbara M. "An Integrated Approach to the Hierarchial Order of the Cognitive and Affective Domains." Journal of Educational Psychology, 72 (1980): 293-303.

Cites research evidence to indicate that cognitive skills and attitudes are integrally related and built on each other. When analyzing learning tasks it is necessary to analyze both cognitive and affective components and the relationships between them.

877. Inlow, Gail M. Values in Transition: A Handbook. New York: Wiley, 1972.

Presents an approach to values education in the schools where the aim is mental health.

878. Johnson, David W. "The Affective Side of the Schooling Experience." The Elementary School Journal, 73 (1973): 306-313.

Discusses the relationships between affective and cognitive dimensions of schooling and provides an observation framework for assessing the affective dimension of the classroom.

879. Johnson, David W. Reaching Out. Englewood Cliffs, NJ: Prentice Hall, 1972.

Stresses the importance of interpersonal skills for self-actualization and presents a long list of practical activities designed to assist individuals in improving in this area. Includes chapters on self-disclosure, developing and maintaining trust, increasing communication skills, expressing feelings, listening and responding and constructive confrontation.

880. Johnson, David W. and Frank P. Johnson. Joining Together: Group Theory and Group Skills. Englewood Cliffs, NJ: Prentice Hall, 1975.

A practical guide to the effective implementation and maintenance of groups. The focus is practical throughout with chapters on leadership, decision making, problem solving, power, controversy, cohesion, team building, etc.

881. Johnson, David W. and Roger T. Johnson. Learning Together and Alone: Cooperation, Competition and Individualization. Englewood Cliffs, NJ: Prentice Hall, 1975.

Meant to assist teachers in selecting the proper goal structure for classes so as to maximize student emotional and intellectual growth. The positive benefits of a cooperative goal structure is presented and ways of implementing this structure in the class is presented.

882. Johnson, David, and Roger T. Johnson, eds. "Social Interdependence in the Classroom: Cooperation, Competition, and Individualism." Journal of Research and Development in Education, 12,1 (Fall 1978).

Contains a collection of papers on dimensions of cooperative, competitive and individualistic learning.

883. Jones, Richard M. Fantasy and Feeling in Education. New York: Harper Colophon Books, 1970.

Focuses on the failure of the Man: A Course of Study curriculum to recognize the potential that the materials have for fostering the emotional growth of children. Draws heavily upon Erik Erikson's work to butress his criticisms. Specific recommendations for new approaches to affective education are offered.

884. Jordan, D.C., and D.T. Street. "The Anisa Model: A New Basis for Educational Planning." Young Children, 28 (1973): 289-307.

Presents a new vision of the transformation of man. Anisa theories of curriculum and pedagogy are derived from humanistic psychology with the emphasis of translating potentiality into actuality.

885. Joseph, Pamela B. "Teaching Potential Morality: The Problem of Affect." Ph.D. dissertation, Northwestern University, 1978. 39/08, p. 4895.

Argues that affect impedes the development of rational morality and that only by teaching about the emotional and unconscious components of morality can educators help students to establish and live by the ethical system of rational morality.

886. Junell, Joseph S. Matters of Feeling: Values Education Reconsidered. Bloomington, IN: Phi Delta Kappa Foundation, 1979.

Argues that emotions of young children must be made the primary target of public education. Values education must come within the emotional context.

887. Khan, S.B. and Joel Weiss. "The Teaching of Affective Responses." Handbook of Research on Teaching, 2nd ed. Edited by R.M. Travers. Chicago: Rand McNally, 1973, pp. 759-804.

Contains a thorough review of the research on the teaching of affective responses in the schools. Among the topics covered are the concept of attitude and attitude change, antecedents and correlates of school-related affective behaviors and the relationship of affective behavior to learning in different content areas. Problems associated with measurement in the affective domain are discussed and directions for future research are presented.

888. Kirschenbaum, H. "Sensitivity Modules." Media and Methods, 6 (1970): 36-38.

A discussion of the sensitivity module strategy is presented. Examples on the themes of race and poverty are given. The purposes and risks of the strategy are related.

889. Kraft, Arthur. The Living Classroom: Putting Humanistic Education into Practice. New York: Harper and Row, 1975.

A practical book for teachers who wish to become a more humanistic teacher. Contains chapters on leadership styles, self-awareness, facilitating learning, facilitating growth and maturity, reflective listening, congruent message reading, analyzing the underlying needs of students and problem solving.

890. Lickona, Thomas. "Beyond Justice: A Curriculum for Cooperation." Development of Moral Reasoning (item 26), pp. 108-144.

Focuses on the character of relationships in the classroom as a source of moral development. He moves beyond justice and beyond simply reasoning and proposes a curriculum of cooperative moral education. Included are 12 classroom tested strategies for fostering important moral dispositions.

891. Lyon, Harold C. Learning to Feel-Feeling to Learn. Columbus, OH: Charles Merrill, 1971.

Presents a rationale for humanistic education and presents a wide range of approaches for teachers to use in the classroom.

892. Marquess, Alma L. "The Impact of Role Playing on Selected Values Claims Held by Third- and Fifth-Grade Students," Ed.D. dissertation, North Texas State University, 1976. 37/06, p. 3397

On three selected value concepts third graders changed significantly as a result of 30 role-playing episodes on honesty and consideration for others, but not on property. Fifth graders didn't change on any of the concepts.

893. Martin, Barbara L. "Hierarchical Integration of Cognition and Affect." Moral Education Forum, 6 (Fall 1981): 30-35.

Notes that the cognitive and affective domains are rarely integrated in the educational literature. Two hierarchies which integrate cognition and affect are presented as a useful tool for analyzing educational goals.

894. Maslow, Abraham H. Motivation and Personality, 2nd ed. New York: Harper and Row, 1970.

Presents Maslow's influential theory of human motivation based on holistic and dynamic principles. Emphasizing a needs hierarchy and the psychology of health the book offers a standard statement of self-actualization theory and data. Maslow's writings provide the major source of conceptual and theoretical underpinning for the humanistic (third force) movement in psychology.

895. Mich, Thomas B. "Humanities Education for Values Instruction in Light of a Critical Examination of a Values Clarification Technique." Ph.D. dissertation, University of Minnesota, 1977. 38/10, p. 5985.

Reaches the conclusion that humanities education has the potential to assist value development. Claims that humanities education may be a viable alternative to values clarification which is judged as inadequate.

896. Miles, M.B. "The T-Group and the Classroom." T-Group Theory and Laboratory Method. Edited by L.P. Bradford, J.R. Gibb and K.R. Benne. New York: Wiley, 1964.

Contains sensible advice regarding the limitations of applying the T-Group experience in the classroom.

897. Miller, John P. Humanizing the Classroom: Models of Teaching in Affective Education. New York: Praeger, 1976.

Following the presentation of a rationale for affective education four models of teaching for affective goals are presented: Developmental models, self-concept models, a sensitivity and group orientation model and a consciousness expansion model. The book is practical in orientation and represents a good entry point for teachers.

898. Morse, Robert and H.C. Simmons. "Dramatics and Moral Development in Latency-age Children: A Bibliographical Summary." Religious Education, 68 (1973): 69-83.

Presents a review of the literature and concludes that dramatics can make a positive contribution to the emotional, and hence the moral development of the 8 to 12 year old child by enabling him to overcome the sense of inferiority. The literature reviewed is so extensive that the footnotes actually take up more space than the text in the article.

899. Moustakas, Clark E. and Cereta Perry. Learning to be Free. Englewood Cliffs, NJ: Prentice Hall, 1973.

Outlines a philosophy of education which leads to self-awareness and freedom with the concomitant values of commitment, involvement, and active participation. How this philosophy has worked out in two school districts is reported.

900. Ojemann, Ralph H. "Some New Perspectives in Child Development." Theory into Practice, 8 (1969): 192-197.

Suggests that schools should provide opportunities for children to examine critically their ways of living and develop a conception of a plan and purpose for their life.

901. Palomares, Uvaldo H. and Geraldine Ball. Magic Circle: An Overview of the Human Development Program. La Mesa, CA: Human Development Training Institute, 1974.

Provides a description of the Human Development Program with its emphasis on affective educational experiences. The theoretical basis of the program along with descriptions of materials and activities is presented. The "Magic Circle" session, which is at the heart of the program, involves a carefully articulated communications system which encourages individual expression about the childrens feelings about their personal and social world.

902. Palomares, Uvaldo H. and Terri Rubin. "Magic Circle: Key to Understanding Self and Others." Educational Leadership, 32 (1974): 19-21.

Discusses the magic circle which is the key concept in the Human Development Program. The program is designed to develop self-awareness, positive self-concept and supportive interaction in children.

903. Patterson, C.H. Humanistic Education. Englewood Cliffs, NJ: Prentice-Hall, 1973.

A scholarly, tightly reasoned introduction to humanistic education. Contains discussions of early and recent developments in humanistic education, the necessary conditions for learning and self-actualization, necessary changes in educational practice, evaluating humanistic learning and the preparation of humanistic teachers.

904. Phenix, Phillip H. "Perceptions of an Ethicist about the Affective." Feeling, Valuing and the Art of Growing: Insights into the Affective. Edited by Louise M. Berman and Jessie A. Roderick. Washington, D.C.: Association for Supervision and Curriculum Development, 1977, pp. 59-81. ED 133 880.

Proposes five levels or modes of affect and their ethical correlates. For each mode the implications for schooling is also discussed.

905. Presno, Vincent and Carol Presno. The Value Realms. New York: Teachers College Press, 1980.

Presents a unified approach to values based on nine value realms: Psychological, social, economic, ethical, social ethical, esthetic technological and legal. Activities are presented for helping students develop values in each of these realms.

906. Read, Donald A. and Sidney B. Simon, eds. Humanistic Education Sourcebook. Englewood Cliffs, NJ: Prentice-Hall, 1975.

Contains 53 papers covering a wide range of issues and approaches related to humanistic. The papers discuss such topics as the facilitation of learning, confluent education, values clarification, teacher as therapist, sensitivity training, teaching with feeling and experiential learning.

907. Ringness, Thomas A. The Affective Domain in Education. Boston: Little Brown and Co., 1975.

Presents a comprehensive analysis of the role of the affective domain in education. Sections of the book focus on the nature and importance of affective learning, affective behavior from the behavioral point of view, humanism and the affective domain, and improving one's affective competence.

908. Rogers, Carl R. "Toward a Modern Approach to Values: The Valuing Process in the Mature Person." Readings in Values Clarification (item 212), pp. 75-91.

In most adults, it is argued the values held are introjected; that is, absorbed unreflectively from others, mostly adult or parent figures. These introjected values are held without consideration of their relationship to one's inner organismic reactions. Rogers urges that we hold to values that have a direct relationship to our existence as an experiencing being. Also Journal of Abnormal and Social Psychology, 68 (1974).

909. Samples, Robert. "Psychology, Thought, and Morality: Some Limitations of Piaget and Kohlberg." Readings in Moral Education (item 449), pp. 220-229.

Urges a movement away from reductionist psychologies and toward a holistic, synegistic approach to education and humanness.

910. Samples, Robert E. "Values Prejudice: Toward A Personal Awareness." Media and Methods, 2 (September 1974): 14-48; 45-52.

Claims that personal experiences indicate that a person's most significant decisions are based on emotion and intuition and not on logic and rationality.

Argues that teachers should become more sensitive to the emotional drives that engage student value structures.

911. Shaftel, Fannie R. and George Shaftel. Role-Playing for Social Values: Decision-Making in the Social Studies. Englewood Cliffs, NJ: Prentice Hall, 1967.

Presents the theory behind role playing, a practical guide for implementing role-playing in the classroom, and stories to serve as the forms of classroom activities. A well conceived, thoughtful and practical book for teachers.

912. Sharan, S. "Cooperative Learning in Teams: A Critical Review of Recent Methods and Effects in Achievement, Attitudes and Race/Ethnic Relations." Review of Educational Research, 50 (1980): 241-272.

Finds from a review of 28 field evaluations that cooperative education produces better academic achievement, intergroup relations, higher self-esteem, and prosocial behavior.

913. Simpson, Elizabeth Leonie. "Creativogenic School: Developing Positive Human Personality." Readings in Moral Education (item 449), pp. 210-218.

Creativogenic schools are schools which optimize creative human potential--they help students find their identity and become a unified being. Presents descriptions of schools where confluent education is in place and methods used in facilitating confluent development.

914. Simpson, Elizabeth Leonie. "A Holistic Approach to Moral Development and Behavior." Moral Development and Behavior (item 1801), pp. 159-170.

Discusses the need for moral development to be seen as a total personality development, not just a cognitive process. Argues for a cognitive-affective integration in the study and practice of moral education. Gives special attention to imagination in moral life.

915. Simpson, Elizabeth L. and Mary A. Gray. Humanistic Education: An Interpretation. Cambridge, MA: Ballinger Publishing Co., 1976.

Following an attempt to define humanistic education, nine exemplary programs are reviewed. A number of college programs attempting to produce humanistic teachers is also reviewed. Finally an extensive annotated bibliography of sources on humanistic education is reviewed.

916. Slavin, Robert. "A Policy Choice: Cooperative or Competitive Learning." Character, 2 (January 1981): 1-6.

Reports on the beneficial effects of cooperative patterns of learning and suggests that a new shift in educational policy is required to implement this for education to the benefit of students. Also in Character Policy (item 1061).

917. Strasser, Ben E. and Gus T. Dalis. Dalstra Values Awareness Teaching Strategy: Inservice Education Program. Los Angeles: Los Angeles County Superintendent of Schools, 1977. ED 153 956 - ED 153 964.

A series of pamplets comprising an inservice program in values education. The Dalstra program is based on the premise that values arise out of self-awareness. These values are then, in turn, used to understand the world.

918. Tolliver, J. Howard. "Confluent/Humanistic/Affective Education: A Set of Bibliographies." Baltimore, MD: Morgan State University, 1979. ED 170 219.

Contains 250 entries under such headings as values clarification, self-concept, self-actualization, attitudes, self-disclosure and general affective education.

919. Ulshak, Francis and John Nicholos. "Transactional Analysis: A Framework for Ethical Decision-Making." Morality Examined (item 1818), pp. 155-176.

Describes how teachers may use transactional analysis to teach students to view ethical decisions in a direct manner. The goals are to get students and teachers actively examining and making decisions for action. The teacher is to serve as a model of the "integrated adult" for students.

920. Ward, J.K. "Beyond Moral Reasoning and Values Analysis: Toward Affective Social Education." Paper presented at the Annual Meeting of the National Council for the Social Studies, Atlanta, 1957. ED 115 533.

Argues that a purely cognitive approach to values education ignores the affective nature of many of the problems faced by individuals and society.

921. Weinstein, Gerald. "Trumpet: A Guide to Humanistic Psychological Curriculum." Theory into Practice, 10 (1971): 196-203.

A strategy for selecting and sequencing activities that will lead to expansion of an individual's response pattern is described.

922. Weinstein, Gerald and Fantini, Mario D. Toward Humanistic Education: A Curriculum of Affect. New York: Praeger, 1970.

Presents an account of the Elementary School Teaching Project designed to meet the needs primarily of disadvantaged youth which is based on the affective domain of learning. Elucidates a model for developing a curriculum of affect, and explains concrete ways of implementing the model in the classroom.

923. Weller, Richard H., ed. Humanistic Education: Visions and Realities. Berkeley: McCutchan Publishing Co., 1977.

A series of papers delivered at the 1976 Phi Delta Kappa National Symposium on Humanistic Education. Each of the papers is followed by the transcription of lively discussion by conference participants.

924. Wight, Albert R. "Affective Goals of Education." Salt Lake City, UT: Interstate Educational Resource Service Center, 1971. ED 069 733.

Presents a broad overview of noncognitive goals and objectives in education.

Value Analysis: Theory, Practice, and Research

925. Applegate, Terry P. "The Development of a Criterion-Referenced Value Analysis Workshop for Secondary Teachers and Administrators." Ph.D. dissertation, University of Utah, 1980. 41/04, p. 1543.

Teachers and administrators participated in a workshop whose purpose was to achieve correct understanding and correct usage of concepts associated with the four standards of rationality when making a value judgment. Over 90 percent of participants achieved the 80 percent criterion.

926. Aron, Israela. "Curricular Proposals for the Ethical and Political Education of Adolescents: Overcoming Dogmatism and Relativism, and Teaching Deweyan Deliberation." Ph.D. dissertation, University of Chicago, 1975. 36/07, p. 4211.

Focuses on the dogmatism and relativism of adolescents and proposes ways of educationally intervening based on the Deweyan method of deliberation.

927. Bruneau, William A. "The Origins and Growth of the Association for Values Education and Research (AVER)." Moral Education Forum, 2 (September, 1977): 5-8.

928. Casteel, J. Doyle and Robert J. Stahl. Value Clarification in the Classroom: A Primer. Pacific Palisades, CA: Goodyear Publishing, 1975.

Presents an approach to values clarification different from that of Raths, Harmin and Simon (item 227). The approach offered suggests four phases of value clarification: comprehension, relational, valuation and reflective. Major portion of the book consists of thirty-nine interesting value sheets for use in the classroom. The resemblance to values clarification of the approach described is in name only.

929. Casteel, J. Doyle et al. Value Clarification in the Social Studies: Six Formats of the Values Sheet. Gainesville, FL: Florida Educational Research and Development Council, 1974. ED 097 263.

Six different formats are presented: standard, forced-choice, affirmative rank order, criterion and classification. Practical examples of each format are included.

930. Chadwick, James and Milton Muex. "Procedures for Value Analysis." Values Education: Rationale, Strategies and Procedures (item 953), pp. 75-119.

Presents two procedures, the rudimentary and extended, for implementing value analysis in the classroom. Extensive examples are presented.

931. Chapman, Marion L. and Florence V. Davis. "Skills for Ethical Action: A Process Approach to Judgment and Action." Educational Leadership, 35 (1978): 457-461.

A program for developing ethical action--doing something that you have decided is fair after considering the possible effects on self and others--is presented. The six step process is described.

932. Chapman, Marion L. and Florence V. Davis. Skills for Ethical Action: A Rationale. Philadelphia: Research for Better Schools. 1977.

Describes the rationale for the Skills for Ethical Action program. The six step strategy presented is: 1) identify the problem, 2) think up action ideas, 3) consider self and others, 4) judge, 5) act, and 6) evaluate.

933. Coombs, Jerrold R. "Cognitive-Decision Theorists' Approach to Moral/Citizenship Education." Paper presented at Moral/Citizenship Conference, Philadelphia, 1976. ED 178 456.

Presents the cognitive-decision approach which holds that the primary goal of moral education is to teach students to make and act on rational decisions about moral questions. Strengths and weaknesses of the approach are discussed.

934. Coombs, Jerrold R. "Objectives of Value Analysis." Values Education: Rationale, Strategies and Procedures (item 953), pp. 1-28.

Anyone taking a value position commits themselves to certain factual and evaluative statements. Discussed are ways of determining the acceptability of factual and value statements and of the structure of moral reasoning.

935. Coombs, Jerrold R. "Validating Moral Judgments By Principle Testing." Development of Moral Reasoning (item 26), pp. 30-55.

Presents four tests by which one can judge if the principle used in one's moral reasoning meets the necessary standards for moral rules as set out by Coombs. The four tests are: 1) New Cases Test, 2) Role Exchange Test, 3) Universal Consequences Test and 4) Subsumption Test. Each of the tests is explained and general guidelines for using them appropriately are offered. See also item 936.

936. Coombs, Jerrold R. and Milton Meux. "Teaching Strategies for Value Analysis." Values Education: Rationale Strategies and Procedures (item 953), pp. 29-74.

Identifies and discusses the six tasks which must be carried out in any evaluative decision making process.

937. Crittenden, Brian. "A Comment on Cognitive Moral Education." Phi Delta Kappan, 56 (1975): 695-696.

Takes issue with Scriven (item 962) on three points: his argument against the developmentalists, his confidence in a clear-cut rational justification for moral beliefs and his separation of affective and cognitive aspects of moral judgment and action.

938. Ennis, Robert H. Logic in Teaching. Englewood Cliffs, NJ: Prentice Hall, 1969.

Undoubtedly the most thorough and comprehensive analysis of the incorporation of principles of logic and reasoning into the curriculum. The book's approach is grounded in philosophical analysis of logical argument. What it means to engage in teaching for logical thinking is presented in fine detail.

939. Evans, William K. "The Effect of Value Analysis Instruction on the Capabilities of Students for Rational Analysis of Controversial Issues." Ph.D. dissertation, University of Utah, 1978. 39/10, p. 6049.

As a result of training in values analysis high school students increased in the ability to make rational value judgments as measured by a Value Reasoning Test and a class project.

940. Evans, W. Keith and Terry P. Applegate. "Value Decisions and the Acceptability of Value Principles," Value Concepts and Techniques (item 1784), pp. 148-158.

Presents a six-step procedure for making rational value decisions. Borrows heavily from Coombs (item 934).

941. Fraenkel, Jack R. "Analyzing Value Conflict." Values Concepts and Techniques (item 1784), pp. 77-86.

An excerpt from Fraenkel's book How to Teach About Values (item 943) where he presents an example of the values analysis approach to exploring value conflict situations.

942. Fraenkel, Jack R. Helping Students Think and Value, 2nd ed. Englewood Cliffs, NJ: 1980.

One of the standard social studies methods textbooks. Chapter 5, entitled "Teaching Strategies for Developing Valuing" surveys a variety of approaches, but is essentially value analysis in flavor.

943. Fraenkel, Jack. How to Teach About Values: An Analytic Approach. Englewood Cliffs, NJ: Prentice-Hall, 1977.

Presents value analysis as an approach to values education. Also presented is values clarification and a cognitive-developmental approach.

944. Fraenkel, Jack R. "Now Is Not the Time to Set Aside Values Education." Social Education, 45 (1981): 101-108.

Presents the argument that the major failing of contemporary approaches to values education is their overly cognitive emphasis. Moral education should take a more comprehensive approach focusing not only on cognitive ability in analyzing value issues but also on developing the desire to want to analyze value issues.

945. Fraenkel, Jack. "Strategies for Developing Values." Today's Education, 63 (November/December, 1973): 49-55.

Presents an approach to values education which emphasizes helping students to evaluate alternatives, consequences and conclusions.

946. Fraenkel, Jack R., Margaret Carter and Betty Reardon. The Struggle for Human Rights: A Question of Values. New York: Random House, Institute for World Order, 1978. ED 170 180.

Intended for secondary school students this pamphlet examines the status of the world community in upholding the promise of the U.N.'s "Universal Declaration of Human Rights." This booklet exemplifies the value analysis approach to values education.

947. Hullfish, H. Gordon and Phillip G. Smith. Reflective Thinking: The Method of Education. New York: Dodd, Mead and Co., 1963.

Analyzes the act of reflection and the role of synthetic, analytic and value judgments in warrenting belief. Also discussed is how to incorporate reflective thinking into classroom teaching. Contains an excellent discussion on the criteria of warranted judgments.

948. Hunt, Blanch S. "Effects of Values Activities on Content Retention and Attitudes of Students in Junior High Social Studies Classes." Ph.D. dissertation, Arizona State University, 1981. 42/02, p. 646.

Finds that values dilemma activities based upon the Casteel-Stahl approach to values education do have effects on the attitudes of students toward themselves, their values and their personal and social skills in selected areas.

949. Hunt, Maurice and Lawrence E. Metcalf. Teaching High School Social Studies, 2nd ed. New York: Harper and Row, 1968.

Presents an approach to social studies which holds that reflective thought as applied to social areas normally closed to inquiry should be at the heart of social education. A model of value inquiry which focuses on the appraisal of consequences is presented.

950. Irvin, Judith L. "The Effects of Value Analysis Procedures Upon Students' Achievement in Reading Comprehension." Ph.D. dissertation, Florida State University, 1980. 41/07, p. 3025.

No significant differences were detected in reading comprehension in groups which used the value analysis approach and the traditional basal approach.

951. Lange, Deborah. "Moral Education and the Social Studies." Theory into Practice, 14 (1975): 279-285.

Analyzes the contribution of the reflectivists--primarily Hunt and Metcalf (item 949) to the treatment of moral argument in social studies education.

952. Massialas, B.G. and C.B. Cox. "Approaches to a Systematic Analysis of Values." Inquiry in Social Studies. New York: McGraw Hill, 1966, pp. 153-178.

Presents a reflective thinking model for adjudicating value disputes which emphasizes intellectualizing value alternatives--by linking them to more important values, by making explicit certain assumptions and scrutinizing them carefully, by defining terms, and by marshalling evidence when matters of an empirical nature are at issue.

953. Metcalf, Lawrence E., ed. Values Education: Rationale Strategies and Procedures. 41st Yearbook of the National Council for the Social Studies. Washington, D.C.: National Council for the Social Studies, 1971.

A collection of related papers in the objectives, teaching strategies, and procedures of values analysis. Also contains chapter on methods of resolving value conflicts. The approach is highly structured and intricate, and takes a formalistic position on warranting value claims. Much emphasis is devoted to the accumulation and evaluation of evidence.

954. Meux, Milton. "Resolving Value Conflicts." Values Education: Rationale, Strategies and Procedures (item 953), pp. 120-166.

Presents strategies for resolving value conflicts. Includes an example of how suggested procedures operate in a classroom situation.

955. Nelson, Jack L. Introduction to Value Inquiry: A Student Process Book. Rochelle Park, NJ: Hayden Book Co., 1974.

Presents a value analysis approach to analyzing social issues.

956. Newmann, Fred M. Clarifying Public Controversy: An Approach to Teaching Social Studies. Boston: Little Brown, 1970.

Describes an approach to the teaching of social studies which focuses on the discussion of public issues as citizenship education. Included is a section ensuring that one's discussions are productive (leading to greater clarity) and on special problems encountered in dealing with moral-value issues. Over half the book consists of a discussion of the issues related to substantive areas such as equality, property, morality-responsibility, etc. The method advocated is that of the jurisprudential approach of the Harvard Social Studies Project (item 958).

957. Oliver, Don, and Fred M. Newmann. Taking a Stand (Public Issues Series). Columbus, OH: Xerox Education Publications, 1967.

A practical guide to productive discussion of public controversy in pamphlet form. An excellent resource out of the Harvard Social Studies Project for teachers and secondary school students.

958. Oliver, Don W., and James P. Shaver. Teaching Public Issues in the High School. Boston: Houghton Mifflin Co., 1966.

Reports on the curriculum development and evaluation of the Harvard Social Studies Project. The theoretical framework for the jurisprudential approach is presented, as is how the theory was operationalized into curriculum. Finally the evaluation of the curriculum, which was inconclusive, is discussed.

959. Pearce, Janice. "Values Education: Extending the View." Journal of School Health, 49 (1979): 169-173.

Presents a summary of the Shaver and Strong (item 134) approach to values education.

960. Ruggiero, Vincent R. The Moral Imperative. Port Washington, NY: Alfred Publishing Co., 1973.

Presents a method for solving ethical issues and a series of ethical problems for consideration. The author presents moral principles which he feels should be used to make value judgments: obligations should be followed, ideals should be served, harmful actions evaded, and the person and the action should be considered as separate.

961. Sayre, Joan M. Teaching Moral Values Through Behavior Modification: Intermediate Level. Danville, IL: Interstate, 1972.

Has nothing to do with behavior modification, but rather is a values analysis approach where students (grades 3 to 5) are asked to confront problem situations and better understand the value dimensions involved.

962. Scriven, Michael. "Cognitive Moral Education." Moral Education ... It Comes with the Territory (item 1811), pp. 313-329.

Sketches out three approaches to moral education: affectivism, developmentalism and cognitivism. Presents the cognitivist perspective and critiques the other two approaches from that perspective. The cognitive curriculum consists of developing: 1) understanding of facts, arguments and positions, 2) cognitive skills of moral reasoning, and 3) metaethics. Also in Phi Delta Kappan, 56 (1975).

963. Shaver, James P., and A. Guy Larkins. The Analysis of Public Issues: Concepts, Materials, Research. Final Report. Logan, UT: Utah State University, 1969. ED 037 475.

Describes a replication of the Oliver and Shaver study (item 958) of the Public Issues Approach. Again no significant treatment effects were detected.

964. Shaver, James P., and A. Guy Larkins. Decision Making in a Democracy. Boston: Houghton Mifflin, 1973.

A textbook meant for high school social studies which attempts to develop decision making skills from the framework developed in the Harvard Social Studies Project (item 958). Contains section on the nature of public controversy, resolving factual, definitional and valuational disagreements, and improving communication.

965. Shaver, James P., and A. Guy Larkins. Instructor's Manual: The Analysis of Public Issues Program. Boston: Houghton Mifflin, 1973.

Accompanies Decision-Making in a Democracy (item 964).

966. Simon, Frank, and Ian Wright. "Moral Education: Problem Solving and Survivial." Journal of Moral Education, 3 (1974): 241-248.

Presents a problem solving approach to moral education in which the desirability of the policy change contained in the 'should' question is examined through the use of the survival value criterion.

967. Stahl, Robert J. "Achieving Values and Content Objectives Simultaneously Within Subject Matter-Oriented Social Studies Classrooms." Social Education, 45 (1981): 580-585.

Using a cognitive social inquiry approach to values education (item 928) which attempts to integrate values education within ongoing content oriented social studies curriculum it was found that the experimental classes scored significantly higher on the content post-test and possessed significantly more positive attitudes and self reports.

968. Stahl, Robert J. "Developing Values Dilemmas for Content-Centered Social Studies Instruction: Theoretical Construct and Practical Applications." Theory and Research in Social Education, 7 (Summer 1979): 50-75.

A "verbal evidence" or "cognitive" approach to values/moral education is presented. In this approach content centered values dilemmas are used to develop both understanding of subject matter content and values reasoning ability.

969. Stahl, Robert J. "Using Questions to Guide Content-Centered Discussions." NASSP Bulletin, 63 (October 1979): 6-15.

Presents eight types of questions which reflect values/moral education goals and also are compatible with content-centered instruction.

970. Stahl, Robert J. "Values/Moral Education: A Synthesis Model." Washington, DC: ERIC Clearinghouse on Teacher Education, 1976. SP 010 430.

Presents a model that synthesizes values clarification and cognitive moral development is presented. The suggested strategy focuses on the development of moral reasoning in four places: conceptual, relational, moral reasoning and moral reflective phase.

971. Stenhouse, Lawrence. "Controversial Issues in the Classroom." Values and the Curriculum (item 1786), pp. 103-115.

Argues that teachers should avoid indoctrination of all sorts in discussing value issues. Also emphasized is avoiding group exercises because of peer pressure, and protecting the privacy of the students.

972. VanSickle, Ronald L. "Experiental Concreteness and the Presentation of Values Dilemmas to Slow Learning Students." Social Education, 42 (1978): 64-6.

Focuses on the question of given five presentations of a physically, psychologically and socially distant value dilemma, which is the most effective in facilitating the achievement of slow learners of the descriptive preconditions of values analysis? It was found that experientially concrete presentations did not produce greater learning effects.

973. Woods, Michael J. "The Categorization of Students' Points of View in the Process of Value Analysis." Ed.D. dissertation, University of Illinois, 1979. 40/10, p. 5395.

Assessed the point of view (personal, social and moral) that subjects bring to bear in making a moral judgment as a result of the process of value analysis. It was found that students were the most rational in three cases which were furthest from their experience. Because level of proximity was so influential to point of view it was not possible to identify the impact of values analysis.

974. Wright, Ian. "There's More to Moral/Values Education than ..." History and Social Science Teacher, 13 (1977): 33-42.

Argues that values clarification and the cognitive-developmental approaches do not go far enough in teaching the skills and procedures for reasoning intelligently about value questions and moral issues. AVER's components of moral competency are presented. These components place Wright and AVER in the value analysis school.

975. Wright, Ian. "Value/Moral Education in Canada: The Work of AVER" Journal of Moral Education, 6 (1976): 32-42.

Discusses the work of the Association for Values Education and Research--an interdisciplinary group of researchers located at the University of British Columbia. Their program is based on a list of components of moral competency somewhat similar to Wilson's (item 1116). Curriculum units and teacher training are described.

976. Alabama State Department of Education. Guide for Teaching Ethics and Moral Values in the Alabama Schools. Montgomery, AL: State Department of Education, 1974. ED 191 768.

Presents nine values lessons suitable for all grade levels. The thrust of the lessons is to develop proper attitudes in such areas as sportsmanship, honesty, respect for others, reverence etc.

977. Allport, Gordon. "Values and Our Youth." Teachers College Record, 63 (1961): 211-217.

Defines value as "meanings perceived as related to self" and relates this to curriculum and to teachers as exemplar. Discusses learning values as an internalization process.

978. Arnspiger, Robert H. "Education in Human Values." School and Community, 58 (May 1972): 16-17.

Describes a theoretical framework and outlines a program in values for a junior high school which is based on Laswell's eight values (item 1018). It is argued that all individuals must come to share these values or they will not be able to achieve a satisfying life in our society.

979. Bennett, William J. "The Teacher, the Curriculum, and Values Education Development." New Directions in Higher Education, Rethinking College Responsibilities for Values, no. 31 (item 1593), pp. 27-34.

If one wants to influence character in schools one must provide people who know what good behavior is, who make some effort to live a good life, and have some interest in instilling in others the same set of dispositions. Curriculum, program, courses and the like have none of the moral power of example.

980. Bensley, Marvin L. Coronado Plan: Teacher's Guide. San Deigo: Pennant, 1974.

Consists of four teacher's guides and one unit guide which attempt to fuse drug abuse instruction with a valuing program based on the Laswell-Rucker categories (item 1041). The approach described attempts to inculcate specific values in students.

981. Berkowitz, Leonard. Development of Motives and Values in the Child. New York: Basic Books, 1964.

Argues that to attempt to raise children in a home in which every childish desire is gratified or to put one's faith in some mystical growth process is to do the child a disservice. Research is cited to show that parents and teachers must impose standards on children for them to become achievement oriented and socially responsible.

982. Beversluis, Eric H. "The Dilemma of Values Clarification." Philosophy of Education 1978 (item 1792), pp. 417-427.

Argues that values clarification theorists cannot hold to a commitment to extreme moral autonomy and at the same time put certain constraints on the behavior of children. The way out of this dilemma for Beversluis is to hold that there is some objective basis for morality--thus one can help children to understand the basis for values. This way one can impose values on children when they do not yet have a full understanding.

983. Blackham, Garth J. and Aldolph Silberman. Modification of Child and Adolescent Behavior, 2nd ed. Belmont, CA: Wadsworth Publishing Co., 1975.

Presents a detailed and practical guide to the use of behavior modification in the classroom. Many examples of the shaping of social behaviors are presented. The book contains excellent references on the theory and practice of behavior modification.

984. Block, Virginia. "Responsibility Management: The Primary Object of Moral Education." Journal of Moral Education, 7 (1978): 166-181.

Argues that people should be held unconditionally or "ascriptively" responsible, eliminating all excusing conditions. Holds that moral education is best understood as a persuasive cultural influence. Excusing conditions increase social deviance, teachers should hold students morally responsible for their actions.

985. Brandt, Elizabeth R. et al., eds. Value-Sharing: A Creative Strategy for American Education. Evanston, IL: National College of Education, 1969.

Describes an approach to values education based on Laswell's eight universal values. The focus of the approach is to have the teacher and school, through curriculum and school practices to share and examine the eight values.

986. Brayer, Herbert O. and Zella W. Cleary. Valuing in the Family: A Workshop Guide for Parents. San Diego: Pennant Press, 1972.

A workshop guide designed to help parents or teachers instill the eight universal values identified by Laswell (item 1018). Each of the values receives attention in a separate chapter which presents specific activities for developing the value.

987. Bruening, William H. "Can Values Be Taught?" No source or date. ED 164 397.

Argues that it is doubtful that schools can teach values. The philosophic and psychological literature suggest that students will best learn values by observing the behavior of ethical people.

988. Bull, Norman J. Moral Education. Beverly Hills, CA: Sage Publications, 1969.

One of the few sources on moral education which faces straight on the need for heteronomy (morality imposed from without) as a prerequisite for latter autonomy in adult morality. Presents a four stage theory of moral development (anomy, heteronomy, socionomy and autonomy) based on author's own interview data. Argues that only through the imposed discipline of the heteronomy stage can the necessary internal discipline develop. Practical guidance for the practice of moral education at different developmental levels is offered.

989. Burkholder, Suzanne, Kevin Ryan and Virgil E. Blanke. "Values, the Key to a Community." Phi Delta Kappan, 62 (1981): 483-485.

Reports on the work of the Phi Delta Kappa Commission on the Teaching of Morals, Values, and Ethics. The work of the Commission has been primarily to help communities to discover core values and to develop a questionnaire which would identify a common attitude toward the teaching of values.

990. Campbell, Donald T. "On the Conflicts Between Biological and Social Evolution and Between Psychology and Moral Tradition." American Psychologist, 30 (1975): 1103-1126.

Argues that human evolution has to a great extent been due to social evolution which is based on cooperation. Social evolution has occurred due to the resolution between the necessity for biological selfishness balanced by the need for social cooperation. Argues that socialization should not be seen as bad but rather as necessary.

991. Caws, Peter. "On the Teaching of Ethics in a Pluralistic Society." Hastings Center Report, 8 (October 1978): 32-39.

Argues that people need to be told that there are such things as moral principles, that they ought to be followed, and that to first approximation, they say thus and so. Ours is not a morally pluralistic society because it is not a rationally pluralistic society. What we do have is a pluralism of values, but this does not imply a pluralism of morals. Morality can best be understood as the system of rules under which the competition for value takes place.

992. Christenson, Reo M. "McGuffey's Ghost and Moral Education Today." Phi Delta Kappan, 58 (1977): 737-742.

Argues that there exist values that all members of a community can accept. These values, it is argued, should be the focus of moral education. Books stressing important values are seen as significant means for transmitting these values to children.

993. Clark, David B. "Social Education: An Experiment with Early School Leavers." Journal of Moral Education, 2 (1973): 243-253.

Argues that inspite of the appearance of new and valuable moral education material for use in the schools, nothing can take the place of an extended opportunity to live out and identify with an adult role in a real life situation. Such a program is described.

994. Donovan, C.F. "On the Possibility of Moral Education." Educational Theory, 12 (1962): 184-186.

Morality cannot be taught as facts can. It can however be inculcated by example, inspiration, contagian. If virtue cannot be taught in the school, it cannot be taught anywhere.

995. Drakeford, John W. Integrity Therapy. Nashville, TN: Broadman Press, 1967.

A model of therapy which emphasized individual responsibility for change, acceptance of a set of American values, group processes and modeling of behavior is presented. The therapy described is taken from the work of O. Hobart Mower.

996. Dunlop, Francis. "Moral Personhood: A Tentative Analysis." Journal of Moral Education. 11(1981): 3-17.

Presents a brief analysis of moral experience and moral agency yielding a set of 'moral components'. The analysis stresses the importance of moral character and the need to instill in children a fundamental moral character based on social consensus.

997. Educational Policies Commission. Moral and Spiritual Values in the Public Schools. Washington, DC: National Education Association, 1951.

In a response to the cold war mentality of the 1950s an appeal is issued for a renewed appreciation and dedication to the common faith of American democracy. Ten values are listed that are held to be generally accepted by all Americans. Moralization and the use of reactions are recommended to gain allegiance to the values suggested.

998. Eysenck, H.J. "The Development of Morality in Adolescence." <u>McGill Journal of Education</u>, 15 (1980): 163-168.

Argues that the decline in the moral character of youth is due to either weaker conditioning in the home and society or a genetic factor which renders individuals less susceptible to the influence of conditioning. Argues that there is a need to strengthen our conditioning procedures, especially, stronger conditioning is needed for those with genetic defects.

999. Farr, Bernard. "Is Moral Education an Impossible Dream?" <u>Journal of Moral Education</u>, 3 (1974): 223-228.

Presents observations on moral education and autonomy with reference to the Schools Council Moral Education Project 'Lifeline'. Argues that moral education because it is essentially social, is incompatible with autonomy. Social training is the essence of moral education.

1000. Fiordo, Richard. "Integrity Training: A Moral Code and Method for Moral Education." <u>Journal of Educational Thought</u>, 15 (1981): 47-60.

Relates O. Hobart Mower's Integrity Training (item 995) to moral education. In this form of therapy it is held that moral education must take a position--some morals are superior to others. In integrity training, a standard for superior conduct is presented as well as a methodology for attaining it.

1001. Gayer, Nancy. "On Making Morality Operational." <u>Phi Delta Kappan</u>, 46 (1964): 42-47.

Discusses teaching strategies related to planned and unplanned modes of instruction. Distinguishes between the words "authoritarian" and "authority" and recommends the latter as being extremely important in a program of moral education. Proposes a program of children-made rules but insists that the teacher's manditory rules must circumscribe the children's area of freedom.

1002. Gordon, J.W. "Values in the Classroom." National Elementary Principal, 42 (1962): 30-34.

Describes forces that affect values development in the classroom. An illustrative list of values children should hold is presented. Teacher behaviors which strengthen childrens' valuing processes are presented

1003. Gorsuch, Richard L. "Moral Education from a Psychological View of Man as an Ethical Being." Educational Forum, 37 (1973): 169-181.

Argues that the kind of ethical principles found in the mature individuals of our society should be what schools should communicate to children.

1004. Gow, Kathleen. Yes Virginia, There is a Right and Wrong. New York: Wiley, 1980.

Presents a criticism of the three major approaches to values education: values clarification, moral reasoning approach and the reflective inquiry approach. These approaches are criticized for their lack of substantive values and implementation without community input. Gow also eschews sanctimonious lists of pious platitudes. Instead she favors acceptance of the existence of a certain core of moral principles and the need to use this base in order to examine situations. Gow spells out eight objective values which all societies hold in common.

1005. Hawley, Robert C. Human Values in the Classroom: Teaching for Personal and Social Growth. Amherst, MA: Education Research Associates, 1973.

While urging some clarification of values, Hawley emphasizes the internalization of love, cooperation, trust, compromise, truth, dignity, joy, and reverence. Suggestions are presented for teaching and structuring the educational environment to inculcate these values.

1006. Hogan, Robert and David Schroeder. "The Joy of Sex and Other Modern Fables." Character, 1 (August 1980): 1-8.

Examines critically the permissive value-free orientation to sexual behavior and sex education. Argues that sexual behavior has always been regulated by society for obvious and socially beneficial reasons. Suggestions for a socially responsible approach to sex education are presented. Also in Character Policy (item 1061).

1007. Hudson, W.D. "Trusting to Reason: An Unfashionable Approach to Political, Moral and Religious Education." New Universities Quarterly, 34 (1980): 241-257.

Argues that it is doubtful that one can teach pupils how to think without teaching them what to think. It is shown how, in one sense, teaching students what to think is not indoctrination and will not inhibit pupils reasoning powers or critical facilities. Teachers must show school children how to hold beliefs in a reasonable manner.

1008. Jensen, Larry C. What's Right? What's Wrong?: A Psychological Analysis of Moral Behavior. Washington, D.C.: Public Affairs Press, 1975.

A review of how to teach people to be moral is presented. Based on psychological evidence it is concluded that the process of induction is the preferred way.

1009. Jensen, Larry C. and Norma P. Johnston. "Moral Education in the Elementary School: Sharing Behavior as an Exemplar." Education, 100 (1980): 314-325.

Empirical and theoretical literature about sharing behavior is reviewed and practical suggestions for implementing instruction are derived. Teacher modeling and reinforcing student behavior are emphasized.

1010. Junnell, Joseph S. "Can Our Schools Teach Moral Commitment?" Phi Delta Kappan, 50 (1969): 446-451.

Argues that the drift of college students from traditional to emergent values is leading to social disaster. He argues that by offering models for identification, key basic values could be fostered in schools.

1011. Kay, William A. Moral Development. New York: Schocken Books, 1969.

Describes and discusses the principal research studies of children's moral development. Argues that there are three clearly discernable stages of moral development present in school age children: amoral, premoral and moral. It is seen as necessary that school compensate for the failure of families and inculcate middle class values. Beyond that, schools should develop autonomy, rationality, responsibility and rational autonomy.

1012. Kehoe, John. "Multiculturalism and the Problems of Ethical Relativism." History and Social Science Teacher, 13 (1977): 33-42.

Argues that schools should teach children to be cultural relativists on all issues but ethical issues. On ethical issues be advocates teaching specific moral rules--with reservations, of course.

1013. Kohn, Kanwar H., and Joseph C. Canegemi. "Social Learning Theory: The Role of Imitation and Modeling in Learning Socially Desirable Behavior." Education, 100 (1979): 41-46.

Argues that modeling and imitation learning is the method by which the majority of socially desirable behaviors are learned. The concepts of identification and imitation are discussed.

1014. Kristol, Irving. "Moral and Ethical Development in a Democratic Society." Moral Education ... It Comes with thc Territory (item 1811), pp. 370-395.

Laments the current permissive attitude of letting morality happen. Urges that teachers should educate from a position of moral authority--if they do not they abrogate their responsibility.

1015. Kupperman, Joel J. "Inhibition." Oxford Review of Education, 4 (1978): 277-287.

Presents the argument that there are strong practical reasons for centering the teaching of morality on simple moral rules, and for inculcating inhibitions about breaking these rules. The thrust of the article is Aristotelian in nature.

1016. Lampe, Philip E. "Values, Morals, and Religion in the Social Studies." Social Studies, 68 (1977): 193-196.

If a teacher fails to admit the existence of society's values to students, then he or she is teaching them by omission that either there are no values or that it really does not matter what one's values are. The teacher must convey a sense of moral norms.

1017. Larsen, Todd S. "The Development of a Values Assessment Device Based upon the Assumptions Underlying the Direct Approach to Moral Education." Ph.D. dissertation, Utah State University, 1981. 42/04, p. 1600.

An objective test was developed for use in grades 5-12 of the Salt Lake City School District which would identify students who exemplify values viewed by the community as essential to adequate socialization. The validity and reliability of the test are reported.

1018. Laswell, H. The World Revolution of Our Time. Palo Alto, CA: Stanford University Press, 1951.

In an attempt to develop a framework for evaluating the world revolution of our time, Laswell proposes eight values which are universal to mankind and enhance human dignity. These values have served as a basis for many of the more directive approaches to moral education.

1019. Leming, James S. "Moral Advocacy and Social Education." Social Education, 45 (1981): 201; 205-207.

Presents an argument for social studies teachers' advocacy of specific moral values in the classroom.

1020. Leming, James S. "On the Limits of Moral Education." Theory and Research in Social Education, 9 (Spring 1981): 7-34.

After noting the paucity of evidence regarding the impact of moral education curricula on social behavior, it is argued that the literature on the development of prosocial behavior provides insights into the essential ingredients for effective moral education.

1021. Liles, Jessee. "A Dilemma of Teaching Values to Young Children." Contemporary Education, 45 (1974): 296-298.

In teaching values to young children teachers must use nonrational strategies such as conditioning and modeling, yet they must not damage the ability of the pupil to achieve rational understanding of his/her value system at a later time.

1022. MacMillan, Donald L. Behavior Modification in Education. New York: Macmillan, 1973.

Presents a readable discussion of the principles upon which behavior modification is built and then translates those principles into practice.

1023. Malikail, J.S. "A Philosophy of Mind Adequate for Discourse on Morality: Iris Murdoch's Critique." Journal of Educational Thought, 15 (1981): 61-72.

Murdoch's views in moral education are summarized. Murdoch holds that the separation of thought and action present in contemporary philosophy is erroneous. For moral dispositions to be developed there should be appropriate motivation, and for appropriate motivation there should be proper and worthy objects of attention. A central task for moral education is seen as deciding what objects are worthy of attention and how best to induce children to attend to these objects.

1024. Malott, Richard W. et al. Contingency Management in Education. Kalamazoo, MI: Behaviordelia, 1972.

Presents in cartoon format the principles of contingency management and the implications for shaping student behavior. This book is both amusing and highly informative. Many of the applications discussed deal with the shaping of social behavior.

1025. Moline, Jon. "Classical Ideas About Moral Education." Character, 2 (June 1981): 1-8.

Argues that there is more to morality and moral education than solving moral dilemmas. We should begin to shift our emphasis to the qualities of character needed to cope with situations which are too complex to anticipate. We should only feel constrained when told what to do--being told what to avoid should not unnecessarily constrain or intimidate us. Practical widsom is more than skill, expertise or know how. After Aristotle, Moline argues that the wise person is the serious person. Being serious implies caring enough to make a place for it in one's life. To be serious about morality is to make a place for it. Moral education must be an invitation into seriousness--an invitation to care for good judgment and a keen sense for moral mistakes. What values to be taught and how they are to be determined is briefly discussed. Also in Character Policy (item 1061).

1026. Oldenquist, Andrew. "Indoctrination and Societal Suicide." The Public Interest, 63 (1981): 81-94.

Argues that the rejection of directive moral education by moral educators is a good formula for societal suicide. It is essential that youth acquire the 'moral core' rather than simply talk about them. Concludes with objections and answers on the topic of directive moral education.

1027. Oldenquist, Andrew. "Moral Education without Moral Education." Harvard Educational Review, 49 (1979): 240-247.

In a review of recent books on moral education, an Aristotelian perspective on moral education is put forth. It is argued that a content-free moral education is impossible and that the shared morality that binds society together should be the focus of moral education. Moral virtues are seen as developed through habituation.

1028. Oldenquist, Andrew. "On the Nature of Citizenship." Educational Leadership, 38 (1980): 30-34.

Argues that there is a need to inculcate certain basic values in all youth. One does not acquire affection for our country by being constantly told of the countries weaknesses and inconsistencies. Concern and affection survive this sort of knowledge. Argues that we can instill values and still respect ethnic pluralism.

1029. Oldenquist, Andrew and Michael Lynn. "Tribal Morality." Character, 2 (March 1981): 1-8.

Argues that the cultivation of the potential for guilt and remorse in learners is an important part of all significant instruction. Moral teachings must be transmitted in ways that prepare learners to resist vital temptations. Societies which reject guilt and shame are suicidal. We are genetically programmed to be socialized and only then can we exist as productive members of a moral community. Also in Character Policy (item 1061).

1030. Oliner, Pearl. Compassion and Caring: Missing Concepts in Social Studies Programs." Journal of Education, 161, 4 (Fall 1979): 36-60.

Argues that social studies curricula need to include the study of prosocial behaviors. If this is omitted then the impression is that all actions are self-serving. Such a curriculum should provide opportunities for students to conceptualize prosocial behaviors, develop social cognition skills and provide access to prosocial models. Examples of topics and strategies are presented.

1031. Orr, John B. "Cognitive-Developmental Approaches to Moral Education: A Social Ethical Analysis." Educational Theory, 24 (1974): 365-373.

Criticizes cognitive-developmental theories because of their rejection of socialization into adult society as a viable educational goal. Children should not be taught that they can shape their own morality--they need to find out the patterns of respectability available to them.

1032. Pekarsky, Daniel. "Education and Manipulation." Philosophy of Education 1977 (item 1817), pp. 354-362.

Using Rousseau's Emile as a base point, the issue of the justification of manipulation in educational contexts is discussed. It is held that relations of authority are necessary in education and to endorse such does not prejudge the question of the importance of freedom in education.

1033. Peters, R.S. "Freedom and the Development of the Free Man." Psychology and Ethical Development (item 1809), pp. 336-359.

Explores the concept of freedom in education and the relationship of the social and school environment to the concept and also discussed is the relationship between Piaget's and Kohlberg's moral development. Concludes that conventional morality probably sustains most mundane conduct and unless the person is bedded in this level his principled thought is likely to be unrelated to his conduct.

1034. Peters, R.S. "Moral Development and Moral Learning." The Monist, 58 (1974): 541-68.

Argues against Kohlberg and Piaget in their view that moral development involves forms of reasoning over content. Peters argues instead that content is essential and unavoidable with young children and that proper moral education at this age should consist of a combination of induction and positive reinforcement. The actual content should be those 'basic rules' which can be defended as necessary to the continuance of any tolerable form of social life.

1035. Peters, R.S. "Rules with Reasons: The Bases of Moral Education." The Nation, 208 (January 13, 1969): 49-52.

Attempts to distinguish moral from legal and religious considerations by emphasizing basic moral concepts and the reasoning process used in their support. Emphasizes the importance of initiation into the code of the community through instruction and explanation. Argues that the method of discovery is inappropriate for the learning of moral codes.

1036. Phillips, D.Z. "Not in Front of the Children: Children and the Heterogeneity of Morals." Journal of Philosophy of Education, 14 (1980): 73-75.

Argues that it is essential to give children a firm foundation of values for only in this way will children come to see values themselves as important.

1037. Poteet, James A. Behavior Modification: A Practical Guide for Teachers. Minneapolis: Burgess Publishing, 1973.

A practical guide for teachers designed to present enough behavior modification information to enable the classroom tacher to launch his/her program in shaping students social behavior.

1038. Ravitch, Diane. "Educational Policies that Frustrate Character Development." Character, 1 (July 1980): 1-4.

The experience of a teen age son forced her to see the error of the position of holding that one never should impose values on others. Educational policies which emphasize the intrinsic value of learning do not emphasize standards and hurt the character formation of youth. Also in Character Policy (item 1061).

1039. Riles, Wilson. "The Role of the School in Moral Development." Moral Development-ETS (item 1795), pp. 69-79.

The superintendent of schools for California states that the school must take responsibility for the transmission of a unifying set of values for a diverse society as well as the teaching of values concerning the intrinsic worth and dignity of the individual.

1040. Rokeach, Milton. "Toward a Philosophy of Value Education." Values Education: Theory/Practice/Problems/Prospects (item 1795), pp. 117-126.

Proposes that value education cannot and should not remain value free and that educators are not performing their educational functions unless they change values in certain directions. A list of terminal and instrumental values are identified as educational values. Also in Understanding Human Values (item 1812).

1041. Rucker, W. Ray, V. Clyde Arnspiger, and Arthur J. Brodbeck. Human Values in Education. Dubuque: IA: William C. Brown, 1969.

Presents a framework, based on Laswell (item 1018) that identifies eight basic values which are seen as universal human needs: Affection, respect, skill, enlightenment, power, wealth, well-being, and rectitude. The goal of the approach is to help students develop these values and 'distribute' them among other persons. Methods for achieving this goal are presented. Ways that systematic thinking and problem solving can be integrated into the values framework is presented. Finally a prototype of a school that adheres to the scheme of value shaping and sharing is presented.

1042. Schimmels, Cliff and Gary Andres. "Man's Will: The Intervening Variable in Moral Education." Journal of Thought, 12 (1977): 9-13.

Argues that the human will is determined by the strength of the conscious perception of the individuals interpretation of the universal "good life" at the moment of impulse or choice. Moral education should seek to instill this concept of a universal value system.

1043. Senesh, Lawrence. "The Challenge of Value Commitment." Values Concepts and Techniques (item 1784), pp. 277-287.

Discusses the values underlying our political, economic and social systems. Argues that in spite of challenges to these values we should work for value commitments through which our best aspirations can be reached. Presents a list of values which should be transmitted.

1044. Shaver, James P. "Citizenship, Values and Morality in Social Studies." The Social Studies: 80th Yearbook of the National Society for the Study of Education. Edited by Howard D. Mehlinger and O.L. Davis. Chicago: University of Chicago Press. 1981, pp. 105-125.

Contrasts the views of the social studies intelligentsia with the views of public school teachers. Emphasizes that how citizenship values and morality are viewed in the social studies depends on the perspective. Shaver argues that teachers have a legitimate concern for passing on traditional values while university professors emphasize critical analysis of those values.

1045. Sieferth, Bernice. "Religion and Morality." _Educational Horizons_, 3 (1960): 99-108.

Argues that although schools are secular they must teach morality. In order for society to survive, a code of moral and ethical behavior must be transmitted from one generation to the next.

1046. Silver, Michael. "Education in Human Values: The Laswell Value Framework." _Values Education: Theory/Practice/Problems/Prospects_ (item 1805), pp. 141-148.

Contains a clear exposition of using Laswell's eight universal values (item 1018) as a focus for value inquiry. Students are encouraged to validate their own value system through value exploration and value sharing.

1047. Simpson, Bert K. _Becoming Aware of Values_. San Diego, CA Pennant Press, 1974.

Based on the Laswell (item 1018) value framework eight universal values are seen as needs that all persons should possess, enhance, and share with others. A practical guide is provided for teachers and administrators.

1048. Simpson, Elizabeth L. "The Right to Individual Judgment." _Educational Leadership_, 35 (1978): 453-456.

Education for judgment may involve clarification and personal development; however, it must also distinguish and utilize the positive basic social values. No groups can survive without a core of mutuality.

1049. Skidmore, Charles E. "Analysis of a Model for Implementing Value Learning in a School District." Ph.D. dissertation, U.S. International University, 1970. 31/05, p. 2080.

Attempts to teach responsible moral behavior through a form of values sharing which in fact is a form of indoctrination. No significant changes were detected.

1050. Staub, Ervin. "The Development of Prosocial Behavior: Directions for Future Research and Applications to Education." Paper presented at Moral/Citizenship Education Conference, Philadelphia, 1976. ED 178 458.

Discusses a wide range of research on the determinants of prosocial behavior and relates findings to procedures for increasing prosocial behavior in children. Actual school programs are described.

1051. Staub, Ervin. "To Rear a Prosocial Child: Reasoning, Learning by Doing and Learning by Teaching Others." Moral Development: Current Theory and Research (item 1790), pp. 113-135.

Reports the results of research designed to enhance prosocial behavior. The techniques used ranged from positive induction, engagement in socially responsible behavior, and peers teaching peers. The implications of such research for educational planning is discussed.

1052. Thomas, M. Donald and Rafael Lewy. "Education and Moral Conduct: Rediscovering America." Character, 1 (January, 1980): 2-7.

Takes a cynical look at value free education (Kohlberg and Simon) and argues that teachers, like parents, are expected to assert control and provide direction. It is this potential for assertion that permits them to care deeply. The efforts of Salt Lake City to foster specific values is described. A Code of Ethics for faculty is presented and a "pro-American" curriculum is briefly described. Also in Character Policy (item 1061).

1053. Thomas, M. Donald and Arthur I. Melvin. "Community Consensus is Available on a Moral Valuing Standard." Phi Delta Kappan, 62 (1981): 479-485.

Argues that without consensus on a standard of desirable behavior, there can be no effective moral education. Describes results of the Century III community workshop process as applied in Salt Lake City in 1979 which encourages participants to discover common ground on moral issues. It was found that participants reached an 81% consensus on the existence of a moral valuing standard.

1054. Thompson, Brenda. "Discipline and Contract in Schools." Progress and Problems in Moral Education (item 1820), pp. 184-191.

Argues that we should not fear the discipline society requires: "... (it) is not nasty green medicine, it is not the jack-booted sadist, it is the respect we all owe each other."

1055. Varenne, Herve. "Symbolizing American Culture in Schools." Character, 2 (April 1981): 1-9.

Argues that ritual has a central role to play in education. Individualism and communalism are contrasting, but essential ingredients of our society. Children must be presented with examples of how to organize their lives, and then invited to demonstrate competence in recreating examples of this organization. It is concluded that at present the mix of rituals and symbols placed before students is not a fair representation of the pattern of values that currently prevail in adult life. Also in Character Policy (item 1061).

1056. Warnock, Mary. "Can Virtue Be Taught?" New Society, 32 (1975): 421-423.

In reviewing a number of contemporary books on moral education the question of whether virtues can be taught is explored. It is concluded that it can but the process is largely by example and by the experiencing of the difference between good, fair, and honest acts, and the opposite.

1057. Warnock, Mary. Schools of Thought. London: Faber and Faber, 1977.

Argues in Chapter 4 that moral education should not be treated in a systematic way in the curriculum. Morality primarily involves practice, and as a result teaching about morality should only occur in the context of teaching to be moral. To do otherwise is to distort. The chapter offers a strong argument against teacher neutrality.

1058. Wees, W.R. "Values in the Curriculum." Education Canada, 20, 1 (Spring 1980): 23-27.

Argues that there are certain categories of values that persist as permanent aspects of the humanity in man. What the school might do to enhance the values in there areas is discussed.

1059. Wiles, Kimball. "Values and Our Destiny." Educational Leadership, 21 (1964): 501-504; 554-555.

Presents five values which, it is argued, are essential for human survival in our current situation. Implicit is the idea that schools should be involved in the process of affirming these values.

1060. Woody, R.M. Behavioral Problem Children in the Schools: Recognition, Diagnosis and Behavior Modification. New York: Appleton-Century-Crofts, 1969.

1061. Wynne, Edward A. Character Policy. Washington, DC: University Press of America, 1982.

Contains papers originally in the short-lived newsletter Character. An excellent collection on the directive approach to moral or character education.

1062. Wynne, Edward, Ed. "Symposium on Sex and Children and Adolescents." Character, 1 (September 1980): 1-7.

Contains responses to Hogan and Schroeder's article on sex education (item 1006). Also in Character Policy (item 1061).

1063. Yudof, Mark G. "The Dilemma of Children's Autonomy." *Policy Analysis*, 2 (1976): 387-407.

Argues that while freedom and autonomy for children are essential, they must be balanced against other legitimate interests including the transmission of culture from generation to generation.

Other Approaches: Theory, Practice, and Research

Beck: Ultimate Life Values

1064. Beck, Clive. Moral Education in the Schools: Some Practical Suggestions. Toronto: Ontario Institute for Studies in Education, 1971.

Proposes a series of mini-courses in values by age groups. Within each age group, a list of appropriate topics is included. Practical suggestions are offered regarding teaching methodology. The suggested approach is eclectic involving the ideas of Kohlberg, Wilson and others. The volume concludes with a short chapter on a theory of values for the schools.

1065. Beck, Clive. "The Reflective Approach to Values Education." Philosophy and Education. Eightieth Yearbook of the National Society for the Study of Education. Edited by Jonas F. Soltis. Chicago: National Society for the Study of Education, 1981, pp. 185-211.

Outlines an approach to values education where the goal is to constantly identify enduring basic human values such as survival, happiness and fellowship, that can be used in reflecting on particular moral questions.

1066. Beck, Clive. "The Reflective, Ultimate Life Goals' Approach to Values Education." Reflections on Values Education (item 1804), pp. 149-161.

Argues that ultimate life goals (survival, happiness, health, love, etc.) must be central to any viable program of value education. A process only approach to values education is rejected, it is claimed that values education must involve content. Reflection should be carried out either upon ultimate life goals or in the light of such goals.

1067. Beck, Clive, et al. The Moral Education Project (Year 5): Final Report 1976-77. Toronto: Ontario Institute for Studies in Education, 1978. ED 166 832.

Reports on the fifth year of a Canadian program designed to help students reflect on their own values in light of fundamental life goals.

Lipman: Philosophy for Children

1608. Evans, Clyde. "The Feasibility of Moral Education." Growing Up with Philosophy (item 1075), pp. 157-173.

Demonstrates that philosophy can bring children to a mastery of skills and a fruition of attitudes that are valuable in the development of moral individuals. It can help children perceive the strength of their commitments in ways that were not before apparent.

1069. Evans, Clyde. "Philosophical Thinking: An Ally for Parental Values." Growing Up with Philosophy" (item 1075), pp. 368-376.

Since parents want children to grow up free, autonomous and reasonable they should support moral philosophy in schools since these are the exact outcomes.

1070. Katzner, Louis, I. "Social Philosophy and Children." Growing Up with Philosophy (item 1075), pp. 194-206.

Argues that if proper caution is used the introducing of social philosophy in the classroom can be a highly constructive endeavor. It is not enough to merely examine injustice; however, children must learn at some point to evaluate the criteria employed by those who wield rights and authority.

1071. Lipman, Matthew. Harry Stottlemeier's Discovery. Upper Montclair, N.J.: Institute for the Advancement of Philosophy for Children, 1974. ED 103 298.

Through a novel a model is offered of dialogue of philosophical inquiry. The events of the novel are a recreation of the ways children might find themselves thinking and acting. It respects the value of inquiry and reasoning, encourages the development of alternative modes of thought and imagination and suggests how children might learn from each other. This novel is meant to be used at grade 5 or 6.

1072. Lipman, Matthew. Lisa. Upper Montclair, N.J.: Institute for the Advancement of Philosophy for Children, 1976.

A novel for children with the focus on ethical and social issues such as fairness, naturalness, lying, and truthtelling, and the nature of rules and standards. Other issues explored include the rights of children, job and sex discrimination, and animal rights. Lisa is concerned with the interrelationship of logic and morality.

1073. Lipman, Matthew. "Philosophy for Children." Upper Montclair, N.J.: Montclair State College, 1973, ED 103 296.

Develops a rationale for teaching philosophy to children and then reports the results of a study which shows that such a course leads to more logical thinking and increased reading scores.

1074. Lipman, Matthew and Ann M. Sharp. "Can Moral Education Be Divorced from Philosophical Inquiry?" Viewpoints on Teaching, 56 (Fall, 1980): 1-31.

Argues that the teachers role should be as a facilitator and clarifier of the child's valuing process. Through the use of philosophic reasoning the child can reach a deep and meaningful understanding of his moral situation. Also Montclair Education Review 6,2 (1977) and Philosophy in the Classroom (item 1078), Chapter 9.

1075. Lipman, Matthew and Ann M. Sharp, eds. Growing Up with Philosophy. Philadelphia: Temple University Press, 1978.

A collection of papers, many of which, explore dimensions of teaching moral philosophy to children.

1076. Lipman, Matthew, Ann M. Sharp, and F.S. Oscanyan. Ethical Inquiry: Instructional Manual to Accompany Lisa. Upper Montclair, NJ: Institute for the Advancement of Philosophy for Children, 1977. ED 148 665.

Emphasizes children learning to think as clearly as possible about moral conduct. Attempts to show the relevance of philosophical thinking to daily moral concerns. The major philosophical themes covered include truth, fairness, consistency, free will, naturalness, change and growth, and standards and rules. The manual is divided into fiften chapters on important themes in _Lisa_. Each chapter contains useful hints for teaching.

1077. Lipman, Matthew, Ann M. Sharp and F.S. Oscanyan. _Philosophical Inquiry: Instructional Manual to Accompany Harry Stottlemeier's Discovery_. Upper Montclair, NJ: Institute for the Advancement of Philosophy for Children, 1979.

1078. Lipman, Matthew, Ann M. Sharp and Frederick S. Oscanyan. _Philosophy in the Classroom_, 2nd ed. Philadelphia: Temple University Press, 1980.

Contains a thorough introduction to the Philosophy for Children Curriculum of the Institute for the Advancement of Philosophy for Children. Through guided discussion based in the novels children are to eke out for themselves the laws of reasoning and the discovery of alternative philosophical views that have been presented through the centuries.

1079. Munby, Hugh. "Philosophy for Children: An Example of Curriculum Review and Criticism." _Curriculum Inquiry_, 9 (1979): 229-249.

Contains a critique of Lipman's Philosophy for Children program.

McPhail: School's Council/Lifeline

1080. McPhail, Peter. "The Moral Education Curriculum Project." Let's Teach Them Right (item 1803), pp. 130-137.

Presents the rationale and curriculum development considerations underpinning the School's Council Moral Education Curriculum Project which resulted in the "Lifeline" Series (item 1085). Developing consideration for others among adolescents is the major focus.

1081. McPhail, Peter. "Moral Education or Education for a Better Life?" Journal of Moral Education, 1 (1972): 109-115.

The main goals of the School's Council Moral Education Lifeline" project are outlined. It is argued that the academic response to moral education has been too philosophical. There is a need to build upon the actual needs and motives of young people.

1082. McPhail, Peter. "The Morality of Communication: Authority and Method in Situational Morality." International Review of Education, 26 (1980): 135-152.

Reviews his work in developing his "Lifeline" and "Startline" moral education programs. Holds that children are naturally honest, caring and morally imaginative and describes his significant situation approach and how to develop in children a 'morality of communication' comprising the abilities to receive, interpret, respond and transmit messages and thereby generate further concern and choice.

1083. McPhail, Peter, David Middleton and David Ingram. Moral Education in the Middle Years. London: Longman, 1978.

Describes "Startline" of the Schools Council Moral Education 8-13 Project. The project is based on a well-reasoned approach to social learning through social conditioning. It argues that choice, reason and decision making should be positively reinforced and encouraged as soon as the capacity for it begins to emerge.

1084. McPhail, Peter, J.R. Ungoed-Thomas and Hilary Chapman. Learning to Care. Niles, IL: Argus Communications, 1975.

Describes the theory and rationale behind the Lifeline curriculum. Although part of the curriculum deals with adjudicating moral conflicts the major focus is on the importance of caring and learning to understand other people's needs. The central task of moral education is seen as to build on the fundamental core of consideration that all people possess, and demonstrate that the differences among people are superficial and the similarities great.

1085. McPhail, Peter, et al. Moral Education in the Secondary School. London: Longman, 1972.

Discusses the nature of adolescence, a rationale for moral education, practical suggestions for implementing a program of moral education and a description of the Lifeline program. The approach outlined is designed to help secondary students learn to care and to choose.

1086. Peters, R.S. "Review of Moral Education in the Secondary School." Journal of Moral Education, 3 (1973): 413-416.

Peters takes a critical view of McPhail's School's Council handbook on moral education. Claims that the theoretical and empirical foundations are muddled. Things are much more complex.

1087. Ungoed-Thomas, J.R. The Moral Situation of Children. London: MacMillan, 1978.

Final report from the School's Council Moral Education 8-13 Project (1972-6). Reports the results of a national survey to assess the moral situation of children so as to have a basis for curriculum development which would be relevant. Contains a rich collection of insights into world of childhood.

Social Action/Community Involvement

1088. Aoki, T. "Controlled Change: A Crucial Component in Social Education." Paper presented at the annual meeting of the National Council of the Social Studies, Denver, 1971. ED 065 404.

Calls for a transactional approach to social studies education in which students interact with their world with a view toward developing participatory commitment to the process of change.

1089. Barr, Robert D. "The Development of Action Learning Programs." NASSP Bulletin, 60 (May 1976): 106-109.

Provides ideas for out-of-classroom learning programs and suggests ways such programs can be organized; a very general treatment.

1090. Corbett, Frederick C. "The Community Involvement Program: Social Service as a Factor in Adolescent Moral and Psychosocial Development." Ed.D. dissertation, University of Toronto, 1977. 39/03, p. 1410.

Reports the results of an evaluation of the impact of a program designed to lead students to a commitment to the solution of social problems through community involvement. It was found that the major discernable impact was on emotion and task competence. No impact on moral reasoning was detected.

1091. Dickson, Alec. "Altruism and Action." Journal of Moral Education, 8 (1979): 147-155.

Argues that the only way to get youth to become good is to have them do good through community service projects.

1092. Enright, Robert D. and Darwin D. Hendel. "An Evaluation of Growth in a University Programme." Journal of Moral Education, 9 (1979): 50-52.

Examines the influence of a combined full-time helping and full-time academic experience on the moral judgment of college undergraduates. On the Defining Issues Test no increase in moral development was detected.

1093. Graham, Richard. "Youth and Experiential Learning." Youth: 74th Yearbook of the National Society for the Study of Education. Edited by Robert J. Havinghurst and Philip H. Dreyer. Chicago: University of Chicago Press, 1975, pp. 161-192.

After reviewing current "action learning" programs Graham suggests a program in which the focus would be on arranging optimal match between the action learning experience and developmental stage.

1094. Hedin, Diane P. "Evaluating Experiential Learning." Character, 1 (February 1980): 1-9.

Thirty experiential education programs involving over 4,000 students are evaluated. Evaluation consisted of assessments of social development, psychological development and intellectual and academic growth. In the majority of the programs youth showed a positive change in attitudes toward adults. Students were also found to develop a heightened sense of responsibility, a heightened self-esteem and increased sense of autonomy. The factors in the programs accounting for positive growth were identified. Also in Character Policy (item 1061).

1095. Jones, W. Ron. Finding Community: A Guide to Community Research and Action. Palo Alto, CA: James E. Freel, 1971.

A practical guide to community action learning and value activities. The basic purpose is to help students explore how well existing institutions are serving the needs of people.

1096. Kelly, Thomas E. "The Problems Experienced by Adolescents Engaged in Civic Action Projects." Ph.D. dissertation, The University of Wisconsin, 1980. 41/09, p. 3980.

Four general problems interfering with productive group work in social action projects were identified: commitment, competence, concreteness and leader-follower relations.

1097. National Association of Secondary School Principals. 25 Action Learning Schools. Washington, D.C. National Association of Secondary School Principals, 1974. ED 103 299.

Presents an overview of the rationale for action learning, suggested objectives and tips for getting started. Reports on 25 exemplary programs are included.

1098. National Commission on Resources for Youth. New Roles for Youth in the School and Community. New York: Citation Press, 1974.

Describes seventy community action and service projects carried out by students.

1099. Newmann, Fred. Education for Citizen Action: Challenge for Secondary Curriculum. Berkeley, CA: McCutchan, 1975.

Builds a strong, theoretically based, case for social action and a goal for secondary education. Social action is seen as action directed toward exerting an influence in public affairs. Involved in the formulating of policy goals is moral deliberation. The rationale and context for such a program is presented as well as a general description of a program in operation.

1100. Newmann, Fred M. "Social Action and Humanistic Education." Humanistic Education (item 923), pp. 65-99.

Proposes a social action curriculum to build students' competence to affect his or her environment. Relates social action curriculum to notions of humanistic education.

1101. Newmann, Fred. "Student Intentions in Social Action Projects." SSEC Newsletter, 12 (February 1972): 1-4.

Discusses the motivational base of individuals as they come to be involved in a school based social action curriculum. Points out that there are a variety of reasons why students get involved in a social action experience and these student intentions have implications for teachers within social action curriculum programs.

1102. Newmann, Fred, Thomas A. Bertocci, and Ruthanne M. Landesness. Skills in Citizen Action. Skokie, IL: National Textbook, 1977.

Outlines Newmann's citizen action program in more detail and describes how such a program can be implemented in a school setting.

1103. Oliver, Don and Fred Newmann. Social Action (Public Issues Series). Columbus, OH: Xerox Education Publications, 1972.

Contains a series of case studies of social action where social action was taken. Designed to get students to think carefully about ones obligations and the problems associated with taking social action.

1104. Scharf, Peter and Thomas C. Wilson. "Work Experience: A Redefinition." Adolescent's Development and Education (item 1806), pp. 433-446.

Uses cognitive-developmental psychology as the basis for redesigning the objective of work experience and the curriculum in which such experiences are integrated. A concrete program to create a new work experience program at Newport Harbor High School is reported.

1105. Ubbelohde, Robert. Social Studies and Reality: A Commitment to Intelligent Social Action. Greensboro, NC: Humanistic Education Project, University of North Carolina, 1973. ED 081 711.

Argues that teachers should help students deal with society in an effort to bring about needed social change. The knowledge and skills required for such a curricula approach are discussed.

1106. Wynne, Edward. "Values Education: Old Answers, New Packages." Curriculum Review, 15 (1976): 222-224.

Argues that the answer to the current values malaise of youth is not values curriculum packages but rather lies in a movement toward restructuring the social experiences of youth. This will involve different social relations in schools and more real away-from-school alternatives of a positive social nature.

Wilson: Components of Moral Competence

1107. Bryden-Brook, Simon. "Moral Studies in the Secondary School: An Experiment." Journal of Moral Education, 1 (1972): 117-121.

Using Wilson's components of a morally educated person, exercises for use in the classroom were devised, tried out, and imformally evaluated.

1108. Bullen, E.L. "House System as an Aid to Values Education." Education Canada, 20 (Summer 1980): 30-34.

Discusses Wilson's organizational form for shaping the hidden curriculum and making it effective. Wilson refers to this organizational form as the House System. This house system involves themes such as sense of community, shared rituals, territoriality, and teachers in a role similar to parents.

1109. Harrington, John L. "Review Article: John Wilson as Moral Educator." Journal of Moral Education, 7 (1977): 50-63.

The rationale and conceptual status of Wilson's components of the morally educated person are discussed. Weaknesses and strengths are pointed out and comparisons made with the views of McPhail, Peters, Frankena and Kohlberg. A final note by Wilson himself reacting to the review is appended.

1110. Harrison, John. "Moral Education: Thinking (and Feeling)." The Teaching of Values in Canadian Education (item 1797), pp. 47-54.

Reviews several of the major research enterprises in moral education in England and Canada and concludes that we should pay more attention to the discrete components of thinking and feeling which are employed in moral issues. Wilson's analysis is seen as useful in this regard (see item 1115).

1111. Wilson, John. "Approach to Moral Education." Religious Education, 65 (1970): 467-473.

Argues that the basis for moral education should be the criteria by which we judge. Wilson's moral components are presented and possibilities for the practice of moral education are discussed.

1112. Wilson, John. The Assessment of Morality. Windsor, Berks, England: NFER Publishing, 1973.

Intended as a guide to researchers in the field of moral education, Wilson lists his moral components and describes techniques for formally measuring each one.

1113. Wilson, John. Moral Education and the Curriculum. London: Pergamon Press, 1969.

Presents an analytic model for the curriculum. By answering the questions given in the model and comparing them with the moral competencies a detailed picture of what actually goes on in the school curriculum will emerge. The teacher will be able to judge what features of the curriculum contribute to moral education.

1114. Wilson, John. "Moral Education and the Curriculum." Progress and Problems in Moral Education (item 1820), pp. 35-47.

Advocates the direct teaching of moral methodology through a wide variety of teaching methods. The methodology and curriculum are to be structured around the authors logical components of moral behavior (item 1112).

1115. Wilson, John. Moral Thinking. London: Heinemann Education Books, 1973.

Intended as a guide for students this book describes the nature of moral thinking from the perspective of Wilson's moral components.

1116. Wilson, John. Practical Methods of Moral Education. London: Heinemann Educational Books, 1972.

Outlines an approach to moral education based on the components of moral competence. Analyzes the use of language, rules and contracts and the school community in the process of moral education. Wilson's components involve such attributes as EMP (ability to identify emotions), GIG (knowing facts relevant to moral situations) and PHIL (concern for people as equals). See also item 167.

1117. Benson, G.C., and T.S. Engeman. "Practical Possibilities in American Moral Education: A Comparison of Values Clarification and the Character Education Curriculum." Journal of Moral Education, 4 (1974): 53-59.

The Character Education Curriculum of the American Institute for Character Education is contrasted with the values clarification approach. Values clarification is judged to be too relativistic and character education is viewed as a bag of virtues approach.

1118. Colby, Anne. "Two Approaches to Moral Education." Moral Education ... It Comes with the Territory (item 1811), pp. 275-290.

Compares Kohlberg's theory of moral development with Simon's work on values clarification. Argues that although the two approaches seem incompatible in some areas, integration of the two is both possible and desirable. Also Harvard Educational Review, 45 (1975): 134-143.

1119. DeBenedittis, Suzanne M. "Styles of Moral Education: An Ethical Analysis." Ph.D. dissertation, University of Southern California, 1978. 39/01, p. 209.

Analyzes the work of Simon, Kohlberg and Wilson and critiques their theoretical and methodological foundations.

1120. Forcinelli, Joseph and Thomas S. Engeman. "Value Education in the Public School." Thrust for Educational Leadership, 4 (October 1974): 13-16.

Reviews four approaches to values education (values clarification, cognitive-developmental, Lifeline and character education) and finds that the Character Education Curriculum of the American Institute for Character Education is the most desirable.

1121. Greenberg, J.S. "Behavior Modification and Values Clarification and Their Research Implications." Journal of School Health, 45 (1975): 91-95.

Each methodology is defined. They are compared and contrasted and the potential for research in these areas is sketched out.

1122. Hartoonian, Michael. Working with Value and Moral Teaching Strategies. Paper presented at the annual meeting of the National Council for the Social Studies, 1975. ED 115 562.

Four models for interpreting values education strategies are provided: Examples from curriculum projects are analyzed in light of these conceptual models. A disclosure approach to valuing is put forth which holds that one must understand the individual and collective human being before values can be adequately explained.

1123. Hemmer, William B. "Values Education Processes." Values Concepts and Techniques (item 1784), pp. 59-74.

Reviews inculcation and contemporary approaches to values education. Points out similarities among the approaches.

1124. Jones, C. "Can Schools Teach Ethics?" Christian Scientist Monitor, December 23, 1974, pp. 1-2.

Looks at how value clarification and moral development is being taught and comments on both approaches.

1125. Kohlberg, Lawrence. "Psychoanalytic and Cognitive-Developmental Approaches to Moral Education." Paper presented at the annual meeting of the American Educational Research Association, San Francisco, 1976. ED 133 039.

Explores the similarities and differences between cognitive developmental and psychoanalytic views on moral development. Concludes that much of childrens conception of reliability is cognitively determined rather than the result of deeper emotions or fantasies.

1126. Kohlberg, Lawrence and Sidney B. Simon. "An Exchange of Opinion Between Kohlberg and Simon." Readings in Values Clarification (item 212), pp. 62-64.

Many points of similarity and difference are noted. The second feeling is that the approaches complement each other. Also in Learning, 1 (December 1972).

1127. Lewis, Frank W. "A Piagetian Critique of Kohlberg's 'Moral Development' and Simon's Values Clarification." Paper presented at Eighth Annual International Interdisciplinary UAP Conference on Piaget and Its Implications for the Helping Professions, Los Angeles, 1978. ED 157 809.

Discusses the major differences between Piaget and Kohlberg and Simon on the nature of moral development and purposes of moral education. The major criticisms of Kohlberg and Simon are discussed.

1128. Pellino, Glenn R. "Student Development and Values Education." Counseling and Values, 22 (1977): 41-51.

The developmental schemes of Kohlberg and Perry and the implications for education are compared and contrasted.

1129. Scharf, Peter. "Indoctrination, Values Clarification, and Developmental Moral Education as Educational Responses to Conflict and Change in Contemporary Society." Readings in Moral Education (item 449), pp. 18-35.

Overviews the philosophic and empirical foundation of developmental moral education and contrasts it to indoctrinative and values clarification approaches.

1130. Shaver, James P. "A Cognitive Decision-Making Approach to Ethics Education: Focus on Public Issues." Paper presented at National Conference on Education and Citizenship. Responsibilities for the Common Good, Kansas City, 1976. ED 144 917.

Reviews the public issues approach to ethics education and contrasts it with values clarification and the cognitive developmental approach.

1131. Smith, Marion. "Kohlberg and McPhail--A Comparison." Journal of Moral Education, 3 (1973): 353-359.

McPhail's (item 1084) "Lifeline" approach with its emphasis on emotion and action is contrasted with Kohlberg's developmental perspective with its emphasis on reasoning.

1132. Wehlage, Gary and Alan L. Lockwood. "Moral Relativism and Values Education." Moral Education ... It Comes with the Territory (item 1811), pp. 330-347.

Argues that moral relativism is an unacceptable position and analyzes the following curricula for relativism: values clarification, Taba Strategies, Science Research Associates, Reflective Thinking, and Public Issues Curriculum.

1133. Bono, Francis V. "The Effects of Two Teaching Approaches on the Moral Judgment of 6th Grade Children." Ph.D. dissertation, Ohio University, 1975. 36/10, p. 6436.

Two approaches to facilitating moral judgment were compared: discussion of moral dilemmas and inculcation. It was found that only the moral discussion group experienced significant moral development.

1134. Cravens, Linda B. "A Comparison of Two Educational Interventions on the Cognitive Interpersonal, and Moral Reasoning Development of Urban Fifth Graders." Ed.D. dissertation, Boston University, 1979. 40/05, p. 2465.

A philosophy for children curriculum was compared with a curriculum where children discussed moral dilemmas. The control group scored higher on interpersonal reasoning. No significant change was found on measures of cognitive development, moral judgment, logical reasoning and achievement tests.

1135. Doornink, J.D., and N.H. Hamm. "Generalized and Nongeneralized Changes in Moral Judgment." Journal of Genetic Psychology, 132 (1978): 277-282.

Two treatments, cognitive conflict and reinforcement, were used to stimulate moral development. It was found that both resulted in significant upward shifts in moral reasoning, but these shifts did not generalize to new situations. It is concluded that moral opinion was changed but not moral reasoning.

1136. Dozier, Martha S. "The Relative Effectiveness of Vicarious and Experimental Techniques on the Development of Moral Judgment with Groups of Desegregated 6th Grade Pupils." Ph.D. dissertation, University of Miami, 1974. 35/04, p. 2045.

Both the vicarious treatment, discussing dilemmas relevant to one's age, and the experimental treatment, increasing subjects' awareness of one's values and how they influence behavior, were found to increase subjects' level of moral development.

1137. Ehman, Lee H. "Research on Social Studies Curriculum and Instruction: Values." Review of Research in Social Studies Education: 1970-1975. Edited by F.P. Hunkins et al. Washington, DC: National Council for the Social Studies, 1977.

Reviews research on values as they relate to learning in social studies classrooms. Separate sections discuss beliefs and attitudes of teachers and students moral development, values curriculum and bias in social studies materials.

1138. Enderle, Glenda R. "A Study of the Effects of Didactic, Discussion and Experimental Group Learnings on Moral Development." Ph.D. dissertation, Kent State University, 1974. 35/10, p. 6510.

With three groups of practicing teachers it was found that didactic lectures about values theory, moral discussions, and T-group exercises all produced significant moral growth pre to post-test.

1139. Forisha, Billy E. "The Facilitation of Moral Growth and Development." Ph.D. dissertation, University of Maryland, 1976. 37/06, p. 3515.

Three approaches comprised the treatment situation. The approaches tested were based on the work of Kohlberg, Dreikurs and Carl Rogers. No significant differences were found as a result of the approach used in growth in moral development. Peer leaders did, however, appear to make a difference.

1140. French, Maynard. "A Study of Kohlbergian Moral Development and Selected Behaviors among High School Students In Classes Using Values Clarification and Other Teaching Methods." Ed.D. dissertation, Auburn University, 1977. 38/5, p. 2521.

It is found that neither lecture, regular teaching methods nor values clarification has any significant impact on moral development.

1141. Harris, David E. "Psychological Awareness and Moral Discourse: A Curriculum Sequence for Moral Development." Ph.D. dissertation, University of Wisconsin at Madison, 1976. 37/09, p. 5562.

It is found that moral discussion in the classroom can be made highly effective if preceeded by activities designed to increase psychological awareness, trust and openness of communication.

1142. Johnson, Xan S. "The Effect of Three Classroom Intervention Strategies on the Moral Development of Pre-adolescents: Moral Dilemma Discussion, Creative Dramatics, and Creative Dramatics/Moral Dilemma Discussion. Ph.D. dissertation, Northwestern University, 1978. 39/08, p. 4597.

The combination of creative dramatics and moral discussion was the only treatment to produce significant gain in moral reasoning of fifth grade subjects.

1143. LeCapitaine, John E. "The Differential Effects of Three Psychological Education Curricula on Affective and Moral Development." Ed.D. dissertation, Boston University, 1980. 41/05, p. 2017.

Three interventions, one focusing on moral development, one on affective development, and the third a combination of the two, were implemented with children ages 9 to 11. It was found that all treatments stimulated affective development and the combination treatment stimulated moral development more than the other two.

1144. Leming, James S. "Curricular Effectiveness in Moral/Values Education." Journal of Moral Education, 10 (1981): 147-164.

Reviews 33 studies on the effectiveness of values clarification and 26 studies which attempt to stimulate moral development using Kohlbergian strategies. The findings from the values clarification research indicate that the approach is ineffective in achieving the stated goals. The findings from cognitive development research are found to be more encouraging.

1145. Leming, James S. "Research in Social Studies Education: Implications for Teaching Values." Social Education, 43 (1979): 597-598; 601.

Presents five generalizations derived from research regarding the teaching of values in the classroom.

1146. Leming, James. "Teaching Values." Practical Applications of Research, 1,4 (June 1979): 3.

A brief review of research which suggests that only the cognitive-developmental approach to moral education has been successful in achieving stated curricular goals.

1147. Leming, James S. "The Uniqueness of the Findings of the Developmental Approach to Moral Education: A Review of Research on the Cognitive Conflict Approach Versus Alternative Forms of Moral Instruction." Paper presented at the Annual Meeting of the American Educational Research Association, Los Angeles, 1981.

Reviews twelve studies in which the moral dilemma discussion approach to moral education was compared, using the same sample, with alternative approaches to moral education. The general finding was that regardless of the approach used all were equally effective in stimulating moral development.

1148. Lockwood, Alan L. "The Effects of Values Clarification and Moral Development Curriculum on School-Age Subjects: A Critical Review of Recent Research." Review of Educational Research, 43 (1978): 325-364.

Critically evaluates the research methodology of studies using values clarification and cognitive-developmental educational interventions. Finds flaws in many of the studies and concludes that the research base for values clarification is weak. Suggestions for improving research are proffered.

1149. Lockwood, Alan L. "Notes on Research Associated With Values Clarification and Value Therapy." Personnel and Guidance Journal, 58 (1980): 606-608.

Examples of research used to support effectiveness claims of values clarification and values therapy

(Rokeach) are carefully analyzed. Questions are raised about the interpretation of the findings of this research. Counselors are urged to be cautious regarding acceptance of claims of treatment effects.

1150. Lorimer, Rowland M. "The Acquisition of Moral Judgments In Adolescence: The Effects of An Exposition of Basic Concepts Versus Exposure to and Discussion of a Filmed Dramatic Example." Ph.D. dissertation, University of Toronto, 1968. 31/05, p. 2187.

One group viewed the film "Fail Safe" and discussed the moral conflicts in the film. Another group heard lectures on normative philosophy. Both groups experienced moral growth on the immediate post-test, but the change disappeared on a delayed post-test. See also _Canadian Journal of Behavioral Science_, 3 (1971): 1-10.

1151. McKellar, Dolores L. "A Study of Two Methods of Training Upon the Development of Moral Judgment in Young Children." Ed.D. dissertation, University of Houston, 1976. 37/08, p. 4828.

Neither cognitive conflict nor indoctrination had any significant impact on the moral development of 7 year old children.

1152. McKenzie, Timothy A. "A Curriculum for Stimulating Moral Reasoning in High School Students Using Values Clarification and Moral Development Interventions." Ed.D. dissertation, Boston University, 1980. 41/05, p. 2020.

Examined the effect of values clarification activities combined with the discussion of moral dilemmas has on the development of moral reasoning. It was found that the curriculum had a significant impact on development of moral reasoning.

1153. Maricle, Robert S. "The Effect of Two Modes of Instruction on Value Change of Secondary School Students While Studying Literature." Ed.D. dissertation, University of Nebraska, 1972. 33/07, p. 3482.

Literature taught by teacher-led discussions using a question/answer method has a significant impact on students' values when compared with independent study.

1154. Medford, Bobby L. "A Comparison of the Rokeach and Values Clarification Methods of Values Change." Ph.D. dissertation, University of North Carolina at Greensboro, 1975. 36/09, p. 5783.

No significant value shifts in either group are found as a result of the two treatments at a three day religious conference.

1155. Search, Paul F. "An Experimental Study in Developing Moral Judgment Through the Comparative Effectiveness of Three Methods: Role Playing, Discussion and Didactic Instruction." Ed.D. dissertation, The Catholic University of America, 1973. 34/03, p. 1139.

Three different methods of instruction, role playing, discussion of moral dilemmas and didactic methods, were all found to be equally effective in stimulating moral development.

1156. Strong, Linda J. "The Impact of Value Education on Preadolescents' Moral Judgment." Ed.D. dissertation, Wayne State University, 1975. 36/05, p. 2608.

Using a combined values clarification and moral dilemma discussion approach it was found that the experimental classes experienced significant growth in stage of moral reasoning.

1157. Weber, Carol R. "A Comparison of Values Clarification and Lecture Methods in Teaching Health at the College Level." Ph.D. dissertation, University of Maryland, 1976. 38/06, p. 3306.

Neither method, lecture or values clarification, resulted in significant differences in attitudes, knowledge of subject material or evaluation of instruction.

Moral Education in Subject Matter Content Areas

English

1158. Aitkin, Johan L. <u>English and Ethics: Some Ideas for Teachers of Literature</u>. Toronto: Ontario Institution for Studies in Education, 1976.

A theoretical defense of and practical guide to the teaching of English and Ethics together.

1159. Arbuthnot, May H. "Developing Life Values Through Reading." <u>Elementary English</u>, 43 (1966): 10-16.

Argues that through identification with the characters and themes in literature children can develop to exemplify those values. Specific values and pieces of literature are suggested for different age groups in the elementary school.

1160. Beach, Richard. "On Literature and Values." Paper presented at the Annual Meeting of the National Council of Teachers of English, San Diego, 1975. ED 117 752.

Demonstrates how developing response to literature approaches to values education are compatible.

1161. Biskin, Donald and Kenneth Hoskisson. "Moral Development through Children's Literature." <u>The Elementary School Journal</u>, 75 (1974): 152-157.

Presents a rationale for fostering moral development (a la Kohlberg) through childrens literature.

1162. Culp, Mary B. "A Study of the Influence of Literature on the Attitudes, Values and Behavior of Adolescents." Ph.D. dissertation, Florida State University, 1975. 36/12, p. 7915.

It was determined through case studies and interviews that a majority of students had been influenced to some extent in their attitudes, values and/or behavior by reading literature.

1163. Feder, Hebert A. "The Place of Literature in Moral Education: An Examination of the Moral Aspects of Literature, Their Significance for Aesthetic Value, and Their Influence on Moral Development." Ph.D. dissertation, University of Toronto, 1978. 39/07, p. 4161.

Argues that literature can provide the basis for establishing a program of moral education. Discusses how it can broaden sympathies, sharpen rationality, and strengthen moral identity.

1164. Garrod, A.C. and G.A. Bramble. "Moral Development and Literature." Theory Into Practice, 16 (1977): 105-111.

Uses Huckleberrry Finn to illustrate how Kohlberg's model can be applied to the teaching of literature in high school.

1165. Gosa, Cheryl. "Moral Development in Current Fiction for Children and Young Adults." Language Arts, 54 (1977): 529-563.

Argues for the need to have the moral themes in novels correspond to the level of moral development of the child. Appropriate books for given age levels are presented.

1166. Gupton, Sandra L. "Moral Education as a Part of the Study of Children's Literature: An Inservice Model and Case Study." Ed.D. dissertation, University of North Carolina at Greensboro, 1979. 40/04, p. 2011.

Explores the relationship between moral education and childrens' literature and develops a model for inservice education to assist teachers to integrate the two.

1167. Hoskisson, K. and D.S. Biskin. "Analyzing and Discussing Children's Literature Using Kohlberg's Stages of Moral Development." Reading Teacher, 33 (1979): 141-147.

1168. Jantz, Richard K. "Moral Judgments and Basal Readers." The Reading Teacher, 30 (1976): 299-305.

Analyzes basal readers for the presence of moral conflict. It is concluded that an ample number of stories in basal readers could be used to facilitate the moral development of children.

1169. Kelley, Marjorie. In Pursuit of Values: A Bibliography of Children's Books. New York: Paulist Press, 1973.

An annotated bibliography of books oriented for elementary, junior and senior high schools which present themes related to moral dilemmas.

1170. Kirschenbaum, Howard. "The Free-Choice English Curriculum." Readings in Values Clarification (item 212), pp. 130-138.

Argues that the only way to make the English curriculum relevant to students is to get them involved in curriculum planning. Urges that the English curriculum move to a free-choice option with a multitude of course offerings, most of which the students had some say in creating.

1171. Kirschenbaum, Howard and Sidney B. Simon." Teaching English with a Focus on Values." Readings in Values Clarification (item 212), pp. 120-129.

1172. Kupfer, J. "Aesthetic Experience and Moral Education." Journal of Aesthetic Education, 12,3 (1978): 13-22.

Describes a case in which aesthetic experince (poetry) is used as a basis for moral education. It is argued that the search for agreement in aesthetic issues is similar to the search for agreement in moral issues.

1173. Legow, Ruth G. "The Ethical Dimension: Developing Moral Awareness in High School Literature Classes." Ed.D. dissertation, Fairleigh Dickinson University, 1981. 42/04, p. 1621.

Describes a rationale and strategies for teaching ethics in the high school English classroom.

1174. Lower, Frank J. and Jerry L. Winsor. "Kohlberg's Theory of Moral Development: A Pedagogical Paradigm." Paper presented at the annual meeting of the Conference of College Composition and Communication, Washington, DC, 1980. ED 188 202.

Applies the Kohlberg methodology to the teaching of English.

1175. McLaughlin, F. "The Place of Fiction in the Development of Values." Media and Methods, 7 (March 1980): 18-21.

Argues that the creative use of fiction assists the young in their struggle for truth and a moral way to be.

1176. Milgrim, Sally-Anne. "A Comparison of the Effects of Classics and Contemporary Literary Works on High School Students' Declared Attitudes Towards Certain Moral Values." Ph.D. dissertation, New York University, 1967. 28/10, p. 3899.

Using the Havinghurst and Taba Student Belief Test it was found that the type of literature being read had no significant impact on students' moral values.

1177. Moir, Hughes. "If We've Always Had Books that Taught All These Virtues, Why is Our Society in Such Lousy Shape?" Language Arts, 54 (1977): 522-528.

Argues that teachers, schools and books have been less effective than hoped for. Perhaps with the new ideas of Lawrence Kohlberg the full impact of good teachers and good literature can be realized.

1178. Newton, Beatryce T. "Critical Reading and Moral Development." Reading Improvement, 16 (1979): 320-323.

Argues that the cognitive-developmental approach to moral education can be directly applied through the skills of critical reading.

1179. Oliver, R.G. "Knowing the Feelings of Others: A Requirement for Moral Education." Educational Theory, 25 (1975): 116-124.

Argues that developing in pupils the ability to know how other people feel is of central importance to the task of moral education. Literature is seen as a central area of the curriculum related to this educational task.

1180. Pillar, A.M. "Using Children's Literature to Foster Moral Development." Reading Teacher, 33 (1979): 148-151.

1181. Pitts, Ben E. and Rhonda York. "Teaching Values Through the Use of Books." Macomb: Western Illinois University, 1978. ED 160 606.

Specific books are suggested to help students develop a sense of honesty and sense of responsibility.

1182. Rearick, William D. "An Exploratory Study of Selected Responses of Sixth Graders to Personal Moral Responsibility as a Social Value in Short Stories." Ed.D. dissertation, University of Washington, 1969. 30/11, p. 4694.

It was found that children are sensitive to the moral questions in short stories and that about half the time teachers see the same issues in the stories as do the children.

1183. Rosenweig, Linda W. and Josephine Harris. "A Cognitive-Moral Developmental Approach to the Teaching of Literature." Moral Education Forum, 2 (April, 1977): 10-12.

Describes a three-year developmental sequence of literature courses which are a part of a pilot program in civic education headed by Edwin Fenton.

1184. Scharf, Peter. "Moral Development and the Literary Interests of Adolescent Readers." Paper presented at the Annual Meeting of the California Library Association, San Diego, 1974. ED 105 890.

Argues that at different levels of moral development adolescents will have different literary interests.

1185. Schwartz, Sheila. "Using Adolescent Fiction That Deals with Current Problems and Lifestyles to Explore Contemporary Values." Paper presented at the Annual Meeting of the English Teachers on Creative Survival, Rutherford, NJ, 1976. ED 119 199.

Argues that literature which incorporates humanistic values, can assist the schools in developing the value structure of students. Examples of books containing humanistic values is provided.

1186. Shachter, Jaqueline. "Themes and Values in Selected Children's Literature." Philadelphia: Temple University, 1979. ED 173 866.

How to use four books by Newbery Medal winners to stimulate discussions of ethical values and moral issues.

1187. Shuman, R. Baird. "Values and the Teaching of Literature." _Clearing House_, 48 (1973): 232-238.

Encourages English teachers to incorporate questions of value into the teaching of literature. Specific steps are suggested with the emphasis on values clarification.

1188. Simon, Sidney B. and Merrill Harmin. "Subject Matter with a Focus on Values." _Readings in Values Clarification_ (item 212), pp. 113-119.

Subject matter must be relevant, that is, it must illuminate a student's values. Gives examples of how _Hamlet_ can be taught at a facts level, a concepts level and a values level.

1189. Simon, Sid, Robert Hawley and David Britton. _Composition for Personal Growth: Values Clarification Through Writing_. New York: Hart Publishing Co., 1973.

Practical values clarification strategies geared for the English classroom.

1190. Sorensen, Marilou R. "Teaching Young People about the Law Through Literature: An Annotated Bibliography." Salt Lake City, UT: Utah State Department of Education, 1980.

Intended for preschool, elementary and middle school this bibliography contains large sections dealing with values and conflict resolution. It features fiction, non fiction, poetry and fantasy.

1191. Swenson, William G. The Search for Values Through Literature: A Practical Teaching Guide. New York: Bantam, 1973.

Objectives and discussions of seven works of literature are presented which have a focus on values. High school students are encouraged to examine values, value sources and value conflicts through the study of literature.

1192. Valentino, Beth A. "An Investigation of the Relationship between Preadolescents' Levels of Reading Comprehension as Defined by Barrett's Taxonomy and Their Existing Levels of Moral Development as Defined by Kohlberg's Stages of Moral Development." Ph.D. dissertation, Pennsylvania State University, 1979. 40/11, p. 5808.

Explores the use of literature to enhance moral development and simultaneously strengthen reading comprehension skills. A significant positive correlation was found between preadolescents' level of reading comprehension (Barrett) and levels of moral development with general academic ability held constant.

1193. Widner, Barbara D. "The Effectiveness of a Freshman Composition Values Curriculum for Developing Competency in the Presentation of Alternative Ideas in Writing." D.A., State University of New York at Albany, 1981. 42/03, p. 1037.

A curriculum using the Moffett curriculum with Kohlberg's moral dilemmas was developed and taught to a class of college freshmen. It was found that the curriculum did not stimulate moral development, nor develop the ability to present alternative ideas in writing.

Health Education

1194. Betof, Edward H. and Howard Kirschenbaum. "A Valuing Approach." School Health Review, 5 (January/ February 1974): 13-14.

Describes the use of facts, concepts, and values in teaching students the importance of feeling, thinking, choosing and acting in their daily lives.

1195. Dalis, Gus T. and Ben B. Strasser. Teaching Strategies for Values Awareness and Decision Making in Health Education. Thorofare, NJ: Charles B. Slack, 1977.

Presents a detailed approach to health education which utilizes the values awareness strategy.

1196. Fox, Robert A. "An Experience with Values Clarification." Health Education, 10 (January-February 1979): 40-41.

Suggests that values clarification can be a useful tool for focusing on the motivation for self-abusive behavior.

1197. Hopp, Joyce W. "Values Clarification and the School Nurse." The Journal of School Health, 45 (1975): 410-413.

In an informal research project five school nurses were trained in values clarification.

1198. Hopp, Joyce and David Abbey. "The Applicability of Value Clarifying Strategies in Health Education at the Sixth Grade Level." Paper presented at the annual meeting of the American School Health Association, 1974. ED 099 384.

Teachers trained in values clarification try it out in their health education classes and enjoy the experience. Student values did not become significantly more clear as a result of the experience.

1199. Murphy, M.L. "Values and Health Problems." Journal of School Health, 43 (1973): 23-31.

Discusses how Lasswell's values framework (item 1018) can be applied to curriculum areas to increase understanding by implementation of relevant skills.

1200. Osman, Jack D. "A Rationale for Using Value Clarification in Health Education." Journal of School Health, 43 (1973): 621-623.

1201. Osman, Jack D. "Teaching Nutrition with a Focus on Values." Readings in Values Clarification (item 212), pp. 340-347.

1202. Osman, Jack. "The Use of Selected Value Clarifying Strategies in Health Education." Journal of School Health, 44 (1974): 21-25.

Describes the use of value clarifying strategies in a college health education class for prospective teachers. The results of the intervention are reported as positive, however no control group was used.

1203. Rees, Floyd D. "Teaching Values Through Health Education." School Health Review, 1 (February 1970): 15-17.

Presents the case for the use of values clarification strategies in health education classes.

1204. Russell, Robert D. "Values and Health Education." Values Concepts and Techniques (item 1784), pp. 249-256.

Discusses the problems posed to health education by the clash of dominant health values and variants on those values.

1205. Schlaadt, Richard G. "Implementing the Values Clarification Process." School Health Review, 5 (January-February, 1974): 10-12.

Reducing Prejudice/Multiculturalism

1206. Alexander, Robert. "Moral Education to Reduce Racial and Ethnic Prejudice." Moral Education: A First Generation of Research and Development (item 428), pp. 126-145.

Describes a course designed to reduce prejudice by stimulating cognitive moral development. Research indicated that the course was successful in achieving its goals with high school students.

1207. Anderson, Norma J. and Barbara Love. "Psychological Education for Racial Awareness." Personnel and Guidance Journal, 51 (1973): 666-670.

Describes activities designed to explore racist attitudes, sources and forms of racism and overcoming racism. The suggestions are very general and lack detail.

1208. Baker, Gwendolyn C. "Multiculturalism in Moral and Values Education." Values Concepts and Techniques (item 1784), pp. 204-207.

Discusses the ways in which moral or values education can be relevant to multicultural education.

1209. Condon, E.C. "Cultural Conflicts in Values, Assumptions, Opinions." New Brunswick, NJ: Rutgers Graduate School of Education, 1973. ED 117 205.

Argues that since values of subcultures in American society vary, teachers should develop cross-cultural understanding and not impose their values on minority groups.

1210. Francis, Mary E. "The Role of Values Education in Multicultural Education." Ph.D. dissertation, University of Toronto, 1980. 42/01, p. 129.

Argues that multicultural education necessarily involves values education. Proceeds to elaborate three objectives common to both in schools: reflectiveness, empathy and psychological maturity.

1211. Goodman, Joel, Sidney B. Simon, and Ron Witort. "Tackling Racism by Clarifying Values." Today's Education, 62 (January 1973): 37-38.

Argues that courses in human relations must deal with more than facts and concepts, they must also deal with values. Examples of how to clarify students values related to racism are presented.

1212. Halverson, Claire B. "Multiculturalism--Should We Clarify or Seek Values." Values Concepts and Techniques (item 1784), pp. 209-224.

Discusses the implications of values clarification and the cognitive-developmental approach for multicultural education. Concludes with four practical activities for classroom use.

1213. Kohlberg, Lawrence and Florence Davidson. "The Cognitive-Developmental Approach to Inter-Ethnic Attitudes." Cambridge, MA: Harvard University, 1974. ED 128 536.

Uses a cognitive-developmental framework to explain how prejudice arises in all cultures and why it has been found to decline with age. The educational implications of this analysis are presented.

1214. Locke, Don C. and Yvonne V. Hardaway. "Moral Perspectives in the Interracial Classroom." Development of Moral Reasoning (item 26), pp. 269-285.

Discusses the conditions under which moral education can be more effective in interracial classrooms. They make practical suggestions for facilitating classroom discussions of race relations.

Science

1215. Allen, Rodney F. "But the Earth Abideth Forever: Values in Environmental Education." Values Education: Theory/Practice/Problems/Prospects (item 1805), pp. 1-24. Also ED 059 300.

Describes how environmental educators can incorporate values education into their classroom. Ten specific teaching processes for guiding student thinking are presented.

1216. Barman, Charles R. "Four Values Education Approaches for Science Teaching." American Biology Teacher, 42 (1980): 153-156.

Focuses on moral development, values clarification, social action, and values analysis. Gives examples of how each can be used in the science classroom.

1217. Barman, Charles R. "Integrating Value Clarification with High School Biology." American Biology Teacher, 37 (1975): 150-153.

Describes a study designed to test if values clarification would affect attitudes toward science and biology and would improve achievement.

1218. Barman, C.R., John P. Guckin and John J. Rusch. Moral Development and Its Implications for Biology Teaching." American Biology Teacher, 38 (1976): 436-439.

1219. Brady, H.S. "Science and Human Values." Science Teacher, 36 (1969): 23-28.

Argues that the role of science in general education should be the interdisciplinary exploration of value.

1220. Brooks, D.W., et al. "Values in Chemical Education." Journal of Chemical Education, 57 (1980): 16.

Describes the use of taped teaching vignettes with subsequent discussion as a way of humanizing future chemistry teachers.

1221. Clawson, Elmer U., et al. "A Framework and Strategy for Examining Environmental Values." Values Concepts and Techniques (item 1784), pp. 235-242.

Suggests that the antropological perspective may provide the best vehicle for helping students understand the value-laden problems that confront people in a technological, industrial society.

1222. Clements, Frank W. "Science Education for Responsible Social Action: A Developing Model." Ph.D. dissertation, University of North Carolina at Greensboro, 1977. 38/09, p. 5212.

Presents a model of science teaching where science is a means and method of dealing with social issues.

1223. Dispoto, R.G. "Moral Valuing and Environmental Variables." Journal of Research in Science Teaching, 14 (1977): 273-280.

Relates levels of moral reasoning to three aspects of environment-related behavior (environmental knowledge, emotionality and activity).

1224. Dispoto, Raymond G. "Socio-Moral Valuing and Environmental Activity, Emotionality, and Knowledge." Ed.D. dissertation, Rutgers University, 1975. 36/07, p. 4380.

It was found that moral reasoning and valuing were related to students' concern over the state of environmental quality.

1225. Fox, F.W. "The Recolored Mentality-Ethical Lessons from Science." The Science Teacher, 43, 6 (1976): 22-24.

Drawing upon the ideals of Whitehead, Erickson and Schilling it is proposed that there are ethical lessons arising from conceptual science as well as from misapplied technology. A program in which these ethical dimensions were explored within science class is described.

1226. Genge, B.A. and J.J. Santosuosso. "Values Clarification for Ecology." The Science Teacher, 41,2 (1974): 37-39.

Describes the application of the values clarification methodology to a unit on pollution.

1227. Gennaro, E.D. and A.D. Glenn. "Science and Social Studies: An Interdisciplinary Approach to Values and Value Decisions." Science Education, 59,1 (1975): 85-93.

Three models of values question analysis are presented and related to science and social studies education.

1228. Harmin, Merrill, Howard Kirschenbaum and Sidney B. Simon. "Teaching Science with a Focus on Values." Readings in Values Clarification (item 212), pp. 150-160.

1229. Herron, J.D. "Implicit Curriculum--Where Values are Really Taught." The Science Teacher, 44,3 (1977): 30.

The value system associated with science is identified and seven typical classroom episodes are presented which illustrate how these values are often taught implicitly.

1230. Iozzi, Louis A., et al. "The Socio-Scientific Reasoning Model: Past, Present and Future." Paper presented at the annual meeting of the National Association for Research in Science Teaching, Atlanta, 1979. ED 173 075.

The socio-scientific reasoning model is described which combines scientific problem solving with the socio and moral concerns of decision making. The model has a developmental flavor.

1231. Jacobsen, M.S. "Relating Science and Values." The Science Teacher, 39,3 (1972): 52-3.

Makes the case for relating the study of science to the value structure of our society. Six objectives designed to achieve this goal are presented.

1232. Knopp, Clifford E. "Teaching Environmental Education with a Focus on Values." Readings in Values Clarification (item 212), pp. 161-174.

1233. Kuhn, David J. Value Education in the Sciences: The Step Beyond Concepts and Processes. Kenosha, WI: University of Wisconsin-Parkside, 1973. ED 080 317.

Centers around the introduction of a values approach to science instruction. Teaching strategies are included which are compatible with a values clarification approach. Also School Science and Mathematics, 74 (1974): 583-588.

1234. Kuhn, David J. "Value Systems in Life Science Instruction." Science Education, 57 (1973): 343-351.

Demonstrates how values clarification techniques can be used in life sciences instruction to develop the necessary student awareness to enable them to make ecologically sound decisions.

1235. Lamb, William. "Classroom Environmental Value Clarification." Journal of Environmental Education, 6 (Summer 1975): 14-19.

Describes a program in which science fiction was used to impel pupils to clarify some of their environmental/ecological values.

1236. Offurum, Robert S. "Science and Moral Education: How Science Teaching Can Address Itself to the Problem of Moral Responsibility." Ed.D. dissertation, Rutgers University, 1977. 38/07, p. 4075.

Formulates a rationale and curriculum design for science teaching where moral responsibility is faced while at the same time teaching for scientific knowledge.

1237. Pilburn, Michael D. "Values Education: Insights from the Social Sciences." Science Teacher, 43 (March 1976): 18-20.

Argues that the teaching of science is value laden and that the values of science teachers are quite different than those of other adult Americans. Compares and contrasts three approaches to values education (development, values clarification and values inquiry) and concludes that value inquiry is the best suited for the teaching of science.

1238. Raisner, Arnold. "The Left Hand of Science." *Science and Children*, 11 (May 1974): 7-9.

Argues that the study of science can also be a tool for the development of moral and social values.

1239. Shattuck, J. Bruce. "Using the Sciences for Value Clarification." *Science Education*, 54 (1970): 9-11.

Sex Education

1240. DeSanto, C. "Sex Education within a Social Context." Journal of Moral Education, 3 (1973): 345-352.

Argues that sex education should be taught in the schools with the facts of life being the focus at the elementary level and the social and moral context of sexual intercourse receiving major attention at the secondary level.

1241. DiStefano, Ann. "Adolescent Moral Reasoning about Sexual and Interpersonal Dilemmas." Moral Education: A First Generation of Research and Development (item 428), pp. 146-164.

Describes the rationale for and theory behind a high school course entitled "The Psychology of Ethics in Relationships."

1242. Harris, Alan. "What Does Sex Education Mean?" Journal of Moral Education, 1 (1971): 7-11.

The concept of the purpose of education is applied to sex education and some of the main implications are drawn out. It is suggested that viewpoint of John Wilson on moral education is a useful approach to sex education.

1243. Hayman, Howard S. "Sex Education and Our Core Values." Journal of School Health, 44 (1974): 62-69.

Ties the teaching of sex education to certain key core values of our democratic society such as free speech, freedom and responsibility, individualism and the common good, etc.

1244. Hoffman, Alan, John J. Pietrofesa and Howard Splete. "Human Sexuality: Can Values Be Clarified in the Schools?" Behavioral and Social Science Teacher, 2 (Fall 1974): 40-47.

Offers three approaches for helping children deal with their sexuality: values clarification, moral education (Kohlberg) and consultation activities.

1245. Morrison, Eleanor S. and Mila U. Price. Values in Sexuality: A New Approach to Sex Education. New York: Hart Publishing Co., 1974.

Contains a series of practical classroom activities designed to get pupils to become more clear about the values underlying their attitudes toward sex.

1246. Rees, Floyd D. "Teaching the Valuing Process in Sex Education." Readings in Values Clarification (item 212), pp. 217-224.

Students must be allowed to decide for themselves what constitutes acceptable sexual behavior.

1247. Regan, Patricia A. "Does Sex Education Change Student's Values?" Salt Lake City, UT: University of Utah, 1980. ED 189 039.

Found that an instructor who "considers herself liberal in sexual matters" and who teaches a sex education course in a "nonmoralistic manner" has no impact on students sexual values.

1248. Risby, J.F. "The Moral Considerations Affecting Sex Education in the Primary School." Journal of Moral Education, 3 (1973): 325-343.

The general background to and justification for sex education in primary schools is discussed. The inevitability of moral guidance in sex education is pointed out, but teachers are warned not to be too obtrusive about it at the primary level.

1249. Roberts, D.F. and G. Roberts. "Techniques for Confronting Sex-Role Sterotyping." School Psychology Digest, Summer (1973): 47-54.

Emphasizes the need to examine traditional sex-role stereotypes, and provides examples of values clarification techniques to meet this objective.

1250. Sadker, David and Myra Sadker. "Nonsexist Teaching: Strategies and Practical Applications." Values Concepts and Techniques (item 1784), pp. 189-203.

Presents a taxonomy of goals for reducing sexism in classrooms: Awareness, clarification and action. Contains practical ideals for classroom practice.

1251. Sadker, David, Myra Sadker and Sidney Simon. "Clarifying Sexist Values." Social Education, 37 (1973): 756-760.

Shows how values clarification activities can be used to help individuals confront sexist values.

1252. Samson, Jean-Marc. "The Objectives of Sex Education in the Schools." Journal of Moral Education, 3 (1974): 207-222.

The lack of precise identification of objectives for sex education is noted. A literature review suggests five categories of objectives. A sixth objective based on the work of Kohlberg is presented.

1253. Samson, Jean-Marc. "Sex Education and Values: Is Indoctrination Avoidable?" Development of Moral Reasoning (item 26), pp. 232-268.

Discusses four general approaches to the question of sexual values. Samson prefers a developmental approach because of its defensible theoretical base.

Social Studies

1254. Beddington, Tony. "Empathy and the Teaching of History." British Journal of Educational Studies, 28 (1980): 13-19.

Discusses a variety of definitions of empathy with a view to arriving at a definition which is usable in the teaching of history.

1255. Barr, Robert, ed. Values and Youth: Teaching Social Studies in An Age of Crisis. Washington, DC: National Council for the Social Studies, 1971. NI

Presents a collection of papers on the values of youth and on ways that social studies can help students with their value crises.

1256. Bauer, Nancy W. "Guaranteeing the Values Component in Elementary School Social Studies." Social Education, 31 (1967): 43-46.

Presents a framework for developing social studies curriculum that guarantees that values goals will be achieved.

1257. Black, Hedda. "Moral Judgments and History Teaching." Australian Journal of Education, 21 (1977): 34-40.

Discusses the potential role of history in the moral development of youth.

1258. Brown, R.A. and Brown, M.R. "Biography and the Development of Values." Social Education, 36 (1972): 43-48.

Argues that by exposing children to biography, teachers can assist them in seeing the important role that values play in individuals lives. A list of recommended biographies is included.

1259. Cirrincione, Joseph M. "The Role of Values in the Teaching of Geography." Ph.D. dissertation, Ohio State University, 1970. 31/09, p. 4377.

It was found that geography education is devoid of theories associated with values and valuation. To reduce the current state of confusion, a Deweyian theory is proposed.

1260. Clark, Todd. "Whose Job is Values Education?" _Social Education_, 41 (1977): 405-406.

Argues that since almost every human act represents a value choice, it is better if that choice has been examined rather than it occur reflexively. The source of our values should come from the Constitution and the Bill of Rights.

1261. Cole, Richard A. _A New Role for Geographic Education: Values and Environmental Concerns_. Oak Park, IL: National Council for Geographic Education, 1974.

Presents a value clarification approach to teaching geography.

1262. Duffey, Robert V. "Moral Education and the Study of Current Events." _Social Education_, 39 (1975): 33-35.

Demonstrates the inevitability of moral issues in current events and presents some operational principles for handling these moral questions in the classroom.

1263. Elder, Carl A. _Making Value Judgments: Decisions for Today_. Columbus, OH: Charles E. Merrill, 1972.

Presents an inquiry--values analysis approach. Students are asked to choose from alternatives, consider consequences and act on one's decisions. Intended as a text for high school use, it has chapters on such topics as drugs, prejudice, citizenship, consumerism, and the like.

1264. Endres, Raymond J. "The Humanities, the Social Studies, and the Process of Valuing." _Social Education_, 34 (1970): 544-548.

Argues that the humanities play an important role in developing and reinforcing a value system. The current status of the humanities presents a bleak and negative view of man.

1265. Fenton, Edwin. "A Developmental Approach to Civic Education." Values Education: Theory/Practice/Problems/Prospects (item 1805), pp. 41-50.

Claims that the reason the new social studies failed was its lack of an adequate psychological base for civic education. Argues that the new civic education should be grounded in developmental psychology.

1266. Fraenkel, Jack. "Value Education in the Social Studies." Phi Delta Kappan, 50 (1969): 457-461.

Argues for a greater clarity among teachers concerning their goals for moral education. The proper focus should be on the process of decision making.

1267. Gray, Charles E. "Curricular and Heuristic Models for Value Inquiry." Bloomington, IL: Illinois State University, 1972. ED 070 737.

Presents a rationale for organizing a social studies program in such a way as to encourage students to analyze and compare cultural value systems and value judgments. A heuristic model for dealing with value judgments in a logical manner is presented.

1268. Gray, Charles E. "Value Inquiry and the Social Studies." Education, 93 (November/December 1973): 130-137.

In the value analysis tradition, two models are presented.

1269. Harmin, Merrill, Howard Kirschenbaum and Sidney B. Simon. "Teaching History with a Focus on Values." Readings in Values Clarification (item 212), pp. 139-144.

1270. Hoskisson, K. and Biskin, D.S. "Structuring Historical and Current Event Lessons Using Kohlberg's Stages of Moral Development." Peabody Journal of Education, 53 (1976): 289-295.

1271. Jervis, Jack and Brad Wideman. "Values and the Social Studies Curriculum." Social Studies, 62 (1971): 328-329.

In a very general discussion, the authors suggest we should infuse the social studies with values, but we should not teach specific values--only about values.

1272. Jones, Clive. "The Contribution of History and Literature to Moral Education." Journal of Moral Education, 5 (1976): 127-138.

Argues that there is a certain connection, concerned with the technique of sympathetic imagination, called Verstehen, which is used identically in moral, historical and literary reasoning. Recommendations for moral education are offered based on this technique.

1273. Kickbusch, Kenneth K. "Values Education in a Confluent Social Studies Curriculum." Values Concepts and Techniques (item 1784), pp. 48-58.

Describes a curriculum approach at Nicolet High School in Wisconsin which attempts to integrate the cognitive and affective domains of learning.

1274. Kirkhorn, Judith and Patrick Griffin. "Exploring Social Issues: A Values Clarification Simulation Game." Values Concepts and Techniques (item 1784), pp. 159-170.

1275. Kohlberg, Lawrence. "Moral Development and the New Social Studies." Social Education, 37 (1973): 369-375.

Five basic postulates of the new social studies derived from Deweyan thinking are presented and it is shown how the new social studies has neglected two central assumptions of Dewey. The cognitive-developmental theory is presented and the ways it can assist educators in achieving the goals of social studies education is discussed. Also in 1709.

1276. Ladenburg, Muriel, and Thomas Ladenburg. "Moral Reasoning and Social Studies." Theory Into Practice, 16 (1977): 112-117.

Presents a developmental conception of the study of history. Within this conception the study of history is viewed as a process comprised of four steps: understanding the context of events, knowing the nature of the event, making judgments about the moral and ethical basis for decisions and actions, and attempting to understand the underlying causes and motives.

1277. Ladenburg, Thomas. "Cognitive Development and Moral Reasoning in the Teaching of History." Moral Education: A First Generation of Research and Development (item 428), pp. 113-125.

Discusses how moral conflicts in history can be used as a focus for stimulating cognitive moral development. Also in The History Teacher, 10(1977), Developmental Counseling and Teaching (item 784), and Adolescent's Development and Education (item 1806).

1278. Ladenburg, Thomas. "Cognitive Development and the Teaching of Social Studies." Readings in Moral Education (item 449), pp. 98-109.

Argues that the time has come for social studies educators to apply the developmental educator's knowledge, insights and techniques to their own disciplines.

1279. Lieberman, Phyllis and Sidney B. Simon. "Current Events and Values." Social Education, 29 (1965): 532-533.

Discusses the application of the values clarification approach to the study of current events.

1280. Lockwood, Alan L. "Values Education and the Study of Other Cultures." Washington, DC: National Education Association, 1976.

Discusses culture study from the perspective of five values education approaches.

1281. McAulay, J.D. "Values and Elementary Social Studies." Social Studies, 65 (1974): 61-64.

Argues that through the social studies the child becomes aware of the values which comprise the web of relationships between man and his world. Presents a method by which teachers can lead students, through social studies, to see how those values relate directly to the individual and the social group.

1282. McCoy, Norma. "A View on the Theory and Process of Value Education." History and Social Science Teacher, 11 (1975): 15-26.

Presents a general description of values education and describes how to integrate it into the history curriculum.

1283. Mackey, James A. "Using Moral Dilemmas to Study the American Revolution." Curriculum Review, 15 (1976): 100-104.

Presents Kohlbergian theory and two dilemmas based on incidents drawn from the American Revolution for use in the classroom.

1284. Miller, Lebern N. "A Law Case Approach to Ethical Education." Educational Forum, 21 (1957): 421-428.

Reports the results of the use of law cases as a basis for ethical education. It was found that the approach produced more positive attitudes toward the law.

1285. Shire, Rossie J. "Three Curriculum Projects and Values Education." Ed.D. dissertation, University of Illinois, 1969. 31/02, p. 668.

Analyzes the perspective on values education of three social studies curriculum projects: The Harvard Public Issues Project, Inquiries in Sociology and Holt Social Studies Curriculum.

1286. Simon, Frank. "Moral Development: Some Suggested Implications for the Social Studies Teacher." Social Studies, 66 (1975): 150-153.

Discusses how a developmental framework entails age-specific practices for effective social education.

1287. Simon, Sidney and Alice Carnes. "Teaching Afro-American History with a Focus on Values." Readings in Values Clarification (item 212), pp. 145-149.

1288. Van Scotter, Richard D. and Jan Cauley. "Future Values for Today's Curriculum." Values Concepts and Techniques (item 1784), pp. 257-267.

Discusses classroom activities oriented toward predicting changes in values as a result of probable futures.

1289. Ward, L.O. "History-Humanity's Teacher?" Journal of Moral Education, 4 (1975): 101-104.

An exploratory essay on the role of history in moral education. Examines the psychological evidence for the value of history in developing moral judgment. The possible role of identification in this process is explored.

1290. Weaver, V. Phillips. "Moral Education and the Study of United States History." Social Education, 39 (1975): 36-39.

Through case studies on Truman, M.L. King and Native Americans it is shown how moral questions are an integral part of U.S. history.

Other Areas

1291. Ally, Louis E. "Athletics in Education--The Double Edged Sword." Phi Delta Kappan, 56 (1974): 102-105; 113.

Argues that athletics can contribute to the development of positive behavior patterns, but that it requires coaches of the highest integrity.

1292. Appell, George N. "Teaching Anthropological Ethics: Developing Skills in Ethical Decision-Making and the Nature of Moral Education." Anthropological Quarterly, 49 (1976): 81-88.

The case-discussion method grafted upon anthropology courses is seen as a means of developing greater knowledge, awareness of ethics, and skills for ethical decision making.

1293. Cullen, Greta T. "Moral Education Through Art." Journal of Moral Education, 3 (1974): 143-150.

Suggests that art education can make a contribution to moral education through developing feelings and awareness. It can also help mental health and stimulate creativity and imagination.

1294. Curry, Charles W. "Vocational Education and the Changing American Work Ethic." Values Concepts and Techniques (item 1784), pp. 225-234.

Discusses the eroding work ethic and how vocational education can be a factor in strengthening it.

1295. Donaldson, Jay. "Working with Parents: A Values Clarification Approach." Paper presented at the Annual International Convention of the Council for Exceptional Children, Chicago, 1976. ED 122 567.

Presents sample workshop materials for use with parents of exceptional children to assist them and their children in personal growth.

1296. Epp, Ronald H. "An Approach to the Teaching of Philosophy." Understanding Human Values (item 1812), pp. 270-274.

Discusses how increasing understanding about one's own and others' values is used to heighten interest and participation in a course dealing with traditional ethical theories.

1297. Frost, Reuben B. and Edward J. Sims, eds. Development of Human Values Through Sports. Washington, DC: American Alliance for Health, Physical Education and Recreation, 1974. ED 099 352.

Contains a series of papers presented at a nation conference held at Springfield College in October 1973. The papers all agree that sport can develop values but such development is not automatic. Relevant research is cited in the papers as well as suggestions for designing sports activities for maximum effectiveness in cultivating values.

1298. Glashagel, Jerry, et al. Digging In ... Tools for Value Education in Camping. New York: National Board of Young Men's Christian Association, 1976. ED 165 965.

Presents a guide for training a camp staff to incorporate values education into the camping experience. Contains a variety of well-designed activities for use in a variety of camping situations.

1299. Greenberg, Herbert J. "The Objectives of Mathematics Education." Mathematics Teacher, 67 (1974): 639-643.

Discusses the role that mathematics education can play in the development of values.

1300. Gurry, Joanne. Speech Communication and Values Clarification. Paper presented at annual meeting of the Eastern Communication Association, 1975. ED 113 762.

1301. Harmin, Merrill, Howard Kirschenbaum and Sidney B. Simon. "The Search for Values with a Focus on Math." Readings in Values Clarification (item 212), pp. 175-184.

How to squeeze values clarification into the multiplication tables.

1302. Howe, Leland W., et al. "Clarifying Values Through Foreign Language Study." Hispania, 56 (1973): 404-406.

Contains values questions en espanol.

1303. Kirschenbaum, Howard. "Teaching Home Economics with a Focus on Values." Readings in Values Clarification (item 212), pp. 185-189.

1304. Kirschenbaum, Howard and Sidney B. Simon. "Values and the Futures Movement in Education." Learning for Tomorrow. Edited by Alvin Toffler. New York: Random House, 1974. pp. 257-271.

Presents standard values clarification fare and applies it to futures education.

1305. Kniker, Charles R. "The Values of Athletics in Schools: A Continuing Debate." Phi Delta Kappan, 56 (1974): 116-120.

Reviews research and concludes that there is a lack of evidence whether athletics is harmful or beneficial to youth.

1306. Ropko, Frederick A. "An Introductory Secondary School Ceramics Curriculum Model Derived from Four Contemporary Value Education Sources." Ph.D. dissertation, University of Maryland, 1977. 38/11, p. 6476.

An introductory secondary school ceramics course developed as a vehicle for improving human relationships through values education techniques was judged by a jury to be relatively effective.

1307. Rudd, Josephine B. Teaching for Changed Attitudes and Values. Washington, DC: Home Economics Education Association, 1971. ED 078 203.

Designed as helpful guide for home economics teachers who wish to teach for values. The approach is eclectic.

1308. Shea, Edward. Ethical Decisions in Physical Education and Sport. Springfield, IL: Thomas, 1978.

Argues that ethical issues are central considerations in evaluating the educational effects of physical education and sport. Presents a model of ethical decision making and varied case studies relating ethical and physical education. Intended for use in college level courses.

1309. Simon, Sidney, Geri Curwin, and Marie Hartwell. "Teaching Values." Readings in Values Clarification (item 212), pp. 336-339.

How values clarification can be used within the Girl Scouts.

1310. Tamminga, Harriet L. "Moral Education Through Gaming-Simulation in Sociology Courses." Teaching Sociology, 4 (1977): 251-270.

The use of gaming-simulation to teach moral values is discussed. The major focus of the paper is on how simulation-gaming is compatible with the goals of moral education.

1311. Walker, Joseph J. "Developing Values in Gifted Children." Teaching Exceptional Children, 7 (1975): 98-100.

Argues that there is a need to develop cooperative as well as competitive values in gifted education. Presents a number of possible activities for use drawn largely from affective education.

1312. Wolfe, David E. and Leland W. Howe. "Personalizing Foreign Language Instruction." Readings in Values Clarification (item 212), pp. 190-206.

Startegies, based primarily on values clarification, are presented which are designed to make the teaching and learning of foreign languages more humane and personally involving for the student.

ADDITIONAL TOPICS AND ISSUES IN MORAL EDUCATION

Survey Data on Moral Education

1313. Atkin, Eugene L. "Students' Views of Objectives for Teaching Value-Development in College Humanities Courses." Ph.D. dissertation, University of Minnesota, 1977. 38/06, p. 3308.

1314. Bayer, Gerald A. "The Perceptions of Parents of Teachers Regarding School Practices Related to Stages of Moral Cognitive Development." Ed.D. dissertation, Wayne State University, 1980. 41/10, p. 4263.

Finds that teachers and parents attribute different stages of moral reasoning concerning what is being taught in the hidden curriculum.

1315. Beck, Clive, et al. The Moral Education Project (Year 4): Annual Report 1975-76. Toronto Institute for Studies in Education, 1978. ED 151 285.

Reports the results of an opinion survey administered to 12,000 Ontario educators. Most respondants agreed that respecting others and developing social responsibility were the primary goals for moral education. Additionally the survey collected information on materials currently being used in moral education.

1316. Blum, Mark. Ethical-Citizenship Education Policies and Programs: A National Survey of State Education Agencies. Philadelphia: Research for Better Schools, 1977. ED 156 592.

Reports the results of a national survey of state education agencies. What's going on in 46 states is reported, as well as names and addresses of contact people in each state. The diversity of approaches reported makes for interesting reading.

1317. Boyd, Dwight. "Teachers' Reflections on Morality: An Exploratory Study." Moral Education Forum, 5 (Winter 1980): 4-15.

Describes an interview format and preliminary results of an attempt to find out what teachers understand as the domain of moral education and what they see as their place within this domain.

1318. Britt, Rodney C. "A Survey and Analysis of the Values/Moral Education Approaches Currently being Recommended and Sponsored by the Fifty State Departments of Education." Ed.D. dissertation, Auburn University, 1977. 38/08, p. 4722.

All state departments of education were found to recognize values education as a viable part of the state's social studies program.

1319. Chester, Richard D. "A Report on National Programs in Citizenship and Four-Related Education." Martin, TN: University of Tennessee-Martin, 1980. ED 194 411.

Presents a selective overview of current programs in moral, legal, and citizenship education.

1320. Cistone, Dominick. "Levels of Moral Reasoning Compared with Demographic Data Among Teachers, Administrators, and Pupil Personnel Employees Enrolled in Graduate Schools." Ed.D. dissertation, University of Southern California, 1980. 40/06, p. 2367.

No significant differences in moral reasoning were found among a cross section of teachers, administrators and pupil personnel employees. It was concluded that moral reasoning is not a factor influencing communication among these groups.

1321. Dow, Owen B. "Moral Education: A Comparative Assessment of the Public Schools in Salt Lake County." Ed.D. dissertation, Brigham Young University, 1980. 40/12, p. 6223.

Examined the stated philosophies of public secondary schools in Salt Lake County in Utah, and compared their philosophies with what is actually being taught as evidenced by statements in course descriptions. 32 moral values were identified as being consistent across all levels of analysis.

1322. Elcott, Ross E. "The Importance of Moral Education Goals as Perceived by Constituencies at the Local School District Level." Ed.D. dissertation, State University of New York at Albany, 1979. 40/03, p. 1240.

A "Moral Education Goals Assessment" instrument was developed and administered to constituents in a local school district. It was found that there was agreement only about autonomous goals for moral education--disagreement existed about the priority for pre-conventional and conventional goals.

1323. Hersh, R.H., and S. Pagliuso. "A Comparison of Two Moral Education Surveys: U.S. and Ontario Educators." Phi Delta Kappan, 58 (1977): 773-774.

Similarities and differences are noted between a U.S. and Canadian survey of teachers. Canadians seem more in favor of instilling agreement with society's rules.

1324. Hildebrand, Verna. "Value Orientations for Nursery School Programs." Reading Improvement, 12 (1975): 168-178.

Describes a research instrument developed to ascertain the value orientation of individuals interested in nursery school programs. The value orientation of individuality was preferred by a majority of the respondents.

1325. Hill, Trios G. "A Study of Moral Education Perceptions of Elementary and High School Principals in Missouri." Ed.D. dissertation, University of Mississippi, 1976. 37/03, p. 1330.

It was found that principals were generally supportive of the schools being involved in moral education as an aid to the family and church.

1326. Kay, William. "Some Changes in Primary School Teachers' Attitudes to Religious and Moral Education." Journal of Moral Education, 3 (1973): 407-411.

Finds that teachers are moving away from religious education and more toward an emphasis on moral content alone.

1327. Kuhmerker, Lisa. "We Don't Call it Moral Education: American Children Learn about Values." Journal of Moral Education, 3 (1973): 359-365.

Documents the increasing attention values education is receiving in the United States.

1328. Mackay, J. Keiller. Religious Information and Moral Development. Toronto: Ontario Department of Education, 1969.

Presents a major study of religion in public schools in Ontario: the "Mackay Report." The report concluded that the commonly accepted characteristics of moral reasoning can be distinguished and taught independently of moral beliefs.

1329. May, P.R. "Teachers' Attitudes to Moral Education." Educational Research, 11 (June 1969): 215-218.

Reports the results of a survey of British teachers on the possible content of moral education lessons. It appears many teachers are willing to experiment in this area and favor teaching about general ethical principles, the law of the land, Christian ethics, and sexual morality.

1330. Michigan State Department of Education. Education in Moral Values in Michigan: A Report on a Survey. Lansing, MI: Author, 1968. ED 052 119.

In the results of a survey of 269 school districts it was found that superintendents felt that schools should be teaching values, its place in the curriculum is in the social studies, English and home economics, and teachers should set a moral example.

1331. Mignogra, William D. "Teaching Moral and Spiritual Values in the Public Schools of New Jersey." Ed.D. dissertation, Temple University, 1964. 31/10, p. 5086.

Using a questionnaire to administrators it was found that a majority of the techniques used to teach moral and spiritual values are legal according to Supreme Court decisions.

1332. Mulkey, Young J. "Reactions of Parents of Different Ethnic and Socio-Economic Groups to Instruction in Values Education in a Metropolitan Area." Ph.D. dissertation, University of Texas at Austin, 1979. 40/07, p. 3746.

It was found that parents want values education. No appreciable difference was found to exist between ethnic groups nor socio-economic-status groups.

1333. Olmo, Barbara G. "Values Education in the New Jersey Secondary Curriculum." 1974. ED 099 263.

Finds that teachers feel the schools should teach specific attitudes, values, and morals, but that there has been little increase in attention to this matter in the last ten years.

1334. Rose, Stephen A. "A Study of Current Practices of Ohio Public Secondary Social Studies Teachers Engaged in Values Education." Ph.D. dissertation, Ohio State University, 1979. 40/04, p. 1995.

1335. Ryan, Kevin, and Michael G. Thompson. "Moral Education's Moddled Mandate." _Moral Education ... It Comes with the Territory_ (item 1811), pp. 405-418.

Analyzes the 1975 Gallup poll results on moral education. Argues that the apparent public endorsement for moral education is more complex than appears at first glance. Also _Phi Delta Kappan_, 56 (1975): 663-666.

1336. Sanders, N.M., and M. Klafter. _The Importance and Desired Characteristics of Moral/Ethical Education in the Public Schools: A Systematic Analysis of Recent Documents_. Philadelphia: Research for Better Schools, 1975.

Analyzes the philosophic statements of 36 state departments of education and 7 professional education organizations regarding the goals of public education as they relate to moral education.

1337. Sanders, N.M., and J. Wallace. Teacher and Parent Opinion Concerning Moral/Ethical Education in the Public Schools: A Report of an Institute for Survey Research Study. Philadelphia: Research for Better Schools, 1975. ED 178 441.

Summarizes a study to determine societal perceptions of the role of the school in moral education. Consensus was found on a wide range of issues related to moral education. Both parents and teachers supported moral education in the schools.

1338. Smith, Jean E. "Moral Reasoning Capability of High School Seniors as Related to Priority of School Goal for Moral Education and Classroom Environment." Ed.D. dissertation, State University of New York at Albany, 1980. 41/05, p. 1930.

When teachers and parents share a felt importance of the need for moral education, students reflect principled moral reasoning in accord with that level of importance.

1339. Snider, Steven C. "The Cognitive Developmental Moral Judgment of Public Senior High School Principals in the State of Indiana. Ph.D. dissertation, Indiana State University, 1977. 38/08, p. 4499.

Most principals think at the conventional level and additional graduate hours beyond the undergraduate degree has no impact on their moral development. Years of experience also has no impact on moral development.

1340. Tallman, George R. "A Study of Elementary Teachers' Attitudes Toward Three Approaches to Values Education in the Social Studies." Ed.D. dissertation, Temple University, 1978. 39/04, p. 2055.

Finds that teachers have the least favorable attitude toward current analytical/process approaches to values education. These are the approaches that experts are most favorable toward.

1341. Wallace, Michael V. "A Survey of the Attitudes of Public High School Teachers Regarding Moral Education in Public High Schools." Ed.D. dissertation, Temple University, 1980. 41/06, p. 2547.

1342. Weaver, Andrew M., and Rodney C. Britt. "Values/ Moral Education Approaches Currently Being Recommended by State Departments of Education." Auburn, AL: Auburn University, 1978. ED 183 466.

Questionnaires were mailed to the highest ranking state social studies supervisor identified. Data was received indicating that all states are involved in values education to varying degrees.

Issues and Instruments in the Evaluation of Moral Education

1343. Allport, G.W., P.E. Vernon and G. Lindzey. A Study of Values. Boston: Houghton Mifflin, 1960.

Reports on the development of an instrument to assess values. In this instrument subjects indicate preferences between carefully chosen alternatives. From this choice the subjects relative value orientation is indicated in six areas: Theoretical, economic, religious, political, aesthetic and social. The results of extensive use of this instrument are reported.

1344. Barton, Alan. "Measuring the Values of Individuals." Religious Education, 57 (July-August 1962): 562-597.

Attempts to map the terrain of research on values, character and religion. Identifies dimensions within these broad areas along which variation among individuals is to be found and discusses the quantification of this variation. An annotated bibliography of value scales and related indices is included.

1345. Beatty, Wolcott H., ed. Improving Educational Assessment and an Inventory of Measures of Affective Behavior. Washington, D.C.: Association for Supervision and Curriculum Development, 1969.

1346. Beck, Clive. "Developing Curriculum for Value Education in the Schools." Developmental Counseling and Teaching (item 784), pp. 128-133.

Argues that the traditional model of educational research is too limiting for values education one can't wait for basic research before beginning dissemination. Also Counseling Psychologist, 6,4 (1977): 30-31

1347. Berkowitz, Marvin. "The Role of Transactive Discussion in Moral Development--The History of a Six-Year Program of Research--Part II." Moral Education Forum, 5 (Fall 1980): 15-27.

Describes the development of the "Transactive Coding Manual."

1348. Bode, James R. and Roger A. Page. "The Ethical Reasoning Inventory." Evaluating Moral Development (item 1391), pp. 139-149.

Discusses the rationale, development, reliability and validity of the Ethical Reasoning Inventory ERI. The ERI presents Kohlbergian dilemmas followed by force-choice stage prototypic responses.

1349. Brandhorst, Allan R. "Reconceptualizing the Affective Domain." Paper presented at the Eastern Educational Research Association Meeting, Williamsburg, VA, 1978. ED 153 891.

Argues that the Bloom/Krathwohl taxonomies are inadequate and three new taxonomies which recognize goals as ends in themselves should be created: a taxonomy of educational objectives with an ego-involvement orientation, a motivational orientation and a moral-development orientation.

1350. Brunkhorst, Herbert K. "Development of a Bioethical Issues Test for Assessing the Effectiveness of Instruction of a Bioethics Unit on the Moral Reasoning Patterns of Secondary Biology Students." Ph.D. dissertation, University of Iowa, 1979. 40/12, p. 6220.

1351. Carroll, James L., and Edward A. Nelson. "Explorations into the Evaluation of the Moral Development of Pre-Adolescents." Evaluating Moral Development (item 1391), pp. 121-130.

Discusses a variety of means of assessing the moral development of pre-adolescents and proposes a new method based on the phenomena of rejection of lower stage immature reasoning.

1352. Cheu, Janey, et al. "The Socio-Scientific Reasoning Model: Instruments for Evaluation." Paper presented at the annual meeting of the National Association for Research in Science Teaching, Atlanta, 1979. ED 173 076.

Describes the development of the Environmental Issues Test to assess moral and ethical reasoning within a scientific or technological context.

1353. Cline, Hugh, and Robert A. Feldmesser. "Problems of Evaluation in Selected Moral and Civic Education Programs." Paper presented at the conference of the Association for Moral Education, Philadelphia, 1979. ED 187 712.

Points out the difficulties of evaluating existing moral education programs and concludes that observation and multiple evaluation techniques would be the most appropriate methods.

1354. Coder, R. "Moral Judgment in Adults." Ph.D. dissertation, University of Minnesota, 1975. 36/03-B, p. 1402.

In a validity study of Rest's Defining Issues Test it was found that the DIT was neither a measure of intelligence nor of left of center political thought.

1355. Colangelo, Nicholas. "Identifying Moral Judgment in Interview Content." Ph.D. dissertation, University of Wisconsin, 1977. 38/06, p. 3283.

Finds that stage of moral judgment can be identified from interview content about actual conflicts in clients' lives.

1356. Colby, Anne, et al. _Standard Form Scoring Manual_, Parts One, Two, Three and Four. Cambridge, MA: Center for Moral Education, June 1979.

Consists of the latest, and supposedly last, of a long string of scoring manuals for the moral judgment interview of Lawrence Kohlberg. The manual reflects Kohlberg's latest revisions of the theory with stages 5A and 5B as the highest form of moral reasoning.

1357. Damon, William. "Measurement and Social Development." _Developmental Counseling and Teaching_ (item 784), pp. 87-93.

Focuses on the methods, problems, uses and misuses of measurement of moral development. It is stressed that one measures development from the child's actual everyday social experience. Also <u>Counseling Psychologist</u>, 6,4 (1977): 13-14.

1358. Damon, William. "Measurement and Social Development." Paper presented at the Annual Meeting of the American Psychological Association, Chicago, 1975. ED 119 812.

Describes the development of dilemmas which tap young childrens' (4-10) social-conceptual development. To accomplish this children are engaged in real situations with practical consequences. The limitations of Kohlbergian hypothetical dilemmas are noted.

1359. Daniels, L.B. "Psycho-Normative Concepts and Moral Education Research." <u>The Teaching of Values in Canadian Education</u> (item 1797), pp. 21-36.

Argues that those who are engaged in research in moral education must understand and correctly use such terms as 'attitudes', 'values' and 'emotions'. Four maxims of conceptual analysis to which anyone must adhere in doing adequate research on moral education are presented.

1360. Davison, M.L. and S. Robbins. "The Reliability and Validity of Objective Indices of Moral Development." <u>Applied Psychological Measurement</u>, 2 (1978): 391-403.

Compares Rest's and Kohlberg's measures of moral development (see items 1356 and 1422). Correlations within age homogeneous groups suggest that the two tests cannot be considered equivalent measures of the same construct. Kohlberg's measure was found to be the most sensitive to change.

1361. DeCosta, Sandra B. "A Study of Developing Moral Opinions in Young Children." Ed.D. dissertation, West Virginia University, 1979. 40/12, p. 6141.

An instrument to measure developing moral opinion was developed incorporating modifications and alterations of Piaget's and Kohlberg's compatible theories of moral development.

1362. Doris, Dennis A. "The Construction of a Model to Develop and Assess the Classroom Teaching of Moral Education." Ph.D. dissertation, University of Utah, 1974. 35/11, p. 6969.

Using primarily the work of Kohlberg and Wilson a model of moral education is developed.

1363. Dukes, William F. "Psychological Studies of Values." Psychological Bulletin, 52 (1955): 24-50.

After brief consideration of the problem of measurement of values, results of studies are reported concerned with value differences between some of the traditional social groupings as well as of studies reporting the relationship between value measures and other tests.

1364. Educational Testing Service. Moral Education: Development of a Model. Final Report. Princeton, NJ: Educational Testing Service, 1972. ED 085 285.

Evaluates the existing literature on moral education and development and develops a model to clarify the concepts of moral judgment, development and commitment.

1365. Erickson, V. Lois. "The Case Study Method in the Evaluation of Developmental Programs." Evaluating Moral Development (item 1391), pp. 151-176.

Presents excerpts from longitudinal case studies selected from a five year follow-up on 21 women who participated in an experimental developmental education course while in high school. Includes data on moral and ego development which reflect significant ego development, but only 1/3 stage growth in moral development was found over a five year period.

1366. Fenton, Edwin. "Moral Development in the Context of Broad Educational Goals." Evaluating Moral Development (item 1391), pp. 205-211.

Argues in opposition to Lockwood (item 1393) that we need evaluation procedures and data that meet the needs of those in whose hands the future of moral education rests--teachers, administrators, board members, parents and students. If moral education is not to be another short lived educational movement the evaluations of programs must sell the approach to the community.

1367. Freeman, S.J. and J.W. Giebink. "Moral Judgment as a Function of Age, Sex, and Stimulus." Journal of Psychology, 102 (1979): 43-47.

An objective measure to assess moral judgment based on Kohlberg's theory was developed. The Objective Assessment of Moral Development (OAMD) was found to be a valid means of assessing moral development.

1368. Geisinger, Robert W. Interaction Analysis of Value-Clarification Behaviors." Houesburg, PA: Pennsylvania State Department of Education, 1970. ED 055 030.

Describes the development of the "Interaction Analysis of Value Clarification Responses" instrument. This instrument enables one to analyze the patterns of discourse during values clarification lessons.

1369. Gephart, William G., et al., eds. Evaluation in the Affective Domain. Bloomington, IN: Phi Delta Kappa, 1976. ED 157 911.

Contains a collection of papers presented at the National Symposium for Professors of Educational Research in 1976 which deal with the nature of affect and principles and guidelines for measureing individual affect and learning environment.

1370. Getzels, J.W. and P.W. Jackson. Creativity and Intelligence. New York: John Wiley and Son, 1962.

Attempts to differentiate between those students who are outstanding in adjustment and those who are outstanding in moral character. Contains the "Do You Agree?" morality test which measures the degree to which subjects will choose correct responses in hypothetical situations.

1371. Gibbs, John C., Keith F. Widaman and Anne Colby. "The Socio-Moral Reflection Measure." Evaluating Moral Development (item 1391), pp. 101-111.

Presents a progress report on the development of the Socio-Moral Reflection Measure--an attempt to develop a systematic instrument which through slightly limiting the subjects' responses, results in an instrument which is more time-efficient to administer but will yield stage of moral reasoning data. The instrument involves asking for the importance of general normative values followed by justification of that evaluation.

1372. Gordon, L.V. _The Survey of Interpersonal Values_. Chicago: Science Research Associates, 1960.

Designed to measure values which involve a social or interpersonal dimension. The scale attempts to assess the relative importance one ascribes to different values.

1373. Gordon, L.V. _The Survey of Personal Values_. Chicago: Science Research Associates, 1960.

Attempts to determine the relative importance one ascribes to six personal values. The development and validation of the scale is described.

1374. Greif, E.B. and R. Hogan. "The Theory and Measurement of Empathy." _Journal of Counseling Psychology_, 20 (1973): 280-284.

Reviews studies supporting the idea that empathy is an important dimension of interpersonal behavior and moral conduct, and reports on factor analysis to determine the underlying structure of Hogan's empathy scale.

1375. Handy, Rollo. _The Measurement of Values_. St. Louis: Warren H. Green, 1970.

Argues that past the attempts to assess values have been marked by vagueness of definition and imprecise measurement instruments. A variety of techniques used to assess values are discussed and critiqued.

1376. Hartnett, J. and M. Shumate. "Ethical Attitudes and Moral Maturity Among Prison Inmates." _Journal of Psychology_, 106 (1980): 147-149.

The construct validity of Hogan's Survey of Ethical Attitudes was tested by employing prison inmates and nonoffenders.

1377. Hartshorne, Hugh and Mark A. May. Studies in the Nature of Character: I. Studies in Deceit. New York: Macmillan, 1930.

Contains the classic inquiry into the effects on children of character education efforts in the early years of the twentieth century. Up to the present this study still stands as the most comprehensive, and creative study of the nature of character.

1378. Hartshorne, Hugh, Mark May and Julius B. Maller. Studies in the Nature of Character: II. Studies in Service and Self Control. New York: MacMillan, 1929.

Studied the more positive human qualities of co-operative and charitable behavior.

1379. Hartshorne, Hugh, Mark A. May, and Frank K. Shuttleworth. Studies in the Nature of Character: III. Studies in the Organization of Character. New York: MacMillan, 1930.

Attempts to synthesize the findings from the two earlier volumes of the study and reach some conclusions regarding the nature of character and the appropriate methodologies for studying it. The situationally specific nature of character is described.

1380. Higgins, Ann. "Research and Measurement Issues in Moral Education Interventions." Moral Education: A First Generation of Research and Development (item 428), pp. 92-107.

Reviews the findings of the studies used to evaluate the Danforth Project (item 481), offers substantive and methodological suggestions, and discusses implications for planning further research and intervention projects.

1381. Hill, Russell A., et. al. Research Studies Reporting Experimental Effects in the Moral/Ethical/Values Domain: An Annotated Bibliography. Philadelphia: Research for Better Schools, 1977.

Contains abstracts of research studies, mostly from the field of psychology and conducted in non-educational settings.

1382. Hogan, Robert. "Development of an Empathy Scale." Journal of Consulting and Clinical Psychology, 33 (1969): 307-316.

Reports on the development of 64-item self-report measure of empathy. It is argued that the instrument is reliable and valid and that it assesses an important dimension of moral character.

1383. Hogan, Robert, and Ellen Dickstein. "A Measure of Moral Values." Journal of Consulting and Clinical Psychology, 39 (1972): 210-214.

Describes the development of a brief, semi-projective measure of moral judgment based on the degree to which subjects responses matched a conception of mature moral concern.

1384. Hunter, William J. "An Initial Validation of a Forced Choice Test of Moral Judgment as Defined by Lawrence Kohlberg." Ph.D. dissertation, Kent State University, 1974. 36/01, p. 187.

Describes the development of an objective means of assessing stage of moral reasoning--Decision Survey. Reliability and validity tests did not support the practical or experimental use of the instrument.

1385. Iozzi, Louis A., and June Paradise-Maul. "Issues at the Interface of Science, Technology and Society." Evaluating Moral Development (item 1391), pp. 131-137.

Discusses the development, reliability and validity of the Environmental Issues Test (E.I.T.). The E.I.T., modeled after Rest's Defining Issues Test, is an objective measure of moral development which uses dilemmas centering on environmental issues.

1386. Johnson, R.C., and J.D. Kalafat. "Projective and Sociometric Measures of Conscience Development." Child Development, 40 (1969): 651-655.

Affective-projective stories, a newly developed set of projective pictures, is used to determine the relationships between guilt and resistance to temptation.

1387. Kavanagh, Harry B. "Some Appraised Instruments of Values for Counselors." Personnel and Guidance Journal, 58 (1980): 613-616.

Reviews six instruments of potential use for counselors: The Study of Values, the Survey of Personal Values, the Survey of Interpersonal Values, the Differential Value Profile, the Personal Orientation Inventory and Ways to Live. The strengths and weaknesses of the approaches are assessed and the potential utility discussed.

1388. Kelley, Harold H. "Moral Evaluation." American Psychologist, 26 (1971): 293-301.

Wishes to bring moral evaluation into the range of psychological analysis and research. The central thesis is that the moral evaluation process (judgments of right and wrong, good and bad) derive their properties in part from the same processes as are involved in judgments of correct and incorrect (reality evaluations) and in judgments of personal success or failure (achievement evaluations).

1389. Kerlinger, Fred N. "The Study and Measurement of Values and Attitudes." Paper presented at the annual meeting of the American Educational Research Association, Chicago, 1972. ED 079 618.

The definition of values and the distinction between attitudes and values is necessary for furthering the progress of values research. Evidence supporting the structural theory of attitudes and values is presented.

1390. Krathwohl, D., B. Bloom and B. Masia. Taxonomy of Educational Objectives: The Classification of Educational Goals, Handbook II: Affective Domain. New York: McKay, 1964.

Presents a taxonomy of the affective domain consisting of five levels: Receiving (attending), responding, valuing, organization and characterization by a value or value complex. The examples of relevant behaviors at each level provide a potential means of assessing the specific levels.

1391. Kuhmerker, Lisa, Marcia Mentkowski, and V. Lois Erickson, eds. Evaluating Moral Development and Evaluating Educational Programs That Have A Value Dimension. Schenectady: Character Research Press, 1980.

Presents a collection of papers delivered at a 1979 conference on the "state of the art" in the evaluation of moral education programs. The papers range from reports of the evaluation specific curriculum projects to more broad considerations regarding the future of evaluation in moral education.

1392. Lieberman, Marcus. "New Directions in Evaluating Moral Education Programs." Evaluating Moral Development (item 1391), pp. 13-26.

After a brief discussion of the current status of educational evaluation and in particular the evaluation of moral judgment, the paper describes the evaluation of a Brookline Massachusetts title IV-C project entitled "Facing History and Ourselves: Holocaust and Human Behavior."

1393. Lockwood, Alan L. "The Original School Board Position in the Evaluation of Moral Education Programs." Evaluating Moral Development (item 1391), pp. 193-203.

Argues that the basis for the evaluation of moral education programs should be from a perspective where rationally self-interested persons, unaware of the status they hold in the educational setting select evaluational foci which are fair to all parties concerned.

1394. Loevinger, Jane. "Issues in the Measurement of Moral Development." Moral Development-ETS (item 1795), pp. 57-68.

Presents a critical analysis of three competing models of moral development and their implications for measuring moral maturity. She stresses the close interrelationship of moral development, interpersonal development, development of self-concept and inner life as a single integrated structure.

1395. McClintock, C.G. "Social Values: Their Definition, Measurement and Development." Journal of Research and Development in Education, 12,1 (1978): 121-13.

Discusses the weaknesses of the Prisoners Dilemma Game for a measure of cooperation and prepares a more complex means of conceptualizing and measuring cooperative and competitive behavior.

1396. Marcia, James. "Development and Validation of Ego-Identity Status." Journal of Personality and Social Psychology, 3 (1966): 551-558.

Four modes of reacting to the late identity crisis were described, measured and validated. The modes of reacting were based on Erikson's formulation of the identity crisis as a psychosocial task.

1397. Martin, R.M., M. Shafto, and W. Vandeinse. "The Reliability, Validity and Design of the Defining Issues Test." Developmental Psychology, 13 (1977): 460-468.

Presents data which may suggest that preference for statements of moral reasoning may reflect a prior commitment to action choice.

1398. Meddin, Jay. "Attitudes, Values and Related Concepts: A System of Classification." Social Science Quarterly, 55 (1975): 889-900.

Attempts to dispell the apparent conceptual confusion regarding the study of subjective phenomena by offering a system of classification of subjective terminology that may be consistently applied in all the social sciences.

1399. Melvin, Arthur I. "Discovering Consensus on a Moral Valuing Standard: A Descriptive and Experimental Study of Century III's Valuing Analysis Papers." Ph.D. dissertation, Northwestern University, 1979. 40/06, p. 3255.

An approach designed to help communities discover and use existing agreed upon universal moral standards without identification with any specific religious political or cultural bias. A complete description of the 12-year history of the Valuing Analysis process is provided.

1400. Mentkoski, Marcia. "Creating a 'Mindset' for Evaluating a Liberal Arts Curriculum Where 'Valuing' is a Major Outcome." Evaluating Moral Development (item 1391), pp. 27-61.

Describes the valuing component of the Liberal Education Curriculum at Alverno College in Milwaukee. As of the writing of this paper the evaluation of the program was unfinished.

1401. Meux, Milton, et al. "The Development of a Value Observation System for Group Discussion in Decision Making: Final Report." Salt Lake City: University of Utah, 1972. ED 066 389.

Reports the results of the development of an observation system which describes some of the important phenomena in groups that have as a task the making of a decision about a controversial issue involving value conflict. It was found that individuals played two sorts of games in such groups: The rationality game and the ego game.

1402. Moran, J.J., and A.J. Joniak. "Effect of Language on Preference for Responses to a Moral Dilemma." Developmental Psychology, 15 (1979): 337-338.

Reports the results of a study which finds that preference for moral statements in moral judgment instruments is an artifact of language sophistication, not a preference for different stages of moral reasoning.

1403. Morris, Charles W. Varieties of Human Value. Chicago: University of Chicago Press, 1956.

Contains the Ways to Live Values questionnaire. The respondent is asked to evaluate 13 different ways to live as described in separate paragraphs. The instrument is designed to yield data on the individual's philosophy of life.

1404. Mosher, Ralph L. "Moral Education: Let's Open the Lens." Evaluating Moral Development (item 1391), pp. 213-222.

Discusses the limitations of moral education achievements to date and argues that if the movement is to remain healthy and grow in the future it will need to be mainstreamed, that is, integrated into the broad goals of schooling.

1405. Murphy, Maribeth L. "Measurement of Values through Responses to Selected Visual Stimulus Materials." Ph.D. dissertation, United States International University, 1970. 30/12, p. 205.

Reports the development and piloting of the Murphy Inventory of Values--an instrument to measure student growth in values development according to the Lasswell/Rucker framework.

1406. Napier, John D. "Effects of Knowledge of Cognitive-Moral Development and Request to Fake on Defining Issues Test P-Scores." Journal of Psychology, 101 (1979): 45-52.

Found that the request to fake higher on the Defining Issues Test has no impact, but knowledge of cognitive developmental theory did have an effect on test scores on the D.I.T.

1407. Page, Roger and James Bode. "Comparisons of Measures of Moral Reasoning and Development of a New Objective Measure." Educational and Psychological Measurement, 40 (1980): 317-329.

The Ethical Reasoning Inventory, an objective instrument for assessing moral reasoning derived from Kohlberg's scoring manual was compared with the Rest Defining Issues Test and the Martland and Goldman Moral Judgment Survey. It was found that the ERI demonstrated a higher internal consistency than the other measures and the testretest reliability compared favorably.

1408. Page, Roger and James Bode. "An Objective Assessment of Moral Reasoning." Moral Education Forum, 3 (November, 1978): 14-15.

Describes the development of the Ethical Reasoning Inventory, an objective instrument to assess moral reasoning. Unlike the Defining Issues Test, this instrument yields stage scores.

1409. Parish, T.S., R.R. Rosenblat and B.M. Koppes. "The Relationship between Human Values and Moral Judgment." Psychology, 16 (Winter 1979/1980): 1-6.

In a comparison of the Rokeach Value Survey and the Rest Defining Issues Test it was found that the students demonstrating higher levels of moral judgment placed a significantly higher priority on the values of equality and mature love.

1410. Pearson, Lea and Colin Elliott. "The Development of a Social Reasoning Scale in the New British Ability Scales." Journal of Moral Education, 10 (1980): 40-48.

Describes the theory behind and the development of the Social Reasoning Scale. The scale has a developmental emphasis and takes a broader, more comprehensive perspective of the social environment than Kohlberg.

1411. Pittel, Stephen and Gerald A. Mendelsohn. "Measurement of Moral Values: A Review and Critique." Psychological Bulletin, 66 (1966): 22-35.

Reviews the literature of efforts to assess strength of moral values and concludes that existing instruments have major weaknesses.

1412. Platek, Theresa F. "The Responses of Six Adolescents to Value Situations in Selected Short Stories: A Case Study of the Valuing Process." Ed.D. dissertation, State University of New York at Buffalo, 1975. 36/06, p. 3245.

Explores the observable aspects of the valuing process as adolescents respond to short stories, value sheets and moral dilemmas. Five stages of valuing response were noted.

1413. Power, Clark. "Further Reflections on Values Assessment." Personnel and Guidance Journal, 58 (1980): 616-617.

Outlines a systematic approach to values research drawing from the Taxonomy of the Affective Domain (item 1390). Specific instruments are used to illustrate how particular dimensions of the values domain may be investigated.

1414. Prince, Richard. "A Study of the Relationships Between Individual Values and Administrator Effectiveness in School Situation." Ph.D. dissertation, University of Chicago, 1957.

Discusses the creation of the Prince Differential Values Inventory, a forced choice values inventory which places students' values along a continuum ranging from emergent to the traditional in value orientation.

1415. Raths, James. "Values and Valuing." Educational Leadership, 21 (1964): 543-546.

Discusses the problems of measurement involved in attempting to study values. Reviews some of the major instruments used in assessing values and points out the problems involved with all of them.

1416. Rest, James. "An Assessment for Moral Judgment." Moral Education Forum, 1 (May, 1976): 1-14.

A brief overview of the rationale behind and development of the Defining Issues Test--an objective measure of cognitive moral development.

1417. Rest, James R. "Basic Issues in Evaluating Moral Education Programs." Evaluating Moral Development (item 1391), pp. 1-12.

Presents arguments for expanding the evaluation of moral education beyond assessing growth in cognitive development. Argues out that since such factors as ego strength, moral sensitivity, moral confusion, unconscious motives and competition from non moral values have all been shown to influence behavior, evaluation of moral education programs should look at multiple outcome variables.

1418. Rest, James R. "The Defining Issues Test: A Survey of Research Results." Evaluating Moral Development (item 1391), pp. 113-120.

Discusses in general terms the results of several hundred studies utilizing the D.I.T. (the definitive discussion of the results of these studies is to be found in item 1419). Also discusses the strengths and weaknesses of the use of the D.I.T. in the evaluation of moral education programs.

1419. Rest, James R. Development in Judging Moral Issues. Minneapolis: University of Minnesota Press, 1979.

As noted by Rest in the preface "the journal articles, dissertations, and manuscripts that report findings on the Defining Issues Test now form a stack over ten feet high." This book condenses and interprets those findings. In a foreward Lawrence Kohlberg compares the Harvard moral judgment interview technique with the Defining Issues Test. The references section is exhaustive and an appendix contains the Defining Issues Test.

1420. Rest, James R. "Development in Moral Judgment Research." Developmental Psychology, 16 (1980): 251-256.

Replies to recent critiques of cognitive developmental interpretations of moral judgment using preference data.

1421. Rest, James R. "Recent Research on an Objective Test of Moral Judgment: How the Important Issues of a Moral Dilemma are Defined." Moral Development: Current Theory and Research (item 1790), pp. 75-93.

Reviews the development of the Defining Issues Test, an objective test measure of level of moral development. Data on reliability and validity are included.

1422. Rest, James. Revised Manual for the Defining Issues Test. Minneapolis: University of Minnesota, 1979.

Describes how to administer and score the questionnaire. Also included are model computer card layouts and programs, how to interpret the scores and data on the reliability and validity of the test.

1423. Rest, James. "Validity of Tests of Moral Judgment." Values Education: Theory/Practice/Problems/Prospects (item 1805), pp. 103-116.

Compares Kohlberg's test with the Defining Issues Test in terms of power of results, replications and sample size of the studies.

1424. Rest, James, et al. "Judging the Important Issues in Moral Dilemmas--An Objective Measure of Development." Developmental Psychology, 10 (1974): 491-501.

Describes the development of the Defining Issues Test.

1425. Rokeach, Milton. "From Individual to Institutional Values: With Special Reference to the Values of Science." Understanding Human Values (item 1812), pp. 47-70.

Proposes an approach to the conceptualization and measurement of institutional values. Data is reported on the instrumental value rankings of science obtained by five methods.

1426. Rokeach, Milton. The Nature of Human Values. New York: The Free Press, 1973.

Discusses the development of an instrument in which one rank orders his/her instrumental and terminal values. The appendix includes a copy of the Rokeach Value Survey and national norms for the instrument.

1427. Roost, Harold C. "An Instrument for Assessing Impact of Curricular Experience on Values." Ph.D. dissertation, Michigan State University, 1975. 36/06, p. 3369.

An instrument is developed--"Values Impact Assessment"--to assess the impact of curricular experience on students. A paper and pencil group assessment of moral reasoning as related to specific curricula (in this case drug abuse) was found to be reasonably reliable and valid.

1428. Ross, John A. "Selecting a Values Education Framework." The History and Social Science Teacher, 15 (1979): 17-25.

Presents a decision making formula to assist school systems in choosing between different approaches to values education.

1429. Sanders, Nicholas M. "Designing Moral Education Program Evaluations to Go Beyond Determining Program Effectiveness." Paper presented at annual convention of the association for moral education, Philadelphia, 1979. ED 194 551.

Discusses four issues which neeed attention when assessing the program effectiveness of moral education curricula: How it will help school personnel deal with a perceived problem, placement of moral education within the total school curriculum, community reaction, and qualifications of those in charge of moral education.

1430. Shostrom, Everett L. Personal Orientation Inventory. San Diego: Educational and Industrial Testing Service, 1963.

Through 150 paired value and behavior judgment items, scores are obtained on twelve bipolar measures of personal values. The score on the Self-Actualizing Value sub-scale is frequently cited as an indicator of self-actualization.

1431. Sprinthall, Norman A. "Fantasy and Reality in Research: How to Move Beyond the Unproductive Paradox." Counseling Education and Supervision, 14 (1975): 310-322.

After reviewing the major flaws in the methods of evaluation of counselor education a model for research designed to assess developmental change is presented.

1432. Stanton, M. "The Assessment of Moral Judgments: Cultural and Cognitive Considerations: Religious Education, 71 (1976): 610-62.

Argues that the focus of research on moral judgments should be on everyday events covering positive and negative situations.

1433. Sullivan, Arthur P. "Measurement of Moral Judgment: Using Stimulus Pairs to Estimate Inter- stage Distances." Paper presented at annual meeting of American Educational Research Association, Toronto, 1978. ED 157 941.

The development of the Sullivan Ethical Reasoning Scale is reported. This scale contains three dilemmas with response pairs representing stages of moral development.

1434. Sullivan, Wilbur H. "The Validation of and Utilization of an Objective Test of Moral Judgment for Students Ten to Fifteen Years of Age." Ed.D. dissertation, University of Arkansas, 1978. 40/03, p. 1267.

1435. Summers, Gene F., ed. Attitude Measurement. Chicago, IL: Rand McNally, 1970. NI

Contains thirty-five articles on various dimensions of attitude measurement. The papers discuss such topics as self-report techniques, indirect tests, direct observation techniques and physiological reaction techniques.

1436. Taylor, Cheri M. "Development of an Instrument to Assess Degree of Principled Moral Thinking about Moral Dilemmas--The Bioethical Issues Test." Ph.D. dissertation, Georgia State University, 1979. 40/10, p. 5390.

Using Rest's Defining Issues Test as a model a Bioethical Issues Test was developed to assess the degree of principled moral thinking of college students on bioethical issues.

1437. Thomas, W.L. The Differential Value Profile. Chicago: W. and J. Stone Foundation, 1963.

The Differential Value Profile is aimed at measuring six factors: Aesthetic, humanitarian, intellectual, material power, and religious. The scale is included along with information on its theory and development.

1438. Thomas, Walter L. "The Initial Development of the Differential Value Profile." Ed.D. dissertation, University of Tulsa, 1970. 31/05, p. 2119.

Discussed the development and validation of the 134 item, six factor Differential Value Profile.

1439. Tyler, Ralph W. "Assessing Educational Achievement in the Affective Domain." East Lansing, MI: National Council on Measurement in Education, 1973. ED 099 394.

Offers suggestions on how best to assess feelings and in doing so draws upon a variety of measurement techniques.

1440. White, Charles B. "Moral Judgments in College Students: The Development of an Objective Measure and its Relationship to Life Experience Dimensions." Ph.D. dissertation, University of Georgia, 1973. 34/07-B, p. 3480.

College students were administered the moral judgment interview and an objective measure of moral reasoning. The results indicate that the objective instrument may be a useful valid discriminator of stage groups.

1441. Whiteley, John M. "Evaluation of Character Development in an Undergraduate Residential Community." Evaluating Moral Development (item 1391), pp. 63-74.

Discusses the impact on seven students of the Sierra Project--a curriculum aimed at character development in college residence hall life at University of California at Irvine. A multi-dimensional evaluation procedure is used involving moral reasoning, ego development, sex role choices, sense of community, locus of control, participant information and student experience at college.

1442. Wight, A.R., and J.R. Doxsey. "Measurement in Support of Affective Education." Salt Lake City, UT: Interstate Educational Resource Service Center, 1972. ED 069 731.

Discusses general concerns and considerations regarding measurement in affective education.

1443. Williams, D., and I. Wright. "Values and Moral Education: Analyzing Curriculum Materials." The Social Studies, 67 (1977): 166-172.

A schema for analyzing and comparing values/moral education curriculum materials is presented. The major components of the schema are antecedent conditions, rationale and objectives, descriptive characteristics, pupil activities, teaching strategies and diagnosis and evaluation needs.

1444. Wilmoth, Gregory H., and Sam G. McFarland. "A Comparison of Four Measures of Moral Reasoning." Journal of Personality Assessment, 41 (1977): 396-401. ED 134 621.

Compares Kohlberg's Moral Judgment Scale, Gilligan et al.'s Sexual Moral Judgment Scale, Maitland and Goldman's Objective Moral Judgment Scale and Hogan's Maturity of Moral Judgment Scale.

1445. Wright, Ian, and David Williams. "An Analysis of Selected Curriculum Materials in Values/Moral Education." Vancouver: University of Britsh Columbia, 1977. ED 143 569.

Develops a model (Curriculum Materials Analysis System) for evaluating values education materials and then uses the model on selected materials.

1446. Ziv, Abner. "Measuring Aspects of Morality." Journal of Moral Education, 5 (1976): 189-201.

A group test reviewing five aspects of morality in children is presented. Aspects are resistance to temptation, stage of moral judgment, confession after transgression, reaction of fear or guilt and severity of punishment for transgression. Data on the validity of the test are presented.

1447. Barton, Douglas L. "A Comparison of Moral Judgment and Student Teacher Effectiveness." Ph.D. dissertation, University of Utah, 1979. 40/03, p. 1414.

It was found that there was no relationship between a student teachers' level of moral judgment and ratings of their student teacher effectiveness.

1148. Bellanca, James A. Values and the Search for Self. Washington, D.C.: National Education Association, 1975.

An inductively structured, experientially based, self-paced, individualized book intended for teachers designed to help the readers discover themselves, their values, and their stance on key issues.

1449. Bensley, Marvin L. "Value Enhancement for Children through Nondirective Inservice Teacher-Training." Ph.D. dissertation, United States International University, 1970. 31/05, p. 2224.

Classes taught by teachers trained in non-directive techniques resulted in positive changes in academic achievement, intelligence scores, value enhancements and behavior patterns of children.

1450. Betof, Edward H. "The Degree of Implementation of Values Clarification by Classroom Teachers Following an Intensive Thirty-Six Hour Workshop." Ed.D. dissertation, 1976. 37/04, p. 2118.

Generally it was found that a high degree of implementation followed participation in the teachers workshop.

1451. Bloom, R.B. "Morally Speaking, Who Are Today's Teachers?" Phi Delta Kappan, 57 (1976): 624-625.

Using the Defining Issues Test it was found that only about 30 percent of the moral reasoning of teachers was at the principled level. This is about ten percent lower than other samples of college graduates. The implications for moral and teacher education are discussed.

1452. Bower, P. Kenneth. "Evaluation of a Competency-Based Self-Instructional Module Designed to Prepare Pre-Service Elementary Teachers to Use Questioning Skills in Conducting Moral Discussions in the Elementary School Classroom." D.Ed. dissertation, Pennsylvania State University, 1974. 36/03, p. 1445.

1453. Burton, John K., Thomas C. Hunt, and Terry M. Wildman. "Who Transmits Values? The Public Schools." Educational Leadership, 37 (1980): 314-318.

Argues that both historically and in response to current social needs, there has been and will continue to be a need for affective education in the schools.

1454. Costello, Marjorie F. "The Valuing Process in the Classroom: The Role of the English Teacher in Facilitating Student Growth in the Valuing Process." Ed.D. dissertation, University of Massachusetts, 1974. 35/05, p. 2821.

Describes one component of a teacher education program designed to generate in the prospective teacher of English an awareness of values and the valuing process and of his/her role in values teaching in literature study.

1455. Crabtree, Walden B. "Why and How Teachers Teach Values." American Secondary Education, 2 (June 1972): 16-20.

Argues that the teaching of values is a core function of teachers lives as professionals. Eight ways that teachers influence students' values are presented.

1456. Crow, Marsha L. "A Survey and In-Service Workshop Package on Moral Education." Boise, ID: Boise State University, 1979. ED 171 631.

Reviews moral education literature, presents a questionnaire on moral education for Seventh-day Adventist elementary school teachers, and provides an inservice workshop package in moral education.

1457. Daly, Brian E. "Values Education in Teacher Preparation: The 'State of the Art' in Higher Education." Ed.D. dissertation, University of Arkansas, 1978. 39/06, p. 3523.

1458. Delatte, Edwin J. "Moral Education: A Response to Burton, Hunt and Wildman." Educational Leadership, 37 (1980): 319-320.

Responding to item 1453, Delatte isn't sure that doing something about values is better than doing nothing at all. It is argued that the proper preparation for teachers to do values education would be very demanding and if education is not ready to make teachers be well-prepared, it might be well to do nothing.

1459. Elliot, Richard J. "Causality, Values and Education." Journal of Thought, 14 (1979): 29-32.

Argues that teachers, if they are to be effective as moral educators must understand that value choices of children are made to protect and enhance individuals. Teachers should not be critical of children in this regard.

1460. Fraenkel, Jack. "Teacher Approaches to the Resolution of Value Conflicts." Paper presented at the Annual Meeting of the National Council for the Social Studies, Boston, 1972, ED 092 445.

Reports the results of a study where teachers were asked to resolve a value conflict. It was found that teachers were unable to perceive a situation from the author's viewpoint and resolved conflict by authority or avoidance. Questions are raised regarding the use of values education materials if teachers manifest this outlook.

1461. Freiberg, H. Jerome and Dennis Foster. "Who Should Facilitate Values Education?" Journal of Teacher Education, 30,3 (May-June 1979): 37-40.

Argues that too little attention has been paid to the teachers importance and competence in the scheme of values and moral education. Five skills are presented which are essential for becoming an effective facilitator of student values.

1462. Galbraith, Ronald E. "An Appraisal of Two Approaches for Training History Teachers to Apply Kohlberg's Theory of Moral Development." D.A. dissertation, Carnegie-Mellon University, 1977. 36/07, p. 3908.

Two approaches, self instructional versus traditional teacher education workshop format, were found to be equally effective in preparing teachers to conduct moral reasoning discussions.

1463. Galbraith, Ronald E. and Thomas M. Jones. "Teaching for Moral Reasoning in the Social Studies: A Research Report." Developmental Counseling and Teaching (item 784), pp. 348-355.

Presents a study in which teachers were trained to be developmental educators either through a handbook or through a training institute. No difference in student's moral development occured as a result of the training received. Also Counseling Psychologist, 6,4 (1977).

1464. Gennell, Marylouise. "Value and Moral Development for Elementary and Secondary School Teachers." Values Pedagogy in Higher Education (item 1558), pp. 187-194.

Describes a program designed to assist teachers in developing skills for understanding the values implicit in their teaching environment. The major emphasis appears to be on values clarification.

1465. Gray, Charles E. "Value Education Outcomes: Implications for the Social Studies Methods Course." Ph.D. dissertation, University of Illinois, 1968. 30/01, p. 188.

Concludes that in spite of available value related knowledge, most social studies educators pay it little attention in their teaching. Presents educational outcomes related to values which provide the basis for a methods course which deals with values inquiry.

1466. Griffore, R.J., and J. Lewis. "Characteristics of Teachers' Moral Judgment." Educational Research Quarterly, 3,3 (1978): 20-30.

Practicing teachers were administered the Defining Issues Test. It was found that teachers level of principled moral reasoning was no higher than that of other adults.

1467. Guy, Hattie J. "An Attitudinal Survey of Teachers Toward Teaching the Process of Valuing in Schools Based on the Values Clarification Approach." Ph.D. dissertation, University of Iowa, 1975. 36/08, p. 4989.

Teachers responded that they generally have a favorable attitude to the schools being involved in values education and toward values clarification in particular.

1468. Harris, Sandra C. "An Evaluative Study Involving the Development and Field-Testing of a Values Clarification Module for Teacher Education Students Which Offers Alternative Paths Based on Cognitive Style." Ed.D. dissertation, University of Georgia, 1974. 36/05, p. 2613.

1469. Hawley, Robert C. "Values and Decision Making." Independent School Bulletin, 32 (October 1972): 19-23.

Walks the reader through a values clarification workshop. Demonstrates a variety of values clarification methods.

1470. Hersh, R.H. and M. Mutterer. "Moral Education and the Need for Teacher Preparation." Values Education: Theory/Practice/Problems/Prospects (item 1805), pp. 65-70.

Discusses the roles of the teacher and of the teacher training institution in the education of teachers to conduct moral education. The perspective is Kohlbergian throughout.

1471. Hodgkinson, Christopher. "Values Education at One Remove." Phi Delta Kappan, 58 (1976): 269-271.

Argues that the values education of children must logically begin with the values education of teachers. A exploratory course designed for such a purpose is described.

1472. Hughes, Richard L. and Daniel Casper. "Implementing a Moral Education Program through Attitude Change Theory." Clearing House, 52 (1979): 431-434.

Analyzes the obstacles to inservice training for teachers in moral education from the perspective of four theories of attitude change.

1473. Hurt, B. Lance "Psychological Education for Teacher-Education Students: A Cognitive-Developmental Curriculum." Developmental Counseling and Teaching (item 784), pp. 339-347.

Provides an overview of a preservice teacher education program which had a significant impact on both the skill levels and developmental levels of the students. Also Counseling Psychologist, 6,4 (1977).

1474. Hurt, B. Lance and Norman A. Sprinthall. "Psychological and Moral Development for Teacher Education." Journal of Moral Education, 6 (1977): 112-120.

Attempts to link moral and psychological education with a teacher training program. A course in educational psychology was adapted to teach counseling techniques as a means of stimulating ego and moral development.

1475. Jones, H. Lawrence. "Morality Development: A Self-Paced Learning Module for Training Facilitators." Ed.D. dissertation, West Virginia University, 1979. 40/12, p. 6153.

Training public school teachers by use of self-paced learning modules in the techniques of moral education can be as effective as a single session in-service session.

1476. Jones, Thomas M. "An Appraisal of Two Approaches for Training American History Teachers to Apply Kohlberg's Theory of Moral Development." D.A. dissertation, Carnegie-Mellon University, 1980. 41/03, p. 1028.

The effects of a one week intensive workshop were contrasted with the use of a teacher training handbook. Teachers perceptions, knowledge and performance indicated that both methods were effective.

1477. Joseph, Pamela. "Value Conflict: The Teachers Dilemma." Morality Examined (item 1818), pp. 141-15.

Discusses how value conflicts in the classroom frequently lead to anxiety reactions on the part of the teacher because of his/her uncertainty in how to deal with them. Presents ways teachers can overcome this anxiety and ways of dealing positively with value conflict in the classroom.

1478. Joy, Maureen A. "Inservice Education in the Cognitive Developmental Approach to Moral Education." Ed.D. dissertation, Harvard University, 1972. NR

1479. Jurich, Anthony P., and Kim M. Kadel. "Moral Development in the Adolescent Years." Manhattan, KS: Kansas State University, 1979. ED 160 214.

Describes a foster parent curriculum designed to develop foster parent competencies in dealing with adolescent values.

1480. Lehman, Ross J. "Examination of Values for Teachers." Ed.D. dissertation, Utah State University, 1980. 41/04, p. 1374.

An instructional package designed to help prospective and practicing teachers identify and understand the teaching implications of their values was developed. The package was then successfully field tested.

1481. Lickona, Thomas. "Helping Teachers Become Moral Educators." Theory into Practice, 17 (1978): 258-266.

Presents evidence which suggests that teachers identify moral development and values education as a high inservice priority. A two weekend course on moral education is presented in some detail. The course focuses on moral development (Kohlberg) and Fairness Meetings (Glasser).

1482. Lickona, Thomas. "Preparing Teachers to Be Moral Educators: A Neglected Duty." New Directions for Higher Education, Rethinking College Responsibilities for Values, no. 31 (item 1593), pp. 51-64.

Argues that there is a pressing need to train teachers to be competent in socio-moral education. Sketches out the major concepts involved in such an effort and proposes a four component process model of moral education.

1483. Loggins, Dennis C. "The Relationship of Teacher Attitude to Teacher Success in the Values Awareness Teaching Strategy Workshop." Ed.D. dissertation, University of Southern California, 1978. 35/05, p. 2725.

A Dalstra Values Awareness Teaching Strategy Workshop was shown to be effective in inducing greater skill in values awareness teaching.

1484. Marks, Merle. "Moral Development. Educational Attitudes and Self-Concept in Beginning Teacher Education Students." No location, 1980. ED 190 486.

Found a relationship between level of moral development and progressive educational attitudes.

1485. Masters, James S. "An Investigation of the Opinions of Open-Minded and Close-Minded Teachers About Which Moral Values Are Most Important for Children to Learn." Ph.D. dissertation, University of Missouri at Kansas City, 1963. 28/02, p. 501.

The hypotheses that close-minded teachers would prefer restructive-preventive values and open-minded teachers would prefer releasing-diversifying moral values was not confirmed; the opposite pattern was found.

1486. Miller, Brian. "Moral Education and the Training of Teachers." Journal of Moral Education, 1 (1971): 27-32.

A short statement on the aims of moral education is given, followed by a discussion of the skills and knowledge needed by teachers if these aims are to be achieved.

1487. Miller, Harry G., and Samuel M. Vinocur. A Method for Clarifying Value Statements in the Social Studies Classroom: A Self-Instructional Program. Carbondale: Southern Illinois University, 1972. ED 070 687.

A self instructional program designed to be used in teacher workshops to teach the value analysis approach to values education.

1488. Olmo, Barbara. "Values Education or Indoctrination." Thrust for Education Leadership, 5 (October, 1975): 17-19.

Attempts to develop a greater awareness in the teacher of his/her definition of value and philosophy/psychology of education. Argues that teachers need to understand how their values influence their teaching.

1489. Pine, G.J., and A.V. Boy. "Teaching and Valuing." The Clearing House, 49 (1976): 313-315.

Argues that education is a value laden activity and that teachers should get in touch with their values if they wish to be effective. Teacher caring is seen as the central value that teachers hold.

1490. Pines, A. Leon. "A Conceptual Approach to Moral Education: A Mini-Course Trainers Manual." Portsmouth, NH: New England Teacher Corp Network, 1979. ED 184 910.

Describes a college level mini-course on moral education designed to develop an appreciation for moral education and the ability to incorporate moral education into the classroom. The approach is eclectic.

1491. Reinert, Paul C. "Faculty Development and Values Education." Values Pedagogy in Higher Education (item 1558), pp. 23-28.

Discusses the authors conclusions, drawn from his work at church related St. Louis University, regarding faculty characteristics needed for effective teaching of religious values.

1492. Rusin, James F. "Curriculum Planning to Improve the Valuing Process." Ed.D. dissertation, State University of New York at Buffalo, 1981. 42/02, p. 534.

Finds that although teachers believe that schools have a responsibility for values education teachers encounter many difficulties in carrying out their ideas into practice.

1493. Rybash, John M. "How Teachers Help Children Resolve Moral Dilemmas." Journal of Moral Education, 10 (1980): 18-23.

Investigated the strategies that elementary school teachers employ when they help other people resolve moral dilemmas. Teachers were asked to respond to the Defining Issues Test as if they were helping a 10 year old child or a 40 year old adult. It was found that teachers made no differentiation in their responses to the D.I.T.

1494. Sadker, Myra and David Sadker. "Microteaching for Affective Skills." The Elementary School Journal, 76 (1975): 91-99.

Presents eight skills by which teachers can help students clarify their feelings about issues. How micro-teaching can develop these skills in teachers is presented.

1495. Simon, Sidney. "The Teacher Educator in Value Development." Phi Delta Kappan, 53 (1976): 649-651.

Six strategies for clarifying values are outlined. An argument is made for bringing to teacher education an emphasis on values clarification.

1496. Sizer, Nancy. "Can Values be Taught? Unkaging Kids." Independent School Bulletin, 35 (October, 1975): 23-24.

Discusses workshops on developmental moral education offered to teachers. The approach and difficulties encountered are covered.

1497. Sprinthall, Norman A. and Joseph E. Bernier. "Moral and Cognitive Development for Teachers: A Neglected Area." Values/Moral Education: Schools and Teachers (item 1794), pp. 119-143.

States that the moral and cognitive development of teachers is of vital importance for moral education. Points out the current inadequacies in teacher education in this regard. Results of a summer workshop are reported.

1498. Stewart, James D. "The Teacher as Moral Advisor." Ph.D. dissertation, Michigan State University, 1974. 35/11, p. 7184.

A conceptual analysis of what it means (what is involved) in the idea of a teacher giving moral advice to students. Argues that it is possible to give advice and avoid using imperative sentences.

1499. Stonehouse, Catherine, M. "An Evaluative Study of Instruction in Moral Development Education for Paraprofessionals." Ph.D. dissertation, Michigan State University, 1976. 37/12, p. 7519.

Attempts to develop a training program for paraprofessionals to assist in moral education. Results of the developed training program were mixed.

1500. Tierney, Dennis S. "A Study of the Relationship Between Levels of Teacher Moral Development and Selected Variables." Ph.D. dissertation, Claremont Graduate School, 1979. 40/04, p. 1975.

It was found that the single best predictor of principled moral reasoning was the Graduate Record Exam Score. Other factors were parent educational level and racial group.

1501. Toffee, Stephen J. "Strategies for Clarifying the Teaching Self." Values Concepts and Techniques (item 1784), pp. 87-94.

Presents techniques designed to assist teachers in achieving clarity about their teaching self.

1502. Traviss, Mary P. "The Principal, Moral Education and Staff Development." Momentum, 6 (December 1975): 16-20.

Argues that the principal is the proper individual to lead staff development in the area of moral education and then provides advice on how to go about leading an inservice program.

1503. Wayne County Intermediate School District. "Values Clarification (Decisions, Drugs, Values)." Lansing, MI: Michigan State Department of Education, 1971. ED 159 526.

A how-to-do-it booklet for teachers on how to use values clarification in drug education.

1504. Wilkins, Robert A. "If the Moral Reasoning of Teachers is Deficient, What Hope for the Pupils?" Phi Delta Kappan, 61 (1980): 548-549.

Cites evidence from Australian teacher education students which shows that the normal distribution curve of moral reasoning scores overlaps the moral reasoning scores of many junior high and senior high students. The question is raised whether one can raise the reasoning of another if one is at his/her level or below.

1505. Witherell, C.S., and V.L. Erickson. "Teacher Education as Adult Development." Theory into Practice, 17 (1978): 229-238.

Discusses the need for using developmental theory as a conceptual paradigm for teacher education. Kohlberg is discussed, however the major thrust of the paper is on Loevinger's Theory of Ego Development. In two case studies the relationship between ego development, teaching behavior and interpretations of teaching behavior is illustrated.

1506. Zabierek, Henry. "Staff Development in Moral Education." Moral Education: A First Generation of Research and Development (item 428), pp. 83-91.

Discusses why moral education is needed and some of the obstacles which must be overcome for it to be successful. The need for support from school administrators, teachers and the community is pointed out.

1507. Zahner, Carl J. "Moral Judgment: A Comparison of Training Effects on Professional and Paraprofessional Counselors." Ph.D. dissertation, University of Florida, 1977. 38/07, p. 4067.

Professional counselors were found to be significantly higher in level of moral judgment than paraprofessionals, but this difference could not be attributed to training.

The Role of the School Counselor in the Moral Education Process

1508. Biggs, D., C. Pulvino, and C. Beck, eds. Counseling and Values. Washington, DC: American Personnel and Guidance Association, 1976.

Contains a collection of articles taken from issues of Counseling and Values which deal with major value questions facing counselors, values education in schools, and problems of meaning on the campus and in the community.

1509. Counseling and Values. "Cognitive Developmental Moral Education," 19 (October, 1974).

Contains a collection of papers, some with a religious theme, which explore the implications of developmental psychology for the role of counselors in schools.

1510. England, C.L. "Using Kohlberg's Moral Developmental Framework in Family Life Education." Family Relations, 29 (1980): 7-13.

It is argued that Kohlberg's principles of moral development meet the needs of family life educators in dealing with diverse value-laden subject matter. Examples are presented of how Kohlberg's principles can be integrated into family life curriculum.

1511. Erney, Tom. Drugs, Youth and the Group Rap: An Overview of the Drug Situation in Our Schools and Suggestions for Local Educators. No location, 1972. ED 103 746.

A practical guide to assist counselors with drug-abused youth. Has a values clarification emphasis.

1512. Glaser, Barbara, and Howard Kirschenbaum. "Using Values Clarification in Counseling Settings." Personnel and Guidance Journal, 58 (1980): 569-574.

1513. Hart, G.M. Values Clarification for Counselors. Springfield, IL: Charles C. Thomas, 1979.

Presents the theoretical background to values clarification and relates the seven steps of the clarifying process to the act of counseling others.

1514. Hennessy, Thomas C. "The Counselor Applies the Kohlberg Moral Development Model." Values/Moral Education: Schools and Teachers (item 1794), pp. 145-165.

1515. Hennessy, Thomas C., ed. "Values and the Counselor." Personnel and Guidance Journal, 58 (May 1980).

Contains a wide ranging collection of papers on values education and the role of the counselor. Contains papers on the cognitive-developmental approach, values clarification, Christian counseling, problems of measurement and evaluation, and other related topics.

1516. Howard, Tina U. "Professional Socialization and Cognitive/Moral Development: A Study of the Relationship Between Level of Moral Thought and Humanistic Attitudes." D.S.W. dissertation, University of Alabama, 1980. 42/02, p. 858.

Finds that post-conventional individuals are more likely to have a strong indentification with (humanistic) social work concerns.

1517. Hultman, Kenneth E. "Values as Defenses." Personnel and Guidance Journal, 54 (1976): 268-271.

Intended for counselors this article provides guidance for detecting when values are used as defenses against irrational beliefs. How to make this awareness a useful factor in one's helping relations with others is discussed.

1518. Ivey, Allen E. "The Counselor as Psychoeducational Consultant: Toward a Value-Centered Advocacy Model." Personnel and Guidance Journal, 58 (1980): 567-568.

Argues that counselors should be advocates and points to the work of Kohlberg and Wasserman as a prime example of advocacy with an impact.

1519. Katz, Bernard, and Robert P. Beech. "Values and Counselors 1968-1978: Stability or Change?" Personnel and Guidance Journal, 58 (1980): 609-612.

Using Rokeach's Survey of Values it was found that over a ten year period counselors' trend in values seems to be from social to personal concerns and from moral to competence ones.

1520. Kohlberg, Lawrence, and Elsa Wasserman. "The Cognitive-Developmental Approach and the Practicing Counselor: An Opportunity for Counselors to Rethink Their Roles." Personnel and Guidance Journal, 58 (1980): 559-567.

Presents cognitive-developmental theory, the educational implications and reports on the just community efforts of the Cluster School. Recommends that counselors work to help build community in schools and encourage school faculty to broaden their view of their function in schools to include the moral and ego development of students.

1521. Morris, Margaret. "A Study of Moral Development and Social Role Perspectives in a Counselor Education Program." Ph.D. dissertation, The University of Wisconsin-Madison, 1980. 42/04, p. 1493.

Finds a significant relationship between the number of years in a counselor education program and level of principled moral thinking.

1522. Pine, Gerald J., and Angelo V. Boy. "What Counselors Might Like to Read about Counseling and Values: An Annotated Bibliography." Personnel and Guidance Journal, 58 (1970): 631-634.

The major sections focus on values and ethics in counseling and cognitive-developmental theory.

1523. Rokeach, Milton, and John F. Regan. "The Role of Values in the Counseling Situation." Personnel and Guidance Journal, 58 (1980): 576-582.

The theory and research behind the Rokeach Value Survey and an application to the counseling situation is presented. It is recommended that the Value

Survey be used to highlight for the client inconsistencies between values and life patterns.

1524. Simon, Sidney B. "Values Clarification--A Tool for Counselors." Personnel and Guidance Journal, 51 (1973): 614-618.

Presents six values clarification exercises which may be of use to counselors.

1525. Stanford, Susan, and Peter Gillan. "The Morality of Counseling: Implications for Teachers." Morality Examined (item 1818), pp. 177-198.

Explores the question of whether or not teachers should counsel students on matters related to personal and social problems. Discusses possible moral implications of such a role and offers guidelines for teachers.

1526. Sullivan, Edmund V. "Values and Issues in Counseling and School Psychology." Values and Moral Development (item 387), pp. 74-101.

Sullivan presents a critical analysis of the role of the psychologist in the schools. The psychologist is pictured as an unwitting agent for social conformity and as the elite expert in psychological technology which is often oppressive in nature.

1527. Alverno College Faculty. Assessment at Alverno College. Milwaukee: Alverno Productions, 1979. NR.

1528. American Association for the Advancement of Science. EVIST Resource Directory. A Directory of Programs and Courses in the Field of Ethics and Values in Science and Technology. Washington, D.C.: American Association for the Advancement of Science, 1978. ED 165 724.

Contains a listing and description of over 120 programs and 900 courses at over 500 institutions of higher education which have a focus on ethics and values. The focus of the offerings is on the relationship between science and technology and values.

1529. Barksdale, Milton, K. "Values and Higher Education." Richmond, KY: Eastern Kentucky University, 1977. ED 145 787.

Traces higher educations traditional concern with value development and reviews current thinking and program development on the topic.

1530. Barnett, John. "The Influence of Community." Values and Moral Development in Higher Education (item 1554), pp. 198-205.

Discusses an experiment in the college of education of Culham College in which a sense of community was developed.

1531. Barton, Bruce. "The Effects of Place of Residence Upon Value Development in College Students." Ph.D. dissertation, University of Connecticut, 1972. 33/06, p. 2727.

No generalized differences in values were found between resident and commuting students.

1532. Baum, Robert J. Ethics and Engineering Curricula. Hastings-on-Hudson, NY: The Hastings Center, 1980.

Discusses the teaching of ethics as a part of the engineering curriculum in higher education. One of eight monographs from the Hastings Center's Teaching of Ethics Project (item 1545).

1533. Beausang, Kenneth R. "The Place of Moral Education in the Curriculum of a Community College." Moline, IL: Black Hawk College, 1977. ED 161 506.

Reviews relevant literature and collects questionnaire data from college faculty on moral education. Concludes that support for moral education is present, but the exact approach which should be taken is unclear.

1534. Bell, Mark A. and Edward D. Eddy. "Values Education: A Student's Perspective, An Administrator's Response." New Directions for Higher Education, Rethinking College Responsibilities for Values, no. 31 (item 1593), pp. 17-25.

Mark Bell, a student leader, argues that the role of higher education in the teaching of values is incidental. There is no agreed upon set of values to be taught and besides, values are a matter for individual choice anyway. Edward Eddy, college administrator, argues that values have a proper place and that place is in the focus on the process of valuing rather than specific values.

1535. Bergoffen, Debra B. "The Moral Value of Philosophy." Journal of Moral Education, 9 (1980): 122-129.

Shows how, in an introductory college-level philosophy course, appealing to Socrates and Bertrand Russell can show students the intimate relationship between rational reflection and the living of a moral life.

1536. Bok, Derek. "Can Ethics Be Taught?" Change Magazine, 8 (1976): 26-30.

Argues that higher education has largely ignored moral education. States that courses in moral education can help students to become more alert to issues of day, reason more carefully and clarify individual moral aspirations.

1537. Bok, Sissela. "Whistleblowing and Professional Responsibilities." Ethics Teaching in Higher Education (item 1542), pp. 277-295.

Whistleblowing is defined as the act of sounding an alarm from within the organization in which one works, in order to spotlight neglect or abuses that threaten the public interest. The nature of whistleblowing is examined and the uses of whistle-blowing case studies in the teaching of applied ethics is discussed.

1538. Broady, Maurice. "Sociology and Moral Education: The Conditions of Impartiality." Values and Moral Development in Higher Education (item 1554), pp. 58-76.

Argues for a conception of impartiality in higher education--one in which the student is inducted into arguments within intellectual disciplines. Politics and education should remain separate in higher education.

1539. Brown, Robert D., and Harry J. Canon. "Intentional Moral Development as an Objective of Higher Education." Journal of College Student Personnel, 19 (1978): 426-429.

The lack of moral education in higher education due to the abandonment of in loco parentis is noted. A model for confronting moral and ethical issues in higher education is presented.

1540. Callahan, Daniel. "Ethics and Value Education." Values Pedagogy and Higher Education (item 1558), pp. 35-42.

Discusses the questions which will be asked by the Hasting Center's study of training in values in college (item 1545).

1541. Callahan, Daniel. "Goals in the Teaching of Ethics." Ethics Teaching in Higher Education (item 1542), pp. 61-80.

Argues that the goals of a course in ethics should be to stimulate moral imagination, provide the ability to reorganize ethical issues, develop analytic skills, elicit a sense of moral obligation and promote tolerance.

1542. Callahan, Daniel, and Sissela Bok, eds. Ethics Teaching in Higher Education. New York: Plenum Press, 1980.

Presents the series of papers which provided the background for Hastings Center's study of the status of the teaching of ethics in American higher education (see item 1545). Contains sections on general issues in the teaching of ethics, the teaching of ethics in the undergraduate curriculum, and recommendations on the teaching of ethics. See item 1584 for critique.

1543. Callahan, Daniel and Sissela Bok. "Hastings Center Project on the Teaching of Ethics: Summary Recommendations." Ethics Teaching in Higher Education (item 1542), pp. 299-302.

Summarizes the seven most important recommendations of the Hasting Center's Project on the Teaching of Ethics (item 1545).

1544. Callahan, D., and S. Bok. "The Role of Applied Ethics in Learning." Change, 11(September 1979): 23-27.

Presents an overview of the goals and methods of the Hastings Center study of the teaching of ethics. The problems of accommodating problems and avoiding indoctrination are discussed. Five goals for the teaching of ethics are presented: 1) stimulating the moral imagination; 2) developing analytic skills; 3) recognizing ethical issues; 4) eliciting a sense of moral obligation and personal responsibility; and 5) tolerating and resisting abstraction and ambiguity.

1545. Callahan, Daniel, and Sissela Bok. The Teaching of Ethics in Higher Education. Hastings-on-Hudson, NY: The Hastings Center, 1980.

Presents an analysis of the state of the art and of the main problems confronting the teaching of ethics in higher education. This volume grew out of a two year systematic study of the state of teaching ethics in American higher education by the Hastings Center funded by the Rockefeller Brothers Fund and the Carnegie Corporation of New York. In addition to this volume this project published eight monographs on the teaching of ethics in subject areas and a collection of articles (item 1542).

1546. Cantrell, Douglas D. "Impact of University Departments or Students Values." Ph.D. dissertation, University of Michigan, 1974. 36/11, p. 7229.

University departments are found to have a significant impact on students' values. Factors influencing this change are discussed.

1547. Caplan, Arthur L. "Evaluation and the Teaching of Ethics." Ethics Teaching in Higher Education (item 1542), pp. 133-150.

Discusses a series of issues related to the evaluation of ethics courses. Argues that behavior is an inappropriate focus of evaluation and that traditional means of evaluating student performance (tests, essays, classroom performance) are as appropriate for courses on ethics as for other subject areas.

1548. Charan, Gabriel. "Literature." Values and Moral Development in Higher Education (item 1554), pp. 106-115.

Explores the potential contribution of the study of literature to moral development.

1549. Chickering, A.W. Education and Identity. San Francisco, Josey-Bass, 1972.

Summarizes the primary areas of student development during the college years. Seven developmental tasks are outlined and recommended as an agenda for student development theory and practice: competence, emotions, autonomy, identity, interpersonal relations, purpose and integrity.

1550. Christians, Clifford G. and Catherine L. Covert. Teaching Ethics in Journalism Education. Hastings-on-Hudson, NY: The Hastings Center, 1980.

Discusses the place of ethics in teaching journalism in higher education. One of eight monographs from the Hastings Center's Teaching of Ethics Project.

1551. Clauser, K. Danner. _Teaching Bioethics: Strategies, Problems and Resources_. Hastings-on-Hudson, NY: The Hastings Center, 1980.

Discusses the teaching of ethics as a part of medical education. One of eight monographs from the Hastings Center's Teaching of Ethics Project.

1552. Coe, Denis. "The Role of Student Services in Student Development--A Polytechnic View." _Values and Moral Development in Higher Education_ (item 1554), pp. 206-211.

Argues that though the sense of caring communicated, and the assistance provided in helping students adjust to society, student services play a significant role in the development of polytechnic students.

1553. Colavechio, Xavier G. "Education By Objectives: Focus on Values." _Values Pedagogy in Higher Education_ (item 1558), pp. 55-61.

Describes the Education by Objectives program at St. Norbert's College. The purpose of the program to help students become more clear about their values and the relations of these values to the college experience.

1554. Collier, Gerald, John Wilson, and Peter Tomlinson, eds. _Values and Moral Development in Higher Education_. London: Croom Helm Ltd., 1974.

A collection of papers on moral education as a function of higher education. Topics covered are the understanding of moral development from the perspective of different disciplines and the potential contributions of specific subject areas and institutional contexts on moral development. The volume features an introduction and postscript by John Wilson.

1555. Collier, K. G. "Experiments in Moral Education at College Level." _Journal of Moral Education_, 2 (1972): 45-51.

An outline of a program of moral education is presented. The program involved discussion of moral questions based on texts and films. It was judged that the course increased awareness of the issues involved.

1556. Cross, Patricia K. "Student Values Revisited." Berkeley, CA: University of California, Berkeley. Center for Researched Development in Higher Education, 1968. ED 025 205.

Using the Omnibus Personality Inventory, 10,000 high school graduates were followed for four years following graduation. College students were found to become more tolerant, flexible and autonomous in their thinking. Individuals who embarked on jobs or homemaking were found to be uninterested in flexible thought.

1557. Dalton, John C. "Student Development from a Values Education Perspective." Counseling and Values, 22 (1977): 35-40.

Argues that three goals of values education appear to be directly related to the issue of integrity in student development.

1558. Donnellan, Michael and James Ebben, eds. Values Pedagogy in Higher Education. Adrian, MI: Swenk-Tuttle Press, 1978.

Report of a conference held at Sierra Heights College in 1978. The general theme of the papers is the relationship between value inquiry and general education in higher education. Small liberal arts and religious affiliated schools are the participants.

1559. Dye, G. R. and J. B. Stephenson. "An Experienced Based College Course on Ethics." Values Pedagogy in Higher Education (item 1558), pp. 117-125.

Describes a political science course which was combined with a public policy oriented internship.

Students experienced a tension between principles learned in the classroom and living out those principles in their internships.

1560. Earley, Margaret. "Valuing in an Outcome-Oriented Liberal Arts College." Values Pedagogy in Higher Education (item 1558), pp. 47-53.

Discusses the values in the liberal arts curriculum at Alverno College. Relates how the total institutional structure makes provisions for the development of valuing.

1561. Earley, M., M. Mentkowski and J. Schafer. Valuing at Alverno: The Valuing Process in Liberal Education. Milwaukee: Alverno Productions, 1980. NR

1562. Ecklund, Kent E. "Value Development: Faculty, Administrators, Students." Values Pedagogy in Higher Education (item 1558), pp. 179-185.

Describes a non-curricular, out-of-the-classroom program for value development in freshmen and sophomores. Interaction between students, faculty and administration are the key elements.

1563. Edge, David. "Science." Values and Moral Development in Higher Education (item 1554), pp. 147-159.

Argues that the education of scientists must confront the unavoidable moral dimensions of the scientific enterprise.

1564. Faust, Clarence H. and Jessica Feingold, eds. Approaches to Education for Character: Strategies for Change in Higher Education. New York: Columbia University Press, 1969. NR

1565. Feldman, Kenneth and Theodore Newcomb. The Impact of College on Students, 2 vols. San Francisco, Jossey-Bass Publishers, 1968.

In an exhaustive review of the impact of college it was found that the personality growth of students, when it does occur, is primarily the result of peer influence. Formal curriculums were found to have relatively little impact on the students personality and values.

1566. Fiske, Edward B. "Growth of Ethics Courses Shows Major Changes on U.S. Campuses." New York Times, February 20, 1978, pp. 1 and B8.

Reviews college ethics courses in the United States.

1567. Flanagan, Dan. "The Impact of American Higher Education on Undergraduate Student Valuing." Amherst, MA: University of Massachusetts, 1975. ED 118 033.

Reviews research on the influence of higher education on student values and concludes that different research methods are called for.

1568. Fleishman, Joel L. and Bruce L. Payne. Ethical Dilemmas and the Education of Policymakers. Hastings-on-Hudson, NY: The Hastings Center, 1980.

Discusses the possible role of ethical dilemmas in the education of policymakers. One of eight monographs from the Hastings Center's Teaching of Ethics Project (item 1545).

1569. Glick, Oren and Jay M. Jackson. "A Longitudinal Study of Behavior Norms and Some of Their Ramifications in a Small Liberal Arts College." Kansas City: Institute for Community Studies, no date. ED 019 678.

Finds that with college students in a small liberal arts college that the most preferred or ideal behavior was highly stable over the course of the study.

1570. Hamblin, Douglas. "The Relationship of Depth Psychology to Moral Development." Values and Moral Development in Higher Education (item 1554), pp. 40-57.

Discusses the role of the depth psychologist in promoting mental health and therefore moral development.

1571. Harshman, Ellen. "Values and Career Education." Values Pedagogy In Higher Education (item 1558), pp. 173-178.

Describes a program at St. Louis University which helps students confront values and career issues. An internship brings college and work cultures closer together.

1572. Hastings Center Staff. "The Teaching of Ethics in American Higher Education: An Empirical Synopsis." Ethics Teaching in Higher Education (item 1542), pp. 153-169.

Surveyed offerings in ethics at one-fourth of all colleges and universities. Categorized 2,757 courses concerned with the teaching of ethics: The results of the surveyed. A profile of the teaching of ethics in seven professional areas (medicine, law, business, social science, engineering, nursing and journalism) is included.

1573. Hatch, Stephen. "Institutional Contexts." Values and Moral Development in Higher Education (item 1554), pp. 192-197.

Argues that the creation of institutions capable of making a distinctive impact on their students depends on the articulation of moral commitments, organizational arrangements and staff and student needs and aspirations.

1574. Henderson, James. "History." Values and Moral Development in Higher Education (item 1554), pp. 137-146.

Argues that the study of history, through the awe, clarity and time-transcendence that it elicits, is conducive to moral development.

1575. Hendrix, Jon R. "How to Add the Value Dimension to Science Content Courses." Value Pedagogy in Higher Education (item 1558), pp. 127-134.

Describes a course in human genetics and bioethical decision making.

1576. Hofmann, Justin. "The Case for Moral Education." Religious Education, 63 (1968): 207-213.

Presents a survey of opinion from diverse sources which mostly favor the teaching of morality in colleges.

1577. Hyman, Herbert H. and Charles R. Wright. Education's Lasting Influence on Values. Chicago: University of Chicago Press, 1979.

Using data collected from national opinion surveys conducted between 1949 and 1975, the authors find that amount of formal education effects values and this effect is positive and lasting.

1578. Jacob, Phillip E. Changing Values in College: An Exploratory Study of the Impact of College Teaching. New York: Harper & Row, 1957.

In a major study of the values of college youth finds that the major impact of a college education is to further homogenize the already homogeneous value orientation of students.

1579. Jones, George W. ed. "Values Education." Counseling and Values, 22 (October 1977).

Contains five noteworthy articles on dimensions of moral/values education in institutions of higher education.

1580. Katz, Joseph and Associates. No Time for Youth. San Francisco: Jossey-Bass Publishers, 1968.

Contains a collection of papers based on in depth interviews of a random sample of 200 college students. The lives and problems of the youth are described with the focus on the development of the students within the institutional setting of higher education.

1581. Kelly, Michael J. Legal Ethics and Legal Education. Hastings-on-Hudson, NY: The Hastings Center, 1980.

Discusses the place of ethics in the education of the legal profession. One of eight monographs from the Hastings Center's Teaching of Ethics Project.

1582. Klinefelter, Donald S. "The Place of Value in a World of Fact." Soundings, 58(1975): 363-79.

Argues that one false assumption of the teaching of ethics in higher education has been that colleges can remain value neutral. Since the college cannot avoid being the purveyor of certain values, these assumptions should be initially examined so that students, teacher and administrators become more aware of the relationship between what is taught and one's view of social commitment.

1583. Knight, Roy. "Drama." Values and Moral Development in Higher Education (item 1554), pp. 116-125.

Argues that the study of drama offers unique contexts for the investigation of the impact of schooling on moral development.

1584. Kohlberg, Lawrence. "Should the College Stimulate Moral Development?" Education and Moral Development, (item 395), Chapter 6.

A brief statement of the place of moral discussion in liberal education and a report on a pilot undergraduate course in ethics.

1585. Kreyche, Gerald F. "A Proposal for College Value Studies." Religious Education, 72 (1977): 74-84.

Presents a curriculum for colleges based on the concept that values are relative but not arbitrary--they are seen to be created and grounded on what is perfective of the person. The program emphasizes critical thinking.

1586. Kuh, George D. "Persistence of the Impact of College on Attitudes and Values." Journal of College Student Personnel, 17 (1976): 116-122.

The Omnibus Personality Inventory was administered to a group of students as freshmen, seniors and five year alumni. It was found changes occured as a result of the college experience.

1587. Laramee, William. "Values Clarification and Self-Understanding through Student Work Related Experiences." NASPA Journal, 17 (Spring 1980): 41-45.

Describes the need to reorganize the potential of student work experiences for values education and makes some suggestions as to the kinds of learning which can take place. This is not an application of standard values clarification theory.

1588. Ledebur, Larry C. "Value Change in College and the Impact of Simulations on Value Systems of Students." Paper presented at annual meeting of the American Educational Research Association, New York, 1977. ED 143 311.

Argues that simulations can be a vehicle for stimulating values growth in college students.

1589. Leininger, C. Earl. "Values in a General Education Program." Values Pedagogy in Higher Education (item 1558), pp. 65-76.

Sketches a rationale for relating general education and values. Points out that the failure to incorporate affective learning experiences into the curriculum places students at the mercy of teachers' hidden values.

1590. Lickona, Thomas. "What Does Moral Psychology Have to Say to the Teacher of Ethics?" Ethics Teaching in Higher Education (item 1542), pp. 103-132.

Discusses the implications of two themes in moral psychology for the teaching of ethics: Cognitive-developmental stage psychology and social psychology.

1591. Loxley, J.C., and J.M. Whiteley. Character Development in College Students II. Schenectady, NY: Character Research Press, 1980. NR

1592. McBee, Mary L. "Higher Education: Its Responsibility for Moral Development." National Forum, 2 (1978): 30-33.

Argues that more important than any course in ethics is the kind of model the institution and its faculty provide.

1593. McBee, Mary L., ed. New Directions for Higher Education, Rethinking College Responsibilities for Values, no. 31. San Francisco: Jossey-Bass, Inc., 1980.

Contains a diverse and interesting collection of papers assessing the role and responsibilities of colleges in the development of student values.

1594. McBee, Mary L. "The Values Development Dilemma." New Directions for Higher Education, Rethinking College Responsibilities for Values, no. 31 (item 1593), pp. 1-7.

Presents a general polemic for the place of values in higher education, its recent neglect, and a call for renewed effort.

1595. McGrath, Earl J. "Institutional Alternatives for an Education in Values." Counseling and Values, 22 (1977); 5-19.

After discussing the shortcomings of current approaches to values education in colleges an approach based on combining teaching and counseling is proposed.

1596. Macklin, Ruth. "Problems in the Teaching of Ethics: Pluralism and Indoctrination." Ethics Teaching in Higher Education (item 1542), pp. 81-101.

Argues that the teaching of ethics neither rules in, nor rules out, in principle, espousal of a particular moral viewpoint. In a series of eleven objections and replies to the question of the teaching of ethics the author addresses the relationship of religion to ethics, the potential for indoctrination, and problems involved by virtue of living in a pluralistic society.

1597. Marlowe, Anne F. "Greek Membership: Its Impact Upon the Value Orientations and Moral Development of College Freshmen." Ph.D. dissertation, University of Kentucky, 1979. 40/06, p. 3202.

1598. Martin, J. Paul. "Moral Values and University Education." Counseling and Values, 22 (1977): 20-34.

Reviews a broad range of approaches to values education and notes that although there are some areas of argument there is little consensus regarding the content of values teaching. It is concluded that institutions of higher education might be the best place for moral education to take place.

1599. May, William F. "Professional Ethics: Setting, Terrain, and Teacher." Ethics Teaching in Higher Education (item 1542), pp. 205-241.

Argues that the teaching of professional ethics needs to go beyond individual guardians and problems. It should also include concerns and structural criticism, the clarification of character and virtue, and the enforcement of professional standards and discipline.

1600. Moore, Robert M. "Value Change Among Junior College Students," Ed.D. dissertation, University of Florida, 1967. 29/01, p. 126.

Using the Allport-Vernon-Lindzey Study of Values instrument it was found that those students who changed a great deal were not significantly different from those who changed little on a variety of demographic variables.

1601. Moran, J.D. "Higher Education and Moral Choices in the 80's." Liberal Education, Summer (1979): 266-271.

The president of Boston College argues that faced with the current moral crisis in society universities must move from a position of moral concern to the assumption and expression of a moral position. Enabling students to make social ethical decisions should be a stated goal and final test of liberal education.

1602. Morgan, G.W. "Higher Education and Moral Development." AAUP Bulletin, 63 (1977): 37-38.

In a response to Trow (item 1628), it is argued that moral life is essentially personal and Trow's emphasis on impersonal rules lowers the quality of moral life.

1603. Morrill, Richard L. Teaching Values in College. San Francisco: Jossey-Bass, 1980.

Following succinct sketches of the major approaches to values education he finds these approaches lacking because of their failure to unify knowing, feeling and doing. Based on a phenomenological interpretation of value theory a notion that focuses on the centrality of human choice is presented. Pedagogical principles and practices consistent with his view and appropriate for higher education are presented.

1604. Morrill, Richard L. "Values, Relativism, and Higher Education: Defining the Issues." Values Pedagogy in Higher Education (item 1558), pp. 5-21.

Attempts to define values and show how they are an appropriate responsibility of higher education. The responsibility of colleges is to foster those values which make collective human life possible.

1605. Nichols, John. "Values, Objectives and Pedagogy in a Core Curriculum." Values Pedagogy in Higher Education (item 1558), pp. 77-86.

Describes the elements of core curriculum at St. Joseph's College. This curriculum is based on an integrated and interdisciplinary approach to general education where values are seen as an integral part of curriculum.

1606. O'Brien, Goel M. "Colleges Concern Grows over Ethical Values." Chronicle of Higher Education, Feb. 23, 1976: 5.

Discusses how small liberal arts colleges and church-related institutions are responding to societal concern over values by incorporating a focus on values in the curriculum.

1607. Parr, Susan R. "The Teaching of Ethics in Undergraduate Nonethics Courses." Ethics Teaching in Higher Education (item 1542), pp. 191-203.

Discusses the issues and problems involved in teaching about ethical questions in courses not designated as ethics courses-the primary examples presented are derived from history and literature.

1608. Phillips, Ellis L. "Improving Decision Making in Business and the Professions." New Directions for Higher Education; Rethinking College Responsibilities for Values, No. 31 (item 1593), pp. 65-70.

Argues that decision making in the business world requires a social consciousness. A seminar program held at C.W. Post College which gives awards for corporate responsibility is described.

1609. Pitt, Valerie. "Polytechnics: Moral Education?" Values and Moral Development in Higher Education (item 1554), pp. 184-191.

Analyzes the rise of technical and commercial education and critically questions the moral dimensions of this form of schooling.

1610. Powers, Charles W. and David Vogel. Ethics and the Education of Business Managers. Hastings-on-Hudson, NY: The Hastings Center, 1980.

Analyzes the place of ethics in the professional preparation of business managers in higher education. One of eight monographs from the Hastings Center's Teaching of Ethics Project.

1611. Read, Joel. "Alverno's Collegewide Approach to the Development of Valuing." New Directions for Higher Education, Rethinking College Responsibilities for Values, no. 31, (item 1593), pp. 71-79.

Describes a program at Alverno College in which a holistic approach to moral development is practiced.

1612. Reek, Carrell. "The Issues-Oriented Values Course." Values Pedagogy in Higher Education (item 1558), pp. 135-142.

Proposes an issue oriented approach to teach values in an ethics course. Argues that students learn about values through relationships with peers and contrasting their own value systems with alternative systems.

1613. Reisman, David. "Egocentrism." Character, 1 (March, 1980): 3-9.

Describes the societal and historical factors which have lead to the increase of egoism in American society. Argues that a stiff code of ethics for colleges could help reverse the trend. Also in Character Policy (item 1061).

1614. Rest, James. "The Impact of Higher Education on Moral Judgment Development." Minneapolis: University of Minnesota, 1979. ED 196 763.

Contains discussions of the relevance of the cognitive-developmental theory of moral reasoning for higher education, the place of rationality in moral behavior, and the research findings of the impact of college on the development of moral reasoning.

1615. Richardson, Robin. "World Studies." Values and Moral Development in Higher Education (item 1554), pp. 162-171.

Discusses the ways that world studies can be said to be of concern to the moral educator. Two clusters of practical approaches (simulations and community education) are reviewed.

1616. Robertson, James. "Theology." Values and Moral Development in Higher Education (item 1554), pp. 126-136.

Explores the question of how the study of theology (religion) in higher education institutions can contribute to the study and furtherance of moral development. A variety of approaches to the issue are presented.

1617. Rosen, Bernard. "The Teaching of Undergraduate Ethics." Ethics Teaching in Higher Education (item 1542), pp. 171-203.

Discusses the recent history of ethics and problems faced by teachers of ethics. Among the problems discussed (and solutions offered) are amoralism and skepticism, pluralism and relativism, indoctrination and indispensibility, and evaluation.

1618. Rosen, Bernard and Arthur L. Caplan. Ethics in the Undergraduate Curriculum. Hastings-on-Hudson, NY: The Hastings Center, 1980.

Analyzes the role of formal courses in ethics in the undergraduate curriculum. Problems are posed and solutions offered. One of eight monographs from the Hastings Center's Teaching of Ethics Project.

1619. Roth, Robert J. "Moral Education at the College Level: A Blueprint." Values/Moral Education: The Schools and the Teachers (item 1794), pp. 73-93.

Presents the background, rationale, description and evaluation procedures for Fordham College's Values Program. The goal of the program is to promote a reflective awareness of values and develop critical skills with which to appraise those values.

1620. St. Clair, Reginald E. "A Study of the Changes in Moral Judgment Patterns of College Students." Ed.D. dissertation, University of Virginia, 1975. 36/09, p. 5656.

No impact on moral reasoning was detected as a result of instruction in ethics and ethical theory among community college students.

1621. Schomberg, Steven F. "Moral Judgment Development and Freshman-Year Experiences." Ph.D. dissertation, University of Minnesota, 1978. 39/06, p. 3482.

The research question was, is moral judgment development a factor in understanding freshmen's behaviors?

1622. Singer, Marcus G. "The Teaching of Introductory Ethics." The Monist, 58 (1974): 616-629.

Argues that to engage in moral education is not the same as teaching ethics. The purpose of teaching ethics through the recommended 'case study' method is to discover through a study of actual behavior the moral principles upon which men conduct their lives.

1623. Straub, Cynthia, and Robert F. Rodgers. "Fostering Moral Development in College Women." Journal of College Student Personnel, 19 (1978): 430-436.

Student personnel workers taught a combined English/Psychology course according to Kohlbergian developmental principles. Students in the class mastered subject matter, grew in cognitive moral reasoning, and confronted identity issues.

1624. Straub, Cynthia A., and Robert F. Rodgers. "The Student Personnel Worker as Teacher: Fostering Moral Development in College Women." Columbus, OH: Ohio State University, 1976. ED 160 930.

Describes a project in which student personnel workers were involved in the design, implementation and evaluation of an English-psychology course premised on the concepts of deliberate psychological education.

1625. Thompson, Dennis F. "Paternalism in Medicine, Law, and Public Policy." Ethics Teaching in Higher Education (item 1542), pp. 245-272.

Paternalism, the imposing of constraints on an individuals liberty for the purpose of promoting his or her own good, is used to illustrate how one might proceed in the teaching of ethics in courses in professional schools and in the study of public policy.

1626. Tomlinson, Peter. "Some Perspectives from Academic Psychology." Values and Moral Development in Higher Education (item 1554), pp. 20-39.

Presents five psychological theories which present models of the forms of moral and social judgment.

1627. Tomlinson, Peter. "Using Formal Knowledge in Education." Values and Moral Development in Higher Education (item 1554), pp. 77-94.

Discusses the application of social science in education, offers a critique and proposes an open, higher-order or reflexive viewpoint on the relation of knowledge and reality. Urges a critically aware image of formal knowledge, especially with respect to the moral aspects of higher education.

1628. Trow, Martin. "Higher Education and Moral Development." Moral Development-ETS (item 1795), pp. 15-31.

Argues that by what we teach, how we teach and who we are colleges and their faculty have a significant impact on moral development. Also in AAUP Bulletin, Spring (1976): 20-27.

1629. Wagschol, Harry, and Robert Beagle. "Changing Values and Higher Education." Paper presented at Global Conference on the Future, Toronto, 1980. ED 194 393.

Contains the transcript of a two-member panel on changing values and higher education. The authors argue for more awareness among colleges of their potential impact on student values. Suggestions for improvement and new directions are offered.

1630. Warwick, Donald P. The Teaching of Ethics in the Social Sciences. Hastings-on-Hudson, N.Y.: The Hastings Center, 1980.

Analyzes the role of the teaching of ethics in courses on social science in higher education. One of eight monographs from the Hastings Center's Teaching of Ethics Project.

1631. Webster, Harold et al. "Personality Changes in College Students." The American College. Edited by Nevitt Sanford. New York: John Wiley and Sons, 1962, pp. 811-846.

Contains a section which discusses research on changes in attitudes and values which occur as a result of the college experience.

1632. Whiteley, John M. "Extracurricular Influences on the Moral Development of College Students." New Directions for Higher Education, Rethinking College Responsibilities for Values, no. 31 (item 1593), pp. 45-50.

Reports the results of a study where it is found that students, on a self-report instrument, perceive extracurricular experiences as having a significant impact on their thinking about moral issues.

1633. Whiteley, John M., Barbara D. Bertin and Bridgette A. Berry. "Research on the Development of Moral Reasoning of College Students." New Directions for Higher Education, Rethinking College Responsibilities for Values, no. 31 (item 1593), pp. 35-44.

Describes a series of research studies on the moral development of college students which all use Kohlbergian scaling procedures. Receiving special attention is the Sierra Project of the University of California, Irvine.

1634. Whiteley, J.M., et al. Character Development in College Students, Vol. 1. Schenectady, NY: Character Research Press, 1980. NR

Contains a collection of papers on the Sierra Project (see item 601) which discuss the freshman year of the project.

1635. Widick, Carole, L. Lee Knefelkamp, and Clyde A. Parker. "The Counselor as a Developmental Instructor." Counseling Education and Supervision, 14 (1975): 286-296.

Using Perry's model of ethical and intellectual development the impact of a course on "identity" on college students was assessed. The course was taught using principles of psychological education. Twenty-eight of thirty-one students showed positive change.

1636. Wilson, John. "Philosophy." Values and Moral Development in Higher Education (item 1554), pp. 96-105.

Presents a position on the moral effects on students of doing philosophy.

1637. Wilson, John. "The Study of 'Moral Development'." Values and Moral Development in Higher Education (item 1554), pp. 5-19.

Presents the components of morality and discusses how higher education can assist in developing these dimensions.

1638. Wilson, Robert and Jerry Goff. College Professors and their Impact on Students. New York: Wiley, 1975.

Presents empirical data supporting the claim that college professors have a considerable impact on students beyond the roles of transmitter and receiver of knowledge.

1639. Yankelovich, Daniel and Ruth Clark. "College and Noncollege Youth Values." Change, 6 (September 1974): 45-47; 64.

Reports on the recent shifts in values which have taken place in college and noncollege youth. The major shift found is that students are now satisfied with their lot and vocationally oriented. The new privatism is noted among college youth. What these trends mean for the college educator is discussed.

1640. Ashton, Diane P. "The Influence of Mental Age and Social Experience on the Moral Judgment Decisions of the Educable Mentally Retarded." Ph.D. dissertation, University of Southern California, 1979. 39/11, p. 6639.

A significant association between mental age and level of moral judgment in EMR and nonretarded subjects, matched for chronological age, was found.

1641. Benka, Phyllis B. "Value Differences and Value System Changes in Incorrigible Girls." Ph.D. dissertation, Washington State University, 1979. 40/01, p. 101.

Showing incorrigible girls the rankings of noncorrigible girls on the Rokeach Value Survey had no impact on their rankings.

1642. Brion-Meisels, Steven. "Reasoning with Troubled Children: Classroom Meetings As a Forum for Social Thought." <u>Moral Education Forum</u>, 4 (1979): 17-23.

Describes how classroom meetings are used with troubled children at the Manville School.

1643. Derr, Alice M. "The Moral Judgment and Conduct of Learning Disabled Adolescent Boys as Compared to Average Achieving Adolescent Boys." Ed.D. dissertation, University of Arizona, 1980. 41/07, p. 3045.

The learning disabled group scored significantly lower than the average achieving group on the Moral Judgment Interview. Teachers rated learning disabled students lower in social/moral conduct on predicted behavior.

1644. Eshroghi-Tahari, Gity, A. "Structures in the Development of Moral Judgment in Delinquent Children." Ph.D. dissertation, University of Texas at Austin, 1975. 36/05, p. 2710.

Tests the hypothesis of sequentiality of stages in the development of moral thinking with delinquent children. It was found that delinquent children have a significantly lower rate of development than non-delinquents.

1645. Finkenover, James O. "Scared Straight? James O. Finkenover Talks about the Juvenile Awareness Program." Moral Education Forum, 4 (1979): 1-7.

Finekenover describes the rationale and methods of the "scared straight" program and includes data on the surprising finding that those incarcerated but not attending the program (controls) had a lower recidivism rate than those supposedly "scared straight."

1646. Freeman, Sue J., Beverly B. Bliss and John W. Giebink. "Moral Reasoning in Young Adolescents with Special Needs." Counseling and Values, 25 (1980): 47-56.

Found that middle school students in special education programs lag behind peers in moral development.

1647. Gerrity, Bernard P. "The Use of Principled Moral Reasoning by Learning Disabled and Emotionally Disturbed High School Students." Ph.D. dissertation, Fordham University, 1979. 39/11, p. 6620.

It was found that mainstream students scored significantly higher than LD or ED high school students.

1648. Hickey, Joseph and Peter Scharf. Toward A Just Correctional System. San Francisco: Jossey-Bass, 1980.

Discusses the potential of democratic programs for correctional reform. The authors take a strong developmental position. Based on practical experience suggestions are offered for implementing such a program.

1649. Joseph, David A., and Pamela B. Joseph. "Teaching Children with Deficient Value Systems." Morality Examined (item 1818), pp. 105-119.

Discusses four case studies, from the psychoanalytic perspective, which illustrate the abnormalities which can occur in the development of moral behavior. Makes suggestions on how teachers can relate to and help these kinds of children.

1650. Jurkovic, Gregory J. "The Juvenile Delinquent As a Moral Philosopher: A Structural-Developmental Perspective." Psychological Bulletin, 88 (1980): 709-727.

Reviews available research on the relationship between moral maturity and juvenile delinquency. Finds that delinquency only moderately relates to a premoral ideological orientation. The distinction is drawn between the underlying sociomoral capabilities and the tendency to exercise these capabilities. Factors mediating various components of the moral judgment process in juvenile offenders are discussed.

1651. Kenney, James F. "The Relationship among the Cognitive Role Taking, and Moral Development Abilities of Emotionally Disturbed Adolescents." Ed.D. dissertation, College of William and Mary, 1980. 41/08, p. 3529.

Finds that when emotionally disturbed youth are compared with normal youth there are only slight differences on moral judgment skills.

1652. Kohlberg, Laurence, Peter Scharf, and Joseph Hickey. "The Justice Structure of the Prison--A Theory and an Intervention." The Prison Journal, 51 (1972): 3-14.

Discusses the "Cheshire Experiment" and the "Niantic Intervention" where prisons are approached from a justice perspective with the hope that a more effective rehabilitation program can be developed. Also in Collected Papers (item 1798) and Education and Moral Development (item 395).

1653. Kohlberg, Lawrence, Kelsey Kauffman, Peter Scharf and Joseph Hickey. "Understanding and Diagnosing Moral Stages--Chapter 5 of The Just Community Approach to Corrections: A Manual, Part II," Moral and Psychological Education (item 448), pp. 241-301.

Presents the basic information on the nature of the stages, the moral judgment interview and scoring interviews for stage of moral reasoning.

1654. Leming, James S. "Moralization Paradigms, Poverty, and School Crime: Analysis and Implications." Final Report, Contract No. HEW-100-76-0132. Hackensack, NJ: National Council on Crime and Delinquency, 1978. ED 157 187.

Four moralization paradigms are presented as explanatory hypotheses for the relationship between poverty and school crime. It is concluded that an awareness of the complexities involved in the moral orientations of those who commit school crime is essential for effective intervention.

1655. Parlett, T.A., J.D. Ayers, and D.M. Sullivan. "The Development of Morality in Prisoners." The Teaching of Values in Canadian Education (item 1797), pp. 76-84.

Reports the results of an experimental university humanities program on the moral development of prisoners. Since no pretest was used it is difficult to interpret the results, however the prisoners manifested a higher level of moral reasoning than three comparison groups following the program.

1656. Scharf, Peter. "The Moral Education of the Juvenile Offender: A Social Dilemma." Development of Moral Reasoning (item 26), pp. 209-231.

Describes a body of emerging work on a cognitive-developmental interpretation of juvenile delinquency. Points out the "moral gap" between the world view of the offender and that of society. Since youthful offenders cannot understand society's perspective this raises questions regarding possible approaches of rehabilitation.

1657. Scharf, P., and J. Hickey. "The Prison and the Inmate's Conception of Legal Justice: An Experiment in Democratic Education." Criminal Justice and Behavior, 3 (1976): 107-22.

Describes the developmental rationale and operational framework for the Niantic Project. Using a new method of scoring environmental perceptions (moral Atmosphere Scoring System) it was found that 75 percent of the inmates accepted the fairness of the political structure of the cottage. Over a five month period an increase in moral reasoning of .39 of a stage was observed.

1658. Scharf, Peter, Joseph E. Hickey, and Thomas Moriarty. "Moral Conflict and Change in Correctional Settings." Personnel and Guidance Journal, 51 (1973): 660-663.

Describes the application of Kohlbergian just community abnd moral dilemma discussion techniques to correctional settings.

1659. Selman, Robert L., and Don Jaquette. "To Understand and To Help: Implications of Developmental Research for the Education of Children with Interpersonal Problems," Readings in Moral Education (item 449), pp. 124-134.

Discusses how basic developmental research informs and guides the effort to construct an educational model for children at a school for children experiencing learning problems and interpersonal adjustment difficulties.

1660. Strong, William J. "A Comparative Study of Moral Judgments of Mentally Retarded Subjects in Institutional and Community Settings." Ed.D. dissertation, Boston University, 1968. 29/11, p. 3783.

Explored the effects of institutionalization on the moral judgment of educable mentally retarded youth. It was found that institutional subjects made significantly more judgments in terms of moral realism than those from the community in the area of immanent punishment.

1661. Turner, Francis J. "Values and the Social Worker." Reflections on Values Education (item 1804), pp. 201-210.

Clients and therapists manifest a range of value orientations to therapy and such diversities must be taken into account as a part of the process. Implications of differing value orientations for treatment of value stress situations is discussed.

1662. Tziahanas, Tom. "Moral Development of Emotionally Disturbed Children." Ph.D. dissertation, University of Michigan, 1971. 32/11, p. 6230.

Older emotionally disturbed elementary school children were more inclined to use reciprocity as a justice principle than "moral" subjects. On other Piagetian dimensions no significant differences were detected.

1663. Wallin, Gloria J. "Learning Disabilities, Religious Training and Moral Judgment of Junior High School Boys," Ph.D. dissertation, Fordham University, 1978. 38/12, p. 7276.

It was found that normal students had higher Defining Issues Test P scores than learning disabled students. There were no differences found by type of school (Jewish or secular) and there were no interactions between learning disability and type of school.

1664. Wright, Ian. "Moral Reasoning and Conduct of Selected Elementary School Students." Journal of Moral Education, 7 (1978): 199-205.

Delinquents and non-delinquents were assigned to three treatment groups: moral discussion, social studies games, and control. It was found that delinquents reason predominantly at the preconventional level and non-delinquents at stage 3. The different treatments had no significant impact on moral development.

1665. Academy of Religion and Mental Health. Today's Youth and Moral Values. New York: Academy of Religion and Mental Health, 1969. ED 164 428.

Contains the report of the tenth annual meeting of the Academy of Religion and Mental Health. Contains thirteen papers on a wide range of subjects such as courses of youth alienation, moral values in secular education, moral values in religious education, youth and drug usage, sex education and the like. A religious theme is contained in many of the papers.

1666. Advisory Council for the Ministry of the Church of England. Teaching Christian Ethics. London: SCM Press, 1974.

Presents the rationale for a course for teaching Christian ethics to ordinands of the Church of England.

1667. Altilia, Leonard. "Education in Christian Morality: A Developmental Framework." Religious Education, 71 (1976): 488-499.

Argues that since moral thinking has been shown to develop through a series of stages, Christian moral teaching, to be effective, must follow the same pattern.

1668. Andreasen, Samuel G. "An Analysis of Change of Adult Values Utilizing Religious Treatments." Ed.D. dissertation, Arizona State University, 1976. 36/11, p. 7127.

On the Study of Values instrument (item 1343) no changes were identified as a result of a Christian Education program held on a military base.

1669. Bachmeyer, T.J. "The Golden Rule and Developing Moral Judgment." Religious Education, 68 (1973): 348-365.

Using interpretations of the Golden Rule based on stage of moral development, it is shown how the rule takes on different meaning at different periods of a person's development.

1670. Bask, Marvin I. "Effects of the Teaching of Ethics on the Moral Judgment of Students." Ph.D. dissertation, The American University, 1973. 35/02, p. 879.

On a researcher constructed test of moral judgment, after a course on Jewish Ethics, an immediate increase in severity of moral judgment was detected.

1671. Belckens, Jef. "Moral Education in Private Schools: A Christian Perspective." Toward Moral and Religious Maturity (item 1793), pp. 517-548.

Explores the possibilities of moral education in schools. Argues that it can occur two ways in schools. The indirect way involves familiarization with the Christian religion. The direct way focuses on moral judgments, moral dispositions and the capacity to perform moral acts.

1672. Blishen, Edward. "The School as Experimental Community." Let's Teach Them Right (item 1803), pp. 202-211.

Discusses the negative impact on moral education of the requirement that teachers teach religion. The problem lies with the emphasis on exhortation and dogmatism.

1673. Brownfield, Rod. "Those Old-Time Values," Readings in Values Clarification (item 212), pp. 231-236.

In a position compatible with values clarification Brownfield argues that no teacher or curriculum should stand in the way of the individuals search for an interpretation of basic core of Christian values.

1674. Chazan, Barry. "Study and Moral Action in Contemporary Jewish Education." Journal of Curriculum Studies, 12 (1980): 307-321.

Examines six programs of Jewish moral education. The programs are analyzed from the perspective of the relationship between knowledge and action. The approaches either emphasize knowledge, action or a dialectic between the two. Contains citations to all the approaches discussed. This paper is an excellent source of information on current Jewish education with an emphasis on morals.

1675. Covey, Stephen R. "Effects of Human Relations Training on the Social, Emotional, and Moral Development of Students, with Emphasis on Human Relations Training Based on Religious Principles." D.R.E. dissertation, Brigham Young University, 1976. 37/09, p. 5892.

Two sections of human relations training, one traditional the other with a religious bent, were found to have no impact on social, emotional or moral development.

1676. Dorff, Elliot N. "Study Leads to Action." Religious Education, 75 (1980): 171-192.

Explores one method for teaching morality used by one tradition in human culture--classical text study within Judaism. How Jews have justified and applied this methodology is explained.

1677. Fernando, Peter. "Effects of a Weekend Religious Experience on the Values of High School Students as Measured by the Allport-Vernon-Lindzey Study of Values." Ph.D. dissertation, Kent State University, 1973. 34/09, p. 5625.

A weekend religious experience was found to have a long term positive impact on religious and social values.

1678. Gentile, Michael. "Moral Judgment Throughout Adulthood Among Four Jewish Religious Affiliations." Ph.D. dissertation, Fordham University, 1978. 39/03, p. 1435.

It was found that the youngest age group (20-34) was significantly higher in stage of moral reasoning than the older groups. Also the Orthodox subjects scored significantly higher in stage of moral reasoning than other religious affiliations (conservative, reform and non-affiliative).

1679. Gerard, Bert S. "Values Teaching: The Hidden Agenda in Religious Education." Religious Education, 69 (1974): 219-227.

Bemoans the bankrupt condition of Jewish religious education and recommends that a whole new look be taken. This new look should involve better relationships in the classroom and allowing students some choice in choosing values.

1680. Goodman, Arnold M. "Potential for Growth and Development: A Rabbinic View." Counseling and Values, 19 (October 1974): 30-35.

Argues that the entire thrust of the Jewish Rabbinic Tradition is to accept the reality of development. Behavior flows from values and the source of all values is seen as the Torah.

1681. Gorman, Margaret. "Moral and Faith Development in Seventeen-Year-Old Students." Religious Education, 72 (1977): 491-504.

Finds no correlation between type of school (religious and nonreligious), attendance at church, and either level of faith or moral development.

1682. Hall, B. and M. Smith. Values Clarification as Learning Process: Handbook for Christian Educators. New York: Paulist Press, 1973.

Explores the theological bases of the value clarification methodology. Applications of the values clarification process for religious education, parish renewal, liturgy and personal prayers are discussed.

1683. Hall, Robert T. "Moral Education and Religion Studies." Distinguishing Moral Education (item 1810), pp. 15-28.

Describes major differences and interrelations between moral education and religion studies.

1684. Harris, Alan. Teaching Morality and Religion. London: George Allen and Unwin, 1976.

Presents a clear analytical examination of what is meant by religious and moral education and argues that the object of both should be to help students form their own judgments. This is a practical introduction to the subject intended for teachers.

1685. Harris, Anton T. "A Study of the Relationship between Stages of Moral Development and the Religious Factors of Knowledge, Belief and Practice in Catholic High School Adolescents." Ed.D. dissertation, University of Oregon, 1981. 42/02, p. 638.

Finds that religious knowledge scores are positively correlated with moral development, but religious belief and practice are not.

1686. Hinton, M.G. "Religious Education and the Teaching of Morality." Let's Teach Them Right (item 1803), pp. 81-92.

Argues that the teaching of morality to sixth-formers should be done in an open manner, rely on discussion, yet should be directed toward certain socially acceptable principles by the teacher.

1687. Hollerorth, Hugo J. "A Programme for Moral Education is Alive and Well at the Unitarian Universalist Association." Journal of Moral Education, 2 (1973): 123-129.

Describes a program of moral education which emphasizes situational ethics.

1688. Horder, Donald. "The Lancaster RE Project." Journal of Moral Education, 1 (1971): 43-47.

Presents an undogmatic approach to religious education with special attention devoted to the project's attitude toward moral education.

1689. Karin, Val E. "An Empirical Investigation of the Relationships between Exposure to Formal Jewish Education, Personal-Social Factors and Moral Judgment." Ph.D. dissertation, New York University, 1973. 34/06, p. 3171.

Extent of religious instruction was found not significantly related to moral maturity.

1690. Kealey, Robert J. "Christian Values and Social Studies: A Redundant Title?" Paper presented at annual meeting of the National Catholic Education Association. Philadelphia, 1979. ED 171 162.

Presents argument for and methods of integrating Christian values into social studies education in Catholic schools.

1691. Kohlberg, Lawrence. "Moral and Religious Education and the Public Schools: A Developmental View." Religion and Public Education. Edited by T. Sizer. Boston: Houghton-Mifflin, 1967, pp. 164-183.

Argues that moral development is nondenominational and that the purpose of religious education should not be to develop moral character, but to develop religious belief and sentiment. Also in Collected Papers (item 1798) and The Philosophy of Moral Development (item 1799).

1692. Koolyk, Shirley. "A Comparison of the Underlying Philosophical Assumptions Concerning the Concept of Justice in Kohlberg's Theory of Moral Development with Those of Jewish Ethical Theory from the Halakhic Perspective." Ed.D. dissertation, Boston University, 1978. 39/05, p. 2813.

Kohlberg's theory of justice is compared to and contrasted with a pluralistic ethical model which puts a greater emphasis on the principle of benevolence and less on adjudicating between disputes.

1693. Kustusch, Donna and Patricia Walter. "A Developmental Approach to Values Education." Values Pedagogy and Higher Education, (item 1558), pp. 143-168.

Describes a 3 stage course sequence in a religious education context at Sienna Heights College. The courses are designed to help students engage in personal value clarification, moral decision making, and systematic religious thinking. The rationale and evaluation of these courses is described.

1694. Little, Lawrence C. Religion and Public Education: A Bibliography. Pittsburg: University of Pittsburgh Book Center, 1968.

Presents an extensive but unannotated bibliography of the field. Features sections on Supreme Court Cases and publications of religious bodies and of public school systems. The lack of an index and of topical organization limits its usefulness.

1695. Lombaerts, Herman. "Reciprocal Relationships Between Moral Commitment and Faith Profession in Worship." Toward Moral and Religious Maturity (item 1793), pp. 251-276.

Presents an account of adolescents designing their own liturgy and the effect it has on moral commitment. The implications for religious education are discussed.

1696. Meyer, John R. "Religion in Ontario's Public Schools: A Critique of the Mackay Report." Religious Education, 65 (1970): 44-49.

Summarizes the Mackay report on religious information and moral development (item 1328) and critiques it for being too simplistic in theory and too optimistic in its goal setting.

1697. Miller, Donald E. "Bargaining with the Divine." Educational Horizons, 56 (Winter 1977-78): 95-100.

Presents a clarification of morality, ethics and moral development along with a definition of justice. A theological perspective on moral development is presented and the implications of this perspective for the education of youth is discussed.

1698. Mischey, Eugene J. "Faith Development and Its Relationship to Moral Reasoning and Identity Status in Young Adults." Ph.D. dissertation, University of Toronto, 1978. 39/07, p. 4146.

It was discovered that there was a rough parallel in moral and religious development with faith development tending to precede the development of parallel forms of moral reasoning in 57 percent of the cases.

1699. Pattison, E. Mansell. "The Development of Moral Values in Children." Pastoral Psychology, 20 (February, 1969): 14-30.

Argues that Christian education should not aim at the transmission of moral values per se, but at providing a vehicle for responsible moral dialogue and presenting children with a model for grappling with morality as an ongoing existential process. A psychoanalytic/existential interpretation of Christian education is presented.

1700. Prunty, Kenneth G. "Values Education in the Local Church." Counseling and Values, 22 (1977): 52-59.

Describes three similar phases in churches' development of ways to deal with the faith/values crises. The effects of this reaction and the implications for the future are discussed.

1701. Rowntree, Stephen. "Faith and Justice and Kohlberg." Readings in Moral Education (item 449), pp. 230-247.

Attempts to place Kohlberg's theory of moral judgment into the tradition of Catholic education. Attempts to reconcile the education of faith with that of ethical reasoning.

1702. Schmidt, Stephen A. "Law-Gospel: Toward a Model of Moral Education." Religious Education, 65 (1970): 474-482.

Focuses on how one teaches Christian morality within the setting of the formal religion period in a Christian classroom. A Lutheran "law-gospel" model is presented. The aim is to do law as accusation, gospel as rebirth and renewal toward freedom as the natural response of new natures.

1703. Selig, Sidney and Gerald Teller. "The Moral Development of Children in Three Different School Settings." Religious Education, 70 (1975): 406-415.

Students in conservative and traditional Jewish schools were tested for level of moral development. Developmental trends were detected.

1704. Shane, Harold G. "The Moral Choices Before Us: Two Theologians Comment." Phi Delta Kappan, 56 (1975): 707-711.

Two theologians (Martin E. Marty and Father David Tracy) comment on the moral crises of contemporary life and theologies potential role in solving these crises.

1705. Sholl, Doug. "The Contributions of Lawrence Kohlberg to Religious and Moral Education." Religious Education, 66 (1971): 364-372.

Analyzes Kohlbergs theory and supplements it with ideas of Tillich and Bellah to develop a perspective on religious and moral education.

1706. Simon, S.B. "Three Ways to Teach Church School." Colloquy, 3 (1970): 37-38.

Three levels of teaching are discussed (facts, concepts, values) and examples are taken from the story of Jesus' triumphant entrance into Jerusalem and the life of St. Francis of Assisi. Also in Readings in Values Clarification (item 212).

1707. Simon, Sidney. "Value Clarification: A New Mission for Religious Education." Readings in Values Clarificaiton (item 212), pp. 241-246.

Shows how Christian education can be strengthened through the inclusion of values clarification techniques.

1708. Simon, S.B., P. Daitch, and M. Hartwell. "Values Clarification: New Mission for Religious Education, Parts I, II and III." Catechist, 1971: 5(1): 809; 5(2): 36-38; and 5(3): 28-29.

Contains three articles designed for religious educators which integrate values clarification with Christian religious education.

1709. Smith, Robert B. "The Theory and Practice of Moral Education: A Manual for Use in the United Church of Canada." Ed.D. dissertation, University of Toronto, 1975. 39/03, p. 1384.

Discusses the relation of religion and morality, insights from the psychologies, and an approach to Christian moral education based on ideas from Freire, Hampden-Turner, Evans, Kohlberg and Erikson.

1710. Sosevsky, Morris. "Incorporating Moral Education into the Jewish Secondary School Curriculum." Ed.D. dissertation, Yeshiva University, 1980. 41/08, p. 3519.

Develops source material for a program of Jewish moral education. Although Kohlberg's personal philosophy is rejected in favor of a more collective Judaic emphasis, his methodology is adopted and incorporated into the program.

1711. Speedy, Graeme W. "Church Programs and Moral Education." Religious Education, 65 (1970): 485-492.

Three issues related to the churches' potential for success in moral education are discussed as an evaluation mode of church programs at two levels (local and societal).

1712. Stauffer, S.A. "Identification Theory and Christian Moral Education." Religious Education, 67 (1972): 60-67.

Argues that the place of models in moral education needs more attention from churches. The concept of identification is presented and research on identification theories is reviewed.

1713. Stoop, David A. "The Relation Between Religious Education and the Process of Maturity Through the Developmental Stages of Moral Judgments." Ph.D. dissertation, University of Southern California, 1979. 40/07, p. 3912.

Conservative Christian education appears to stimulate Stage 4 moral reasoning, causing early acceleration to this stage. Lutheran religious education appears to stimulate principled moral reasoning. No appreciable trends in moral development were detected for Catholic and public high school youth.

1714. Swyhart, Barbara A. "The Paradox of Moral/Values Education and Religion Studies: A Critical Overview." Distinguishing Moral Education (item 1810), pp. 29-70.

Critiques the various approaches to values education and suggests a rationale for a methodology for bringing values education and religious studies together.

1715. Taylor, Marvin J. Religious and Moral Education. New York: The Center for Applied Research in Education, Inc., 1965.

Review the history of American religious education, legal questions surrounding religion morality and the schools and moral and character education in schools. Protestant, Jewish and Catholic religious education practice is described and compared.

1716. Theroux, Susan S. "Beyond Dogmatism and Unbelief: A Redefinition of Moral Education." Journal of Moral Education, 4 (1975): 231-242.

Claims that moral education must be based on universal religious values if it expects to have an impact on character development. A moral education program (the Anisa project) with an emphasis on cooperation is discussed. The joint use of the methods of ground rules, modeling and moral reasoning is described.

1717. Walters, Thomas P. "A Study of the Relationship between Religious Orientation and Cognitive Moral Maturity in Volunteer Religion Teachers from Selected Suburban Catholic Parishes in the Archdiocese of Detroit." Ph.D. dissertation, Wayne State University, 1980. 41/04, p. 1517.

Religious orientation was not found to correlate to level of moral reasoning.

1718. Westerhoff, John H. "How Can We Teach Values?" Readings in Values Clarification (item 212), pp. 225-230.

The author attempts to show that values clarification and religious education are compatible.

1719. Wilcox, Mary M. Developmental Journal: A Guide to the Development of Logical and Moral Reasoning and Social Perspective." Nashville, TN: Abington Press, 1979.

Combines developmental perspectives (Piaget, Kohlberg and Fowler) and arrives at an approach for introducing religion into the schools. Sees Kohlberg's stages as a way of teaching religion to students based on the idea that the higher stages are more cosmic.

1720. Wolf, Richard J. "A Study of the Relationship between Religious Education, Religious Experience, Maturity and Moral Development." Ph.D. dissertation, New York University, 1979. 40/12, p. 6219.

It was hypothesized that subjects exposed to a high degree of religious education, with a high degree of commitment to their religion and with a high degree of maturity integration would score higher on a test of moral development than subjects without those religion related characteristics. The opposite was found to be the case.

1721. Broudy, Harry S. "Moral/Citizenship Education: Potentials and Limitations. Occasional Paper No. 3." Philadelphia: Research for Better Schools, 1977. ED 160 480.

Discusses the problems with implementing a moral/citizenship education program in a pluralistic society and suggests conditions which would make such programs acceptable to communities.

1722. Durlo, H.F. "A Taxonomy of Democratic Development." _Human Development_, 19 (1976): 197-219.

Points out the necessity to view democratic socialization from a cognitive-developmental perspective.

1723. Eyler, Janet. "Citizenship Education for Conflict: An Empirical Assessment of the Relationship between Principled Thinking and Tolerance for Conflict and Diversity." _Theory and Research in Social Education_, 8 (Summer 1980): 11-26.

Finds that principled moral thinkers surpass non-principled thinkers in applying democratic principles in concrete controversial situations.

1724. Fenton, Edwin. "The Relationship of Citizenship Education to Values Education. Occasional Paper No. 2." Philadelphia: Research for Better Schools, 1977. ED 178 448.

Defines six major goals of citizenship education and relates the major approaches to values education to these goals. It is found that the most effective programs of citizenship education are not a part of the values education programs. Concludes by outlining a comprehensive approach to citizenship education.

1725. Harmon, Carolyn P. "The Development of Moral and Political Reasoning Among 10, 13 and 16 Year Olds." Ph.D. dissertation, Yale University, 1973. 34/05, p. 2718.

Uses the cognitive-developmental theory to challenge traditional conceptions of political socialization.

1726. Kutnick, Peter. "The Myth of the Democratic Leader: An Insight into Political Socialization of the Primary School." Journal of Moral Education, 10 (1981): 173-185.

Presents a discussion of the political socialization literature and findings fom two studies on the child's developing conception of leadership. The author's research indicates that children's knowledge of leadership is generated through actual life and school experiences. It is argued that the more the child is involved in shared authority the better his/her moral development.

1727. Lockwood, Alan. "Moral Reasoning and Public Policy Debate." Moral Development and Behavior (item 1801), pp. 317-325.

Explores the relationship between normative moral philosophy and public policy controversy. Examines ways that moral reasoning is applicable to public policy debate, psychological research on the relationship between moral views and policy positions and actions, and the adequacy of certain moral points of view for resolving public policy disputes.

1728. Mancuso, James C., and Theodore R. Sarbin. "A Paradigmatic Analysis of Psychological Issues at the Interface of Jurisprudence and Moral Conduct." Moral Development and Behavior (item 1801), pp. 326-341.

Reviews the literature on the relationship between psychological development and law-related behavior. They point out the great difficulty involved over the use of the terms "disease of the mind," "know" and "wrong." They urge a contextualist view of legal culpability--consideration of the total ecology of rule-following conduct.

1729. Merelman, Richard M. "A Critique of Moral Education in the Social Studies." Journal of Moral Education, 8 (1979): 182-192.

Argues that the moral education approach to social studies is pedagogically and politically unsound. Political decision making is shown to be a quite different process than moral decision making.

1730. Nelson, Jack L. "The Uncomfortable Relationship between Moral Education and Citizenship Instruction." Moral Development and Politics (item 1821), pp. 256-285.

Examines the uneasy relationship between moral education and citizenship education. Contains an account of historical relationships between moral and citizenship education. Possible relationships between moral and citizenship education are discussed. It is concluded that traditional means of citizenship instruction have acted to impede rather than enhance the capacity for the development of mature moral individuals.

1731. Oldenquist, Andrew. "On the Nature of Citizenship." Educational Leadership, 38 (1980): 30-34.

Citizenship education should foster group loyalty and white, middle-class values, especially in black and poor white neighborhoods. Discusses the simularity and differences between moral and citizenship education. Moral and citizenship education must be based on a foundation of a sense of belonging to local and national communities and a loyalty to their norms.

1732. Puz, Susan K. "Women's Role in the Quest for Justice in American History: A Civic Education Curriculum." D.A. dissertation, Carnegie-Mellon University, 1981. 41/11, p. 4675.

Presents four core curriculum units prepared to facilitate growth in students' knowledge of women's history as well as advance students' intellectual skills, participatory skills, democratic values, and personal development.

1733. Scheffler, Israel. "The Moral Content of American Public Education." Moral Education ... It Comes with the Territory (item 1811), pp. 20-29.

Moral education in a democracy does not shape, it liberates. An anology is drawn with the scientific method--moral education should develop a critical moral point of view.

1734. Tapp, June L., ed. "Socialization, the Law and Society." Journal of Social Issues, 27,2 (1971).

A special edition containing excellent articles on role of law as socializer, legal development, and socialized values in law and society.

1735. Tapp, June L., and Lawrence Kohlberg. "Developing Senses of Law and Legal Justice." Journal of Social Issues, 27,2 (1971): 65-92.

A theory of developing conceptions of law and legal justice is presented. The theory is based on Kohlberg's congitive-developmental approach to moral reasoning. Research is cited to support the arguments presented.

1736. Wallace, John D., ed. Report on the National Conference on Planning for Moral/Citizenship Education. Philadelphia: Research for Better Schools, 1976. ED 129 767.

The conference findings are summarized under the headings of public policy, theory, research, development and dissemination. This document only summarizes. The papers delivered are not included here.

1737. White, Pat. "Political Education and Moral Education or Bringing Up Children to be Decent Members of Society." Journal of Moral Education, 9 (1980): 147-155.

Argues that political education is an essential part of moral education and supplies the context and content of moral education. Rational morality commits one very concretely to a democratic form of society. The concepts, forms of argument and dispositions necessary for democratic society are the focus of moral/political education.

Critiques of the Enterprise of Moral Education

1738. Bereiter, Carl. "The Morality of Moral Education." Hastings Center Report, 8 (April 1978): 20-25.

Argues that the cognitive-development approach and values clarification, contrary to their claim of neutrality, do in fact teach values. In classrooms this means the majority opinion will prevail. If the teacher does not teach the child what to believe, someone else will.

1739. Bereiter, Carl. Must We Educate? Englewood Cliffs: Prentice-Hall, 1973.

Argues that the school should do what it does well, develop skills, and leave the rest alone. Especially moral education should be left to the family.

1740. Bereiter, Carl. "Schools Without Education." Harvard Educational Review, 42 (1972): 390-413.

Argues that since schools are not successful in influencing the way children turn out anyway, they shouldn't try to influence such things as values. Schools should concentrate only on providing child care and skill training.

1741. Blocher, D.H. "Toward an Ecology of Student Development." Adolescents' Development and Education (item 1806), pp. 490-496.

Warns against narrow views of human development. Suggests that the total development of the person is the proper concern of education and this requires an ecological view of the schooling process.

1742. Broughton, J.M. "Beyond Formal Operations." Teacher's College Record, 79 (1977): 87-97.

Presents five reasons why educating people up to the final stage of operational thought may not be justifiable as the central aim of postchildhood education.

1743. Broughton, John M. "Dialectics and Moral Development Ideology." Readings in Moral Education (item 449), pp. 298-307.

Analyzes existing critiques of Kohlberg and offers his own Marxian perspective.

1744. Broughton, John M. "The Limits of Formal Thought." Adolescents' Development and Education (item 1806), pp. 49-60.

Argues that if we are to have a comprehensive of adolescent and adult rationality we must broaden the construct of formal operations as a mode of consciousness. As it is construed by Piaget it is a mode of consciousness involving only logical empiricism. Formal operations should be seen as the culmination of a destructive socialization that alienates our thinking and being.

1745. Crabtree, Walden. "Establishing Policy in the Values Education Controversy." Contemporary Education. 46(1974): 24-27.

Argues that the thing to do with parents who object to schools meddling with their childrens values is to train the parents to accept what is going on.

1746. Cragg, A.W. "Moral Education in the Schools." Canadian Journal of Education, 4 (1979): 28-38.

Introducing moral education exacerbates the problem of the hidden curriculum rather than reducing it. Each approach to moral education is based on philosophic conception of morality which is not openly debated.

1747. Cragg, A.W. "Moral Education in the Schools: The Hidden Values Argument." Interchange, 10 (1978/79): 12-25.

Argues that inspite of new moves into moral education the hidden curriculum will still be with us, it will simply take a new shape for there are also hidden values in Kohlberg and values clarification.

1748. Crittenden, Brian. Bearings in Moral Education, Australian Educational Review No. 12. Hawthorn, Victoria: Australian Council for Educational Research, 1978.

Consists of a brief critical review of recent work in moral education. Reviews recent shifts in moral philosophy and concludes by urging the need for a wider perspective on moral education.

1749. Delattre, Edwin J. and William J. Bennett. "Where the Values Movement Goes Wrong?" Change, 11 (1979): 38-43.

Argues against current approaches to values education. Claims that the goal of values education should not be to develop skilled youth at thinking about morality, but rather to develop youth who are moral. In spite of rapid social change there still exist core values. Teachers should present moral ideals with conviction, not with tentativeness.

1750. Eger, Martin. "The Conflict in Moral Education: An Informal Case Study." The Public Interest, 63 (1981): 62-80.

Examines the question of whether great harm is being done by teaching values by probing the connection between a values education program and the social conflict to which it gave rise. The case centers on the teaching of values clarification in 1979 in Spencer-Van Etten school district in upstate New York. A series of questions on adequate training of teachers, parental control of schools, academic freedom, exclusion of competing moral positions, etc. are posed.

1751. Floy, Joseph. "Can Children Do Moral Philosophy?" Growing Up With Philosophy (item 1075), pp. 145-157.

Argues that moral education is itself immoral. Childhood is a stage of life that must be protected in all its innocence and dependence--it is a world organized and stabilized by adult authority. Ethics introduced too early can fragment this world and lead only to cynicism, skepticism, boredom and alienation.

1752. Gordon, David. "Free-Will and the Undesirability of Moral Education." Educational Theory, 25 (1975): 407-416.

Argues that in order for a teacher to develop pupils' autonomy they must reject moral education. Moral education is taken to mean the development of a pupil's inclination to do what is right.

1753. Grant, Gloria. "Values/Diversity in Education: A Progress Report." Educational Leadership, 35 (1978): 443-448.

Argues that the progress toward integrating educational resources into schools which represent diverse social and cultural values and norms has been slow and inadequate.

1754. Hyland, Eddie. "Towards a Radical Critique of Morality and Moral Education." Journal of Moral Education, 8 (1979): 156-167.

Argues that there is no deductive justification possible for moral rules, therefore no reason for being moral. In morality's place he argues for an analysis of needs and wants as a foundation for a fuller and richer value system.

1755. Lerner, Michael P. "Marxism and Ethical Reasoning." Social Praxis, 2 (1974): 63-88.

It is argued that a historical analysis of the function of ethics reveals its centrality in the struggle between dominant classes and those that challenge them. Lerner claims that the "good-reasons" approach of Kai Nelson's Reason and Practice in Ethics has ideological use in justifying an established order. An alternative view of ethics more complimentary to those involved in the struggle for social change is presented.

1756. Martin, Jane R. "Moral Autonomy and Political Education." Growing Up With Philosophy (item 1075), pp. 174-194.

Argues that traditional philosophy, which prepares children for intellectual autonomy, fails to acquaint children with the social, economic and political realities of which they are a part. If the existing social system is unjust then true education must produce youthful social critics. Philosophical inquiry will lead to only abstract ideals without apparent application to real social and moral issues.

1757. Nielsen, Kai. "Class Conflict, Marxism and the Good-Reasons Approach: A Response to Michael Lerner." Social Praxis, 2 (1974): 89-112.

Argues that the 'good-reasons' approach does not have the conservative ideological--implications attributed to it by Michael Lerner (item 1755). Examines the problems of morality embedded in Marxist ideology and offers a resolution of those problems.

1758. Ofstad, Harold. "Education versus Growth in Moral Development." The Monist, 58 (1974): 581-599.

Argues that moral agency can not be brought about through educational procedures such as instruction or rational dialogue. If the posited ten conditions of moral agency are to come about at all it is more than likely the lucky outcome of a developmental process in which social growth and interaction have been of decisive importance.

1759. Oliver, Donald W. and Mary Jo Bane. "Moral Education: Is Reasoning Enough?" Moral Education ... It Comes With the Territory (item 1811), pp. 349-369.

Questions whether or not most people engage in the kind of moral reasoning advocated by moral education curriculum and if so whether or not this kind of reasoning is a significant part of something we might call the moral personality. Discusses the limits of reason and the need to encourage students to confront the irrationality in life and think metaphorically. Also in Moral Education: Interdisciplinary Approaches (item 1785).

1760. Phillips, D.Z. "Is Moral Education Really Necessary?" British Journal of Educational Studies, 27 (1979): 42-56.

Criticized the view that moral education should make explicit the values in an academic curriculum.

The view that education should be value free is also criticized. The proper focus should be the values enbedded with the subjects being taught. Claims that what is not necessary is moral educationists, especially those who corrupt education by their focus on values in schools rather than in subjects.

1761. Reid, Herbert and Ernest Yanarella. "Critical Political Theory and Moral Development: On Kohlberg, Hampden-Turner and Habermas." Theory and Society, 4 (1977): 505-541.

It is shown that Kohlberg's stages are little more than a continuation of the ideological hegemony of Lockean-Liberalism. When faced with the prospect of their critique becoming merely a demystifying hermeneutics the possibilities and limits of existential radicalism--Hampden-Turner and Habermas--are explored. It is concluded that "the pragmatics of communicative competence must be recontextualized within a larger critical and more deeply dialectical theory of totality and temporality, hopefully illuminating radically democratic modes of struggle with the hegemony of alienating institutions and their 'historical blocks'."

1762. Ruscoe, Gordon C. "Moral Education in Revolutionary Society." Theory into Practice, 14 (1975): 221-223.

Examines some of the features of the moral context in which education in a revolutionary society operates. Discusses the need for changing habitual forms of moral behavior. The inevitable conflicts between economic and ideological concerns is discussed.

1763. Ryan, Kevin. "Is it Going to be Just a Word Game?" The Humanist, 38 (November/December 1978): 21.

Argues that although we know that for moral and value education to take root there must be some affective commitment and involvement yet our intellectual approach to moral education does little to develop these dispositions.

1764. Sullivan, Edmund V. "Can Values Be Taught?" Moral Development and Socialization (item 1822), pp. 219-243.

Argues that institutions project certain kinds of values into education. This projection of values also pervades the content of curriculum which is introduced into schools. It is incumbent on the believer in moral education that he/she address the institutional question when considering moral education. A postcritical approach to moral education is proposed which involves subjecting ones values to "critical awareness." Five broad guidelines for postcritical education are offered.

1765. Sullivan, Edmund V. "The Scandalized Child: Children, Media and Commodity Culture." Toward Moral and Religious Maturity (item 1793), pp. 549-573.

Argues that mass media with its legitimation of mass culture (seen as a commodity culture assults basic human dignity) is so pervasive and influential in the moral socialization that the only way to morally educate children is by means of developing a post critical perspective in children. This involves developing in children a "critical awareness" of their environment.

1766. Wallen, Norman E. "Can Moral Behavior Be Taught Through Cognitive Means?--No." Social Education, 41 (1977): 329-331.

Argues that reasoning alone is merely an intellectual exercise. Thought must be linked with strong emotions if it is to affect behavior.

1767. Walzer, Michael. "Teaching Morality." The New Republic, 178 (June 10, 1978): 12-14.

Points to the fatal weakness in "American liberal approach to moral life" as it affects education. One posture relegates values to private life and leads to intense subjectivity. The other posture reduces values to quantifiable cost/benefit analysis and leads to a radical objectivity. Neither conforms to the realities of our common moral life. Neither can be realized by any imaginable form of social life.

1768. Welton, M. "Is Moral Education Possible in Advanced Capitalist Consumer Society." The History and Social Science Teacher, 13 (1977): 9-22.

Presents a neo-Marxist analysis and concludes that liberal capitalist ideology and its value structure fail to justify the state and the institutions in it--schools do not escape this "legitimation crisis." The interest on form rather than content is seen as merely a diversion from the fact that schools teach values that justify societal immorality--capitalism.

1769. Wynne, Edward. "Adolescent Alienation and Social Policy." Teacher's College Record, 78 (1976): 23-40.

Cites data to show that our social and political institutions are becoming less effective at socializing our young to become mature, wholesome, and committed citizens. The situation is analyzed from a Durkheimian perspective and interpreted as one of increasing social fragmentation. Values education should be on an affective level as opposed to using more formalism, cognition and legalism.

BIBLIOGRAPHIES

1770. Blackham, H.J. Moral Education. London: National Book League, 1971.

An annotated bibliography of 186 items, most of which originate from England. Contains sections on Study of Morality, Study of Moral Education, Studies in Particular Moral Areas and Books for the Classroom.

1771. Bouchard, L.A.M., and W.A. Bruneau, eds. Moral Education: A Bibliography, 3rd ed. Vancouver: Association for Values Education and Research, 1975.

Items are indexed by discipline, components discussed and the nature of publications. Contains 2,500 entries. Currently is out of print.

1772. Canadian Teacher's Federation. Moral and Values Education. Bibliographies in Education, No. 44. Ottawa: Canadian Teacher's Federation, 1974. ED 097 269.

Contains 414 citations compiled from the five year period of 1968-1973. Entries are arranged alphabetically under the headings of books, articles and theses.

* Canfield, John and Mark Phillips. A Guide to Humanistic Education, 1970. ED 067 356. Item 853.

* Canfield, John T. and Mark Phillips. "Humanisticography." Media and Methods, 8 (1971): 41-56. Item 854.

1773. Cochrane, Don. "Bibliography." Moral Education Forum. Spring 1977-1981.

Published every year in the Spring edition, Cochrane presents an extensive but unannotated listing of the major works published over the preceeding year. Sections usually include new books, special issues of journals and articles. Selections are taken from the psychological and philosophical literature. This is probably the best "single shot" means of reviewing the past years publications in the field.

1774. Cochrane, Don. "Doctoral Dissertations in Review." Moral Education Forum, 5 (Winter 1980): 16-38.

A review of 62 doctoral dissertations completed during 1979 on moral development and related topics. The annotations are done carefully.

1775. Cochrane, Don. "Doctoral Dissertations in Review." Moral Education Forum, 6 (Fall 1981): 2-23.

Sixty-three doctoral dissertations completed between 1979 and 1981 and dealing with topics related to moral education are annotated.

1776. Cochrane, Don. Moral/Values Education in Canada: A Bibliography and Directory, 1970-1977. Toronto: Ontario Institute for Studies in Education, 1978.

Contains a collection of hundreds of articles, many in small Canadian journals. Organization is alphabetical and contains no annotations.

1777. Curry, Charles. "An Annotated Bibliography of Instructional Materials Which Emphasize Positive Work Ethics." Blacksburg, VA: Virginia Polytechnic Institute and State University, 1975. ED 115 766.

1778. Hunt, Mate G. Values Resource Guide. Oneonta, NY: American Association of Colleges for Teacher Education, 1958.

Contains annotated lists of books, films, plays, readings, etc. All entries are indexed by the character trait emphasized.

1779. Kelly, Marjorie. In Pursuit of Values: A Bibliography of Children's Books. New York: Paulist Press, 1973. NR

* Kirschenbaum, Howard and Barbara Glaser-Kirscherbaum. "An Annotated Bibliography on Values Clarification." _Readings in Values Clarification_ (item 212), pp. 366-383. Item 211.

1780. Klafter, Marcia. _A Bibliography on Moral Values Education_. Philadelphia: Research for Better Schools, 1976. ED 128 766.

Presents a collection of 1,800 citations published between 1960 and 1975. Entries are organized alphabetically and the collection contains a large number of psychological studies related to moral thought and action.

1781. Kuhmerker, Lisa. _A Bibliography on Moral Development and the Learning of Values in Schools and Other Social Settings_. New York: Center for Children's Ethical Education, 1971. ED 054 014.

A forty-five page bibliography organized around four topics: Moral development, cultural influences on values, moralization, and values in education.

* Little, Lawrence C. _Religion and Public Education: A Bibliography_. Pittsburg: University of Pittsburg Book Center, 1968. Item 1694.

1782. Nicholoson, Sandy. _Values, Feelings and Morals: Part II--An Annotated Bibliography of Programs and Instructional Materials_. Washington, DC: American Association of Elementary-Kindergarten-Nursery Educators, 1974.

An annotated collection of teaching materials most of which are only tangentally related to moral/values education.

* Pine, Gerald J. and Angelo V. Boy. "What Counselors Might Like to Read about Counseling and Values: An Annotated Bibliography." _Personnel and Guidance Journal_, 58 (1970): 631-634. Item 1522.

* Rosenzweig, Linda. "A Selected Bibliography of Materials about Moral Education Based on the Research of Lawrence Kohlberg." _Social Education_, 40 (1976): 208-212. Item 446.

* Sorensen, Marilou R. "Teaching Young People About the Law Through Literature: An Annotated Bibliography." Salt Lake City, UT: Utah State Department of Education, 1980. Item 1190.

1783. Thomas, Walter L. <u>A Comprehensive Bibliography on the Values Concept</u>. Grand Rapids, MI: Northview Public Schools, 1967. ED 024 064.

Cites over 800 articles and books published between 1945 and 1967. Organization is alphabetical only.

* Tolliver, J. Howard. "Confluent/Humanistic/Affective Education: A Set of Bibliographies." Baltimore, MD: Morgan State University, 1979. ED 170 219. Item 918.

COLLECTIONS OF READINGS

1784. Barclay, John G., ed. Values Concepts and Techniques. Washington, D.C.: National Education Association, 1976.

A collection of papers, mostly reprinted elsewhere, dealing with issues in values education and techniques for implementing values education in a variety of settings.

1785. Beck, Clive M., Brian S. Crittenden, and Edmund V. Sullivan, eds. Moral Education: Interdisciplinary Approaches. Toronto: University of Toronto Press, 1971.

Presents papers delivered at a 1968 conference on Moral Education at the Ontario Institute for Studies in Education. Contains sections on the search for norms in a pluralistic society, moral action, psychological processes in moral development and moral behavior and problems of methodology and practice.

* Callahan, Daniel and Sissela Bok, eds. Ethics Teaching in Higher Education. New York: Plenum Press, 1980. Item 1542.

1786. Carr, William G., ed. Values and the Curriculum: A Report of the Fourth International Curriculum Conference. Washington, DC: National Education Association, 1970.

Reports the results of a conference sponsored by the National Education Association's Center for the Study of Instruction. The focus of the conference was the central place that values should play in education. The topic is construed in very general terms by the participants and the distinction between moral and nonmoral issues is frequently blurred.

1787. Chazan, Barry I. and Jonas F. Soltis, eds. Moral Education. New York: Teachers College Press, 1973.

A volume of readings designed to bridge the gap between the moral philosopher and the moral educator by providing discussions of themes in moral philosophy in a way that will enable those in moral education to understand more fully the complex nature of their task.

* Cochrane, Donald B. and Michael Manley-Casimer, eds. Development of Moral Reasoning: Practical Approaches. New York: Praeger Publishers, 1980. Item 26.

1788. Cochrane, Donald B., Cornel M. Hamm and Anastasios C. Kazepides, eds. The Domain of Moral Education. New York: The Paulist Press, 1979.

A series of philosophical essays designed to clarify the parameters of the moral domain and examine the nature and importance of its constitutive elements. Contains sections on the limits of moral education, the nature of moral education, form and content in moral education, and a review of the developmental perspective.

* Collier, Gerald, John Wilson and Peter Tomlinson, eds. Values and Moral Development in Higher Education. London: Croom Helm Ltd, 1974. Item 1554.

1789. Damon, William, ed. New Directions for Child Development, No. 2: Moral Development. San Francisco: Jossey-Bass, Inc., 1978.

A collection of non-traditional and controversial papers on moral development. Especially noteworthy is the paper by Kohlberg (item 410) in which he drops stage 6 from his typology and comes out for indoctrination as an appropriate methodology for moral education.

1790. DePalma, David J. and Jeanne M. Foley, eds. Moral Development: Current Theory and Research. Hillsdale, NJ: Lawrence Erlbaum Associates, 1975.

* Donnellan, Michael and James Ebben, eds. Values Pedagogy in Higher Education. Adrian, MI: Swenk-Tuttle Press, 1978. Item 1558.

1791. Dwain, Hearn D., ed. Values, Feelings and Morals: Part I--Research and Perspectives. Washington, DC: American Association of Elementary-Kindergarten-Nursery Educators, 1974.

Contains papers presented at the 1973 National Research Committee Conference sponsored by the American Association of Elementary Kindergarten, Nursery Educators.

* Erickson, V. Lois and John M. Whiteley, eds. Developmental Counseling and Teaching. Monterey, CA: Brooks/Cole, 1980. Item 784.

* Faust, Clarence H. and Jessica Feingold, eds. Approaches to Education for Character: Strategies for Change in Higher Education. New York: Columbia University Press, 1969. Item 1564.

1792. Fenstermacher, Gary D., ed. Philosophy of Education 1978: Proceedings of the Thirty-Fourth Annual Meeting of the Philosophy of Education Society. Champaign, IL: Philosophy of Education Society, University of Illinois, 1979.

1793. Fowler, J. and A. Vergote, eds. Toward Moral and Religious Maturity: The First International Conference on Moral and Religious Development. Morristown, NJ: Silver Burdette, 1980.

Contains a collection of papers which constitute the best single source of information on recent thought on the interplay between religious and moral development.

* Goodman, Joel, ed. Turning Points: New Developments, New Directions in Values Clarification. Volumes I and II. Saratoga Springs, NY: Creative Resources Press, 1978. Item 186.

1794. Hennessy, Thomas C., ed. Values/Moral Education: The Schools and the Teachers. New York: Paulist Press, 1979.

A collection of articles on effective methods of moral and value education during different levels of schooling.

* Hennessy, Thomas C., ed. Values and Moral Development. New York: Paulist Press, 1976. Item 378.

1795. Holtzman, Wayne H., ed. Moral Development: Proceedings of the 1974 ETS Invitational Conference. Princeton, N.J.: Educational Testing Service, 1975.

1796. Jelinek, James J. The Teaching of Values. The Third Yearbook of the Arizona ASCD. Tempe, AZ: Arizona Association for Supervision and Curriculum Development, 1975. ED 118 512. NI

Contains twenty-seven articles on the teaching of values focusing on theories, teaching strategies, and learning activities.

1797. Kazepides, A.C., ed. The Teaching of Values in Canadian Education, Yearbook of the Canadian Society for the Study of Education. Edmonton, Alberta: University of Alberta, 1975.

Contains a diverse and interesting set of seven papers on issues seldom addressed in moral education.

* Kirschenbaum, Howard and Sidney B. Simon, eds. Readings in Values Clarification. Minneapolis, MN: Winston Press, 1973. Item 212.

1798. Kohlberg, Lawrence. Collected Papers on Moral Development and Moral Education. Cambridge, MA: Center for Moral Education, Harvard University, 1973.

A collection of photocopies of 16 early works by Kohlberg.

1799. Kohlberg, Lawrence. Essays on Moral Development. Volume 1: The Philosophy of Moral Development. New York: Harper and Row, 1981.

A collection of articles by Kohlberg in which the focus is on moral stages and justice. In these papers Kohlberg sets forth his philosophical positions on moral, political, and educational issues underlying his developmental theory. With the exception of one paper on stage 7, all of the papers have been previously published. Each paper has, however, been slightly modified with an introduction linking it to the other papers and to the theme of the book.

1800. Kohlberg, Lawrence. Essays on Moral Development. Volume 2: The Psychology of Moral Development. New York: Harper and Row, forthcoming.

A collection of mostly previously published articles that trace the psychological theory from earlier formulations to the present. Presented is his longitudinal data and the method of scoring it. Accounts of eras in the life cycle from a stage perspective are also included.

* Kohlberg, Lawrence. Essays on Moral Development. Volume 3: Education and Moral Development. New York: Harper and Row, forthcoming. Item 395.

* Kuhmerker, Lisa, Marcia Mentkowski, and V. Lois Erickson, eds. Evaluating Moral Development and Evaluating Educational Programs That Have a Value Dimension. Schenectady, NY: Character Research Press, 1980. Item 1391.

1801. Lickona, Thomas, ed. Moral Development and Behavior: Theory, Research and Social Issues. New York: Holt, Rinehart and Winston, 1976.

A collection of high-quality papers dealing with such issues as how morality is learned, research into the psychological bases of moral thought and behavior, and morality and social issues. Contains papers by Kohlberg, Aronfreed, Bronfenbrenner, Mischel, Eysenck, Hoffman, Selman, Rest, et al.

* Lipman, Matthew and Ann M. Sharp, eds. Growing Up with Philosophy. Philadelphia, PA: Temple University Press, 1978. Item 1075.

* McBee, Mary L., ed. New Directions for Higher Education, Rethinking College Responsibilities for Values, No. 31. San Francisco: Jossey-Bass, 1980. Item 1593.

1802. Macmillan, C.J.B., ed. Philosophy of Education 1980: Proceedings of the Thirty-Sixth Annual Meeting of the Philosophy of Education Society. Normal, IL: Philosophy of Education Society, Illinois State University, 1981.

1803. Macy, Christopher, ed. Let's Teach Them Right. London, Pemberton Publishing, 1969.

Consists of a series of papers on religious education, religious and moral education together, and moral education.

* Metcalf, Lawrence E., ed. Values Education: Rationale, Strategies and Procedures. 41st Yearbook of the National Council for the Social Studies. Washington, DC: National Council for the Social Studies, 1971. Item 953.

1804. Meyer, John R., ed. Reflections on Values Education. Waterloo, Ontario: Wilfred Laurier University Press, 1976.

Contains a series of essays on values education dealing with theoretical problems, the learning environment and the helping facilitator. Contains essays on the development of the theory and a method of assessment of moral judgment (Kohlberg).

1805. Meyer, J.R., B. Burnham and J. Cholvat, eds. Values Education: Theory/Practice/Problems/Prospects. Waterloo, Ontario: Wilfred Laurier University Press, 1975.

1806. Mosher, Ralph, ed. Adolescents' Development and Education. New York: McCutchan, 1979.

Contains a collection of papers on developmental and moral education about half of which were published elsewhere. Witty and sometimes illuminating comments by Mosher preceed the various sections.

* Mosher, Ralph, ed. Moral Education: A First Generation of Research and Development. New York: Praeger, 1980. Item 428.

* Munsey, Brenda, ed. Moral Development, Moral Education and Kohlberg. Birmingham, AL: Religious Education Press, 1980. Item 432.

1807. Niblett, W.R., ed. Moral Education in a Changing Society. London: Faber and Faber Limited, 1963.

Contains a series of addresses presented in London in 1962.

1808. Overly, Norman L., ed. The Unstudied Curriculum: Its Impact on Children. Washington, D.C.: Association for Supervision and Curriculum Development, 1970.

Contains a collection of papers on the nature of the hidden curriculum and its impact on children.

1809. Peters, R.S., ed. Psychology and Ethical Development. London: George Allen and Unwin, 1974.

Contains a collection of papers, all published elsewhere. Part II consists of seven papers on ethical development.

1810. Piediscolzi, Nicholas and Barbara Ann Swyhart, eds. Distinguishing Moral Education, Values Clarification and Religion-Studies. Proceedings of American Academy of Religion, 1976, Section 18. Missoula, MT: Scholars Press, 1976. ED 146 063.

1811. Purpel, David and Kevin Ryan, eds. Moral Education ... It Comes With the Territory. Berkeley, CA: McCutchan Publishing Corp., 1976.

A collection of papers focusing on the topics of the hidden curriculum, values clarification, the cognitive-developmental approach, and the cognitive approach to moral education.

* Read, Donald A. and Sidney B. Simon, eds. Humanistic Education Sourcebook. Englewood Cliffs, NJ: Prentice Hall, 1975. Item 906.

1812. Rokeach, Milton, ed. Understanding Human Values: Individual and Societal. New York: The Free Press, 1979.

Contains a collection of eighteen research reports on the conceptualization and measurement of individual and supraindividual values, the major determinants and consequences of value organization and change that are naturally occuring, the effects of inducing awareness about one's own and others' values, and the role that values and value education should play within the context of the educational institution. The reference section of the volume is comprehensive with respect to Rokeach's definition of the value concept and value change.

* Scharf, Peter, ed. Moral and Psychological Education: Theory and Research. No location: R F Publishing, 1978. Item 448.

* Scharf, Peter, ed. Readings in Moral Education. Minneapolis: Winston Press, 1978. Item 449.

1813. Sizer, Theodore, ed. Religion and the Public Schools. Boston: Houghton Mifflin, 1967.

A collection of readings featuring 17 articles on such topics as teaching about religion; the challenge of religion to our educational system; the relationships among secularism, pluralism, and religion; and theological perspectives on public education.

1814. Sizer, Theodore R. and Nancy F. Sizer, eds. Moral Education: Five Lectures. Cambridge, MA: Harvard University Press, 1973.

Contains five lectures presented at Harvard University on moral education by Gustafson, Peters, Kohlberg, Bettelheim and Keniston.

1815. Sloan, Douglas, ed. Education and Values. New York: Teachers College Press, 1980.

A collection of papers dealing with the relationship between values and education. The papers are largely theoretical. The authors are scientists, philosophers, theologians and historians. A version of this volume first appeared as a special issue of Teachers College Record (February 1979).

1816. Sprinthall, Norman A. and Ralph L. Mosher, eds. Value Development ... As the Aim of Education. Schenectady, NY: Character Research Press, 1978.

A collection of papers with the focus on psychological and moral development as a goal for education.

1817. Steinberg, Ira S., ed. Philosophy of Education 1977: Proceedings of the Thirty-Third Annual Meeting of the Philosophy of Education Society. Urbana, IL: Philosophy of Education Society, University of Illinois, 1977.

1818. Stiles, Lindley J. and Bruce D. Johnson, eds. Morality Examined: Guidelines for Teachers. Princeton, New Jersey: Princeton Book Company, 1977.

This book of readings is designed to provide teachers with a background for understanding the complexity of ethical issues as well as to offer specific help for teaching moral values. The papers in this volume grew out of Northwestern University Faculty-Student Seminar. The essays tend to deal with the topics in a somewhat superficial manner.

1819. Strike, Kenneth A., ed. Philosophy of Education 1976: Proceedings of the Thirty-Second Annual Meeting of the Philosophy of Education Society. Urbana, IL: Philosophy of Education Society, University of Illinois, 1976.

* Summers, Gene F., ed. Attitude Measurement. Chicago, IL: Rand McNally, 1970. Item 1435.

1820. Taylor, Monica J., ed. Progress and Problems in Moral Education. Slough, Berks, England: NFER Publishing Company Ltd, 1975.

A collection of readings by British authors centering around the issues of the place of moral education in the curriculum, difficulties in communication about moral education, neutrality, and discipline. The authors react to each others positions.

* Weller, Richard H., ed. Humanistic Education: Visions and Realities. Berkeley, CA: McCutchan Publishing Co., 1977. Item 923.

1821. Wilson, Richard W. and Gordon J. Schochet, eds. Moral Development and Politics. New York: Praeger, 1980.

A fascinating collection of papers exploring the relationship of moral development to political life. The book contains fifteen papers grouped under four general headings: Theory and Context; Moral Development as Liberal Ideology; Institutions, Moral Behavior, and the Polity; and Learning to be a Virtuous Citizen.

1822. Windmiller, Myra, Nadine Lambert and Elliot Turiel, eds. Moral Development and Socialization. Boston: Allyn and Bacon, 1980.

Nine papers on three current theories of moral development, issues that emerge from contradictions among the theories, moral development and the study of values, and the question whether or not morality or values can be taught.

* Wynne, Edward, Character Policy: An Emerging Issue. Washington, DC: University Press of America, 1982. Item 1061.

SPECIAL EDITIONS AND SECTIONS OF JOURNALS
(listed alphabetically by journal title)

1823. Chavez, Linda, ed. "Education and Morality." American Educator, 3 (Winter 1979).

1824. Stephens, Beth, ed. "Symposium: Developmental Gains in the Reasoning, Moral Judgment, and Moral Conduct of Retarded and Nonretarded Persons." American Journal of Mental Deficiency, 79 (September 1974).

Results from a longitudinal study on the development of Piagetian reasoning, moral judgment and moral conduct are presented.

1825. Elliott, John, ed. "Fundamental Issues Underlying Religious and Moral Education." Cambridge Journal of Education, 10 (Easter Term).

1826. Frank, Mary, ed. "Moral Education for Young Children." Children in Contemporary Society, 13 (1980). ED 188 777. NI

Contains seven articles dealing with such subjects as environmental influences on moral development, history of moral education, the role of conflict in moral education, a bibliography of children's books with moral themes, etc.

1827. Grimley, Leon K., ed. "Moral Education." Contemporary Education, 48 (Fall 1976).

* ________________. "Cognitive Developmental Moral Education." Counseling and Values, 19 (October 1974). Item 1509.

* Jones, Goerge W., ed. "Values Education." Counseling and Values, 22 (October 1977). Item 1579.

* Erickson, V. Lois, ed. "Developmental Counseling Psychology." *The Counseling Psychologist*, 6 (No. 4, 1977). Item 783.

1828. ______________. "Values Education." *Curriculum Review*, 15 (1976).

A review of books, teachers materials and commercially prepared curriculum dealing with values education.

1829. ______________. "Values Education." *Curriculum Review*, 18 (February 1979).

Reviews a wide range of commercially available materials for classroom use.

1830. ______________. "Values Education." *Curriculum Review*, 19 (June 1980).

Reviews a wide range of K-12 curriculum materials with an emphasis on values.

1831. Weaver, Gladys C., ed. "The Schools and Moral Development." *Educational Horizons*, 56 (Winter 1977-78).

1832. Leeper, Robert R., ed. "Personal and Social Values." *Educational Leadership*, 21 (May 1964).

1833. Smith, B.O., ed. "Education of Judgment and Action: Personal and Civic." *Educational Leadership*, 35 (March 1978).

1834. Dalis, Gus T., ed. "Feature: Values Clarification Revisted." *Health Education*, 7 (March/April 1976).

1835. Beck, Clive, ed. "Values and Moral Education." *The History and Social Science Teacher*, 11 (Fall 1975).

1836. Cochrane, Don and David Williams, eds. "Moral Education and the Social Studies." *The History and Social Science Teacher*, 13 (Fall 1977).

1837. Kurtz, Paul, ed. "Moral Education for Children." *The Humanist*, 32 (November/December 1972).

1838. Kurtz, Paul, ed. "Moral Education and Secular Humanism." The Humanist, 38 (November/December 1978).

Hall assesses the status of moral education and other members of the symposium reply.

1839. Greenland, J. and K. Robinson, eds. "Problems of Teaching Moral Values in a Changing Society." International Review of Education, 26 (1980): 97-245.

1840. McNeill, John L., and Gary J. de Leeuw, eds. "Moral Education Special Issue." Journal of Educational Thought, 15 (April 1981).

* Johnson, David, and Roger T. Johnson, eds. "Social Interdependence in the Classroom: Cooperation, Competition and Individualism." Journal of Research and Development in Education, 12,1 (Fall 1978). Item 882.

* Tapp, June L., ed. "Socialization, the Law and Society." Journal of Social Issues, 27,2 (1971). Item 1734.

1841. Freeman, Eugene, ed. "The Philosophy of Moral Education." The Monist, 58 (October 1974).

Contains a collection of papers by eminent philosophers on the philosophy of moral education. The papers are of exceptional quality. This volume has not received the attention it justly deserves.

1842. Sharp, A.M., ed. "Moral Education." Montclair Educational Review, Spring 1977. NR

1843. Kuhmerker, Lisa, ed. "Facing History and Ourselves." Moral Education Forum, 6 (Summer 1981).

Contains five articles on the teaching of the Holocaust. The papers deal with integrating the holocaust into the curriculum, developing relevant resources, excerpts from student journals and the evaluation of the curriculum.

* Kuhmerker, Lisa, ed. "Scarsdale Alternative School's Just Community." Moral Education Forum, 6 (Winter 1981). Item 621.

* Ivey, Allen E. and Alfred S. Alschuler, eds. "Psychological Education: A Prime Function of the Counselor." Personnel and Guidance Journal, 51 (May 1973). Item 795.

* Hennessy, Thomas C., ed. "Values and the Counselor." Personnel and Guidance Journal, 58 (May 1980). Item 1515.

1844. Elam, Stanley, ed. "The School's Responsibility for Moral Education." Phi Delta Kappan, 46 (October 1964).

1845. Purpel, David and Kevin Ryan, eds. "Moral Education." Phi Delta Kappan, 56 (June 1975).

1846. Cole, Robert W., ed. "Moral Education: An Emerging Consensus." Phi Delta Kappan, 62 (March 1981).

A collection of five papers featuring descriptions of efforts to arrive a community consensus regarding goals and examinations of Kohlbergian assumptions and programs.

1847. Cook, Stuart, ed. "Review of Recent Research Bearing in Religious and Character Formation." Religious Education, 57 (July-August 1962).

1848. Miller, R.C., ed. "The Open Society: Shaping Religions and Values." Religious Education, 69 (March/April 1974).

1849. Miller, R.C., ed. "Values and Education: Pluralism and Public Policy." Religious Education, 70 (March/April 1975).

* Westerhoff, J.H., ed. "Moral Development." Religious Education, 75 (March-April 1980). Item 162.

* Caroll, M.R., ed. "Special Feature: Psychological Education." School Counselor, 29 (May 1973). Item 768.

* Guidubaldi, John, ed. "Humanizing Education." School Psychology Digest, 1 (Summer, 1972). Item 7900.

* Hart, Stuart N., ed. "Affective Education." School Psychology Digest, 7 (Spring 1978). Item 870.

1850. Jarolimek, John, ed. "The Elementary School: Focus on Values." Social Education, 31 (January 1967).

1851. Joyce, W.W., ed. "Moral Education: Learning to Weigh Human Values." Social Education, 39 (January 1975).

1852. Fenton, Edwin, ed. "Cognitive-developmental Approach to Moral Education." Social Education, 40 (April 1976).

Contains articles on the research base, conducting moral discussions, just community, a bibliography and a critique.

1853. Sloan, Douglas, ed. "Education and Values." Teachers College Record, 80 (February 1979).

1854. ________________. "Review of the Hastings Center Report on Teaching Ethics." Teaching Philosophy, 4:2 (April 1981): 159-178.

Nine philosophers review the nine volumes of the Hastings Center Report (item 1545).

1855. Reagan, Gerald M., ed. "Moral Education." Theory Into Practice, 14 (October 1975).

* Hersh, Richard H., ed. "Moral Development." Theory Into Practice, 16 (April 1977). Item 379.

1856. Graves, W.A., ed. "Special Feature on Values." Today's Education, 66 (September/October, 1977).

1857. Clayton, A. Stafford, ed. "Education and Moral Development." Viewpoints, 51 (November 1975).

1858. Maccia, G.S., ed. "On Teaching Philosophy." Viewpoints in Teaching and Learning, 56 (Fall, 1980).

Contains five papers related to teaching philosophy in public schools and colleges.

AUTHOR INDEX

SUBJECT INDEX